Human Resource Management Ethics

A volume in
Ethics in Practice
Robert A. Giacalone and Carole L. Jurkiewicz, *Series Editors*

Ethics in Practice

Robert A. Giacalone, *Temple University*
Carole L. Jurkiewicz, *Louisiana State University*
Series Editors

Human Resource Management Ethics (in press)
   Edited by John R. Deckop

Positive Psychology in Business Ethics and Corporate Responsibility (2005)
   Edited by Robert A. Giacalone, Carole L. Jurkiewicz, and Craig Dunn

Human Resource Management Ethics

Edited by

John R. Deckop

INFORMATION AGE
PUBLISHING

Greenwich, Connecticut • www.infoagepub.com

Library of Congress Cataloging-in-Publication Data

Human resource management ethics / edited by John R. Deckop.
   p. cm. – (Ethics in practice)
 Includes bibliographical references.
 ISBN-13: 978-1-59311-527-2 (pbk.)
 ISBN-13: 978-1-59311-528-9 (hardcover)
 1. Personnel management–Moral and ethical aspects. 2. Organizational
behavior–Moral and ethical aspects. 3. Organizational justice. I. Deckop,
John Raymond. II. Series: Ethics in practice (Greenwich, Conn.)
 HF5549.H7856 2006
 174'.4–dc22

                                      2006015685

ISBN-10: 1-59311-527-X (pbk.)
          1-59311-528-8 (hardcover)

Printed in the United States of America

CONTENTS

V

Focused Perspectives

FOREWORD

The field of human resource management (HRM) appears to have had little to do with the well-publicized ethical fiascos that came to light over the past several years. Financial malfeasance, lack of effective auditing controls, inattentive boards, and flat out greed are most commonly seen as the culprits. The term "CEO" (chief executive officer) has become increasingly associated with scandal, and the term "CFO" (chief financial officer) perhaps even more so.

Not far beneath the surface of many of these scandals, however, are human resource management (HRM) issues that contributed to, and possibly caused, the more visible problems. At Enron, a cutthroat HRM culture was developed that put tremendous pressure on employees to meet financial objectives or face termination, and selection, promotion, and performance appraisal practices contributed to the disaster (Gladwell, 2002). Compensation practices, and in particular the lure of stock options, have been an important factor in explaining why executives in numerous firms made unethical decisions (Cassidy, 2002). Yet while CFOs and the fields of accounting and finance have been much maligned in the public and media, far less focus has been directed on the field of HRM and top executives in HRM as causes of, and solutions to, ethical problems.

The field of HRM has its share of ethical challenges, and perhaps more. If there is anything positive about the highly visible ethical scandals, it is the increasing focus on ethics in businesses and academia, including HRM ethics. Highly publicized scandals come and go, but ethical problems in organizations continue on. This volume takes on the task of defining, analyzing, and proposing solutions for ethical problems in the field of HRM, both those related to executive levels of the organization, as well as to the organization as a whole.

In a sense, the contents of this volume represent the results an inductive assessment of the most pressing ethical issues in HRM. Highly-regarded scholars in a wide range of fields were invited to address the issue of HRM ethics from the perspective of their expertise. General topics were suggested to each contributor; however the authors were free to develop their ideas in the direction they wished. In several cases the authors chose to pursue a topic different from the one that was suggested to them.

The result as represented in these pages is a fascinating range of scholarship. Macro and micro perspectives are presented, including perspectives from psychology, social psychology, organizational behavior, strategy, law, spirituality, critical studies, public/nonprofit management, and a variety of functional areas within the field of HRM.

Within this range in perspective, several themes that spanned multiple chapters emerged. Perhaps the broadest and most pervasive theme discussed by the authors is the intersection of organizational culture and values, and HRM ethics. It is clear that the authors, many of whom are HRM researchers, see HRM ethics and broader organizational issues as inexorably intertwined. Orlitzky and Swanson discuss how value attunement between the organization and the functional areas of HRM results in superior accomplishment of both economic and social goals. Cardy and Selvarajan analyze the nexus between HRM ethics and organizational culture through the use of performance management, explaining how it can align ethical values of the organization with employee values across functional areas of HRM. Schumann also discusses an integrated management system to promote ethical behavior, but bases his arguments on how organizations through their HRM practices should recognize, adapt to, and improve the moral development of employees.

Other chapters discuss direct effects of organization culture on ethical behavior and policies. Cirka and Messikomer, in a qualitative study of the assisted living industry, draw connections among organization culture, HRM practices, and treatment of clients, concluding that organizations that develop a sustainable, ethical culture provide better treatment of clients, and attain a significant competitive business advantage. Hauserman discusses how organizational culture, as manifested in local norms, can facilitate sexual harassment in organizations. Greenwood, Holland, and Choong argue that some organizations use drug testing in part to reinforce an organization culture of control, as opposed to reduce harm. Kasser, Vansteenkiste, and Deckop show how an organizational culture that creates and exploits the materialist values of employees harms employees and may result in unethical behavior.

Two chapters explore how the "arrow" pointing from organizational culture to HRM ethics can or should be reversed. Kolodinsky draws on theory and literature on wisdom to discuss how wise HR managers and a wise HRM function can affect the ethical culture and values of an organization. Hatcher advocates the central role of the human resource development (HRD) function in producing an ethical organization, and explores the provocative question of whether the HRD function is better able to accomplish this objective than the HRM function.

Another theme that spans multiple chapters relates to the potential of conflict between the goals of profit maximization and the ethical treatment of employees. Though many of the chapters mentioned above provide support for the premise that ethical treatment of employees results in superior financial performance, several chapters analyze the tension between profit maximization and the rights of employees and other stakeholders. Lepak and Colakoglu explore what research in strategic HRM might look like if instead of focusing on profit maximization as the ultimate goal of HRM, this research utilized a multiple stakeholder approach. Montemayor analyzes the implications for compensation policy and practice were a comprehensive relational obligation perspective to be adopted by researchers and practitioners, as opposed to the dominant and traditional competitive market economics perspective. Day proceeds along parallel lines in analyzing what compensation practice would look like if organizations incorporated spirituality principles in the design of compensation policies. Also along similar lines, Pynes explores issues of economic justice and compensation policy, with particular application to the public and nonprofit sectors.

McClendon explores the understudied but important issue of whether typical management conduct in a union-management relations context, and in particular in union organizing campaigns, is ethical. Greenwood et al. question the ethicality of drug testing as typically practiced, particularly given the availability of less morally hazardous and invasive alternatives. Kasser et al. argue that organizations inappropriately treat employees as a means to an ends by exploiting the materialistic values of employees.

This represents only a small taste of the provocative ideas and issues explored in this book. Readers will identify other themes and perspectives shared by the articles, and will agree with many arguments and undoubtedly disagree with others. The goal is to stimulate discussion and debate, as HRM ethics underlies many of the critical ethical challenges in organizations today. HRM may also represent the solution to even more.

—John R. Deckop
Temple University

REFERENCES

Cassidy, J. (2002). The greed cycle. *New Yorker*, 78, September 23, 64–77.

Gladwell, M. (2002). The talent myth: Are smart people overrated? *New Yorker*, 78, July 22, 28–33.

PART I

BROAD-BASED PERSPECTIVES

CHAPTER 1

SOCIALLY RESPONSIBLE HUMAN RESOURCE MANAGEMENT

Charting New Territory

Marc Orlitzky
University of Redlands

Diane L. Swanson
Kansas State University

Corporations face increasing pressure from activists, journalists, and management scholars to take their role as good citizens in society seriously (see also Matten & Crane, 2005). Yet, even in the aftermath of an unprecedented earthquake of corporate scandals, a definitive response from the business community has been slow in coming. One reason for this resistance is that a greater emphasis on corporate social responsibility can be construed as costly (Frederick, 1995; Swanson, 1995). But this perception may be more a force of habit than based on fact. Until recently, theoretical explanations of how managers can simultaneously pursue economic and other social goals have been scarce. The *a priori* assumption that these

Human Resource Management Ethics, pages 3–25
Copyright © 2006 by Information Age Publishing

goals are incompatible may help explain why so few companies are beacons of corporate social responsibility. As some observers have noted, most organizations eschew leadership in this area, preferring the status quo instead (Skeel, 2005; Thomas, 2004).

This habitual reluctance is questionable at best. At worst it suggests that corporate managers may be sabotaging their own firms' potential to honor the social contract (Donaldson, 1989) and increase organizational performance. After all, some empirical evidence substantiates that companies will not necessarily have to sacrifice economic performance to other desirable achievements. In fact, two award-winning meta-analyses have demonstrated that corporate social performance and financial performance may be correlated in cycles of mutual reinforcement (Orlitzky & Benjamin, 2001; Orlitzky, Schmidt & Rynes, 2003),[1] for which several theoretical explanations have been offered (cf. Orlitzky, in press, for an overview of this literature).

Therefore, the good news is the possibility that economic and social performance exhibit synchronicity. The bad news is that this co-existence may cut both ways, as when firms falter in both areas. For instance, during the last wave of corporate scandals, many firms, including Worldcom, Enron, Tyco, Arthur Anderson, and Aldephia, failed to enact even minimal economic and social responsibilities. This failure may point to a broader problem. Many of today's managers may be ill-equipped to leverage the potential synergy between financial and social performance, or they may overlook the opportunity altogether. Unfortunately, neither the academic nor the practitioner literature provides them with many useful guidelines for synergistic *implementation* of high corporate social *and* financial performance—and human resource management is no exception (Peterson, 2004; Rynes, 2004).

Theory is missing in action, so to speak. Needed is a theoretical perspective on corporate social responsibility robust enough to accommodate the simultaneous pursuit of economic and social goals as a frame of reference for benchmarking socially responsible guidelines for managers.

We respond to this challenge in the following three sections. First, we describe irresponsible and responsible corporate postures toward the social environment, using a comprehensive theoretical perspective on corporate social performance. According to this theory, managerial decision making and organizational dynamics can culminate in either neglectful or responsive stances towards society. On the one hand, *neglectful* firms are ill-equipped to respond to opportunities to improve both economic and social performance concurrently; on the other hand, *attuned* organizations embody the potential to pursue both simultaneously (subject to limitations, discussed in the next paragraph). Second, we explore the role of human resource management in this broader context for corporate social responsibility, particularly how recruitment and selection, performance appraisal, compensation, and training and development practices can facilitate *attunement*. Finally, we give some implications for research, education, and practice in these areas.

But first a caveat. Although the relationship between financial and social performance can be synergistic, it can also be subject to tradeoffs. That is, some corporate social responsibilities can be costly, as when public policy stipulates that the expense of rectifying pollution be internalized by firms in an industry. In such cases, public welfare can trump financial goals under the terms of the social contract. We do not deny the possibility of such tradeoffs, many of which are probably endemic to the relationship between business and society. Rather, our aim is to explore a new frontier of potential synergy between economic and social responsibilities in terms of human resource management. After all, it is not far-fetched to think that effective management can help forge more constructively creative organizational dynamics that redefine perceived limitations to corporate social responsibility.

By exploring this possibility, we seek to chart new territory in corporate social responsibility and human resource management that can be referenced for further study. Quite simply, this chapter points to an agenda for future inquiry in this important area.

TOWARD A NEW FRONTIER OF CORPORATE SOCIAL RESPONSIBILITY

In this section we review the two models that shed light on the potential firms have to pursue economic and social goals in tandem. These models, drawn from Swanson's (1999) theoretical perspective on corporate social performance, are broadly termed "value neglect" and "value attunement."[2] We distinguished between these two models in order to explore some socially responsible human resource management practices, discussed later.

Corporate Lack of Responsibility as *Value Neglect*

Swanson's model of *value neglect* is based on understanding the role values play in organizational life and how value dynamics ultimately affect a firm's posture toward society. Her overarching proposition is that when executive managers exhibit *normative myopia* by ignoring, suppressing, or denying the role of values in their decisions, then whole organizations eventually lose touch with stakeholder expectations of social responsibility. These expectations, which are value-based, include calls for economic performance as well as the enactment of other desirable goals, including product safety, respect for human rights, fair employment standards, and sustainable business practices (Swanson, 1999). It is important to note that the values inherent in such calls are the standard currency of business ethics (Frederick 1995; see also Rokeach, 1973). Hence, value-based expectations of business are shaped by and articulated as ethical perspectives, including those of human rights and justice-as-fairness, which prize the sanctity of human life and dignity of personhood as standards that outweigh a singularly narrow pursuit of profit (Swanson, 1995, 1999).

In short, *normative myopia* and an organizational tendency to neglect social values and ethical expectations go hand in hand. Figure 1.1 represents a simplification of Swanson's model. Its logic is as follows. Executives who exhibit *normative myopia* use formal and informal mechanisms to encourage other employees to follow suit and suppress value awareness and ethical analysis. Formally, executives can do so by using their authority to set a narrow range for employee decision making along chain-of-command structures. Practically speaking, this means that executives can discourage employees from including information about stakeholder expectations in official reports, statements, and other feedback mechanisms. In this way, the range of discretion for subordinate decision making gets aligned with the narrow value premises set on a higher level of administration (Simon, 1957). Informally, executives can also signal their approval of *myopia* by using certain cultural mechanisms. For instance, they can promote sycophants who convey only desired information to decision makers and excommunicate or ignore employees who give fuller accountings (Schein, 1992).

The upshot of these formal and informal signals is that myopic decision making gets replicated among employees, a dynamic Chikudate (2002)

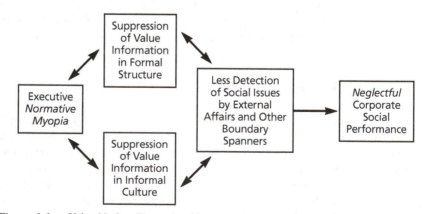

Figure 1.1.   *Value Neglect:* Executive *Normative Myopia* and *Neglectful* Corporate Social Performance. (Adapted from Swanson, 1999)

calls "collective myopia." When boundary-spanning employees, such as public-affairs specialists, align with this shortsightedness, they fail to communicate important information about the social environment to others in the organization (Swanson, 1999). The situation is self-perpetuating in that employees develop a reluctance to convey stakeholder expectations of corporate social responsibility to the executive who signaled disinterest in the first place. Executive and organizational myopia replicate each other, as the executive proclivity to ignore or downplay values is played out as a chronic tendency for the organization to neglect social concerns (see also Scott & Hart, 1979).

As illustrated in Figure 1.1, *normative myopia* and poor social performance are inextricably linked in a theory of *value neglect*. In terms of corporate social performance, *value neglect* represents a violation of the social contract that imputes legitimacy to corporations because they enhance the greater good. Under the terms of the social contract, corporate responsibilities include not only economizing behaviors but also the ability to forge cooperative, symbiotic linkages with the external environment that function adaptively to sustain life (Frederick, 1995). Firms that manifest *value neglect* fail to forge such linkages. They can also fail to economize, as the last wave of corporate scandals demonstrates. Inadequate attention to the economic potential of building and maintaining effective and efficient stakeholder relations may contribute to this failure (Jones, 1995), which is another way of describing the dynamic of *value neglect*.

The Potential for Corporate Responsibility as *Value Attunement*

Essentially, *value neglect* is a benchmark or frame of reference for understanding what can happen to an organization's posture toward society when the chief executive consistently fails to acknowledge and examine the ethical values implicated in his or her decisions. In contrast, Swanson modeled *normative receptivity* to represent executive decision making that consciously strives to include such information. Accordingly, when executives use formal and informal mechanisms to signal that employees should attend to values, the possibility of *attunement* exists. Put differently, when decision makers throughout the organization are directed by formal creed and informal examples to recognize and attend to stakeholders' ethical concerns, then the organization's posture toward the host environment can undergo a change for the better. In terms of the social contract, cooperation and adaptive symbiotic linkages, including those that support economizing, become possible, and a corporation can potentially enact corporate social responsibility.

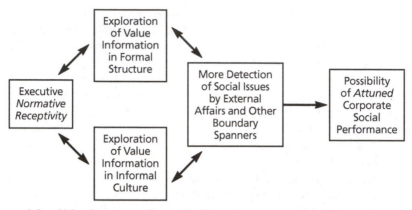

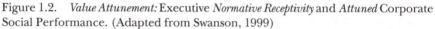

Figure 1.2.   *Value Attunement:* Executive *Normative Receptivity* and *Attuned* Corporate Social Performance. (Adapted from Swanson, 1999)

Although we do not define standards of corporate social responsibility here, *normative receptivity* can be thought of as necessary to a firm's ability to respond constructively to stakeholder expectations. *Receptivity* is the converse of the logic embodied in Figure 1.1 in that it represents an enhanced awareness and appreciation of values in the executive mindset that gets transmitted throughout the informal and formal organization and acted upon by a firm's boundary-spanners. Similarly, in Chapter 4 in this volume, Cardy and Selvarajan suggest that an alignment of values is important to making ethics a reality in organizations. In terms of business and society, *value attunement* implies that a corporation has the potential to carry out its part of the social contract described previously. Figure 1.2 summarizes this possibility.

The dynamics outlined in Figure 1.2 should be viewed as necessary but not sufficient conditions for high corporate social performance. As Swanson (1999) herself noted, *attunement* is not as theoretically developed as *neglect,* probably because it is easier to recognize the dynamics that contribute to irresponsibility than it is to identify all precursors to responsibility. Indeed, one need only look at the history of corporate social performance research to understand that it has been shaped more by a concern for corporate abuse of power and a lack of responsibility than a complete understanding of what responsibility entails (Frederick, 1995; Wood, 1991). Given this history, our exploration of socially responsible human resource management practices is simply part of an agenda to understand the *attuned* pole of corporate social responsibility better.

Illustrating *Neglect* and *Attunement*

It is important to underscore that Swanson modeled *value neglect* and *attunement* as *ideal types.* That is, they represent logical implications drawn from extant research on corporate social performance and organizational theory. In reality, we expect executives to exhibit degrees of *normative myopia* or *receptivity* instead of pure forms of these decision processes. Similarly, organizations manifest tendencies toward *neglect* or *attunement* instead of perfect alignments.

To illustrate how *neglect* and *attunement* can be used as poles of reference for corporate social responsibility, consider the longstanding controversy surrounding Nestle's sales of infant formula. For decades, Nestle Corporation faced social opposition to its marketing of infant formula in developing countries. Critics, including the World Health Organization, claimed that unsanitary water and low rates of literacy rendered the sale of the product unsafe in those countries (Sethi, 1994). Eventually Nestle was the target of intense pressure from stakeholders aimed at forcing the firm to comply with an international code aimed at restricting such sales. This longstanding controversy can be seen as a clash between narrow profit seeking and broader social values and ethical expectations. It appears that Nestle executives adopted a myopic mindset, referencing narrow company objectives to the detriment of broader community values, particularly a respect for the sanctity of infant life (Swanson, 1999).

In terms of Swanson's models, Nestle exhibited *neglect*, instead of striving for *attunement* and engaging critics in a timely, constructive dialogue about their values and ethics. By adhering rigidly to original plans, it seems that top executives myopically failed to consider other options. For example, the controversy might have been averted in an early stage if Nestle had decided to treat the infant formula not as a food product but as a healthcare product, dispensing it by prescription through pharmacies (Husted, 2000). A precedent for this kind of re-evaluation already existed in that pharmaceutical companies such as Abbott Labs had successfully responded to stakeholder concerns by making the switch (Austin & Kohn, 1990). That Nestle was unable to re-envision its identity as a food company can be viewed as a failure of executive managers to exhibit *normative receptivity* and factor compelling social values into their decisions. In this way, *receptivity* and *attunement* can be used as points of reference for emphasizing the need for top managers to attend to stakeholder concerns quickly, adaptively, and creatively. Conversely, the logic embodied in *myopia* and *neglect* helps explain why social control of business, such as the pressure exerted on Nestle, may become necessary in the first place.

MANAGING HUMAN RESOURCES FOR *ATTUNEMENT*

Given the theoretic possibility of *attunement,* we now explore its implications for human resource management (HRM). Specifically, we explore the areas of recruitment and selection, performance appraisal, compensation, and training and development, none of which can be ignored if the goal is to manage human resources for constructive social outcomes. While our focus is on these functional areas, it is important to keep in mind that the role of the executive manager is paramount in providing authentic—and not merely espoused—support for socially responsible programs, policies, and procedures, which might otherwise add up to little more than window dressing. Ultimately, such support should translate into greater employee awareness of and commitment to *value attunement* (see Simmons, 2003). Admittedly, this shift will not be easy because some research suggests that HRM has historically played only a marginal role in the formulation and implementation of corporate social responsibility (Zappala, 2004).

Recruitment and Selection

To recap, corporate social responsibility can be conceptualized as *attunement* processes directed by executives who model receptivity toward ethical values. As a practical matter, these executives will encourage open discussions about values among employees as well as value identification and analysis (Orlitzky & Swanson, 2002; Swanson, 1999). Logically, they will also steer their organizations toward hiring employees who are well suited for such endeavors. The criteria could include (a) employees' cognitive moral development, (b) personality traits associated with *normative receptivity*, and (c) workforce diversity.

As for the first criterion, companies striving for *attunement* could benefit from hiring employees who are comfortable with and adept at factoring values into decisions. In other words, screening for higher levels of cognitive moral development could be an important step in enhancing corporate social responsibility (see Colby & Kohlberg, 1987; Fisher, 1999; Frederick, 1995; Weber, 1990; Weber & Wasieleski, 2001). The logic is as follows. Employees reasoning at the highest ("postconventional") level of moral development would be more likely to act on moral principles rather than narrow egocentric impulses and rewards associated with lower (preconventional) stages. They would also be more inclined to conform to the laws and societal norms that are elements of mid-level, conventional moral reasoning. Our expectation is that employees at the postconventional level would more readily reflect on moral obligations that transcend the legal realm to take into account broader societal and environmental concerns. In short, they would be good candidates for enacting *attunement*.

In this way, screening for moral development may be an effective route to *attunement*. It might be efficient as well. In Chapter 6 in this book, Schumann observes that managers are likely to have employees at any or all of the stages of moral development and that what motivates an employee who is at one particular stage of moral development may not motivate employees at other stages of moral development. Therefore, he suggests that managers who want to motivate employees to behave ethically tailor HRM policies, practices, and procedures to all of the possible stages of moral development. Yet, if employees are screened for moral development in the first place, then managers can focus their time and attention more efficiently on enacting policies, practices, and procedures geared to moral maturity.

Although cognitive moral development seems to be a natural screen for more responsible employees, it may also present a number of unique challenges. First, because contextual factors and issue characteristics affect moral reasoning (Jones, 1991; Weber, 1990), the utility of a screen for moral development could be affected by various contingencies. For example, Jones (1991) argued that moral intensity (the extent of issue-related moral imperative in a situation) might influence all stages of moral reasoning. Second, the measurement of moral development may be confounded by social desirability bias; yet more accurate measures could be time-consuming to develop and administer (Weber & Wasieleski, 2001). Third, some feminist researchers claim that Kohlberg's conceptualization of moral development is gender-biased because women are more likely to score at lower levels (Gilligan, 1982). Although empirical studies have generally not supported this claim (Derry, 1989; Walker, 1984), the possibility of small gender effects remains (Jaffee & Hyde, 2000), which could raise the legal specter of gender discrimination. Finally, if moral development improves with age (Ruegger & King, 1992), screening for it could invite charges of reverse age discrimination.

Given these potential problems, it is important to consider alternative screens for *attuned* hiring. Recent evidence suggests that the personality trait of "agreeableness," which encompasses the proclivity to be other-regarding and considerate, is positively associated with *normative receptivity,* or the predisposition to consider values in decision making (Orlitzky, Swanson, & Quartermaine, 2005; Swanson & Orlitzky, 2006). Because personality inventories are already used in many organizations' selection processes, the inclusion of agreeableness might be relatively easy to implement. An added advantage might be the minimization of legal challenges, since no evidence of gender effects has been found in the relationship between agreeableness and *normative receptivity* (Orlitzky, Swanson, & Quartermaine, 2005; Swanson & Orlitzky, 2006). The potential for charges of age discrimination is also mitigated because, like other personality traits, agreeableness tends to be relatively stable over an individual's lifespan (Costa & McCrae, 1994). Even so, a lot more research is needed before agreeableness and moral reasoning can be treated as interchangeable screens for hiring.

The most important means for promoting *attunement* is probably increasing workforce diversity, which is akin to saying that organizations facing complex social environments need to respond in kind by increasing internal "requisite variety" (Conant & Ashby, 1970; Weick, 1979). By definition, *attunement* requires that employees attend to a wide range of stakeholder issues and concerns. Because "only variety can regulate variety" (Buckley, 1968, p. 495), *attuned* hiring necessarily translates into a deliberate shift away from the current monolithic emphasis on "fit." Although it is beyond the scope of this chapter to critically review the mainstream HRM literature, much of it emphasizes the importance of "supplementary fit" as a predictor of employees' job satisfaction, performance, and career success (Kristof, 1996; Muchinsky & Monahan, 1987). Such fit is said to occur when a person "supplements, embellishes, or possesses characteristics which are similar to other individuals in an environment" (Muchinsky & Monahan, 1987, cited in Kristof, 1996, p. 3). The downside of recruitment and selection practices aimed at such similarity is that they easily create excessively homogeneous cultures that are counterproductive to enacting social responsibility. More pointedly, "groupthink" can sabotage a receptive attitude toward a diversity of stakeholder interests (see Janis & Mann, 1977).

In order to minimize such myopic group dynamics, workforce diversity must be broadly defined so that employees have backgrounds conducive to communicating with stakeholders about views different from those embedded in organizational cultures. Consistent with this posture, executives should direct employees to forego heavy-handed attempts to manage and control stakeholders or force organizational views on them (see Liedtka, 1998). Workforce homogeneity can detract from this effort if employees fail to consider alternative views while striving to fit into a culture that shies away from "undiscussables" (Argyris, 1993; Schneider, 1987; Waddock, 2002). In the case of Nestle, a more heterogeneous workforce led by a receptive executive might have been able to respond to the public outcry over marketing practices in developing countries sooner, helping the firm shift from *neglect* toward a posture of *attunement.*

Eventually, *attuned* recruitment may lead to a "virtuous cycle" of attracting socially responsible employees, especially if a company's reputation for social performance attracts employees who care about social responsibilities in the first place (Greening & Turban, 2000; Turban & Cable, 2003; Smith, Wokutch, Harrington, & Dennis, 2004; Turban & Greening, 1997). To capitalize on this possibility, hiring processes should reinforce employees' receptivity to stakeholder concerns. In this way, value *attunement* can beget *value attunement.* Conversely, reinforcing *myopia* in hiring could contribute to a downward spiral of organizational irresponsibility, which may help explain the coincidence of poor financial and social performance described earlier.

Performance Appraisal

It would be contradictory for *value-attuned* organizations to rely on performance objectives defined solely by financial criteria, especially since such exclusivity can create cultures in which ends justify any means. To grasp this point, one need only consider that a focus on financial goals permeated the culture at Enron before its demise or that Nestle pursued controversial marketing policies in developing countries in the face of widespread public criticism. In contrast, *attuned* performance appraisal systems would encourage employees to attend to both financial and social objectives. A "balanced scorecard" that measures and assesses employee performance in both areas might accomplish this (see also Kaplan & Norton, 1992, 2004). Because these objectives can be industry- and firm specific, it would be ideal for external stakeholders to help design them (Simmons, 2003). Again the case of Nestle comes to mind. For if the firm had engaged critics in the development of performance objectives early in the issue's life-cycle, then employee tasks aimed at ameliorating the crisis might have been designed and implemented, such as assessing and reporting on water conditions for consumers in developing countries.

Broadly speaking, *attunement* requires that employees adopt an external orientation of "search and discover," which formal appraisal systems should encourage. At the same time, these systems should discourage an overemphasis on economic goals.

Compensation

Since performance-based pay is an important element of effective employee management, organizations should reward employees for behaviors consistent with *attunement* (see also Kerr, 1995). The monetary incentives can operate at two levels. One, incentives tied to some measure of stakeholder satisfaction can be applied to specific employees, perhaps based on the aforementioned scorecard approach. On another level, incentives that promote social goals can be applied to teams and/or whole business units. For example, environmental initiatives in firms aimed at waste minimization often translate into cost reductions that could then be passed on to employees in gainsharing plans (see Hawken, Lovins, & Lovins, 1999).

A cautionary note is that companies striving for *attunement* should utilize performance-based pay with moderation. The danger is that pitting employees against each other in what agency theorists call "tournaments" may be counter-productive to their endeavors at social responsibility (see Huselid, 1992, and Baron & Kreps, 1999, for further discussions of tournament systems). This could occur for two reasons. First, tournaments may prompt hyper-competitive behaviors that undermine the collective spirit needed for effective stakeholder engagement (Waddock, 2002). Clearly, firms cannot hope to cultivate enduring cultures of trust, cooperation, solidarity, and teamwork needed for constructive stakeholder relationships when pay tournaments undermine such efforts (see Bloom, 1999; Bloom & Michel, 2002; Shaw, Gupta, & Delery, 2002). Second, our own research has shown that managers who prefer greater pay dispersion in their organizations are considerably more likely to be myopic rather than receptive to the needs of the collective (Orlitzky, Swanson, & Quartermaine, in press; Swanson & Orlitzky, 2006). In other words, vast pay inequalities can undermine social responsibility because these inequalities may drive out or fail to attract those employees who can best implement it.

Finally, it would be consistent with the logic of *attunement* to supplement monetary with non-monetary incentives, especially since there is reason to believe that employees with higher levels of moral development have transcended reward seeking as a sole motivation. Non-monetary incentives could include awards for good citizenship. Additionally, corporations could provide the means for employees to perform voluntary community service of their choice. The Body Shop was one of the first large companies to institutionalize such employee volunteerism, but increasingly more traditional corporations like General Electric and AT&T have followed suit (Roddick, 1991; Schwartz & Post, 2002).

Training and Development

Given what has been said so far, an aggressively heavy-handed approach to stakeholder management would work against *attunement*. Instead, a dialogue-based, open-ended, interactive process of trust building is needed (Calton & Lad, 1995; Waddock, 2002). To enact this process, employees must be trained in the *praxis* of engaging and balancing a multitude of stakeholder interests and issues. Otherwise, employees could easily default to a style of proactive strategic management, which tends to preempt dialogue when based on a condescending, egocentric assumption that the organization "knows best." In contrast, *attunement* is based on a mode of communication that is mutual and respectful of stakeholder needs and claims. For example, Royal Dutch/Shell seems to have taken a step in this

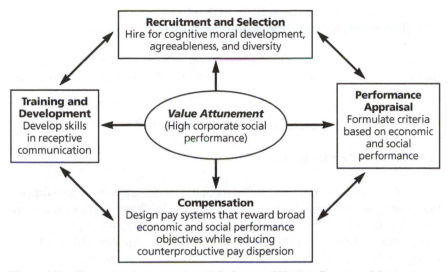

Figure 1.3.   Toward an integrated model of *Attuned* Human Resource Management.

direction by creating various modes for communicating with stakeholders after a number of problems surfaced (Mirvis, 2000). The point is that *attuned* stakeholder dialogue requires a continuous development of employees' communication competencies, including active-listening skills and candid, supportive communication (Senge, 1990, 1994; see also Nichols, 1995), especially for organizational boundary-spanners (Swanson, 1999).

Toward an Integrated Model of *Attuned* Human Resource Management

Through the integration of the four HRM practices described above, we propose that organizations can capitalize on processes that reinforce and perpetuate *attunement* and the coincidence of positive financial and social performance described earlier. The four practices illustrated in Figure 1.3 are as follows:

1. *Recruitment and selection:* Hire employees who exhibit relatively high levels of cognitive moral development and the personality trait of agreeableness, while enlarging workforce diversity.

2. *Performance appraisal:* Formulate criteria based on economic and social performance objectives.

3. *Compensation:* Design pay systems that reward economic and social performance objectives while reducing counterproductive pay dispersion.

4. *Training & Development:* Develop employee skills in receptive stakeholder engagement and communication.

Since our research on *attuned* HRM is preliminary, we offer Figure 1.3 as a
starting point for charting new territory in research, education, and practice.

CHARTING NEW TERRITORY

Implications for Research

Employee retention is a major challenge in today's increasingly competitive, dynamic, and global labor markets (Cappelli, 2000). This would seem
especially true for firms striving for *attunement*, since they would want to
recoup their investments in newly designed and integrated HR systems by
retaining those employees who have benefited from them. Since retention
cannot be assumed in a "new deal" environment in which employee loyalty
cannot be bought (Cappelli, 1999; Orlitzky & Rynes, 2001), employers will
need to find creative ways of retaining employees who can make the greatest contributions to corporate social performance. To complicate matters,
the effectiveness of retention strategies ranging from job customization to
greater emphasis on social ties among employees may be shaped by indus-
try- and firm-specific conditions (Cappelli, 2000; Sheridan, 1992). In other
words, we must learn much more about the specific organizational practices useful for the retention of *socially responsible* employees.

Besides retention, four other areas of inquiry strike us as particularly
pertinent. First, several authors have argued that HR practices should not
only fit corporate missions vertically, but also need to be horizontally consistent with each other (Baron & Kreps, 1999; Pfeffer, 1998). This kind of
internal consistency is represented in Figure 1.3 by the double-headed
arrows between recruitment and selection, performance appraisal, compensation, and training and development. Although theory suggests that
these practices are mutually reinforcing, the superiority of our proposed
"bundle" of practices should be substantiated by empirical studies (cf. Delery & Doty, 1996, and Guest, 1997, for examples of such configurational
research approaches to strategic HRM).

A second area of potential research stems from our broader approach to
employee performance, which is a departure from the more frequently
used criterion of financial objectives. Since we have not offered specific
social performance metrics that can be factored into performance
appraisal evaluations, this area is also ripe for future inquiry. Indeed, Cardy
and Selvarajan's Chapter 4 in this volume includes one approach to generating ethical performance criteria that can also be used to inform recruit-

ment and selection, training and development, and compensation. A third, closely related area is the development of ways to measure the effectiveness of the proposed practices. One practice that might be the most intractable to gauge is training and development for stakeholder engagement and communication. Because it is important to measure changes in outcomes after this practice is adopted, relatively sophisticated longitudinal, experimental, or at least quasi-experimental research designs may be necessary for determining whether individual training in communication translates into departmental or organizational improvements in stakeholder relations and, by extension, higher corporate social performance.

Finally, there is the issue of potential tradeoffs between decision-making efficiency and *attuned* stakeholder engagement. Identifying and attending to multiple stakeholders in fluid environments can conceivably delay organizational actions, causing opportunities to be missed. Moreover, some stakeholder issues may clash, as when local communities in less developed countries could benefit from the economic investments vested in new jobs, but unions push for keeping those same low-wage jobs domestic. Given such predicaments, an integrated approach to *attuned* HRM will likely seek to optimize rather than maximize decision goals and criteria.

Implications for Education

Although values are germane to understanding organizational cultures and ethical issues in domestic and global business, normative analysis is sparse in current business school curricula (Gioia, 2002; Kelly, 2002; Swanson & Frederick, 2005; Waddock, 2003). Indeed, only one third of AACSB-accredited business schools require students to take an ethics course (Willen, 2004), which would be a logical vehicle for such analysis. As a result, students by the thousands graduate each year without a practical knowledge of the role values play in their chosen professions (Windsor, 2002). According to two studies, this myopia becomes worse as students advance through the business school curriculum (Aspen ISIB 2002; Swanson & Orlitzky, 2006). The implication is that students will turn into managers and employees who perpetuate neglectful corporate social performance for generations to come. This could be especially true for human resource managers who hire employees and influence retention through performance appraisals and compensation programs. In their capacity as gatekeepers, in addition to crafting employee training and development, these managers, perhaps more than any other group, assist executives in shaping and maintaining organizational cultures.

The possibility of *attunement* is not coming through in the current environment for business education. Indeed, many ethics courses that stress the need for corporate social responsibility have been cut from degree programs during the past few years, even in the aftermath of corporate scandals (Kelly, 2002). The dilemma is that a myopic attitude in the business sector is reflected in business degree programs and vice versa. Given evidence that ethics and other behaviorally based skills can be taught and learned (Rynes, Trank, Lawson, & Ilies, 2003), and that formal education can enhance moral reasoning (Bebeau, 2004; Fisher, 1997; Rest, 1988), most business schools are missing an opportunity to educate students in their future social responsibilities. Instead, they continue to convey an amoral, even brutish theory of management (Ghoshal, 2003; Gioia, 2002). That students can graduate from business schools with a narrower perspective than they had going in is not lost on the students themselves. Only 22 percent of MBA students polled said that business schools are doing a lot to prepare them ethically, most adding that they would rather change firms than fight for their own values (Aspen ISIB, 2002).

This bracketing of personal values, a behavioral artifact of value-free education, stifles the potential for *normative receptivity* and *value attunement*. Worse, it may produce the very behavior assumed in standard economic theory, which is that decision makers are driven by unfettered, narrow self-interest (Ferraro, Pfeffer, & Sutton, 2005; Ghoshal, 2005; Pfeffer, 2003). Given this theory's long history as a mainstay of business education, ethics courses must not be optional (Swanson & Frederick, 2005). Instead, they must serve as springboards for integrating community-mindedness into other courses, including HRM. Moreover, given the organizational dynamics that shape corporate social performance (viz. *neglect* and *attunement*), HRM professors would be well advised to place more emphasis on such topics as organizational change and development, communications, group behavior, and organizational theory. Otherwise, HRM students will be ill-equipped to carry out one of their most important future roles, which is to help line managers and employees navigate organizational change (Rynes, 2004: 207). They will also be ill prepared to adopt a stakeholder perspective instead of the "me first" self-aggrandizement perpetuated in most business degree programs.

In short, business schools must institutionalize a stand-alone foundational ethics course as a fulcrum for integrating topics of corporate social responsibility across the curriculum (Swanson & Frederick, 2005). That done, students might grasp the importance of values and ethics holistically, instead of in bits and pieces or perhaps not at all. In terms of HRM, a required ethics course helps lay the normative groundwork for how recruitment and selection, performance appraisal systems, compensation, and training and development systems can facilitate *attunement*.

Implications for Practice

Our perspective has several implications for practicing human resource managers. Perhaps the most important is that they need to foster social responsibility by creating the employee buy-in that makes it work (Peterson, 2004), while guiding employees to balance economic and social goals (Rynes, 2004). Although this balancing act may be difficult, it should be reassuring for practitioners to know that economic and social goals are not necessarily at odds but can reinforce each other cyclically over time (Orlitzky, in press, 2005; Orlitzky & Benjamin, 2001; Orlitzky et al., 2003). Armed with this knowledge, HR practitioners should re-envision themselves as change agents (Rynes, 2004; Ulrich, Brockbank, Yeung, & Lake, 1995). In this role they will need to understand that radical changes in organizational posture often prompt employee resistance fueled by fear or cynicism (Kanter, 2001; Skoldberg, 1994). In the case of moving toward a broader performance management model that transcends narrowly defined financial objectives, employees might become uncertain or ambivalent about their jobs. To minimize this possibility, HR practitioners should clearly convey to the entire workforce why such shifts are necessary. Although top executives must initiate and sponsor such shifts, ideas from lower ranks should be invited so that employees are involved in, and committed to, the journey from *neglect* to *attunement.*

CONCLUSION

We have proposed that human resource management can help leverage corporate social responsibility as a simultaneous pursuit of economic and social goals. According to our theoretical perspective, such an effort requires that executives lead their organizations to enact receptively *attuned* postures toward their stakeholder environments. We have identified specific practices in recruitment and selection, performance appraisal, compensation, and training and development designed to harness employee commitment to this project. We offer these practices as part of an agenda for developing a robust perspective on socially responsible human resource management.

NOTES

1. Orlitzky and Benjamin's (2001) study won the 2001 Best Article Award from the International Association for Business & Society (IABS). Orlitzky, Schmidt, and Rynes' (2003) study won the 2004 Moskowitz Award for out-

standing quantitative research relevant to the social investment field. The Moskowitz Prize is awarded each year to the research paper that best meets the following criteria: 1) practical significance to practitioners of socially responsible investing; 2) appropriateness and rigor of quantitative methods; and 3) novelty of results.

2.   Swanson's theory, which was awarded the "The Best Article in Business and Society" in 2001, incorporates and extends other theoretical perspectives on corporate social performance, including Carroll's (1979), Frederick's (1987), Wartick and Cochran's (1985), and Wood's (1991). Our discussion of Swanson's model is drawn partly from Swanson and Orlitzky's (2006) summary of it.

REFERENCES

Argyris, C. (1993). *Knowledge for action: A guide to overcoming barriers to organizational change.* San Francisco, CA: Jossey-Bass.

Aspen Initiative for Social Innovation through Business (ISIB) (2002). *Where will they lead? MBA student attitudes about Business & Society.* New York: Aspen ISIB.

Austin, J. E., & Kohn, T. O. (1990). *Strategic management in developing countries: Case studies.* New York: Free Press.

Baron, J. N., & Kreps, D. M. (1999). *Strategic human resources: Frameworks for general managers.* New York: Wiley.

Bebeau, M. J. (2004). Influencing the moral dimensions of dental practice. In J. R. Rest, & D. Narvaez (Eds), *Moral Development in the Professions.* New Jersey: Lawrence Erlbaum Associates.

Bloom, M. (1999). The performance effects of pay dispersion on individuals and organizations. *Academy of Management Journal, 42,* 25–40.

Bloom, M., & Michel, J. G. (2002). The relationships among organizational context, pay dispersion, and managerial turnover. *Academy of Management Journal, 45,* 33–42.

Buckley, W. (1968). Society as a complex adaptive system. In W. Buckley (Ed.), *Modern systems research for the behavioral scientist* (pp. 490–513). Chicago: Aldine.

Calton, J. M., & Lad, L. J. (1995). Social contracting as a trust-building process of network governance. *Business Ethics Quarterly, 5,* 271–296.

Cappelli, P. (1999). *The new deal at work: Managing the market-driven workforce.* Cambridge, MA: Harvard Business School Press.

Cappelli, P. (2000). A market-driven approach to retaining talent. *Harvard Business Review, 78*(1), 103–111.

Cardy, R. L. & Selvarajan, T. T. (2006). Beyond rhetoric and bureaucracy: Using HRM to add ethical value. In J. R. Deckop (Ed.), *Human Resource Management Ethics.* Greenwich, CT: Information Age.

Carroll, A. B. (1979). A three-dimensional model of corporate social performance. *Academy of Management Review, 4,* 497–505.

Chikudate, N. (2002). Collective myopia and disciplinary power behind the scenes of unethical practices: A diagnostic theory on Japanese organization. *Journal of Management Studies, 39,* 289–307.

Colby, A., & Kohlberg, L. (1987). *The measurement of moral judgment: Vol. 1. Theoretical foundations and research validations.* Cambridge, MA: Cambridge University Press.

Conant, R. C., & Ashby, R. W. (1970). Every good regulator of a system must be a model of that system. *International Journal of Systems Science, 1*(2), 89–97.

Costa, P. T., Jr., & McCrae, R. R. (1994). Set like plaster? Evidence for the stability of adult personality. In T. F. Heatherton & J. L. Weinberger (Eds.), *Can personality change?* (pp. 21–40). Washington, DC: American Psychological Association.

Delery, J. E., & Doty, D. H. (1996). Modes of theorizing in Strategic Human Resource Management: Tests of universalistic, contingency, and configurational performance predictions. *Academy of Management Journal, 39,* 802–835.

Derry, R. (1989). An empirical study of moral reasoning among managers. *Journal of Business Ethics, 8,* 855–862.

Donaldson, T. (1989). *The ethics of international business.* New York: Oxford University Press.

Ferraro, F., Pfeffer, J. & Sutton, R. I. (2005). Economics language and assumptions: How theories can become self-fulfilling. *Academy of Management Review, 30,* 8–24.

Fisher, D. G. (1997). Assessing taxpayer moral reasoning: The development of an objective measure. *Research on Accounting Ethics, 3,* 141–171.

Fisher, D. G. (1999). Tax compliance decisions and the influence of moral reasoning: An experiment. *Research on Accounting Ethics, 5,* 95–112.

Frederick, W. C. (1987). Theories of corporate social performance. In S. P. Sethi & C. Falbe (Eds.), *Business and society: Dimensions of conflict and cooperation* (pp. 142–161). New York: Lexington Books.

Frederick, W. C. (1995). *Values, nature, and culture in the American corporation.* New York: Oxford University Press.

Ghoshal, S. (2003, Fall). B-Schools share the blame for Enron: Teaching brutal theories leads naturally to management brutality. *Business Ethics, 4.*

Ghoshal, S. (2005). Bad management theories are destroying good management practices. *Academy of Management Learning & Education, 4*(1), 75–91.

Gilligan, C. (1982). *In a different voice.* Cambridge, MA: Harvard University Press.

Gioia, D. A. (2002). Business education's role in the crisis of corporate confidence. *Academy of Management Executive, 16,* 142–144.

Greening, D. W., & Turban, D. B. (2000). Corporate social performance as a competitive advantage in attracting a quality workforce. *Business & Society, 39,* 254–280.

Guest, D. E. (1997). Human resource management and performance: A review and research agenda. *International Journal of Human Resource Management, 8*(3), 263–276.

Hawken, P., Lovins, A. B., & Lovins, L. H. (1999). *Natural capitalism: The next industrial revolution.* London: Earthscan.

Huselid, M. A. (1992). The incentive effects of tournament compensation systems. *Administrative Science Quarterly, 37,* 336–350.

Husted, B. (2000). A contingency theory of corporate social performance. *Business & Society, 39,* 24–48.

Jaffee, S., & Hyde, J. S. (2000). Gender differences in moral orientation: A meta-analysis. *Psychological Bulletin, 126,* 703–726.

Janis, I. L., & Mann, L. (1977). *Decision making: A psychological analysis of conflict, choice, and commitment.* New York: Free Press.

Jones, T. M. (1991). Ethical decision making by individuals in organizations: An issue-contingent model. *Academy of Management Review, 16,* 366–395.

Jones, T. M. (1995). Instrumental stakeholder theory: A synthesis of ethics and economics. *Academy of Management Review, 20*(2), 404–437.

Kanter, R. M. (2001). The ten deadly mistakes of wanna-dots. *Harvard Business Review, 79*(1), 91–100.

Kaplan, R. S., & Norton, D. P. (1992). The balanced scorecard: Measures that drive performance. *Harvard Business Review, 69*(1), 71–79.

Kaplan, R. S., & Norton, D. P. (2004). Measuring the strategic readiness of intangible assets. *Harvard Business Review, 82*(2), 52–63.

Kelly, M. (2002, Fall). It's a heckuva time to be dropping business ethics courses. *Business Ethics,* 17–18.

Kerr, S. (1995). An Academy classic: On the folly of rewarding A, while hoping for B. *Academy of Management Executive, 9,* 7–16.

Kristof, A. L. (1996). Person-organization fit: An integrative review of its conceptualizations, measurement, and implications. *Personnel Psychology, 49,* 1–49.

Liedtka, J. M. (1998). Constructing an ethic for business practice. *Business & Society, 37*(3), 254–280.

Matten, D., & Crane, A. (2005). Corporate citizenship: Toward an extended theoretical conceptualization. *Academy of Management Review, 30*(1), 166–179.

Mirvis, P. H. (2000). Transformation at Shell: Commerce and citizenship. *Business and Society Review, 105*(1), 63–84.

Muchinsky, P. M., & Monahan, C. J. (1987). What is person-environment congruence? Supplementary versus complementary models of fit. *Journal of Vocational Behavior, 31,* 268–277.

Nichols, M. P. (1995). *The lost art of listening.* New York: Guilford.

Orlitzky, M. (in press). Links between corporate social responsibility and corporate financial performance: Theoretical and empirical determinants. In J. Allouche (Ed.), *Corporate social responsibility, Vol. 2: Performances and stakeholders.* London: Palgrave Macmillan.

Orlitzky, M. (2005). Social responsibility and financial performance: Trade-off or virtuous circle? *University of Auckland Business Review, 7*(1), 37–43.

Orlitzky, M., & Benjamin, J. D. (2001). Corporate social performance and firm risk: A meta-analytic review. *Business & Society, 40*(4), 369–396.

Orlitzky, M., & Rynes, S. L. (2001). When employees become owners: Can employee loyalty be bought? In D. Rousseau & C. Cooper (Eds.), *Trends in Organizational Behavior* (Vol. 8). New York: Wiley.

Orlitzky, M., Schmidt, F. L., & Rynes, S. L. (2003). Corporate social and financial performance: A meta-analysis. *Organization Studies, 24*(3), 403–441.

Orlitzky, M., & Swanson, D. L. (2002). *Value attunement:* Toward a theory of socially responsible executive decision making. *Australian Journal of Management, 27*(Special Issue), 119–128.

Orlitzky, M., Swanson, D. L., & Quartermaine, L.-K. (in press). Normative myopia, executives' personality, and preference for pay dispersion: Toward implications for corporate social performance. *Business and Society.*

Peterson, R. B. (2004). A call for testing our assumptions: Human resource management today. *Journal of Management Inquiry, 13*(3), 192–202.

Pfeffer, J. (1998). *The human equation: Building profits by putting people first.* Boston, MA: Harvard Business School Press.

Pfeffer, J. (2003). *Economic logic and language in organization studies: The undermining of critical thinking.* Paper presented at the Academy of Management conference, Seattle, WA.

Rest, J. R. (1988) Why does college promote development in moral judgment? *Journal of Moral Education, 17*(3): 183–194

Roddick, A. (1991). *Body and soul: Profits with principles.* New York: Crown.

Rokeach, M.J. (1973). *The nature of human values.* New York: Free Press.

Ruegger, D., & King, E. W. (1992). A study of the effect of age and gender upon student business ethics. *Journal of Business Ethics, 11*, 179–186.

Rynes, S. L. (2004). Where do we go from here? Imagining new roles for human resources. *Journal of Management Inquiry, 13*(3), 203–213.

Rynes, S. L., Trank, C. Q., Lawson, A. M., & Ilies, R. (2003). Behavioral coursework in business education: Growing evidence of a legitimacy crisis. *Academy of Management Learning & Education, 2*, 269–283.

Schein, E. H. (1992). *Organizational culture and leadership* 2nd ed. San Francisco, CA: Jossey-Bass.

Schneider, B. (1987). The people make the place. *Personnel Psychology, 40*, 437–453.

Schumann, P. L. (2006). The role of moral development in motivating ethical behavior by employees. In J. R. Deckop (Ed.), *Human Resource Management Ethics.* Greenwich, CT: Information Age.

Schwartz, R. H., & Post, F. R. (2002). The unexplored potential of hope to level the playing field: A multilevel perspective. *Journal of Business Ethics, 37*(2), 135–143.

Scott, W. G., & Hart, D. K. (1979). *Organizational America.* Boston, MA: Houghton Mifflin.

Senge, P. M. (1990). *The fifth discipline: The art and practice of the learning organization.* New York: Doubleday.

Senge, P. M., Kleiner, A., Roberts, C., Ross, R. B., & Smith, B. J. (1994). *The fifth discipline fieldbook: Strategies and tools for building a learning organization.* New York: Doubleday.

Sethi, S. P. (1994). *Multinational corporations and the impact of public advocacy on corporate strategy: Nestle and the infant formula controversy.* Norwell, MA: Kluwer.

Shaw, J. D., Gupta, N., & Delery, J. E. (2002). Pay dispersion and workforce performance: Moderating effects of incentives and interdependence. *Strategic Management Journal, 23*(6), 491–512.

Sheridan, J. E. (1992). Organizational culture and employee retention. *Academy of Management Journal, 35*, 1036–1056.

Simmons, J. (2003). Balancing performance, accountability and equity in stakeholder relationships: Towards more socially responsible HR practice. *Corporate Social Responsibility and Environmental Management, 10*(3), 129–140.

Simon, H. (1957). *Administrative behavior.* New York: Macmillan.

Skeel, D. (2005). The empty legacy of the corporate scandals. *Challenge, 48*(1), 104–117.

Skoldberg, K. (1994). Tales of change. *Organization Science, 5,* 219–238.

Smith, W. J., Wokutch, R. E., Harrington, K. V., & Dennis, B. S. (2004). Organizational attractiveness and corporate social orientation: Do our values influence our preference for affirmative action and managing diversity? *Business & Society, 43*(1), 69–96.

Swanson, D. L. (1995). Addressing a theoretical problem by reorienting the corporate social performance model. *Academy of Management Review, 20,* 43–64.

Swanson, D. L. (1999). Toward an integrative theory of business and society: A research strategy for corporate social performance. *Academy of Management Review, 24,* 506–521.

Swanson, D. L., & Frederick, W. C. (2005). Denial and leadership in business ethics education. In O.C. Ferrell & R. A. Peterson (Eds.), *Business ethics: The new challenge for business schools and corporate leaders.* New York: M.E. Sharpe.

Swanson, D. L., & Orlitzky, M. (2006). Executive preference for compensation structure and normative myopia: A business and society research project. In R. W. Kolb (Ed.), *The ethics of executive compensation* (pp. 13–31). Malden, MA: Blackwell.

Thomas, D. (2004, July 13). Academy aims to entrench CSR as day-to-day concern. *Personnel Today,* 4.

Turban, D. B., & Cable, D. M. (2003). Firm reputation and applicant pool characteristics. *Journal of Organizational Behavior, 24*(6), 733–751.

Turban, D. B., & Greening, D. W. (1997). Corporate social performance and organizational attractiveness to prospective employees. *Academy of Management Journal, 40,* 658–672.

Ulrich, D., Brockbank, W., Yeung, A. K., & Lake, D. G. (1995). Human resource competencies: An empirical assessment. *Human Resource Management, 34,* 473–495.

Waddock, S. (2002). *Leading corporate citizens: Vision, values, value added.* Boston, MA: McGraw-Hill.

Waddock, S. (2003). *A radical agenda for business in society education.* Presented at the Academy of Management, Social Issues in Management Division, Seattle.

Walker, L. J. (1984). Sex differences in the development of moral reasoning: A critical review. *Child Development, 55,* 677–691.

Wartick, S. L. & Cochran, P. L. (1985). The evolution of the corporate social performance model. *Academy of Management Review, 10,* 758–769.

Weber, J. (1990). Managers' moral reasoning: Assessing their responses to three moral dilemmas. *Human Relations, 43*(7), 687–702.

Weber, J., & Wasieleski, D. (2001). Investigating influences on managers' moral reasoning: The impact of context and personal and organizational factors. *Business & Society, 40,* 79–111.

Weick, K. E. (1979). *The social psychology of organizing* (2nd ed.). New York: McGraw-Hill.

Willen, L. (2004, March 8). Kellogg denies guilt as B-Schools evade alumni lapses. *Bloomberg Press Wire.*

Windsor, D. (2002, October 8). *An open letter on business school responsibility.* [Posted on IABS and SIM newsgroups of the Academy of Management.]

Wood, D. J. (1991). Corporate social performance revisited. *Academy of Management Review, 16,* 691–718

Zappala, G. (2004). Corporate citizenship and human resource management: A new tool or missed opportunity? *Asia Pacific Journal of Human Resources, 42*(2), 185–201.

CHAPTER 2

ETHICS AND STRATEGIC HUMAN RESOURCE MANAGEMENT

David P. Lepak and Saba Colakoglu
Rutgers, The State University of New Jersey

INTRODUCTION

Strategic human resource management (SHRM) is a field of study that examines the relationship between the use of human resource (HR) practices and organizational outcomes, and focuses on the pattern of planned human resource deployments and activities intended to enable an organization achieve its goals (Wright & McMahan, 1992). Based predominantly on the resource-based view of the firm (Barney, 1991) and the behavioral perspective (Jackson, Schuler, & Rivero, 1989), strategic HRM researchers have built a strong body of evidence suggesting that HR practices may directly influence a firm's potential competitive advantage. Specifically, competitive advantage achieved via HR practices results from an increase in the level and type of human capital (knowledge, skills, and abilities) of the workforce as well as an alignment of employee attitudes and behaviors with organizational contingencies. Extending this logic, strategic HRM researchers have made considerable progress demonstrating the validity of

Human Resource Management Ethics, pages 27–45

their arguments by finding apparent links between the use of HR practices and organizational performance (Collins & Clark, 2003; Delery & Doty, 1996; Huselid, 1995).

While understanding the potential value creating capability of an effective HR system for organizational performance is certainly a critical endeavor, the focus of this chapter is to consider the potential role of ethics in strategic HRM research. Although there is certainly nothing ethically wrong about focusing on organizational performance, it is important to recognize that the effectiveness of HR systems may be viewed from a variety of perspectives; perspectives that may vary in terms of the measures of effectiveness they emphasize. At a basic level, one can view an organization as navigating among the needs of various stakeholders. While financial stakeholders have received the most attention in the strategic HRM literature, other stakeholder groups such as unions, customers, and employees themselves are important stakeholders as well. As Wal-Mart has currently been experiencing, for example, it is often difficult to meet the needs of all stakeholders simultaneously. Indeed, we have recently witnessed a flurry of news stories related to organizations' actions that may be questioned from an ethical point of view. While the stories that may have received the most attention have focused on the actions of top managers in companies such as Enron and Tyco, the potential role of ethics for strategically managing employees is potentially more pervasive.

In the remainder of this chapter, we review the key components of a strategic approach to HRM and then integrate stakeholder theory (Freeman, 1984) as a complement to existing frameworks in strategic HRM to explore how strategic HRM may take into account the needs of different stakeholders. At heart of this issue is whether strategic HRM researchers can make use of theories that balance the simultaneous need to be ethical and organizationally efficient. Finally, research and practical implications are discussed.

CONCEPTUAL BACKGROUND

Before we can explore the role of strategic HRM research and ethics in organizations, it is important to have a clear understanding of what strategic HRM research is about. A useful way to understand the focus of this stream of research is in comparison to more traditional HRM research. Even though strategic HRM may be considered as an extension of the traditional HRM literature, there are three main points of departure that differentiates the two.

The first point of departure for strategic HRM research is a focus on HR systems as opposed to individual HR practices. While the terminology may differ across studies, HR systems refer to a configuration or bundle of HR practices that complement and mutually reinforce each other. The emphasis on HR systems is based on the logic that employees are faced with multiple HR practices simultaneously rather than individual HR practices and that the influence of one HR practice on employees is, at least partially, dependent on the impact of other HR practices in place to manage employees.

The second point of departure of strategic HRM from traditional HRM research is its emphasis on both internal and external contingency variables that are argued to moderate the HR system-organizational performance relationship (Baird & Meshoulam, 1988; Miles & Snow, 1984). The logic of this emphasis on internal and external alignment reflects the importance of fit between the needs, demands, goals, objectives and structure of an organization and the needs, demands, and goals of its internal and external environment (Nadler & Tushman, 1977; Wright & Sherman, 1999). Conceptually, HR practices are implemented in response to various contingencies in the environment to encourage the development of needed skills among employees as well as encourage the display of needed role behaviors by employees. Although strategy has been a prominent focus for researchers in this contingency perspective (e.g., Youndt, et al., 1996) other variables such as industry (Datta, Guthrie, & Wright, 2005; Jackson, et al., 1989), technology (Snell & Dean, 1994), and life cycle stage (Baird & Meshoulam, 1988) have also been examined.

The third point of departure is the focus of strategic HRM on organizational performance as the main outcome of interest. In 1998, Rogers and Wright reviewed 59 studies that examined the relationship between HR systems and various organizational outcomes and revealed that only two of those studies used employee outcomes such as turnover as the outcome of interest. On the other hand, 40 of the studies reviewed by Rogers and Wright (1998) used accounting measures and financial market measures of performance such as return on asset, return on equity, and Tobin's Q delineating the importance of financial performance for SHRM research. This focus on performance, in part, reflects the concern of HR departments and practitioners over demonstrating the value of the HR function and proving its contribution to the bottom-line, as well as projecting the importance of shareholders as a critical organizational stakeholder. However, meeting the needs of the shareholders may at times come at the expense of hurting other stakeholders such as employees, customers, or the society at large. Therefore, strategic HRM may benefit from a more balanced emphasis on meeting the demands of other stakeholder groups with diverse needs, interests, and agendas. However, creating this balance among diverse and sometimes conflicting interests is an extremely challenging task for practitioners and researchers alike. One framework that may guide organizations in adapting a more balanced approach is the stakeholder theory and the concept of stakeholder management. Next, we review this theory and discuss its implications for strategic HRM.

Stakeholder Theory and HRM Research

Adopting a stakeholder perspective requires that we cast organizations in the context of all of the stakeholders that have a vested interest in an organization. In his pioneering book on stakeholder theory, Freeman (1984) defines a stakeholder as "any group or individual who can affect or is affected by the achievements of the organization's objectives" (p. 46). Clarifying further the notion of who a stakeholder is, Mitchell, Agle, and Wood (1997) proposed that any group or person who has the power to influence the organization, has a legitimate relationship with the organization and has an urgent claim on the firm can be considered as a stakeholder. Depending on the saliency of the power, legitimacy, and urgency dimensions, Mitchell and colleagues (1997) differentiated between categories of stakeholders as latent (a group or a person that is hardly recognizable on all the dimensions), dormant (a group or a person that is high on the dimension of the power to influence the firm), discretion (a group or a person that has a legitimate relationship with the organization but does not have the power to influence) and demanding (the group or the person has an urgent claim but has no power or legitimacy).

The challenge with adopting a stakeholder perspective is not only to understand what a stakeholder is, but also who the stakeholders are. And while we might conceptualize many different internal and external parties of an organization who have a vested interest in its operations, Hitt, Ireland, and Hoskisson (2005) suggest that there exist three primary groups of stakeholders that exert distinct pressures on organizations. First, companies must attend to the needs of capital-market stakeholders—shareholders and major suppliers of capital such as banks. Second, companies must consider the needs and demands of product-market stakeholders—the primary customers, suppliers, unions, and host communities with whom organizations conduct business. Finally, companies must also consider the needs of organizational stakeholders, the employees and managers within the organization.

According to stakeholder theory, organizations that are capable of adapting to the needs of the key constituencies will outperform those that do not in the long-run (Kotter & Heskett, 1992). This perspective implies that the simultaneous fulfillment of diverse stakeholder needs do not come at the expense of business performance, but that it actually aids organizations to improve their performance. In this sense, it is likely that the importance of the ability to balance and respond to the diverse needs of different stakeholder groups will increase in the future. However, empirical evidence that relates to the achievement of stakeholder management and firm performance is mixed. Research on the closely related concept of corporate social responsibility, which is also discussed by Orlitzky and Swanson (This Issue), reveals that the relation between corporate social responsibility and firm performance is a complex one (Godfrey, 2005; Margolis & Walsh, 2001). As we will discuss, the challenge faced by organizations is that different stakeholder groups often hold disparate interests for how companies should conduct business. As such, meeting the needs of different stakeholders may have important implications for how HR systems are designed. In the next section we review existing strategic HRM related research that has focused on each of the different stakeholder groups and then turn toward research challenges for addressing multiple stakeholder groups simultaneously.

Capital-Market Stakeholders and Strategic HRM Research

Of the three stakeholder groups, capital-market stakeholders have implicitly received a majority of the research focus among strategic HRM researchers. Indeed, the strong emphasis on strategy as a dominant contingency variable as well as financial and market based performance metrics in strategic HRM research reflects the importance placed on meeting the needs of individuals or organizations with a vested interest in the financial performance of companies.

In this stream of research, researchers have emphasized two dominant perspectives for examining strategic HRM—the universalistic perspective and the contingency perspective (Delery & Doty, 1996). The universalistic perspective, also referred to as the best practice approach, rests on the logic that there is a set of HR practices which lead to increased organizational performance regardless of the context in which the organization operates. Pfeffer (1995), for example, identified HR best practices that differentiate successful companies from those that are not. Regardless of the strategy or the industry in which they operate, these successful companies had HR systems that provided employees with employment security, were highly selective in their recruiting, had high wages, relied on incentive pay and employee ownership, ensured information sharing, participation and empowerment, implemented self-managed teams, and had intensive training and skill development programs.

Although there are variations across studies as to what constitutes an HR best practice, HR practices that have been considered as part of a high performance work system traditionally includes selective staffing, intensive training and development opportunities, employee involvement programs, developmental performance appraisals, job security, and the like (Arthur, 1992; Huselid, 1995; MacDuffie, 1995). There are also variations across studies as to the terminology used to refer to such HR systems, but in terms of the empirical evidence, this perspective has received considerable support. For example, researchers have found that high performance work systems (Huselid, 1995), innovative employment practices (Ichniowski, Shaw, & Prennushi, 1997), or high involvement HR practices (Batt, 2002) have direct effects on performance including market based performance measures (Huselid, 1995), productivity (Ichniowski et al., 1997), lower scrap rates (Arthur, 1994), lower quit rates (Arthur, 1994; Batt, 2002), and higher sales growth (Batt, 2002).

The second dominant mode of theorizing—the contingency perspective—is based on the logic that the impact of an HR system on organizational outcomes is contingent upon the alignment of the HR system with contextual factors such as strategy (Arthur, 1992; Youndt et al., 1996), technology (e.g., Snell & Dean, 1992), industry (e.g., Datta, et al., 2005; Jackson, et al., 1989), and life cycle stage (Baird & Meshoulam, 1988). Perhaps the most well-developed contingency in this stream of research is the relationship between strategy and HR systems. This conceptual logic suggests that companies competing with a high-road strategy need to align their HR system with this strategy, and thus invest more in their people. Accordingly, companies that can achieve such an alignment will be more successful than companies who cannot achieve it or fail to do so. While a small number of researchers have found some empirical support for this particular type of alignment, the overall trend of the findings is mixed. In terms of the evidence that supports such an alignment between high-road strategy and high performance work systems, Youndt et al. (1996) examined the relationship between manufacturing strategy, HRM, and operational performance (employee productivity, machine efficiency, and customer alignment) and found a moderating effect of a quality strategy on the relationship between the use of a human-capital-enhancing HR system and operational performance. Similarly Lee and Miller (1999) reported that dedicated positioning strategies work better when they are coupled with a commitment type of HR system. However, some studies did not find any support for this argument at all (Delery, & Doty, 1996; Huselid, 1995, Huselid, & Becker, 1996, 1997).

As opposed to high road strategies, some companies compete on the basis of a low cost approach. Extending the contingency logic to HR, an HR system that supports a low-cost strategy is a system in which employees are viewed not necessarily as an asset to be capitalized on, but as a cost to be minimized. Such systems are characterized by a focus on cost, control, and lack of participation and involvement of employees. For example,

Youndt et al (1996) reported an interaction between the use of a low-cost strategy and administrative HR system on operational performance. That is, companies that implemented a low-road strategy, and aligned this strategy with an administrative HR system which is based on low cost and diminished developmental opportunities performed better. Similarly, Arthur (1992) found a relationship between a low cost strategy and a control oriented HR system among steal mini-mills. While the research emphasis on the contingency perspective is admittedly mixed, this perspective continues to be conceptually attractive for strategic HRM research.

While there remains considerable research to be done in this research domain, an emerging theme is that HR systems do have an impact on financial and market based performance measures as well as intermediate variables such as turnover and labor productivity that directly or indirectly influence these performance measures.

Organizational Stakeholders and Strategic HRM Research

While strategic HRM researchers have focused considerable energy on addressing the capital market stakeholders, several other research domains have paid more attention to organizational stakeholders—in particular, employees as a stakeholder group. On the one hand, there is a long history in more traditional human resource management that examines the implications of various HR practices and activities on employees. A large volume of research has accumulated in this area over the years examining the impact of single HR practices such as selection (e.g., Barrick, Patton & Haugland, 2000), training and development (e.g., Frayne & Geringer, 2000), recruitment (e.g., Philips, 1998), compensation (e.g., Rynes & Bono, 2000), and performance management (e.g., Welbourne, Johnson, and Erez, 1998) on individual level outcomes. Although there is considerable emphasis even within this research stream on the outcome of job performance (Wright & Boswell, 2002), researchers have also examined the impact of these practices on more employee-focused outcomes such as job satisfaction (e.g., Seibert, Silver, & Randolph, 2004), motivation (e.g., Bloom 1999), socialization (e.g., Klein & Weaver, 2000), and career success (e.g., Janasz, Sullivan, & Whiting, 2003). An emphasis on such employee-focused outcomes takes into account the importance of meeting the needs and interests of employees as major stakeholders in the organization.

A secondary stream that has focused on employees, as well as on unions that we discuss below, is the industrial relations literature. Industrial relations research focuses on the employee as the main stakeholder of interest. As noted by Osterman and colleagues (2001, p. 3):

> The institutional perspective recognizes a set of moral values, which individu-
> als seek to realize through work. These values are distinct from economic
> efficiency and are not necessarily promoted by the market. They include
> equity and due process in the management of the workplace, work as a cre-
> ative and dignifying activity, and the right of workers to a voice in the organi-
> zation and governance of the workplace. An institutional perspective
> understands the economy as embedded in the social structure and as
> depending on that structure for its capacity to operate effectively.

The main difference between industrial relations research and strategic HRM research is that while strategic HRM approaches the study of work and employment from the employer's perspective, and thus implicitly the shareholders' or capital market perspective, industrial relations research approaches the same topic from the employee's perspective (Kaufman, 2001) and explains why individual workers may be at a power disadvantage against the corporation and advocates collective forms of dealing between employees and employers.

Interestingly, researchers coming from an industrial relations (IR) perspective often focus on similar issues as strategic HRM researchers, albeit from different philosophical and disciplinary perspectives. For example, IR researchers such as Osterman (1994) and Pil and Ichniowski (1996) examined the use of several innovative or flexible work place practices such as job rotation, quality circles, total quality management, and participation. While these practices have considerable overlap with HR systems studied by strategic HRM researchers, the vantage point of the perspective adopted here emphasizes work practices that benefit the employee rather than solely focusing on the interests of the organization. Nevertheless, the fact that researchers from strategic HRM and IR backgrounds share common interest in a broadly conceived notion of HR practices, this suggests a strong possibility for research opportunities to examine the potential for mutual gains initiatives that may benefit both employees as well as capital market stakeholders.

Product-Market Stakeholders and Strategic HRM Research

One line of research that has been concerned with the interests of the customers as a stakeholder group is the climate research that focuses on the climate for service. Although customer satisfaction is seen as a mediating variable between human resource practices and business performance in this model, climate for service research is different from strategic HRM by its focus on the customer as the main outcome of interest. In general, climate is defined as the incumbents' perceptions of the routines and rewards that characterize a setting (Schneider & Reichers, 1990) and can be understood as the immediate environment surrounding the individuals when they enter an organization. Climate research generally has a strategic target or focus of interest (such as service, justice, or safety), and attempts to identify those elements of the work environment-as described by employees-that correlate, or link, to critically important organizational outcomes such as customer satisfaction. Studies that indicate a significant and positive relationship between how favorably members of an organization describe their work environment and customer satisfaction levels are numerous.

Wiley and Brooks (2000), reviewed the literature on this type of linkage research and found that various dimensions of work climate, such as customer orientation, quality emphasis, teamwork/cooperation, involvement/empowerment have been found to correlate with overall customer satisfaction. What this research stream suggests is that we could identify some practices that simultaneously meet the needs of the customers, employees, and shareholders. For instance, Liao and Chuang (2004), found that service climate and employee involvement explain individual level employee service performance which, in turn, is related to customer satisfaction and loyalty.

Since product-market stakeholders are those stakeholders that are positioned outside the organization, it is useful to consider unions as one of the stakeholders that belong to this group. According to the industrial relations paradigm, collective forms of employee representation are the most efficient ones for promoting industrial democracy. Thus, in essence the interests of unions are no different than the interests of employees. Freeman and Medoff (1979) argued that there are two fundamentally different ways of looking at unions, which they called the two faces of unionism. In the collective-voice view, the unions promote the interests of employees, shareholders, and the society collectively. They do so by improving communication between managers and workers, collecting information about the preferences of all workers and having positive effects on productivity, as well as reducing the inequality of pay among workers, and representing the political interests of lower income and disadvantaged people. On the other extreme is the monopolistic view of unions which views this institution as raising wages above competitive levels, reducing productivity, lowering society's output through frequent strikes, and fighting for their own interests in the political arena. These two faces of unionism put unions in a controversial position within the stakeholder theory: do unions promote its own interest at the expense of the business, economy, and society or do unions help promote the interests of all these groups simultaneously. Although the evidence about the effects of unions on organizational performance and overall economy is mixed, unions are an important stakeholder group that needs to be taken into account along with employees, customers, suppliers, financial institutions, shareholders, and the like.

Research Implications for Strategic HRM

One of the primary objectives of this chapter was to explore the potential value of adopting a stakeholder perspective for strategic HRM research. We argue that a stakeholder perspective can be meaningfully integrated into strategic HRM research due to the descriptive, instrumental, and normative nature of the stakeholder theory (Donaldson & Preston, 1995). This theory is descriptive because it enables the description of an organization as a constellation of cooperative and competitive interests. At the same time, it is instrumental because it builds the corporate connection between stakeholder management and achievement of organizational goals, mainly performance. Third, it has a normative aspect since stakeholders are persons or groups with legitimate interest in procedural and/ or substantive aspects of corporate activity and organizations and all of their interests have intrinsic value. In this normative line of reasoning the questions relate to "what moral obligations do stakeholders place on managers?," "what are the relative importance of the fiduciary duty to shareholders and other stakeholder groups?" (Jones & Wicks, 1999; Goodpaster, 1991), "what is the end an organization pursues and what are the means it can utilize to achieve those ends?" (Freeman, 1994). According to Freeman (1994), stakeholder theory has a strict normative core to it since it nicely blends together central concepts of business with those of ethics. At the same time, however, many challenges remain for considering the needs and desires of various stakeholder groups for strategic HRM research.

Addressing Multiple Stakeholder Demands Simultaneously

Amy Domini, named to the *Time* 100 list of the world's most influential people, is an investment professional who advises individuals and institutions on integrating their social and financial criteria into their investment decisions (*Time*, 2005). The Domini 400 Social Index^{SM}, is an index of 400 primarily large-capitalization U.S. corporations, roughly comparable to the S&P 500, selected based on a wide range of social and environmental criteria such as corporate citizenship, diversity, employee relations, environment, non-U.S. operations, and safe and useful products. In terms of assessing an organization's quality of employee relations, Domini looks closely at how a company treats its employees, evaluates the company's record with regard to labor relations; workplace safety and employee benefit programs including an analysis of the firm's attempts to allow employees to meaningfully participate in profits and decision-making through stock purchase or profit-sharing plans, and other innovative management techniques.

While the Domini example demonstrates that some companies can indeed balance various stakeholder demands, it is important to recognize that within organizations it is extremely challenging to overcome the inherent difficulties with meeting the conflicting needs of these different stakeholder groups. Thus, a logical question that needs to be considered in strategic HRM research is: How well are the universalistic and the contingency perspectives equipped to face this challenge of meeting multiple stakeholder needs?

The ethical implications of existing research adopting a universalistic perspective are straightforward and promising. This perspective suggests that investing in employees, encouraging their participation and involvement, giving them ownership in the organization, empowering them, and having their best interest-such as job security in mind leads to the development of a skillful, committed, and a motivated workforce which, in turn, will engage in positive employee attitudes and behaviors such as improved job performance, and organizational citizenship. Naturally, such a workforce will be a strategic and valuable asset for the organization that will transfer into a source of a sustained competitive advantage. Although there is a tradition, especially within the field of industrial relations to view the goals of employees and owners/managers as naturally conflicting with each other, the universalistic perspective rests on the ground that the goals of employees and owners/managers may actually align with each other. While creating wealth for its shareholders is perhaps the ultimate goal of any for-profit organization, this perspective suggests that if the organization can achieve this end by treating its employees right, high involvement HR systems will work well for both the organization and the employees. That is, both the goal of the organization, which is to create wealth, and the goals of the employees, which is to find meaning in their jobs and to be treated with respect, dignity, and equity may be met simultaneously under the universalistic perspective.

The ethical implications of the prescribed alignment between high-road strategies and high investment HR systems may mirror the implications of the universalistic perspective. That is, because this perspective prescribes the use of HR practices that not only benefit the company, but also the employees, the interests of both of these parties are well respected and represented in this approach. However, we anticipate that achieving alignment between HR systems focusing on cost controls or control oriented systems may be in conflict with meeting the needs of organizational stakeholders and some product market stakeholders. For example, Wal-Mart is a salient example of a company who has successfully achieved the fit between its low-cost strategy and its HR system. Wal-Mart became the world's largest retailer by selling goods to consumers at rock-bottom prices. It is the nation's largest private-sector employer with more than 1.3 million workers and has been among the top 5 *Fortune* "Most Admired Companies" during the last 5 years and has recently been named the #1 globally admired firm (*Fortune*, 2005). Moreover, customers flock to Wal-Mart to take advantage of their extremely low prices.

Despite its apparent financial success, the HR system that is in place which is in line with its strategy is a cost-oriented HR system in which the ultimate goal is to minimize employee costs. Although the business model of Wal-Mart makes business sense, the question is, to what extent is Wal-Mart able to treat its employees with respect, dignity, and care within the boundaries of such a business model? The company has attracted dozens of lawsuits against it alleging pay and labor violations and gender discrimination (*CNNMoney*, 2004), and with regard to its treatment of suppliers, it has also drawn fire for stifling small businesses and squeezing its vendors. Wal-Mart's "vast economic power" allows it to impose price and time requirements on supplier factories that, some have argued, may result in sweatshop conditions. Thus, the business model of Wal-Mart benefits the shareholders with high profit margins, and the customers with low prices at the expense of other stakeholders such as employees and suppliers. This is not to suggest that Wal-Mart is not a fine company or a good employer; rather, from a stakeholder perspective, we use this example simply because it is a highly visible company that has received considerable press and highlights the difficulties of meeting the needs of all stakeholders, particularly for companies pursuing a low cost strategy.

Another example from the same industry, which is in sharp contrast to that of Wal-Mart is Costco Wholesale, the nation's fifth-largest retailer. While Costco seems to be implementing the same type of low cost strategy as Wal-Mart is, its approach to employee relations is fundamentally different (Greenhouse, 2005). Costco's average pay, for example, is $17 an hour, 42 percent higher than its biggest rival, Sam's Club, and Costco workers pay 8 percent toward their health costs, when the retail average is 25 percent. Based on the contingency perspective, such a mismatch between business strategy and HR system is not desirable. Wall Street analysts are also not content with the road that Costco takes, complaining that Costco is overly generous to its employees. Despite this misalignment and criticisms by financial analysts, Costco's stock price has risen more than 10 percent in the last 12 months, while Wal-Mart's has decreased 5 percent indicating either that the contingency perspective does not hold or that the strategy implemented by Costco is not actually low-cost. Indeed, one can argue that Costco's strategy is to target a niche market that is both cost-conscious and also desire the fact that low prices do not come at the workers' expense. In any case, the examples of Costco and Wal-Mart demonstrate the tension between meeting capital market needs and employee needs.

While researchers have examined the tension between meeting capital market needs (financial performance) and investing in meeting employee needs, research is needed that examines how these tensions can be balanced with meeting the needs of the product market stakeholders as well. In particular, issues regarding social responsibility and union relations have not been well integrated into strategic HRM research. The need for meeting customer needs is very obvious—if customers are not happy and purchasing a company's products or services, a company's financial performance will suffer. The relationship between union relations with financial returns, however, is more complicated. Although the proponents of the monopolistic view of unions would argue that the existence of unions would hinder the overall productivity and profitability of the firm, proponents of the collectivist view have tried to come up with evidence against this view. For example, Freeman and Keliner (1999) found very little support that unionization increases the insolvency of firms. They concluded that unions behave in an economically rational manner, pushing wages to the point where union firms may expand less rapidly than nonunion firms, but not to the point where the firm closes down. While it is too early to reach a definitive conclusion regarding this issue, research is needed that investigates the role of social responsibility and union relations in strategic HRM research.

Do All Stakeholder Needs Have to be Met?

Of course, adopting a stakeholder view in strategic HRM research raises an additional question that must be examined. Specifically, do companies have to address all stakeholder needs? While there are conceptual arguments that balancing the needs of multiple stakeholders may prove beneficial for organizations, research is needed to examine if there really is a need to meet these various demands. While from an ethical perspective it may be desirable to do so, it is possible that doing so may compromise the ability to meet any stakeholder's needs by trying to meet all stakeholder needs at once. An alternative approach to meeting all stakeholder needs simultaneously is more of a sequential or life-cycle model for meeting stakeholder needs. In the strategic HRM literature, Baird and Meshoulam (1988) provided a logic that the demands placed on the human resource management activities within a company evolve as companies grow from birth to maturity to decline. Essentially, the HRM needs for companies vary at each stage of the life-cycle.

Extending this logic, it is possible that companies may adopt a life-cycle approach to meeting stakeholder needs and focus on meeting the relevant needs of particularly salient stakeholders during the evolution of the company. For example, early in an organization's existence, capital market stakeholders may be particular salient since they may have funded the organization and look for considerable returns on their investments. More established companies may be in a better position to balance the financial concerns of capital market stakeholders and pay increased attention to their relations with relevant product market stakeholders such as communities, unions, and suppliers. Organizational stakeholders are likely to be important stakeholders through out the life-cycle of an organization but may receive increased attention during high growth periods as well as periods of organizational decline. While there are many stories of mass layoffs, some companies are very pro-active in terms of how their employees are treated and their employment prospects during periods of corporate decline. However the ability of organizations to maintain high involvement work practices with job security pledges may be constrained by the macro-economic context in which the companies are embedded in. For example, Levine and Tyson (1990) discuss the transaction costs of adopting such systems, and discuss the features of product, labor, and capital market conditions that make the adoption of these HR systems feasible. Accordingly, a stable demand for the product, tight labor markets and low unemployment, as well as a long-term orientation in the capital markets may make the adoption of such systems easier.

For example, most of the Japanese organizations were able to adopt and maintain such systems during the post-war years up until mid 90s since their environment was a high-growth one, characterized by relatively small cyclical disturbances. Therefore there was a stable and increasing demand in the product market making it possible for Japanese organizations to offer life-time employment to its employees. Because of rapid, stable growth, such firms operated in tight labor markets in which there was a strong competition for good employees. So, it was in the firm's interest to have healthy labor relations systems to attract and maintain good people. Rapid growth also allowed the firms to offer their workers quick promotion opportunities in return for their commitment to firms' success reinforcing life time employment. The capital market environment in Japan has also supported the adoption and maintenance of high involvement HR systems. Most institutional investors in Japan are other large Japanese firms and large banks that have close ties to product or input markets and have close long-term relations with the organizations that they invest in. Such a capital regime with its long-term orientation makes it favorable to invest in human capital through training and development since such investments materialize over a longer period of time (Hyman, 2004).

On the other hand, the economy of U.S. has been characterized by cyclical periods of growth and recession which made long-range plans or investments less stable for U.S. employers. Similarly, since company financing is obtained from the stock market, the employers are forced to focus on short term goals of its investors making the adoption of such HR systems problematic. Therefore, companies in U.S. who try to maintain their employment prospects during periods of economic decline are, in a way, penalized because of the unfavorable economic context that they operate in.

Another perspective may be that only certain stakeholders really matter. In cost oriented companies, for example, HR systems are often designed to make employees semi-replaceable (Arthur, 1992) and to keep fixed labor costs to a minimum. In this design, do cost oriented organizations really need to treat employees ethically to realize a profit? If the shareholders and customers are happy, what are the real consequences for these types of organizations to not meet the needs of organizational stakeholders? This is not to suggest there are no consequences; rather, from a theoretical and research perspective, what exactly are the consequences? While we would personally agree with a call for the ethical treatment of all stakeholders, research is needed to examine the costs and benefits of trying to meet all stakeholder needs rather than focusing on meeting the needs of a select few particularly salient stakeholder needs. The reality is that despite its ethical and conceptual appeal for a stakeholder approach to help incorporate ethics into strategic HRM research, research is needed to examine whether there is an ethical bonus for companies that strive to address the needs of all parties or a potential penalty for only meeting the needs of a few stakeholders or only partially meeting all stakeholder needs.

CONCLUSION

Ethical issues have not always been explicitly recognized and addressed in strategic HRM research. In this chapter, we tried to take an initial step at filling this very important gap. We did so by showing that stakeholder theory can be a fruitful avenue for strategic HRM researchers. Identifying those HR practices that can simultaneously meet the demands of different stakeholders is of course a very challenging task. Nevertheless, because organizations operate in the context of multiple stakeholders, research is needed that considers the impact of different stakeholder groups on HRM, how HR systems are related to multiple outcomes in addition to financial performance, and describe how HR systems may be designed to achieve multiple stakeholder satisfaction.

REFERENCES

Arthur, J.B. (1992) The link between business strategy and industrial relations systems in American steel minimills. *Industrial and Labor Relations Review, 45,* 488–506.

Arthur, J.B. (1994) Effects of human resource systems on manufacturing performance and turnover. *Academy of Management Journal, 37,* 670–687.

Baird, L., & Meshoulam, I. (1988). Managing two fits of strategic human resource management. *Academy of Management Review, 13,* 116–128.

Barney, J. (1991). Firm resources and sustainable competitive advantage. *Journal of Management, 17,* 99–129.

Barrick, M. R., Patton, G. K., & Haugland, S. N. (2000). Accuracy of interviewer judgments of job applicant personality traits. *Personnel Psychology, 53,* 925–951.

Batt, R. (2002). Managing customer services: Human resource practices, quit rates, and sales growth. *Academy of Management Journal, 45,* 587–597.

Bloom, M. (1999). The performance effects of pay dispersion on individuals and organizations. *Academy of Management Journal, 42,* 25–40.

Collins, C. J., & Clark, K. D. (2003). Strategic human resource practices, top management team social networks, and firm performance: The role of human resource practices in creating organizational competitive advantage. *Academy of Management Journal, 46,* 740–752.

CNNMoney. (2004). http://money.cnn.com/2004/06/04/news/fortune500/wal_mart/

Datta, D. K., Guthrie, J. P., & Wright, P. M. (2005). Human resource management and labor productivity: Does industry matter? *Academy of Management Journal, 48,* 135–145.

Delery, J. & Doty, D. (1996). Modes of theorizing in strategic human resource management: Tests of universalistic, contingency, and configurational performance predictions. *Academy of Management Journal, 39,* 802–835.

Donaldson, T., & Preston, L. (1995). The stakeholder theory of the corporation: Concepts, evidence, and implications. *Academy of Management Review, 20,* 65–91.

Frayne, C. A., & Geringer, J. M. (2000). Self-management training for improving job performance: A field experiment involving salespeople. *Journal of Applied Psychology, 85,* 361–372.

Freeman, R. B., & Kleiner, M. M. (1999). Do unions make enterprises insolvent? *Industrial and Labor Relations Review, 52,* 510–528.

Freeman, R. B., & Medoff, J. L. (1979, Fall). The two faces of unionism. *The Public Interest,* 69–93.

Freeman, R. E. (1984). *Strategic Management: A Strategic Approach,* Boston, MA: Pitman.

Freeman, R. E. (1994). The politics of stakeholder theory. *Business Ethics Quarterly, 4,* 409–422.

Fortune. (2005). http://www.fortune.com/fortune/globaladmired.

Godfrey, P. C. (2005). The relationship between corporate philanthropy and shareholder wealth: A risk management perspective. *Academy of Management Review, 30,* 777–798.

Goodpaster, K. (1991). Business ethics and stakeholder approach. *Business Ethics Quarterly, 91,* 53–73.

Greenhouse, S. (2005, July 17). How Costco became the anti-Wal-Mart. *NYTimes.*

Hitt, M., Ireland, D., & Hoskisson, R. (2005) *Strategic Management: Competitiveness & Globalization: Concepts, 6th edition, Thompson/Southwestern.*

Huselid, M. A. (1995). The impact of human resource management practices on turnover, productivity, and corporate financial performance. *Academy of Management Journal, 38*(3), 635–672.

Huselid, M. A., & Becker, B. E. (1996). Methodological issues in cross-sectional and panel estimates of the HR-firm performance link. *Industrial Relations, 35,* 400–422.

Huselid, M. A., & Becker, B. E. (1997). The impact of high performance work systems, implementation effectiveness, and alignment with strategy on shareholder wealth. Paper presented at the 1997 Academy of Management Annual Conference, Boston, MA.

Hyman, R. 2004. Varieties of capitalism, national industrial relations systems and transnational challenges. In Harzing, A.W., & Ruysseveldt (Eds.), *International Human Resource Management,* Sage Publications, Thousand Oaks, CA.

Ichniowski, C., Shaw, K., & Prennushi, G. (1997). The effects of human resource management practices on productivity: A study of steel finishing lines. *The American Economic Review,* June: 291–314.

Jackson, S. E., Schuler, R. S., & Rivero, J. C. (1989). Organizational characteristics as predictors of personnel practices. *Personnel Psychology, 42,* 727–786.

Janasz, S. C., Sullivan, S. E., & Whiting, V. (2003). Mentor networks and career success: Lessons for turbulent times. *Academy of Management Executive, 17*(4), 78–91.

Jones, T., & Wicks, A. (1999). Convergent stakeholder theory. *Academy of Management Review, 24,* 206–221.

Kaufman, B. E. (2001). Human resources and industrial relations: Commonalities and differences. *Human Resource Management Review, 11,* 339–374.

Klein, H. J., & Weaver, N. A. (2000). The effectiveness of an organizational-level orientation training program in the socialization of new hires. *Personnel Psychology, 53,* 47–66.

Kotter, J. P., & Heskett, J.L. (1992). *Corporate Culture and Performance,* New York, NY: The Free Press.

Lee, J., & Miller, D. (1999). People matter: Commitment to employees, strategy and performance in Korean firms. *Strategic Management Journal, 20,* 579–593.

Levine, D, & Tyson, D.A. (1990). Participation, productivity, and the firm's environment. In Blinder, A. (Ed.), *Paying for Productivity: A Look at the Evidence,* The Brookings Institution, Washington, D.C.

Liao. H., & Chuang, A. (2004). A multilevel investigation of factors influencing employee service performance and customer outcomes. *Academy of Management Journal, 47,* 41–58.

Margolis, J. D., & Walsh, J.P. (2001). *People and Profits? The search for a link between a Company's Social and Financial Performance.* Mahwah, NJ: Lawrence Erlbaum Associates.

MacDuffie, J. P. (1995). Human resource bundles and manufacturing performance: Organizational logic and flexible production systems in the world auto industry. *Industrial and Labor Relations Review, 48,* 197–221.

Miles, R.E., & Snow, C.C. (1984). *Designing strategic human resource systems. Organizational Dynamics, 13,* 36–52.

Mitchell, R., Agle, B., & Wood, D. (1997). Toward a theory of stakeholder identification and salience: Defining the principle of who and what really counts. *Academy of Management Review, 22,* 853–336.

Nadler, D., & Tushman, M. (1977). A diagnostic model for organizational behavior. In J. R. Hackman, E. E. Lawler, & L. W. Porter (Eds.) *Perspectives on Behavior in Organizations.* New York: McGraw-Hill.

Osterman, P. (1994). How common is workplace transformation and who adopts it? *Industrial and Labor Relations Review, 47,* 174–188.

Osterman, P., Kochan, T. A., Locke, M. R., Piore, M. J. (2002). *Working in America. A Blueprint for the New Labor Market.* The MIT Press.

Pfeffer, J. (1995). Producing sustainable competitive advantage through the effective management of people. *Academy of Management Executive, 9,* 55–69.

Phillips, J. M. (1998). Effects of realistic job previews on multiple organizational outcomes: A meta-analysis. *Academy of Management Journal, 41,* 673–690.

Rogers, E.W., & Wright, P.M. (1998). Measuring organizational performance in strategic human resource management research: Problems, prospects, and performance information markets. *Human Resource Management Review, 8,* 311–331.

Rynes, S. L., & Bono, J. E. (2000). Psychological research on determinants of pay. In S. Ryenes & B. Gerhart (Eds.), *Compensation in Organizations* (pp. 3–31). San Francisco: Jossey-Bass.

Schneider, B., & Reichers, A.E. (1990). Climate and culture: An evolution of constructs. In B. Schneider. (Ed.), *Organizational Climate and Culture,* San-Francisco, CA: Jossey-Bass.

Seibert, S., Silver, S., & Randolph, W. A. (2004). Taking empowerment to the next level: A multiple-level model of empowerment, performance, and satisfaction. *Academy of Management Journal, 47,* 332–349.

Snell, S.A. & Dean, J. Jr. (1992). Integrated manufacturing and human resource management: A human capital perspective. *Academy of Management Journal, 35,* 467–504.

Time. 2005. http://www.time.com/time/innovators/business/profile_domini.html

Welbourne, T. M., Johnson, D. E., & Erez, A. (1998). The role-based performance scale: Validity analysis of a theory-based measure. *Academy of Management Journal, 41,* 540–555.

Wiley, J. W., & Brooks, S. M. (2000). The high-performance organizational climate: How workers describe top-performing units. In N.M Ashkanasy, C. Wilderom, & M. F. Peterson, (Eds.), *Handbook of Organizational Culture and Climate,* Thousand Oaks, CA: Sage.

Wright, P. M., & Boswell, W. R. (2002). Desegregating HRM: A review and synthesis of micro and macro human resource management research. *Journal of Management, 28,* 247–276.

Wright, P. M., & McMahan, G. C. (1992). Theoretical perspectives for strategic human resource management. *Journal of Management, 18,* 295–320.

Wright, P. M. & Sherman, W. S. (1999). Failing to find fit in strategic human resource management: Theoretical and empirical problems. In P. Wright, L.

Dyer, J. Boudreau, & G. Milkovich (Eds.), *Research in Personnel and Human Resource Management*. Greenwich, CT: JAI Press.

Youndt, M. A., Snell, S. A., Dean, J.W. Jr., & Lepak, D. P. (1996). Human resource management, manufacturing strategy, and firm performance. *Academy of Management Journal, 39,* 836–866.

CHAPTER 3

WISDOM, ETHICS, AND HUMAN RESOURCES MANAGEMENT

Robert W. Kolodinsky
James Madison University

INTRODUCTION

The greatest good is wisdom.

—St. Thomas Aquinas

The recent increases in corporate misdeeds have given rise to ever-tightening and further-reaching laws and federal sentencing guidelines geared to constrain illicit behavior in organizations. From accounting scandals to sexual harassment complaints, discrimination cases, fairness problems, and breaches of confidentiality, both public and private firms are experiencing mounting legal and ethical scrutiny (Bartels, et al., 1998; Clark, 2004; Sandler, 2005). Given these developments, legal compliance and ethical behavior have increasingly become two of the primary concerns of organizational stakeholders today (Schramm, 2004; Vickers, 2005). Unfortunately, businesses do not survive simply by obeying laws and behaving

Human Resource Management Ethics, pages 47–69
Copyright © 2006 by Information Age Publishing
All rights of reproduction in any form reserved.

ethically. They also must perform well financially. This uneasy tension between satisfactory financial performance and "right" behavior is probably higher than ever before (e.g., Vickers, 2005).

Which organizational function should have responsibility for managing compliance and ethics issues? Despite such obviously critical concerns, CEOs are generally ill-equipped—and much too busy with other issues—to address such matters effectively, as chief executives typically are under ever-increasing pressure from a wide-variety of stakeholders to perform effectively on multiple financial-based measures (e.g., Henry, France, & Lavell, 2005). Though certainly aware of the need for worker compliance and ethics, CEOs alone cannot effectively address the legal and ethical issues facing firms today (e.g., Henry et al., 2005). Instead, due in part to the human resource (HR) function being the primary employee-focused function in most organizations, the responsibility to ensure worker compliance and ethics has commonly fallen squarely on the HR role (Sandler, 2004; Vickers, 2005). Indeed, HR increasingly has become the focus of responsibility for compliance and ethics initiatives and resolution of such problems in organizations (Driscoll & Hoffman, 1998; Nadel, 2004; Wiley, 1993, 2000). As a result, some view the HR role as having become more critical to organizational functioning than ever before (Sandler, 2004; Vickers, 2005; Wiley, 2000).

Notwithstanding these additional concerns and responsibilities, the importance of the HR role is still viewed with wide variance in organizational settings, contingent upon many factors. Paramount among these factors is the differential perception of added value, beyond its routine functions, that the HR role provides the organization. Despite the increasingly obvious notion that workers—particularly workers' knowledge—are most organizations' most valuable resource (Barney, 1991; Nonaka, 1994; Spender, 1996), and despite HR having the most vital and focused worker-oriented role, many organizations still fail to elevate HR to a prominent place in the decision-making hierarchy (Grossman, 2004; Lawler, 2001; Wells, 2005).

This seeming anomaly may stem in part from a top management team legacy, however antiquated, that continues to relegate HR primarily to its traditional functions—staffing, payroll, benefits, training, etc.—and the assurance that these key functions are competently met either internally or properly outsourced. So, despite calls for HR to be involved in organizational strategy and to finally take its rightful place in the boardroom (Grossman, 2004; Wells, 2005), such elevation is not a common occurrence. A second, perhaps more likely reason for being kept out of the boardroom—and out of loop for the most important macro-level decisions—is that many HR professionals simply do not have, or actively manifest, the wisdom necessary to earn such an important decision-making role (cf., Grossman, 2004; Lawler, 2001).

The purpose of this chapter is to offer an alternative, more valuable and prescriptive role for HR—one that commonly has been reserved for just a handful of long-term HR professionals at larger firms. This view is one in which HR departments, and the HR professionals heading them, are sought after for sage advice, decision-making, problem-solving, and constructive action in most areas of organizational functioning—not just common HR functions. To bridge the "tension gulf" between satisfactory financial performance versus "right" ethical decisions and behaviors—seemingly opposing goals—these wise HR sages meticulously weigh the impact worker-related decisions have on various stakeholders and environments, understand the systems-related connectedness of such decisions, and lead in ways that authentically show they care about short- and long-term performance *and* worker development. Just as importantly, the wisest HR professionals realize the incredible opportunity—indeed, daunting responsibility—they have in impacting organization-wide ethical behavior (Bartels et al., 1998; Jose & Thibideaux, 1999) and in leaving an ethical legacy both on their organization and on individual workers.

Drawing on concepts and theories from various literatures, including psychology, philosophy, leadership, and theology, initial ideas on HR wisdom are offered to stimulate further conceptual development among academics, and to encourage practitioners to take action on becoming truly wise HR professionals. First, a conceptual overview of wisdom is offered, particularly in light of its moral and ethical implications. Second, primary challenges and considerations of wise HR professionals are presented, including the balancing of competing interests with impact concerns in various environment contexts, the need for systems-wide thinking, and leadership considerations—all in an ethics context. Last, some concluding remarks and issues for future research consideration are offered.

WISDOM: A BRIEF CONCEPTUAL OVERVIEW

Wisdom has been pondered for thousands of years, as made evident by major philosophers in a variety of cultures and traditions. While it is beyond the scope of this chapter to provide an exhaustive historical review of wisdom, it is helpful to reflect upon a few glimpses into the "wisdom" of the ancient philosophers and other writers.

For example, English translations of the Old Testament of the Bible are replete with phrases—even whole sections—on wisdom. King Solomon especially is called out as having great wisdom, in particular his wise judgment about which of two prostitutes was the mother of a child (1 Kings: 3 &

4; 2 Chronicles 1 & 8). Wisdom is prominent elsewhere in the Bible, including: "Wisdom is more precious than rubies" (Proverbs 8:11); "I, wisdom, dwell together with prudence; I possess knowledge and discretion...counsel and sound judgment are mine; I have understanding and power...I walk in the way of righteousness, along the paths of justice" (Proverbs 8:12–20); and "...with humility comes wisdom" (Proverbs 11:2). People called "wise" in the Bible include, among others, Joseph, Moses, David, Abigail, Solomon, Paul, and Jesus Christ. According to Proverbs (3, 4, 8, 9; Life Application Bible, 1991:1077), the person who has wisdom is loving, faithful, knows right from wrong, does what is right, listens and learns, possesses knowledge and discretion, gives good advice and has common sense, and loves correction and is teachable. The benefits of wisdom include having a reputation for good judgment, success, honor, justice, righteousness, constant learning, and understanding (Life Application Bible, 1991:1077).

Pythagoras (c. 600 BC; cited in Howatson, 1990:476 and in Small, 2004:756) asks a variety of wisdom-related questions, which illustrate wisdom during his lifetime:

> What is the wisest of the things in our power? The answer is medicine. What is the fairest of the things in our power? The answer here is harmony. What is the most powerful? The answer here is knowledge. Lastly, what is the best? The answer here is happiness.

Aristotle (translated 1982:337; in Small, 2004:757; italics added for emphasis) addressed prudence or practical wisdom in the following way: "A truth-attaining rational quality, which was concerned with *action* in relation to things that were good and bad for human beings." Socrates weighs in on the importance of wisdom with the following phrase: "All...things hang upon the soul, and all things of the soul herself hang upon wisdom" (Socrates, 88).

Wisdom can be defined as the "power of judging rightly and following the soundest course of action, based on knowledge, experience, understanding, etc." (*Webster's New World College Dictionary*, 1990:1533). According to Sternberg (1990:ix), "wisdom is about as elusive as psychological constructs get." Among other definitions, it has alternatively been viewed as "expert knowledge involving good judgment and advice in the domain, fundamental pragmatics of life" (Baltes & Smith, 1990:95), "intellectual ability to be aware of the limitations of knowing and how it impacts solving ill-defined problems and making judgments, characteristics of reflective judgment" (Kitchener & Brenner, 1990:325), and "problem-finding ability [and] a fundamental cognitive process of reflection and judgment" (Arlin, 1990:325). Sternberg (2003:*xviii*; italics added for emphasis) views wisdom as "the value-laden *application* of tacit knowledge not only for one's own benefit…but also for the benefit of others, in order to attain a common good." Thus, wisdom is an action-oriented construct that goes beyond simple understanding of information or even expert knowledge. According to Ackoff (1989, p. 9), "Wisdom adds value, which requires the mental function we call judgment." Whereas knowledge can be considered static—resident but not necessarily used—wisdom implies "making decisions (judgments) intended to change the conduct of…actors. Thus, it is an action-oriented construct" (Bierly, Kessler, & Christensen, 2000, p. 597).

Whereas the notion of wisdom has been considered for millenniums, the academic and scientific community has largely avoided research on wisdom. This may be in large part due to wisdom being "about as elusive as psychological constructs get" (Sternberg, 1990:ix). The limited research performed has occurred mostly in the past three decades, primarily in the fields of psychology (e.g., Clayton, 1975, Clayton & Birren, 1980; Rosch, 1975) and information systems (e.g., Ackoff, 1989). Much of the recent organizational research work pertaining to wisdom has been at the macro-level and centered in the knowledge and strategy literatures, and primarily focusing on strategic impact of information, knowledge, and, more recently, wisdom (Grant, 1996; Spender, 1996). Indeed, researchers suggest that there is a "knowledge hierarchy" (also, "learning hierarchy" or "knowledge pyramid"), with wisdom at the pinnacle (Ackoff, 1989; Bellinger, Castro, & Mills, 2005; Bierly et al., 2000; Hey, 2004).

The Data/Information/Knowledge/Wisdom (DIKW) Hierarchy

Regarding this knowledge hierarchy, there appears to be general agreement on the content and order of four primary categories, starting with data at the base of the hierarchy, followed by information, knowledge, and lastly by wisdom (Ackoff, 1989; Hey, 2004).[1] An example of this data/information/knowledge/wisdom (DIKW) hierarchy was explained by Bierly and colleagues (Bierly et al., 2000, p. 597; italics added for emphasis), "A book contains data in its letters and words; reading…a book imparts information; breaking down and integrating that information imparts knowledge, and *using* the knowledge to solve the practical problems of life, both personal and organizational, imparts wisdom." The following is a brief overview of these four concepts.

Data is viewed as merely raw symbols with no inherent meaning or value until processed into a useable form. In other words, data is unprocessed information (Hey, 2004) that, by itself, typically has no value. For example, letters on a page have no meaning until organized into readable information.

Information is "processed data"—collected and organized (McKinney, 2005)—that commonly has meaning based on some "relational connection" (Bellinger et al., 2005). Information answers "questions that begin with such words as *who, what, where, when,* and *how many*" (Ackoff, 1989, p. 3; italics in original) and may or may not be useful.

Knowledge "is the awareness and understanding of facts, truths or information gained in the form of experience or learning" (www.wordiq.com). Some view it as information that is processed, commonly memorized (Bellinger et al., 2005), and given a context (McKinney, 2005). Others make a distinction between "know how" (i.e., tacit knowledge) and "know about," or explicit knowledge (Polanyi, 1966; Nonaka & Takeuchi, 1995). Analogous to distinctions between intuitive and rational decision-making (Agor, 1986; Blattberg & Hoch, 1990; Simon, 1987), wherein intuitive decision-making relies on "gut feelings" to inform the decision-maker (Agor, 1986; Sadler-Smith & Shefy, 2004; Simon, 1987), tacit knowledge is "deep knowledge" that is informed through experience but difficult to express (Polanyi, 1966; Sternberg, 1990). Tacit knowledge has also been viewed as "sticky knowledge"—valuable knowledge that is difficult to express, pass on to others, or "leak" (Liebeskind, 1996; von Hippel, 1994; Wernerfelt, 1984). Sternberg views tacit knowledge as "action-oriented, typically acquired without direct help from others, and allows individuals to achieve goals they personally value" (2000:635; Sternberg, Wagner, Williams, & Horvath, 1995). Thus, tacit knowledge can be viewed as valued procedural "know how" that develops when one learns from experiences rather than instruction (Sternberg 1990). Tacit knowledge is central to the concept of wisdom (Sternberg, 1990).

Wisdom, at the top of the knowledge pyramid, requires all of the above—data, information, and knowledge—but is so much more. As Sternberg (2003) suggests, "the wise person realizes what matters is not just knowledge, or the intellectual skills one applies to knowledge, but *how* this knowledge is *used*" (xviii; italics added for emphasis). Extracting from the definitions and descriptions offered earlier, wisdom can be viewed as an aggregate of traits, behaviors, and focuses, including competence, expertise, knowledge, understanding, reflection, good judgment, ability and action in judging rightly, knowing right from wrong, acting and deciding appropriately, common sense, advising prudently, and continuous and intentional learning.

In this chapter, wisdom is concerned with actions and decisions that benefit many; as in Sternberg's (2003:xviii) words, "...for the benefit of others, in order to attain a common good." As such, a wise person is one who understands morality in each context, considers the impact of decisions on others, and acts in "right" ways that indicate knowledge of right versus wrong, good versus bad, ethical versus unethical. Understanding the relationship between wisdom, morals, and ethics is the focus of the next section.

Wisdom, Morality, and Ethics

Morals refer to principles or standards of right and wrong, good or bad, justice or injustice; what is judged to be right, good, or just; and judgments of goodness or badness related to human action or character (e.g., American Heritage Dictionary; www.aspaonline.organization; www.wordnet.princeton.edu; www.business-words.com). Similarly, ethics is defined as the science or study of morals or moral choices in human conduct; or a set of moral principles (e.g., American Heritage Dictionary; Oxford Dictionary; www.abc.net.au). To be ethical "is to conform to moral standards or to conform to the standards of conduct of a given profession or group" (Cascio, 2003:19). In organizational settings, these concepts are typically considered in relation to decisions and actions of workers—that is, ethical behavior. In the current context, ethical behavior refers to the specific decisions, choices, or actions that can be evaluated based on generally accepted moral principles; also, the degree to which an individual or group adheres to moral principles (e.g., wordnet.princeton.edu). Morals and ethical behavior are viewed here as integral to possessing wisdom—indeed, behaving ethically is essential to being wise and acting wisely. As such, those with wisdom act in ways that are consistent with generally accepted moral principles, and do so in ways that consider the impact that such actions have on others. To not do so would be unwise.

Unfortunately, moral decay is evident throughout many Western societies, infesting our cultures and our organizations, with wisdom in short supply (Chandler & Holliday, 1990). Rather than contemplating the effect on "the common good" important work-related decisions commonly have, organizational decision-makers too often cast aside the moral rightness of decision considerations in favor of financial "imperatives" (cf. Manz, Manz, Marx, & Neck, 2001; Small, 2004; Sternberg, 2003). Linear thinking focused primarily on short-term financial performance too frequently trumps moral considerations. As a result, blinded by such imperatives, unethical behaviors come all too easily.

In the United States, the increasingly obvious attention paid to materialistic values has strongly influenced the ways in which American businesses are run. Our organizational systems are all too often fueled by extrinsic motivations. For example, our organizational rewards systems primarily address extrinsic factors, often unwittingly encouraging workers to "do whatever it takes to meet your financial goals." But, as we now know so painfully (e.g., Enron; WorldCom, Tyco), such ill-advised systems can lead to devastating ethical problems.

Organizational definitions of success, for workers and for the organization itself, must change in order for behavior to change. Too often success is defined in materialistic terms—by increased organizational profits or share price or ROI, and by worker income. But primarily focusing on these material and extrinsic issues will by its nature result in failure to focus on post-material, intrinsic issues (cf. Giacalone & Jurkiewicz, 2003)—worker needs for recognition, for personal and professional development, and for one's search for meaning and purpose in one's work. Perhaps more importantly, attention focused and rewarded on material pursuits, will unlikely result in making ethical behavior a priority. With increasing scrutiny of workplace compliance and ethics, but also with the increasingly obvious adverse effects that a materialistic workplace focus can cause, the time has come to focus on developing wisdom throughout one's organization. Indeed, it is argued here that a wisdom-based approach—balancing various stakeholder interests, considering systems-wide effects, and leading authentically with a serve-first mindset—will be the most successful long-term approach for organizations.

Yet, too few organizational leaders radiate wisdom. Since many CEOs and other top management team (TMT) members experience relentless shareholder pressure to produce satisfactory short-term financial results, and further given the nature of most TMT compensation packages which commonly base the bulk of incentive pay on financial results (e.g., Colvin, 2001; Tosi, Werner, Katz, & Gomez-Mejia, 2000; Useem, 2003), it is unrealistic to expect such individuals to effectively focus on ethical worker behavior. In the absence of the presence of an powerful ethics officer, it is the HR director who must proactively and assertively ensure that ethical behavior is adhered to. But the ethical challenges and issues needing attention can be frightening. The following section addresses some of the most salient issues, and offers some wisdom-oriented ways to bridge the tension gulf between the need for effective financial performance and the long-term imperative for "right" behavior.

HR WISDOM AND ETHICS: CHALLENGES AND CONSIDERATIONS

Wisdom consists in the highest use of the intellect for the discernment of the largest moral interest of humanity. It is the most perfect willingness to do the right combined with the utmost attainable knowledge of what is right.

—Felix Adler (1944)

In practice, the HR function commonly faces myriad challenges and obstacles that must be contemplated in order to have any chance of reasonably smooth organizational functioning. Wise HR professionals are more likely to prevail in such circumstances because their actionable judgments carefully consider the various interests, values, and impacts of their decisions.

In the following sections, I suggest that wise HR professionals—particularly those who work in fast-paced, rapidly changing, and even turbulent environments—are adept at balancing, systems thinking, and leading. Deft handling of each of these activities enables such professionals to shape their organizations in the ethical manner they envision.

HR Wisdom and Balance

To wisely address the challenges encountered in complex HR environments, HR professionals must understand how to balance the various interests and environmental issues potentially impacted by each decision. Sternberg's (1998, 2000, 2003) balance theory of wisdom is beneficial in this context. The balance theory of wisdom "specifies the processes (balancing of interests and of responses to environmental contexts) in relation to the goal of wisdom (achievement of a common good)" (Sternberg, 2000:638). More than just expert knowledge and know how, wisdom is "relevant to the attainment of particular goals people value, not just any goals, but rather, a balance of responses to the environment—adapting, shaping, and selecting—so as to achieve a common good for all relevant stakeholders" (Sternberg, 2000:638). He defines wisdom in this context as "the application of tacit knowledge as mediated by values toward the goal of achieving a common good through a balance among multiple 1. *interests*: (a) intrapersonal, (b) interpersonal, and (c) extrapersonal in order to achieve a balance among 2. *responses to environmental contexts*: (a) adaptation to existing environmental contexts, (b) shaping of existing environmental contexts, and (c) selection of new environmental contexts" (Sternberg, 2000:637; italics in original).

While discussions of equity theory (e.g., Adams, 1963, 1965) are beyond the scope of this chapter, in the current context the goal of HR wisdom—to achieve a "common good"—refers to decisions that are "best for most," but particularly are made with careful consideration regarding the most salient stakeholders affected by each decision.

Following these ideas, HR wisdom only becomes apparent when HR decisions are made taking into account the delicate consideration of multiple—often competing—interests *and* the various resultant environmental responses. For example, the decision to move from paper to an organization-wide web-based HRIS affects not only many current internal and external stakeholders, but also the entire future organizational environment. With such a significant change, the wise HR professional recognizes the need to carefully consider the effects not only on all workers but other stakeholders as well. For instance, some workers will take on new responsibilities, for which extensive training may be required. Some long-time vendors may experience a huge drop in revenues (e.g., paper vendors), while others will reap new rewards (e.g., new HRIS software providers). All workers will now need to learn how to access and use the new web-based intranet system, which likely will result in a large spike in calls to the HR helpline. With regard to balancing of environmental effects, all workers will now need access to a computer and to the Internet, and be provided a password. Office space may need to be adapted and shaped into training rooms (or HRIS access rooms) so that workers can learn and use the new system. The HRIS may have to be implemented in phases, and future environmental issues (e.g., more computers; more space; how to handle all the old hard paper files) will all have to be considered.

Moreover, wise HR decision-making involves recognition of the importance of stakeholder values and careful consideration of what is good for most ("the common good"). According to Sternberg (1990:640), "values mediate how one balances interests and responses and collectively contribute even to how one defines a common good." While extensive elucidation of values and "the common good" is beyond the scope of this chapter, certainly values—along with moral implications (see Kohlberg's stages of moral development; 1969, 1983) and ethical consequences—must be considered in order for wise HR decisions to be made. For example, the degree to which the HR decision-maker values concern for people over technical issues (i.e., task accomplishment) could influence the extent to which HRIS training is provided in multiple ways; for instance, addressing differential learning styles. In addition, staffing decisions are certainly subject to values considerations, as when valuing cognitive ability (e.g., Hunter, 1986; Schmidt & Hunter, 1993) above, for instance, social skills in a hiring decision (e.g., Ferris, Witt, & Hochwarter, 2001; Sternberg, 1985; 1997; Witt & Ferris, 2003). Certainly the use of valid assessment instruments, triangulated with other proven staffing methods, is critical to reducing the probability of unwise employment decisions. Of course, all of this must consider the effect on the "common good" of such a monumental change. Is this the best decision for most? Will this decision help make the organization and its workers more effective? Are more people helped than harmed? As can be seen from this HRIS example, substantial *a priori* considerations precede wise HR decision-making. Ethical considerations for this example are considered below.

The point here is that wise HR professionals understand the concept of balancing, and act in ways that carefully consider salient stakeholder interests and environmental responses in seeking to make prudent decisions with the goal of achieving a common good in their decision-making. Clearly, much HR decision-making has ethical implications; ethics concerns, wisdom, and balancing are the subject of the next section.

HR Wisdom and Balance: Ethical Considerations

Staying on the right side of ethics requires understanding of these balancing concepts, and careful contemplation of "common good" effects. Certainly, ethics involves not only one's own interests, but also the interests of others, particularly those with some stake in the decision or behavior (Cascio, 2003; Cullen, Victor, & Stephens, 1989). The decision-maker should question the degree to which each particular decision is motivated by self-interest—for example, does one alternative solution have more attractive benefits to this person personally or professionally than another viable alternative? Moreover, are certain outcomes of a decision disproportionately beneficial (or hurtful) to some stakeholders more than others? How might alternative solutions help produce a more balanced result?

While seemingly innocuous and beneficial to the "common good," the decision to move from paper to web-based HRIS, for instance, may have important ethical implications. For example, should a family member or close friend of the decision-maker have the potential to benefit in some way from this decision (e.g., a brother is an HRIS software salesperson; a good friend with strong HRIS skills would become a good candidate for a job if the HRIS is implemented), an ethical dilemma is encountered. If the change to a HRIS is motivated in part because it provides the HR director with an opportunity to make obsolete a particularly disliked subordinate's job, or to weed out older workers who in the past have shown resistance to learning new technologies, an ethics breach may occur. Certainly, should the development of criteria for HRIS vendor selection be motivated by some probable personal benefit (e.g., the decision-maker knows that the vendor has a luxury box and season's tickets to the beloved local football team), an ethical situation has been encountered.

Ethical considerations are not limited just to balancing multiple interests; environmental concerns also need to be considered in an ethical light. For example, the decision to shift from paper to HRIS could be motivated by the desire of the decision-maker to move to a newer building or larger office (regardless of whether these areas are better equipped to handle the new technologies). If implemented, this decision could have wide-ranging environmental effects on, for instance, displacement of whole departments, office space requirements, worker access to the latest computers, and even the possibility of some workers now being able to do their work effectively at home. Certainly, this shift has important budgetary considerations, and may give the HR decision-maker more leverage when negotiating for more resources, more space, new equipment and furniture, and—if all goes well—more power. From just these limited examples, it is easy to see the various complexities and potentially devastating ethical problems of HR decisions.

Balancing interests and contextual matters, keeping in mind stake-holder values and what's best for "the common good," all must be considered when making complex HR decisions. In addition to balancing issues, wise HR professionals must consider the possible system-wide effects and ethical repercussions each critical judgment and behavior may have on the organization and its stakeholders. Systemic considerations are the focus of the next section.

HR Wisdom and Systems Thinking

Another separator of those with HR wisdom compared to those without it is that wise HR professionals understand that decision-making can have wide-ranging, and long-term, effects throughout the various systems of an organization. Decisions affecting workers are likely to have a variety of interrelated effects, ranging from effects on worker emotions, motivation, performance, intent to withdraw or not, and more. Such decisional interrelatedness is akin to Senge's (1990) notion of "systems thinking," the idea that much about an organization—and organizational behavior—is interrelated and interdependent. Systems thinking involves the recognition that a wide-variety of forces impacts the interrelationships that shape the behavior of systems (Senge et al., 1994). A systems thinking mindset requires a change in the way one thinks about organizational behavior: understanding interrelationships instead of just seeing simple linear cause-effect relationships; discerning continuously moving processes of change rather than static snapshots.

Most HR decisions have the potential to have system-wide effects. As Senge (1990) suggests, even what may seem like small efforts can act as powerful "levers" and make huge differences to organizational functioning. For example, what started out as a simple General Electric (GE) hiring decision, to hire Jack Welch decades ago, has left an indelible systems-wide mark on GE for likely decades to come. Certainly, the decision to hire any particular worker may have potentially enormous effects on the entire organizational system—consider the potentially catastrophic systemic effects of making a poor hiring decision (e.g., "Chainsaw" Al Dunlap at Sunbeam Corporation; Jeffrey Skilling at Enron Corporation). Or how failing to do an adequate background check on an emotionally unstable job candidate who later turns violent can have devastating long-term effects on other workers and ultimately on the performance of the organization itself. Moreover, a change in rewards systems—from one based on individual performance and competition between workers to one focused on teamwork and collaboration—is likely to affect not only worker motivation and performance, but also turnover, future hiring, methods of managing, office layout and worker proximity, communication systems, and more.

Even seemingly useful decisions can have adverse systems-wide effects, and in retrospect seem unwise. For example, though not unethical, a simple decision such as the adoption of a corporate ethics policy—in the absence of any additional supplementary actions or decisions to complement such a policy, such as training, workshops, and discipline policy changes—is likely to be viewed by workers as a cosmetic symbol that will likely fail to affect organizational behavior in a positive manner. In fact, such a decision may be viewed pejoratively, as yet another example of management's ineptitude. Such isolated HR-related choices reveal a lack of understanding of the system-wide effects of such decisions. While most organizations and academics would agree that having a well-written ethics code is better than not having one (cf. Dean, 1992; Wiley, 2000), positive changes in organization-wide ethical behavior are likely to manifest only when a variety of ethics-related behaviors are evidenced and policies implemented.

HR Wisdom and Systems Thinking: Ethical Considerations

In order to make wise decisions, it is essential that HR professionals understand the moral implications of the choices they make, and how such choices might affect the entire work system. Developing one's moral maturity—progressing further along Kohlberg's (1969, 1983) stages of moral development—is foundationally vital to becoming a wise HR professional. One of the great moral thinkers, Kant, clearly understood the relationship between morals and systems. According to Csikszentmihalyi and Rathunde (1990:33), "Kant urges us to develop a morality based on an understanding of the 'world as an ordered whole of interconnected goals, as a system of final causes.'"

From an HR ethics perspective, being sensitive to the interrelated effects that decisions, policies, and actions have on workers and systems at all organizational levels enables the wise HR professional to better avoid the ethical hazards so many colleagues have suffered. Alternatively, making important decisions while failing to take into account systems-related effects, can have devastating consequences. Few HR-related decisions are immune to such potential problems.

Consider the instance in which an HR director gets wind of the CEO's desire to railroad through a promotion decision of an inadequately qualified candidate, without the approval of HR. Perhaps the decision is based more on friendship—a golf or drinking buddy—than on work performance or qualifications. The wise HR professional would carefully plan out a way to discuss the pros and cons of such a decision, and then act on such a plan by meeting face-to-face with the CEO to discuss the potentially devastating system-wide consequences such a decision would have on the organization. The clear signal this unethical decision would send to other workers is that excellent work performance may not lead to valued rewards—rather, friendship or ingratiation may prove to be a more fruitful endeavor. Perhaps even more devastating are other system-wide effects that this poor decision fails to consider, including adverse effects on worker morale, motivation, and performance, and thus on future organizational performance.

Important decisions in nearly all of the functional areas of HR can serve to help or hurt the organizational system. For example, the failure to ensure that supervisors have sufficient sexual harassment training can have devastating system-wide consequences—as when an inadequately trained but top performing male supervisor makes a quid pro quo faux paux with a female subordinate (e.g., "Date me and I'll give you a better performance review"). Or, for instance, when an HR director fails to intervene when a less qualified candidate who happens to be a relative of one of the organization's vice presidents gets hired over a clearly more qualified candidate—nepotism at its worst. The post-merger decision to reduce or abandon health benefits to retired former employees, while legal in some circumstances, may substantially reduce health-related costs but would likely cause other organizational costs to rise—from the need to defend the probable lawsuits that will occur, from the increase in complaints from older workers nearing retirement age, and from reduced worker productivity and retention due in part to morale problems caused by such insensitivity. Any of these unethical choices, as word spreads, will have potentially debilitating effects system-wide if not immediately rectified and denounced.

Thus, HR wisdom, with a focus on doing what's right for the common good, involves embracing systems thinking. This involves not only *knowing about* such thinking, but more importantly seeks to understand and reflect upon the various relations affected by HR-related decisions—before such decisions are made. It also requires actions that reflect such thinking. It sends up "trial balloons' and "tests the waters' with new ideas, discussing the notion of team incentives, for instance, with workers of a variety of organizational levels prior to recommending implementation. Wise HR professionals also understand that HR-related choices are made each day, at least indirectly, by most—if not all—workers, so devising ways to influence, educate, and train workers to make the right (i.e., ethical) choices are also crucial to evidencing HR wisdom. Moreover, continuous scanning and evaluation must be performed during and following implementation of such programs to monitor system-wide effects, so that prudent adjustments can be made to future decisions and actions.

HR professionals must take a leadership stance in order to affect such changes. The best leadership approach is one that adopts a serve-others-first mindset coupled with skill in influencing others. HR wisdom and leadership is the focus of the next section.

HR Wisdom and Leadership

According to Sternberg (2003), a leader can have many valuable attributes "and still lack an additional quality that, arguably, is the most important a leader can have, but perhaps, the rarest. This additional quality is wisdom" (393). For HR wisdom to manifest, HR professionals must take a leadership role—not just with HR issues but in influencing all in the organization to understand the impact each worker's choices can have on organizational stakeholders. With most top management team members focused on macro-level issues that are not worker-related, it is up to HR to be persuasive about the importance of issues other than financial performance and to articulate how such issues affect financial performance. Taking a leadership role means wise HR leaders are effective at influencing others—particularly top management team members—in acting on the belief that (1) each critical decision made can have system-wide effects that can shape the future of the organization and its stakeholders, and (2) making choices that reflect careful balancing of the various stakeholder interests is in the best interest of all.

For HR leadership to be most effective, it must be with a serve-others mindset rather than one that falls lock-step into the financial performance mantra. One must be careful not to fall into the trap so many HR professionals have found themselves in—that is, being a subservient servant to the top management team (and even peers) while failing to take a leadership role. The best leadership approach to becoming a wise HR professional is to become a servant leader.

A servant leader is an individual with a compelling vision and skilled at influencing others, but also one with a desire to serve others through one's actions and choices (e.g., Autry, 2001; De Pree, 1992; Frick, 2004; Greenleaf, 1977). In stark contrast to most organizational leaders who seek power and have a strong desire to exercise control over others, the servant leader is more concerned with ensuring that workers' needs and values are considered and, to the extent possible and prudent, met (e.g., Doyle, 1997; Fairholm, 1998). The servant leader is less concerned with power over others and more focused on cooperation, while never losing sight of the importance of achieving organizational goals (Kolodinsky, Bowen, & Ferris, 2003). According to Manz and colleagues (Manz et al., 2001:98), "very often cooperation with a spirit of service can supplant competition as the best way to achieve prosperity (financial health, social benefit, and peace of mind) even within seemingly highly competitive situations." Aaron Fuerstein exhibited unmistakable servant leader qualities when he decided to rebuild his Massachusetts-based Malden Mills factory after a devastating fire. Even though most advisors suggested he move his manufacturing plants to overseas locations where labor costs would be substantially cheaper, his decision to place his workers' needs above cost considerations soon paid off in unexpected ways—his workers repaid him with higher-than-ever productivity returns following the rebuilding of his plant.

Consonant with balance approaches to wisdom (e.g., Sternberg, 2003), organizational leaders need to emphasize a balance between the technical (performance) and the social (relationship) needs of organizations and organizational members (e.g., Manz et al., 2001). Relationship building is a hallmark of servant leadership. Employers who adopt such socio-technical balance systems assign both social and task responsibilities and evaluate workers "based on the quality of their social relationships (at work) as well as their task performance. The often-perceived choice between performance and relationship is removed; both are part of the job" (Manz et al., 2001:97). They offer AES corporation, an independent, energy-producing company and one of America's fastest growing large companies, as a good example of a firm that performs extremely well while also treating workers well. AES "encourages an intense team spirit throughout the entire company. AES de-emphasizes profit as a primary motive in favor of a set of what sound like noncompetitive values, including integrity, fairness, fun, and social responsibility….Not only does cooperation create a more positive environment in which to work but it also fosters an ethical spirit of treating others fairly" (98).

How can HR help to achieve this balance? One way, they suggest, is to encourage job rotation, which enables workers to better understand others' job difficulties and to empathize with the challenges others face in their jobs. This can result in a more cooperative and compassionate environment (97). Another way is to foster feedback and evaluation systems that encourage authentic communication between all members. Indeed, along with being vulnerable, accepting, present, and useful, being authentic—being open, truthful, trustworthy, and having integrity—is a critical attitude for servant leaders (Autry, 2001).

Further, it is HR's job to provide leadership on reconciling the tension between "for-profit" and "for the people." HR must take the lead in assertively convincing upper management that servant-oriented empowerment systems with valued rewards logically linked with performance objectives is the best way to secure long-term financial viability. Given the well-documented costs of worker-related problems (e.g., suboptimal worker fit; inadequate training and development; worker withdrawal; worker fears of job security; motivational effects on performance; etc.), it is up to HR to continually and, if necessary, forcefully remind top organizational decision-makers that designing systems that encourage empowerment and self-leadership are in the best long-term interests of the organization. While systems designed to encourage competition and bottom-line thinking often have positive short-term effects, they generally fail to sustain the long-term benefits of more worker-centered organizations. Worker-centered organizations focus on cooperation, self-leadership, teaming where applicable, concern for people more than profits, and value courage, compassion, integrity, and justice. Servant leaders work hard to foster the development of worker-centered organizational cultures.

Moreover, servant leaders are expert at inclusiveness, particularly when it comes to organizational goals and visions. Indeed, developing a vision with the cooperation of others—a *shared* vision—is integral to servant leadership. In Senge's (1990) writings on learning organizations, the notion of *shared vision* is introduced as one of the five core "learning disciplines" necessary for lifelong organizational learning programs. Shared vision is "building a sense of commitment in a group, but [also] developing shared images of the future we seek to create, and the principles and guiding practices by which we hope to get there" (Senge et al., 2004:6). To optimize effectiveness, wise HR professionals must be adept at developing and communicating a vision that is attractive to most workers. Servant-oriented HR leaders do this in a variety of ways, including putting emphasis on community rather than on the individual, on internal cooperation rather than competition, on responsible participative goal setting and ethical goal achievement, and developing both systems and people in ways that offer an attractive future for all. To the degree that wise HR professionals are able to enact such changes, they go a long way toward leaving the kind of ethical legacy that can help his or her organization achieve sustainable competitive advantage.

HR Wisdom and Leadership: Ethical Considerations

According to Burke (1999), ethics is a "leadership imperative." As the primary worker-focused function in the organization, HR has a leadership responsibility to ensure that both implicit and explicit forms of ethics institutionalization take place. Explicit forms include codes of ethics, ethics officers or ombudspersons, ethics committees, ethics hotlines, ethics newsletters, and ethics training. Implicit forms include ethical leadership, open communication channels, and fair reward, promotion, discipline, and performance evaluation systems. While empirical research seems to suggest implicit forms to be more effective (e.g., Jose & Thibodeaux, 1999), many ethics researchers support the use of both forms as a means to optimal ethical effectiveness (e.g., Callan, 1992; Dean, 1992; Ford & Richardson, 1994; Trevino & Nelson, 1995; Weiss, 1994; Wiley, 2000). Moreover, an ethical organizational culture will more likely manifest.

The wise HR professional should not only be aware of this dualistic need, but assertively must take action to ensure that various ethics institutionalization forms are implemented effectively. As some firms have found out the hard way, simply posting a code of ethics does not ensure ethics compliance (e.g., Dean, 1992; Wiley, 2000). Ethics compliance is most likely to come through triangulation; i.e., applying a variety of explicit and implicit forms, led by HR but with the full support of top management.

While CEOs and top management teams may pay lip service to the importance of ethical decision-making and behavior, HR—more than any other organizational function—needs to take a lead role in ensuring that both forms of ethics institutionalization take place. Assertively standing up for one's convictions and visions and leading with a servant-first approach will go a long way in influencing top management team decision-making—and worker behavior throughout—to consider the ethics-related effects of their decisions and actions. Should HR not take a lead role in implementing such multiple forms, ethics is not likely to be given the priority it deserves. As a result, the organization will have a greater likelihood of experiencing unethical behavior. No wise HR professional would want to risk that.

CONCLUDING REMARKS

The purpose of this chapter was to provide an initial overview of the concept of HR wisdom and to articulate its importance in addressing the ethical challenges inherent in today's performance-oriented workplaces. I suggest that wise HR professionals proactively and assertively impact ethical behavior in their organizations. In doing so, they add more value, have more power, and—importantly—positively impact long-term financial performance.

CEOs who value knowledge accumulation and organizational learning should be looking to the HR role for solutions to a wide variety of people-related problems. Because of the nature of the people-focused HR role, wise HR professionals should be in a better position than anyone else (including the CEO) to make the key intra-organizational worker-oriented decisions that affect the "right functioning" of the organization. However, HR wisdom only becomes evident through proactively addressing the following three ethics-related issues: balancing interests, understanding and influencing systems-wide effects, and assertively leading with a servant-first mindset. Carefully attending to such critical matters will help wisdom further accumulate, serving both the individual and the organization in more sound decision-making and more appropriate behavioral modeling to more effectively handle the bumpy compliance and ethics hurdles ahead.

There are several future research considerations worth pursuing. For example, what constitutes having HR wisdom? It may be that HR professionals can be categorized based on their attained level of wisdom, made evident by judgments made and actions taken—particularly in complex or challenging circumstances. Subject to such key factors as knowledge, experience, and time in the HR profession, a typology of HR professional wisdom may be developable. In addition, researchers may explore the various ways in which HR wisdom is developed. For example, in their discussion of wisdom from a strategic management perspective, Bierly and colleagues (Bierly et al., 2000) suggest that wisdom develops in three primary ways: experience, passion to learn, and through spiritual paths. Understanding the ways in which wise HR professionals develop wisdom would be insightful to researchers and practitioners alike. Further, the attributes, antecedents, moderators, and consequences of HR wisdom need further exploration. What are the primary characteristics of wise HR professionals? What are the factors contributing to—or thwarting—wisdom development? How is wisdom best applied? What are the primary outcomes linked to those with wisdom? Moreover, distinctions between wisdom and knowledge, and wisdom and intelligence need to be teased out to offer a more clear view of the nature of the HR wisdom construct.

In conclusion, I suggest in this chapter that wisdom and ethics are critically linked constructs. In an HR context, wise professionals who lead with a servant-first mindset, and labor to understand how best to balance the interests of many while carefully considering systems-related effects of decisions and actions, will have a greater chance of impacting positive long-term organizational outcomes. And they will position themselves to more likely help others understand that bridging the tension gulf between financial performance and "right" behavior is not only doable, but imperative.

NOTE

1. Bellinger and colleagues (Bellinger et al., 2005) suggest that "understanding" is the next step in the hierarchy (after knowledge and before wisdom), and refers to comprehension, discernment, or interpretation of knowledge. According to www.merriam-webster.com, understanding refers "to grasp the meaning of; have the power of comprehension; to achieve a grasp of the nature, significance, or explanation of something. According to www.wordiq.com, understanding "is a psychological state in relation to an object or person whereby one is able to think about it and use concepts to be able to deal adequately with that object. People with understanding are

able to synthesize newly acquired knowledge and reconcile it with previous acquired knowledge; as such, it is similar to the difference between memorization and learning (e.g., Bellinger et al., 2005). While knowledge answers "how" questions, understanding offers those with knowledge an appreciation of "why" something is the way it is (Bellinger et al., 2005).

REFERENCES

Ackoff, R.L. (1989). From data to wisdom: Presidential address to ISGSR, June 1988. *Journal of Applied Systems Analysis, 16,* 3–9.

Adams, J.S. (1963). Toward an understanding of inequity. *Journal of Abnormal and Social Psychology, 67,* 422–436.

Adams, J.S. (1965). Inequity in social exchange. In L. Berkowitz (Ed.), *Advances in Experimental Social Psychology, 2,* 267–299.

Adler, Felix (1944), *Life and Destiny.* NY: American Ethical Union.

Agor, W.H. (1986). The logic of intuition: How top executives make important decisions. *Organizational Dynamics,* Winter, 5–18.

American Heritage Dictionary of the English Language (4th ed.) (2000). Boston: Houghton Mifflin.

Aquinas, St. Thomas (c. 387). *Soliloquies.*

Aristotle (384–322 B.C. [1987]). *The works of Aristotle.* Chicago: Great Books of the Western World, Vols. 8 & 9, Encyclopedia Britannica.

Arlin, P.K. (1990). Wisdom: The art of problem finding. In R.J. Sternberg (Ed.), *Wisdom: Its nature, origins, and development,* (pp. 230–243). New York: Cambridge University Press.

Autry, J. (2001). *The servant leader: How to build a creative team, develop great morale, and improve bottom-line performance.* New York: Prima Publishing/Random House.

Baltes, P.B., & Smith, J. (1990). Toward a psychology of wisdom and its ontogenesis. In R.J. Sternberg (Ed.), *Wisdom: Its nature, origins, and development,* (pp. 87–120). New York: Cambridge University Press.

Barney, J.B. (1991). Firm resources and sustained competitive advantage. *Journal of Management, 17,* 99–120.

Bartels, L.K., Harrick, E., Martell, K., & Strickland, D. (1998). The relationship between ethical climate and ethical problems within human resource management. *Journal of Business Ethics, 17,* 799–804.

Bellinger, G., Castro, D., & Mills, A. (2005). *Data, information, knowledge, and wisdom.* www.systems-thinking.organization/dikw.

Bierly, P.E., Kessler, E.H., & Christensen, E.W. (2000). Organizational learning, knowledge, and wisdom. *Journal of Organization Change Management, 13*(6), 596–618.

Blattberg, R.C., & Hoch, S.J. (1990). Database models and managerial intuition: 50% model + 50% manager. *Management Science, 36,* 887–900.

Burke, F. (1999). Ethical decision making: Global concerns, frameworks and approaches. *Public Personnel Management, 8*(4), 530–537.

Callan, V. (1992). Predicting ethical values and training needs in ethics. *Journal of Business Ethics, 11*(10), 761–769.

Cascio, W.F. (2003). *Managing human resources: Productivity, quality of work life, profits.* New York: McGraw-Hill/Irwin.

Chandler, M.J., & Holliday, S. (1990). Wisdom in a postapocalyptic age. In R. J. Sternberg (Ed.), *Wisdom, its nature, origins and development* (pp. 121–142). Cambridge: Cambridge University Press.

Clark, M.M. (2004). New sentencing guidelines to reward ethical culture, compliance commitment. *HR Magazine,* September, 28.

Clayton, V. (1975). Erikson's theory of human development as it applies to the aged: Wisdom as contradictory cognition. *Human Development, 18,* 119–128.

Clayton, V., & Birren, J.W. (1980). The development of wisdom across the life span: A reexamination of an ancient topic. In P.B. Baltes & O.G. Brim, Jr. (Eds.), *Lifespan development and behavior* (Vol. 3, pp. 103–135). New York: Academic Press.

Colvin, G. (2001). The great CEO pay heist. *Fortune,* June 25.

Csikszentmihalyi, M., & Rathunde, K. (1990). The psychology of wisdom: An evolutionary interpretation. In R.J. Sternberg (Ed.), *Wisdom: Its nature, origins, and development,* (pp. 25–51). New York: Cambridge University Press.

Cullen, J.B., Victor, B., & Stephens, C. (1989). An ethical weather report: Assessing the organization's ethical climate. *Organizational Dynamics, 18,* 50–62.

De Pree, M. (1992). *Leadership Jazz.* New York: Dell.

Dean, P.J. (1992). Making codes of ethics real. *Journal of Business Ethics, 11,* 285–290.

Doyle, R.J. (1997). The case of a servant leader. In R.P. Vecchio (Ed.), *Leadership: Understanding the dynamics of power and influence in organizations,* (pp. 439–457). South Bend, IN: University of Notre Dame Press.

Driscoll, D., & Hoffman, W.M. (1998). HR plays a central role in ethics programs. *Workforce, 77*(4), 121–123.

Fairholm, G. (1998). *Perspectives on leadership: From the science of management to its spiritual heart.* Westport, Connecticut: Praeger.

Ferris, G.R., Witt, L.A., & Hochwarter, W.A. (2001). Interaction of social skill and general mental ability on job performance and salary. *Journal of Applied Psychology, 86,* 1075–1082.

Ford, R., & Richardson, W. (1994). Ethical decision making: A review of the empirical literature. *Journal Of Business Ethics, 13,* 205–221.

Frick, D.M. (2004). *Robert K. Greenleaf: A life of servant leadership.* San Francisco: Berrett-Koehler.

Giacalone, R.A., & Jurkiewicz, C.L. (2003). Toward a science of workplace spirituality. In R.A. Giacalone & C.L. Jurkiewicz (eds.), *Handbook of workplace spirituality and organizational performance,* (pp. 3–28). New York: M.W. Sharpe.

Grant, R.M. (1996). Toward a knowledge-based theory of the firm. *Strategic Management Journal, 17,* 109–122.

Greenleaf, R.K. (1977). *Servant-Leadership: A Journey Into the Nature of Legitimate Power and Greatness.* Mahwah, NJ: Paulist Press.

Grossman, R.J. (2004). HR on the board. *HR Magazine,* June, *49*(6), 56–63.

Henry, D., France, M., & Lavell, L. (2005). The boss on the sidelines: How auditors, directors, and lawyers are asserting their power. *Business Week,* April 25, 2005, 86–96.

Hey (2004). *The data, information, knowledge, wisdom chain: The metaphorical link.* best.me.berkeley.edu/~jhey03/files/reports/IS290_Finalpaper_HEY.pdf.

Howatson, M.C. (1990). *The Oxford companion to classical literature*. Oxford: Oxford University Press.

Hunter, J. E. (1986). Cognitive ability, cognitive aptitudes, job knowledge, and job performance. *Journal of Vocational Behavior, 29,* 340—362.

Jose, A., & Thibodeaux, M. (1999). Institutionalization of Ethics: The Perspective of Managers. *Journal of Business Ethics, 22,* 133–143.

Kitchener, K.S., & Brenner, H.G. (1990). Wisdom and reflective judgment: Knowing in the face of uncertainty. In R.J. Sternberg (Ed.), *Wisdom: Its nature, origins, and development,* (pp. 212–229). New York: Cambridge University Press.

Kohlberg, L. (1969). *Stages in the development of moral thought and action.* New York: Holt, Rinehart and Winston.

Kohlberg, L. (1983). *Essays in Moral Development, vol. 2: The Psychology of Moral Development.* New York: Harper and Row.

Kolodinsky, R.W., Bowen, M.G., & Ferris, G.R. (2003). Embracing workplace spirituality and managing organizational politics: Servant leadership and political skill for volatile times. In R.A. Giacalone & C.L. Jurkiewicz (Eds.), *Handbook of workplace spirituality and organizational performance,* (pp. 164–180). New York: M.E. Sharpe.

Lawler, E. III (2001). *Corporate boards: New strategies for adding value at the top.* San Francisco: Jossey-Bass.

Liebeskind, J.P. (1996). Knowledge, strategy, and the theory of the firm. *Strategic Management Journal, 17,* 93–108.

Life Application Bible (New International Version edition) (1991). Wheaton, IL: Tyndale.

Manz, C.C., Manz, K.P., Marx, R.D., & Neck, C.P. (2001). *The wisdom of Solomon at work: Ancient virtues for living and leading today.* San Francisco: Berrett-Koehler.

McKinney, M. (2005). Where is the wisdom we have lost in knowledge? *www.foundationsmag.com/pvwisdom.html.*

Nadel, M.S. (2004). Refining an "opt in" approach. *The American Journal of Bioethics* 4(4), 51–52.

Nonaka, I. (1994). The dynamic theory of organizational knowledge creation, *Organization Science, 5*(1), 14–37.

Nonaka, I., & Takeuchi, H. (1995). *The knowledge-creating company.* New York: Oxford University Press.

Polanyi, M. (1966). *The tacit dimension.* Garden City, New York: Doubleday.

Rosch, E. (1975). Cognitive representations of semantic categories. *Journal of Experimental Psychology: General, 104,* 192–233.

Sadler-Smith, E., & Shefy, E. (2004). The intuitive executive: Understanding and applying "gut feel' in decision-making. *Academy of Management Executive, 18*(4), 76–91.

Sandler, S.F. (Ed.) (2005). How HR can facilitate ethics. *HRfocus,* April, 1, 11–14.

Schmidt, F.L. & Hunter, J.E. (1993). Tacit knowledge, practical intelligence, general mental ability, and job knowledge. *Current Directions in Psychological Science, 1,* 8–9.

Schramm, J. (2004). Perceptions on ethics. *HR Magazine,* November, 176.

Senge, P. (1990). *The Fifth Discipline: The art and practice of the learning organization.* New York: Doubleday.

Simon, H. (1987). Making management decisions: The role of intuition and emotion. *Academy of Management Executive, 1*(1), 57–64.

Small, M.W. (2004). Wisdom and now managerial wisdom: Do they have a place in management development programs? Journal of Management Development, *23*(8), 751–764.

Spender J.C. (1996). Making knowledge the basis of a theory of the firm. *Strategic Management Journal, 17*(Winter), 45–62.

Sternberg, R.J. (1985). *Beyond IQ, A triarchic theory of human intelligence.* New York: Viking.

Sternberg, R.J. (1990). Wisdom and its relations to intelligence and creativity. In R.J. Sternberg (Ed.), *Wisdom: Its nature, origins, and development,* (pp. 142–159). New York: Cambridge University Press.

Sternberg, R.J. (1997). Managerial intelligence: Why IQ isn't enough. *Journal of Management, 23,* 475–493.

Sternberg, R.J. (1998). A balance theory of wisdom. *Review of General Psychology, 2*(4), 347–365.

Sternberg, R.J. (2000), Intelligence and wisdom. In R.J. Sternberg (Ed.), *Handbook of intelligence,* (pp. 631–649). New York: Cambridge University Press.

Sternberg, R.J. (2003). *Wisdom, intelligence, and creativity synthesized.* Cambridge, UK: Cambridge University Press.

Sternberg, R.J. (Ed.) (1990). *Wisdom: Its nature, origins, and development.* New York: Cambridge University Press.

Sternberg, R.J., Wagner, R.K., Williams, W.M., & Horvath, J.A. (1995). Testing common sense. *American Psychologist, 50*(11), 912–927.

Tosi, H.L., Werner, S. Katz, J.P., & Gomez-Mejia, L.R. (2000). How Much Does Performance Matter? A Meta-Analysis of CEO Pay Studies. *Journal of Management, 26*(2), 301–339.

Trevino, L., & Nelson, K. (1995). *Managing business ethics.* New York: Wiley.

Useem, J. (2003). Have they no shame? *Fortune,* April 28.

Vickers, M.R. (2005). Business ethics and the HR role: Past, present, and future. *Human Resource Planning, 28*(1), 26–32.

Von Hippel, E. (1994). Sticky information and the locus of problem solving: Implications for innovation. *Management Science, 40*(4), 429–439.

Webster's New World College Dictionary (1990) (3rd ed.). New York: Warner Books.

Weiss J.W. (1994). *Business ethics: A managerial, stakeholder approach.* Belmont, CA: Wadsworth.

Wells, S. (2005). Educating the board. *HR Magazine, 50*(2), 46–52.

Wernerfelt, B. (1984). A resource-based view of the firm. *Strategic Management Journal, 5,* 171–180.

Wiley, C. (1993). Employment managers' views on workplace ethics. *The EMA Journal* (Spring), 14–24.

Wiley, C. (2000). Ethical standards for human resource management professionals: A comparative analysis of five major codes. *Journal of Business Ethics, 25,* 93–114.

Witt, L.A., & Ferris, G.R. (2003). Social Skill as a moderator of the conscientiousness–performance relationship: Convergent results across four studies. *Journal of Applied Psychology, 88,* 809–820.

CHAPTER 4

BEYOND RHETORIC AND BUREAUCRACY

Using HRM to Add Ethical Value

Robert L. Cardy
University of Texas at San Antonio

T. T. Selvarajan
University of Houston–Victoria

This chapter focuses on using human resource management (HRM) to improve ethical conduct in organizations. We begin with a general consideration of the status of ethical conduct in organizations. We then address three core topics: 1) highlighting the importance of ethical conduct, 2) directions for improving ethical conduct, and 3) measuring ethical conduct. We then offer implications of the approach for researchers, practitioners, and educators.

Let us begin with a brief quiz! Do not worry, it is not going to be hard, it will not take long, and there really are not any right or wrong answers. Consider the following True or False items.

Human Resource Management Ethics, pages 71–85
Copyright © 2006 by Information Age Publishing
All rights of reproduction in any form reserved.

1. Ethical misconduct is a problem in many of today's organizations. True or False?

2. It is important to assure that conduct in organizations is ethical. True or False?

If you are like most people, you probably answered "True" to both items. But even if your response was "True" to only the second item, the implication would remain that a proactive approach to managing ethical conduct should be taken. Whether trying to reduce misconduct (an action suggested by item 1) or encourage positive conduct (an action suggested by item 2), we must take action in organizations to improve ethical conduct. Unethical conduct is not likely to stop or ethical conduct likely to increase without systematic intervention. However, it is not always clear just what actions should be taken to address ethical conduct.

Perhaps we should focus any actions at the top of the organization? There certainly seem to be no shortage of stories about ethical missteps among top managers in organizations. Dennis Kozlowski had a penchant for excess as chief executive office of Tyco International Ltd., including extravagant parties with x-rated ice sculptures and $6,000.00 shower curtains. The former CEO was recently convicted for stealing millions from the company. Probably most widely known is the case of Kenneth Lay, former CEO of Enron. Lay and other former top Enron executives are facing a variety of fraud charges. The accounting firm of Arthur Anderson was convicted of obstruction of justice in the Enron case. Approximately 4,000 workers at Enron lost their jobs when the house built on inflated profit numbers collapsed. As yet another example, Bernie Ebbers, former chief executive of WorldCom, has been found guilty by a federal jury of securities fraud, conspiracy, and lying to regulators. The WorldCom trial received a great deal of public attention. Part of the media focus is probably a function of human fascination with a fallen leader or with the story of a powerful but greedy person who gets their due. However, the attention is also due to the damage that often occurs in the wake of unethical leadership. In the WorldCom case, for instance, many people lost their jobs and life savings due to a greedy and unprincipled person at the top (Joyner, 2005). Considering the examples given above can lead to the conclusion that there is ethical poverty at the top (see e.g., Gomez-Mejia, Balkin, & Cardy, 2005).

Top management is not the only organizational level which appears to suffer from lapses in ethical conduct. A variety of indicators suggest that ethical misconduct also afflicts the lower ranks (Shellenbarger, 2005). For example, employees calling in sick recently hit a five-year high and it appears that somewhere around 30 to 60 percent of those did so to take care of personal business or because they felt entitled to the time off. Additionally, misrepresentation by job applicants is a growing problem. One estimate places the percentage of resumes that contain false information at 12 percent. Certainly, lower level employees also engage in theft at work. This misconduct might involve relatively minor infractions to complex schemes involving stealing and reselling expensive materials or products. Further, survey information indicates that non-managerial workers are less likely than managers to report observed misconduct (Shellenbarger, 2005). More surveys are being conducted all of the time, but the general conclusion seems inescapable: ethical misconduct is not a problem that primarily resides at only one level in an organization. Certainly, it is important to have positive role models at the top of an organization. However, focusing on ethical conduct at only one level in an organization is not likely to solve ethical issues. What is needed is improvement efforts that cut across the organization and affect every employee.

The need for improving ethical performance might be compelling and persuasive, but just how can the goal be accomplished? We propose a simple model in which the first step toward improving ethical performance in organizations is establishing the importance of ethical conduct. As presented in the model (see Figure 4.1), the next step in improving ethical performance is performance management. In this step we primarily emphasize the establishment of performance criteria. However, we broadly define performance management in the model as a concept that, in addition to performance appraisal, can include selection, training, and compensation. The components, or drivers, of ethical performance in this model parallel the generic performance equation used in the human resource management area: performance = ability × motivation. Establishing the importance of ethical conduct can provide incentive to everyone in the organization to get "on board" with the ethical values of the organization. Recognizing the importance of ethical performance can motivate people, but does not give people the means, or capabilities, to follow through on the conceptual intention. The step of performance management operationalizes the concept of ethical performance and can provide people the ability to improve their ethical conduct. For example, having clear and behavioral criteria can provide explicit guidance for desired conduct. We next address the steps of establishing importance and performance management.

Figure 4.1.   Ethical performance improvement model.

ESTABLISHING IMPORTANCE

One approach to trying to make ethics a reality in organizations is to make organizational survival contingent on aligning with the ethical values of the organization. For example, Harry Jansen Kraemer, CEO of the global health company, Baxter International Inc., believes that ethical conduct can only be assured when employees share the values that guide that conduct (Sisk, 2003). A way to approach this issue and underscore the importance of sharing the right ethical values is with the use of a simple 2×2 matrix which divides employees into four categories, depending on their performance levels and ethical values (see Figure 4.2). The performance factor divides employees into two categories of work performance: either acceptable or unacceptable. Performance might be defined as amount of sales, quantity produced, or according to some other results metric. The ethical value factor divides employees into two categories: those who are aligned with the ethical values of the organization and those who are not. Given this simple 2×2 matrix, there are two cells that might be considered "no-brainers," good performers who take the ethical value system to heart and poor performers who do not align themselves with the ethical value system. Obviously, the former group are "keepers" and the model citizens. The latter group consists of people who need to be moved along to other employment options—not only do they not obtain adequate results, but they also do not approach their tasks in an acceptable manner. There are two more cells in the matrix that require consideration. What about employees who are not obtaining adequate results but are aligned with the ethical values of the organization? These people already embrace the appropriate values, but need to bring up their performance levels. Maybe they deserve a chance to improve and might benefit from additional training. Now for the tough cell in the performance-by-ethical-values matrix. What to do about employees who "hit the numbers" but are

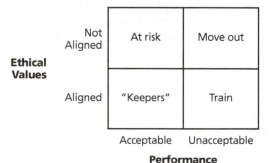

Figure 4.2.   Performance by ethical values matrix.

not on board with the ethical values espoused by the organization? There are cases where top managers have used this type of matrix to get out the message regarding plans for people in this last cell. Jack Welch, the former CEO of General Electric, for example, advocated the use of a performance by value matrix as guidance for managing employee behaviors (Kallish, 2005). If the organization is serious about ethical values, the message for people in this cell is that they will be gone! In other words, getting results is not enough. If an employee gets things done but does it by cutting corners, misrepresenting, being underhanded, and so on, their employment is at risk.

The performance by ethical values matrix is an effective way for top management to bring attention to ethics and to clarify just how important ethics will be treated in the organization. It can certainly get the attention of people to tell them that their job may be at risk, even though they are getting the results. In essence, the message is that performance and productivity are not enough: how one goes about achieving those outcomes can be even *more* important! In other words it is not just ends, but.the means used to achieve the results. While it can take awhile, we are of the belief that it is the process of how an organization goes about its business that can determine the long-term productivity, profitability, and even survival of the business.

The performance by ethical conduct matrix is a tool that can be used to bring home the importance of ethical conduct, but does it give people a path to follow to really improve ethical conduct? Unfortunately, simply classifying people as being aligned or not aligned with ethical values is too ambiguous to provide much direction as to how to improve. The matrix helps to make clear that ethics is important, but just how is ethical conduct in an organization improved? We now turn to the next step in our simple ethical performance model: performance management

PERFORMANCE MANAGEMENT

A reaction to recent ethical scandals is to provide more rules and checks regarding ethical conduct. For example, due to the U. S. Sarbanes-Oxley Act of 2002, many organizations now face additional accounting rules and reporting requirements. Public companies, according to the Sarbanes-Oxley Act, are required to have and disclose a code of ethics (Hoffman, 2005). According to the act, all public companies must document, test, and evaluate their internal controls (Higgins, 2005). Beyond the Sarbanes-Oxley Act, internal auditors are mandated by their professional standards to evaluate the effectiveness of an organization's ethics-related internal controls (Verschoor, 2004). Further, many governments and governing bodies around the world are developing organizational regulations and guidelines that include ethics (Verschoor, 2004). As another indication of the focus on compliance with ethical standards, one can look at membership in a group called the "Ethics Officer Association." This association includes ethics and compliance practitioners and its membership between June 2003 and November 2004 (a period during which several Sarbanes-Oxley statutes were implemented) increased by 17.5 percent for company members and by 22 percent for individual members (Harbert, 2005).

The purpose, of course, of the types of standards and compliance evaluations described above is to assure that organizations and their members adhere to ethical standards. While the intent of standards and compliance assessments is positive, there are some important drawbacks to solely relying on rules to improve ethics. First, rules cannot cover all aspects of performance. Accounting rules can leave open a variety of ways to act unethically. Regulations might provide acceptable standards for numbers but *how* those numbers were obtained is a central ethics issue. Standards of operation might be adhered to, yet the performance of people in the organization could be characterized as underhanded and deceitful. A second and related drawback to a reliance on rules is that they simply cannot cover every possible situation. No matter how detailed and compulsive rule-makers might be, there are bound to be situations that arise that were not anticipated. If standards do not cover a situation, how should people act?

There are limits to a compliance-based bureaucracy. It may not be widely recognized, but Enron had a fine ethics handbook (Jennings, 2005). Unfortunately, a good set of standards did not prevent Enron from being the poster child for ethically corrupt organizations. Simply stated, compliance is not ethics (Hoffman, 2005). Regulations can provide a starting point and indicate the "floor," or minimum expectations. Ethical performance, on the other hand, is a more abstract concept and can mean going beyond rules and legal requirements and doing what is the right and just thing to do according to ethical principles. Relying on compliance to achieve ethics is analogous to relying on inspection to achieve quality. As pointed out by one of the most outspoken proponents of the quality movement, you cannot inspect quality in (Deming, 1986). Similarly, compliance cannot guarantee ethical performance.

While regulations and compliance evaluations have limitations, they are needed but must be recognized as simply starting points. To build and assure ethical performance, an organization must go beyond having rules and compliance audits. As Orlitzky and Swanson argued in Chapter 1 of this book, the performance appraisal system should be attuned to ethical values. That is, ethics must become part of the performance management system. To begin with, this means that criteria for ethical conduct must be generated. People need to see examples of good and bad levels of ethical performance and develop an operational understanding of ethical conduct in the organization. Employees need to internalize the spirit behind the rules, not just adhere to the letter of the rules. Explicit ethical performance criteria can provide concrete examples and a basis for people to internalize the ethical principles they convey.

An approach we recommend for generating ethical performance criteria is the tried-and-true HRM tool for developing behavioral criteria—the critical incident technique (Cardy, 2004).

The critical incident technique can be used to operationally define ethical and unethical conduct when people carry out their duties in an organization. The critical incident technique can easily be adapted to generate examples of ethical, rather than purely task, performance. Incidents can be generated, for example, to reflect ethical aspects regarding how each of the dimensions of a job is carried out. Or, separate ethical dimensions that cut across the job can be identified. Behavioral examples that illustrate each of these independent dimensions can then be generated. As an illustration, ethical dimensions for salespeople have been identified in previous research as including dimensions such as deception, falsification, bribery, and personal use of company resources. A brief description of each of these dimensions is presented in Table 4.1. We used the critical incident technique to generate behaviorally-based rating scales for each of these dimensions (Cardy & Selvarajan, 2004). The same approach could be taken to generate behaviorally-based ethical scales for non-sales positions and to generate company-specific ethical performance measures. An important and positive feature of behaviorally-based ethical scales is that they make clear to people just what is meant by ethical conduct in the organization. The behavioral descriptions move people beyond a set of policies and beyond a conceptual understanding of ethics and provide a behavioral roadmap for the types of actions people should and should not engage in.

Table 4.1. Dimensions and Definitions of Ethicalness of Performance

Dimension	Definition
Bribery	Giving and accepting gifts/favors in exchange for preferential treatment.
Deception	Indulging in cheating, fraudulent and deceitful conduct towards customers.
Falsification	To misrepresent/lie, indulge in falsehood in company matters vis-à-vis company rules, policies and company records.
Ethical dealing with co-workers	Being dishonest/unethical about dealing with coworkers; taking credit for coworkers' effort and passing blame on co-workers for one's mistakes.
Padding expense accounts	Being dishonest about statements related to expense accounts submitted on business trips.
Personal use	Misusing of company resources (e.g., facilities, supplies); using them for personal use.

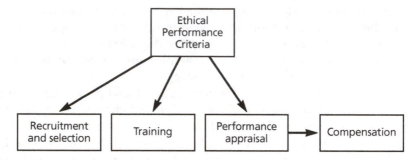

Figure 4.3.   Ethical performance criteria.

The development of behavioral criteria is, in our opinion, a critical and necessary first step in the ethical performance management process. As depicted in Figure 4.3, the criteria feed into all other aspects of the ethical performance management process. The criteria should be the underpinnings for all of the components of performance management. For example, ethical criteria should drive recruitment and selection efforts, if ethical conduct is really to be a serious emphasis in the organization. The ethical criteria can help identify an employment brand (Cardy, 2005) for the organization and attract people who will fit with and embody the ethical principles. The ethical criteria can be the basis for assessment during the selection process. Just as with assessment of task-related knowledge and ability, if ethical performance is to be a real organizational priority, assessments on the ethical dimensions should be made as well. Including ethical conduct assessment in tests and interviews can further clarify the importance of ethics to the organization's employment brand. Further, including ethics in the selection process can help the organization to avoid the difficulties that can occur when "bad apples" get into a good system and engage in unethical conduct.

Behavioral criteria should also be the starting point for the remaining key performance management components: performance appraisal, compensation, and training. As depicted in Figure 4.3, we view behavioral criteria as directly impacting performance appraisal. In turn, performance appraisal should be a driver of compensation, such as merit pay, that is linked to ethical aspects of performance. Training also may need to be provided regarding ethical conduct. At the least, training may be required to assure that everyone understands the ethical dimensions and how ethical performance will be assessed. Additional training may be needed depending on the levels of ethical performance, as measured with the performance appraisal system.

In the remainder of this discussion of ethical performance management, we will focus on performance appraisal, in particular the measurement of ethical performance. Certainly, all of the components of the ethical performance management process can be important. However, measurement of ethical performance is key if ethics is to be managed and improved.

Measuring Ethical Performance

Up to this point, we have stressed that in order to maximize ethics, the importance of ethics needs to be emphasized to organizational members. Further, ethical conduct requires more than rules. People need behavioral examples to "get it" and put the ethics concept into practice. However, importance and capability does not assure that people are going to engage and execute. The ingredient that needs to be added to the above mix is measurement. If the measurement of ethical conduct is not included, the time and effort that management might expend on emphasizing the importance of ethics can simply be viewed as rhetoric by organizational members. From a management perspective, without measurement there is the risk that the resources devoted to enhancing ethics could end up being a sunk cost. Including ethics in the measurement of performance moves ethical concern beyond rhetoric. Including ethical dimensions in the measurement of performance sends the clear signal to everyone that this stuff about ethical conduct is important on a day-to-day basis.

Beyond operationalizing the importance of ethics, measuring ethical conduct is necessary if it is to be managed. Regular measurement of ethical conduct is required if ethics in an organization is really going to be managed. How is the organization doing in terms of ethics? Are things improving? Getting worse? Are there areas of the organization where there seem to be problems? Are there individuals who appear to be cutting corners and who either do not understand or are not on board with our ethical standards? Can we make training, rewards, recognition, and other possible actions contingent on ethical conduct? All of these management questions and more require the measurement of ethical performance.

Consider the typical performance appraisal system in an organization. Do any of the dimensions focus on ethics? Our expectation is that the answer for most of us is "No." While the inclusion of ethics in performance appraisal is certainly doable, it seems to be rarely done. Task performance and achieving outcomes are clearly priorities in organizations. However, how tasks are carried out and outcomes are achieved is also important. Measuring ethical conduct requires assessing the process of performance, such as provided by the behaviorally based approach mentioned previously.

Having a measurement instrument for assessing ethical conduct is not enough. In order to be well managed, ethical conduct must be accurately assessed. Unfortunately, based on initial evidence, it appears that ethical judgments may be systematically biased by the outcomes achieved by a worker, an effect we refer to as "success bias."

Success Bias

Characteristics of workers have long been examined as possible sources of bias in performance evaluations. Of course, worker behavior has been found to be a primary determinant of performance evaluations (Cardy & Dobbins, 1994). Interestingly, the outcomes achieved by workers have also been found to influence ratings of behavioral performance (Cardy, Anderson, & Evans, 1991; DeNisi & Stevens, 1981). In other words, the results obtained can influence judgment of the means used by workers to obtain those ends. It appears that this biasing effect for the results achieved by workers extends to judgments of ethical performance.

An initial study (Cardy & Selvarajan, 1997) examined whether results might bias judgments of ethical performance. There are some important facets of this study that we will briefly describe so that the findings can be better understood. The study described the results and behavioral performance of a fictitious salesperson. The worker either succeeded or failed in making sufficient sales. Behavioral performance depicted either ethical or unethical performance on five of the six dimensions that were presented in Table 4.1. A critical aspect of the study was that no information was provided on one dimension. This design allows the application of signal detection theory (Lord, 1985) in which the tendency to make false positive errors can be calculated. The study used a behavioral observation scale on which evaluators simply indicated whether a worker exhibited each of 12 behaviors. Thus, the design of the study allows examination of whether the actual observations reported by evaluators are veridical, not just whether evaluations about the quality of performance are shifted in an upward or downward fashion. Specifically, the dependent measure used in the study was bias (Snodgrass & Corwin, 1988) and it reflects the extent of directional bias in the observational judgments.

The results of this initial study strongly support the conclusion that outcomes bias judgments of ethical performance. Study participants were significantly more likely to report observing ethical behaviors when the worker was successful than when s/he was unsuccessful. The mean level of bias in the success condition was .84 and in the failure condition was .69. The mean levels of bias in the behavior (ethical or unethical) by outcome (success or failure) matrix are presented in Figure 4.4. Statistical analysis found both behaviors and outcomes to significantly influence the accuracy of the behavioral observations.

Outcome

		Failure	Success
	Unethical	.619	.749
Behavior			
	Ethical	.756	.929

Figure 4.4.   Mean bias scores in initial study.
Note: Higher scores indicate more bias.

The above findings suggest that an outcome schema may have an influence on evaluating the ethicalness of a worker's behaviors. From a schematic perspective (e.g., Neisser, 1967) a worker who achieves excellent work outcomes may be placed in a high performance cognitive category by the rater. Unethical behavior that the worker engaged in may be ignored, discounted or reinterpreted to be consistent with the schema of a high performer. The result would be inordinately positive judgments of the worker's ethical performance. In other words, people may tend to rate the ethics of a successful employee more favorably than that of an unsuccessful employee.

The study described above is only one empirical investigation and had characteristics that may limit its generalizability. Specifically, study participants were undergraduate students and the behavioral descriptions of workers consisted of entirely ethical or entirely unethical behavior. More experienced evaluators and more realistic evaluatee descriptions may reduce or eliminate the effect of outcomes on ethical performance judgments. Another study, similar in design to the initial one, was conducted (Cardy & Selvarajan, 2000). Study participants for this follow-up investigation were full time employees enrolled in a night MBA program. The behavioral descriptions of workers included a, perhaps more realistic mixture of ethical and unethical behaviors, with ethical (unethical) workers being described with ethical (unethical) behavior on four of five dimensions. Again, no behavioral information was provided on a sixth dimension.

The second study again found significant main effects for behaviors and outcomes. The critical finding is replication of the biasing influence of success or failure on behavioral observation judgments. Thus, the influence of outcomes on judgments regarding ethical behaviors was still found to operate with a sample of more experienced raters and with less extreme materials.

Another study also corroborated the hypothesis that judgment of ethical behavior is influenced by outcomes (Selvarajan & Cardy, 2003). This hypothesis was tested with undergraduate business students as a part of lager study on the influences of rater cognitive processing on the accuracy of ethical judgments. The behavioral descriptions and study design were similar to that of the second study discussed above.

To summarize our research on the influence of results on judgments of ethical performance, participants across three studies were more likely to report the occurrence of ethical behaviors (that the worker really did not do) for successful than for unsuccessful workers. To coin a phrase or two, it appears that "nothing succeeds like success" or that "success excuses all." More work is needed before it can be concluded that the success bias is accepted as a general phenomenon. However, at this point it appears that we focus on outcomes achieved and those outcomes color not only the level of our evaluations but also our very perception of whether ethical or unethical conduct occurred.

Based on the studies conducted thus far, our conclusion is that the effect of outcomes on judgments of ethical behavior is a real and significant issue for the measurement of ethical performance. Rationally, whether a worker succeeds or fails should not be a factor in judgments concerning the ethical-ness of behaviors a worker engaged in as the means to achieve those out-comes. However, knowledge of success or failure appears to play a significant role in determining the judgments of the ethicalness of a worker's behavior. It is important to recognize that the effect of outcomes reported here is not just to raise or lower ratings. Rather, success leads evaluators to report observing ethical behaviors that the worker never engaged in.

SOME DIRECTIONS FOR RESEARCH AND PRACTICE

The ethical domain is rich with opportunities for HRM researchers and practitioners. In terms of organizational practice, it seems compelling that ethical conduct needs to be added to the performance management sys-tem. To the extent that ethics is a true priority in the organization, ethical conduct needs to be included in the assessment, feedback, and perfor-mance improvement efforts. Generating ethical dimensions and behavior-ally describing those dimensions is a process that could heighten the sensitivity, appreciation, and understanding of ethics in the organization. As discussed earlier, ethical conduct, by its very nature, has to do with the process of performance. Thus, evaluations of the ethical conduct of a worker should be done by those closest to the process of that worker's per-formance. Peers and customers may be much more aware of the process of a worker's performance while a supervisor may be more aware of and focused on the outcomes achieved by the worker. Peers and customers may be the best and most knowledgeable sources for assessing ethical conduct.

Research directions in the domain of ethics include issues of criteria definition and measurement, among others. In terms of defining ethical performance, what are the underlying dimensions? Is there a core set of ethical dimensions that are generalizable, or do the dimensions change across jobs and organizations? Maybe there are generalizable dimensions, but the behavioral specifics change? Further, should ethical performance be separated from other performance dimensions, or should ethical conduct be intertwined with task performance? That is, should separate and unique ethical dimensions be generated or should ethical conduct be part of how task performance is defined and measured? The latter approach makes ethical conduct integral with task performance and "bakes in" ethics as part and parcel of the performance expectations. However, the integral approach also runs the risk of ethics being less visible as an initiative in the organization. Which approach is best in terms of measures such as efficiency, acceptance, and assessment effectiveness?

Further research on the "success bias" needs to determine if the effect occurs with other materials and participants. The generalizability of the bias and possible moderators of the effect should be investigated. Are some sources of evaluation less susceptible to success bias? For example, for customers, worker outcomes may mean little while the process of performance is of central concern.

In terms of other components of the ethical performance management process, research should examine the assessment of ethical dimensions at the selection stage. For example, might work samples, behavioral interviewing, or some other approach be most effective for assessing the level of ethical characteristics of applicants? Which approach is most effective in terms or validity and utility? Likewise, can ethical conduct be learned through behaviorally based training? If such training works, does it have a long term effect, or does it dissipate. How effective is the training when there is no surveillance or accountability? More fundamentally, can ethics be learned or is it a person characteristic, similar to personality traits, that is largely immutable?

Ethics is an important issue that we should claim as part of our HRM domain. We certainly have the tools and expertise to measure and improve ethics. The topic also offers a wide range of interesting and relevant research issues.

REFERENCES

Cardy, R.L. (2004). *Performance Management: Concepts, Skills, and Exercises*. Armonk, N.Y.: M.E. Sharpe.

Cardy, R. L. (2005). Brand 'Em! HRM Makes the Brand Real. Feature article in Spring Issue of the Academy of Management HR Division Newsletter.

Cardy, R. L., Anderson, J.S., & Evans K.R. (1991). *Judging performance: The impact of Behaviors, Outcomes and Trait Inferences.* Paper presented at the 1991 annual conference of the Society for Industrial and Organizational Psychology, Inc.

Cardy, R.L., & Dobbins G.H. (1994). *Performance appraisal: A consideration of alternative perspectives.* Cincinnati, OH: South-Western.

Cardy, R.L., & Selvarajan, T.T. (1997). *Assessing ethical behavior: The impact of outcomes on judgment bias.* Paper presented at the annual meeting of the Academy of Management, Boston.

Cardy, R.L., & Selvarajan, T.T. (2000). *Assessing ethical behavior revisited: The impact of outcomes on judgment bias.* Paper presented at the annual meeting of the Academy of Management, Toronto.

Cardy, R. L. and Selvarajan, T. T. (2004). Assessing Ethical Behavior: Development of a Behaviorally Anchored Rating Scale. *Proceedings of the Southwest Academy of Management Meeting,* Orlando, March, 2004.

Deming, W. E. (1986). *Out of the Crisis.* Cambridge, MA: MIT Initiative for Advanced Engineering Study.

DeNisi, A.C., & Stevens, G.E. (1981). Profiles of performance, performance evaluations and personnel decisions. *Academy of Management Journal, 24,* 592–602.

Drummond, M. (May 2, 2005). Firms with solid ethical footing can still recover when leaders go astray. Knight-Ridder/Tribune Business News.

Gomez-Mejia, L.R., Balkin, D.B., & Cardy, R.L. (2005). *Management,* 2nd edition, McGraw-Hill, Boston.

Harbert, T. (2005). Oaths of office: Complex regulations prompt more companies to hire compliance chiefs. *Electronic Business, 31,* 13.

Higgins, D. (April 4, 2005). Honesty costs money. *Times Union,* Albany, N.Y., Business News.

Hoffman, D. (2005). Money managers: Chief compliance officer duties could have ethics added to list. *Pensions & Investments, 33,* 4.

Jennings, M. (April 2, 2005) Personal communication.

Joyner, T. (March 16, 2005). Ex-worker applauds Ebber's conviction. Knight-Ridder Tribune business News.

Kallish E. (2005). *Ethics in Corporate America.* http://www.nbc11.com/employment/770947/detail.html

Lord, R.G. (1985). Accuracy in behavioral measurement: An alternative definition based on rater's cognitive schema and signal detection theory. *Journal of Applied Psychology, 70,* 66–71.

Neisser, U. (1967). *Cognitive Psychology.* Englewood Cliffs, NJ: Prentice Hall.

Orlitzky, M and Swanson, D (2006). Socially responsible human resource management: Charting new territory. In J. R. Deckop (Ed.), *Human Resource Management Ethics.* Greenwich, CT: Information Age.

Selvarajan, T. T. & Cardy, R. L. (2003). *Assessing ethical behavior: The influence of schematic, attributional, and affective processes.* Paper presented at the Academy of Management Meeting, 2003. Seattle, WA.

Snodgrass, J.G., & Corwin, J. (1988). Pragmatics of measuring recognition memory: Applications to dementia and amnesia. *Journal of Experimental Psychology: General, 117,* 34–50.

Verschoor, C.C. (2004). The ethical climate barometer: Stormy weather could be ahead if your organization's culture is based on the wrong values. Learn to read, recognize, and evaluate your company's corporate culture to ensure bright days are on the horizon. *Internal Auditor, 61,* 48–54.

CHAPTER 5

AN EXAMINATION OF THE POTENTIAL OF HUMAN RESOURCE DEVELOPMENT (HRD) TO IMPROVE ORGANIZATIONAL ETHICS

Tim Hatcher
North Carolina State University

INTRODUCTION

Unlike HRM and ethics the relationship between Human Resource Development (HRD) and ethics has been largely ignored. According to Tom Donaldson, the well-known business ethicist, "HRD has taken ethics for granted for too long" (Personal communication, September 12, 2001). Only very recently have HRD practitioners and scholars begun to truly understand and embrace the critical nature of ethics. In the not too distant past HRD as a discipline stood idly by as employees and managers faced dilemmas and paradoxes where doing the right thing was not clear, or in cases where personal, organizational and economic and social values clashed. But the profession has begun to take notice of this omission and now provides venues to address moral concerns within organizations. For

Human Resource Management Ethics, pages 87–110
Copyright © 2006 by Information Age Publishing
All rights of reproduction in any form reserved.

example, there are now codes of ethics for professional organizations such as ASTD, International Society for Performance Improvement (ISPI), and the Academy of Human Resource Development (AHRD).

There is a growing library of publications on ethics and HRD including articles, case studies and textbooks intended to help practitioners and scholars better understand what is driving the need for ethics in our organizations and to figure out how to make the right decisions when faced with ethical dilemmas. And most professional conferences related to HRD now offer sessions and/or workshops related to ethics, values and/or morality. More importantly professionals are experiencing real dialogue about ethics and values-laden issues such as globalization, technology and corporate social responsibility.

Using more critical approaches than ever before HRD scholars and practitioners are trying to better understand the "dark side" of organizations and the oft-times malicious socio-economic environment where it resides; to question our assumptions and critically reflect on issues of power and influence. The HRD ground that we thought was so stable is shifting away from the mere rhetoric of compliance and codes—however important to accomplish—towards a "soul searching" for the heart of the HRD profession; where we honestly deal with our espoused values versus values in use and acknowledge and understand the relationship between ethics and HRD.

Training, educating, and developing people and providing organizational development and change initiatives inherently have moral implications. However, HRD professionals have until a short time ago had little or no help from the profession when challenged with on-the-job ethics. As an example, at the conclusion of a needs assessment a trainer coerced by an over-zealous manager to reveal the source of information she considered "negative" had no professional standards to use as moral authority until just a few years ago. For an example of a code of ethics for HRD see the Academy of Human Resource Development *Standards on Ethics and Integrity* at www.ahrd.org.

The HRD profession is no longer ignoring issues of power, confidentiality, equal access to learning and a myriad of other moral issues, but it has yet to fully embrace its full potential as the conscious of the corporation. There is some growing evidence however that because of its unique position as an emerging and relatively new discipline HRD can influence ethics in organizational and work-related systems (Hatcher, 2002), because as Foote & Robinson (1999) implied there is little evidence of HRM's ability to influence organizational ethics.

To presume a causal relationship between industrial training and organizational ethics in the simple and sheltered companies of the past century is implausible. Yet in today's complex organizations HRD is increasingly charged with changing entire organizational cultures, educating and instilling morals in our leaders, and addressing the challenges of globalization and ever-changing technology; all of which have a direct impact on creating either ethical or unethical work environments.

Simultaneously, along with changes in the workplace, HRD professionals have evolved from entertainers posing as stand-up trainers and instructional designers with narrowly defined skills to highly educated change agents, architects of organizational learning and knowledge development and leaders in e-learning. Additionally, they have gone from being a minor player at the strategy table, having little or no accountability, to having more responsibilities for strategic initiatives and being accountable for return on investment of HRD-related interventions and programs (It should be noted that these statements are optimistic in nature; HRD is still nowhere near the strategy table in many companies). In a recent article titled "Why We Hate HR," in the popular magazine *Fast Times* Hammonds (2005) said,

> After close to 20 years of hopeful rhetoric about becoming "strategic partners" with a "seat at the table" where the business decisions that matter are made, most human resource professionals are not nearly there. They have no seat, and the table is locked inside a conference room to which they have no key. HR people are, for most practical purposes, neither strategic nor leaders. (p. 42)

With these changes comes increasing responsibility and influence; the kind of power that, without ethical grounding, can be problematic and potentially abused. HRD is just beginning to realize and address this responsibility; and while we have made good progress, it seems we still have a long way to go.

I suggest and there is evidence that HRD has more potential than other related disciplines to help create organizations where people act in responsible and ethical ways. To support the contention that there is potential for HRD to provide ethical guidance to organizations this chapter will focus on three issues: First, I offer definitions of contemporary HRM and HRD and discuss the evolution of their conceptual frameworks and how the transformation of definitions may be attributing to ethical behaviors especially within HRD. Second is a discussion of the outcomes of HRD research and practice on ethics, both positive and negative. Finally, I discuss the future potential of HRD to help create ethical organizations.

EVOLVING DEFINITIONS AND THEORIES

To better understand its evolution and how HRD is currently defined, I will compare and contrast definitions and concepts of HRD and HRM. But before I define either, the historical foundations and evolution of the two disciplines and how this history may have influenced the way in which each discipline views and practices ethics are discussed.

There are limited publications on the history of HRD and HRM. A brief review of available electronic databases revealed no HRD or HRM related historiographies or true historical scholarship. Thus, historical analysis depends not so much on scholarship, but on the subjective interpretations of scholars and practitioners; piecing together histories from non-empirical trade publications and personal accounts.

It seems reasonable to address the evolution of academic and practitioner HRD and HRM since there is much written about the gap between research that occurs primarily in academic settings and work-based practice. It is especially pertinent in this chapter on ethics and HRD to view historical events such as these through an ethics lens to appreciate how they may have influenced HRM and HRD's moral development and the potential that either has in creating ethical organizations.

Understanding the growth of HRM requires a journey into the evolution of management in general and employee relations and personnel in particular. Marciano (1995) suggested that HRM, as it has been practiced in the U.S., evolved from the management thinking of Peter Drucker and his seminal work *The Practice of Management* (1954). The emergence of industrial psychology in the 1950s, primarily in response to Sputnik and the subsequent "cold war," and the work of Carl Jung, B.F. Skinner, W. Edwards Deming and others, brought scientific approaches to employee management. However, there are several people and/or events that served to influence the development of HRM as a discipline in the early 1900s, some four decades earlier. These include the work of F.W. Taylor and scientific management, Ford's assembly line, World War I and the need to quickly train great numbers of people, and publication of the work of managers by Henri Fayol, to name but a few. In the 1920s, '30s and the early '40s, Follett's seminal work on human factors in management, Western Electric's Hawthorne studies and the start of World War II, further defined the emerging field of personnel and industrial relations. The 1940s saw a multitude of influences on personnel management including publication of *The Future of Industrial Man* (1942) by Drucker, and the early work of Lewin, Lippit, and McGregor from the National Training Labs (human relations concepts). In addition to the work of Drucker in the 1950s, Marciano (1995) suggested that scholars like Bakke (1958), Miles' (1965) "Human Resource Model," and the publication of the American Management Association *Innovative Human Resource Management* (Desatnick, 1972), further influenced and solidified personnel management. It was not until the 1970s that legislation such as OSHA and EEO/affirmative action began to have a considerable impact on HRM. Compliance became the primary focus of HRM in many organizations and significantly changed how it was viewed by management.

Until the 1980s, HRM was synonymous with personnel management and the need to comply with regulations. It was not until the work of Tichy and others at the University of Michigan, and Beer at Harvard in the 1980s, did a "general theory" of HRM as a strategic initiative (SHRM) in organizations emerge and become the standard of contemporary HRM.

The evolution of HRD follows a different path than HRM but is no less complex. Primarily following the history of industrialism in the U.S., the UK and parts of Europe, HRD has emerged from simple skills training to e-learning, knowledge creation and organizational learning. The basic notion of a worker showing another how to perform a task or skill is not a new activity with roots that can be traced to the ancient Middle East. Brought to the New World primarily through British and European apprenticeships and guilds that embraced Luther and Calvin's work ethic, early training was seen primarily as a means to serve a transcendent and theistic purpose. It was not until the shift from community-based work to factory-based work that training eventually became institutionalized in educational and vocational organizations. For example, in the late 1800s, factory schools began as a result of the rise in product and service demands. This was soon followed by a dramatic increase in vocational education programs throughout the U.S. This advancement for vocational education culminated in the Smith-Hughes Act of 1917, the first federal legislation to aid pre-collegiate education. Training has also been greatly influenced by several major U.S. war efforts to systematically train many people well within a short time frame. The work of Channing Dooley and the *Training Within Industry Report of 1940–1945* is considered a major historical event in the evolution of training and HRD (Ruona, 2001).

As technology and increasing demands created needs for more highly educated employees in more complex and multi-faceted organizations, HRD has evolved beyond skills training toward providing organization development, knowledge creation, competence modeling and e-learning for international companies and is an integral part of national initiatives to develop competitive workforces in several developing countries.

As can be seen from these brief and incomplete histories, HRM and HRD have evolved from different historical origins. It is hard to draw definitive relationships between the evolutions and the role that ethics may be playing within the two disciplines as a result. However, considering their history and evolution we can generalize about how the two consider ethics as either an integral theoretical foundation or an externality similar to other compliance or legal issues. For example, since HRM has remained closely aligned with organizational strategies, it is likely more concerned with ethics as it impacts upon a specific organization's success or failure.

Thus, HRM may view ethics in a more businesslike and instrumental manner. HRD, on the other hand, evolving from apprenticeships and a focus on an individual's skills may lead to the discipline addressing ethical issues more in terms of how they may influence individual development and personal growth. Again, these are broad generalities unsubstantiated through historiographic analysis and subject to criticism.

Because of the lack of empirical analyses, to draw definitive conclusions is not prudent. It may not be completely unrealistic however to suggest that HRD and HRM have different views of ethics that at least to a certain extent is based on the focus on the management of personnel issues as a part of both academe and the workplace for HRM scholars and practitioners and for those involved in HRD the focus has been on the long-term development and growth of people in work-related systems.

Evolutions and histories reveal only a part of the overall picture of multifaceted disciplines like HRM and HRD. To fully understand how they differ or may be similar and how their development may impact upon ethics also requires an examination and understanding of their definitions.

Definitions

HRD and HRM have experienced a sometimes intimate, sometimes symbiotic, sometimes tumultuous and sometimes tenuous relationship. The rhetoric is incongruent: HRD is a subset of HRM, or HRD is the overriding concept with HRM as "a part of" organizational learning and performance. Note that some professionals distinguish a difference between HRM (a management activity) and HRD (the profession that develops learning and performance). So, those who vision HRM within HRD, explain HRD as the broader range of activities to develop people inside of organizations, including, career development, training and development, and organization development. Conversely, HRM scholars and practitioners likely view HRM as the prevailing concept that includes the practices that are traditionally considered HRD-related, e.g., training and development, career development and organizational development.

The scant published histories of HRD and HRM previously mentioned provide few clues to the development or revision of respective definitions. Marciano (1995) said that efforts at defining HRM are grounded on current descriptions and do not attempt to resolve the issue of evolution by tracing the term's history. The history of HRD provides even fewer resources that illustrate how its definitions have changed since the 1970s when the term was first used in its familiar context (see Nadler, 1970). Both HRD and HRM scholars agree and are insistent that neither term is well defined (see Table 5.1, Definitions of HRD and HRM). Referred to variously as a "definitional fog," a "quagmire of definitions," and a "discipline in search of itself," McLean lamented that "if we can't define HRD in one country, how can we define it in an international context?" (1998, p. 313). And Lee (2001) suggested that HRD is indefinable; to define it is to misrepresent it as a thing of being rather than a process of becoming; that defining HRD runs the risk of disengaging from its moral dimension (p. 327).

Table 5.1.   Definitions of HRD and HRM

HRD Definitions	HRM Definitions
Human resource development is a series of organized activities conducted within a specified time and designed to produce behavioral change (Nadler, 1970).	"The human resource—the whole man—is, of all resources entrusted to man, the most productive, the most versatile, the most resourceful...when we talk about the management of worker and work, we are talking about a complex subject. First, we are dealing with the worker as the human resource. Second, we must ask what demands the enterprise makes on the worker in its capacity as the organ of society responsible for getting the work done, and what demands the worker makes on the enterprise in his capacity as a human being, an individual and a citizen? Finally, there is an economic dimension grounded in the fact that the enterprise is both the wealth-producing organ of society and the source of the worker's livelihood. This means that in managing worker and work we must reconcile two different economic systems. There is a conflict between wage as cost and wage as income which must be harmonized. And there is the problem of the worker's relation to the enterprise's fundamental requirement of profitability. And the human being has one set of qualities possessed by no other resource: it has the ability to co-ordinate, to integrate, to judge and to imagine" (Drucker, 1954, p. 263–264).
HRD is the integrated use of training and development, organization development and career development to improve individual, group, and organizational effectiveness (McLagan, 1989).	Personnel Management "encompasses the activities of recruitment and employment, manpower planning, employee training and management development, organization planning, organization development, wage and salary administration, health and safety, benefits and services, union-management relations, and personnel research. Personnel Management or Personnel Administration are concerned with all of the above plus applied human behavior areas such as supervision, motivation, work group behavior, communication and managing change" (Beach, 1975, p. 76).

Table 5.1.   Definitions of HRD and HRM

HRD Definitions	HRM Definitions
HRD includes training, education, and development. *Training* is planned learning that is focused on improving current job performance while *education* is planned learning focused on preparing an individual for a future job. *Development* is broader than education, not specifically job-related, learning pertaining to personal growth (Nadler and Nadler, 1989).	"Personnel management is concerned with obtaining, organizing, and motivating the human resources required by the enterprise; with developing an organization climate and management style that will promote effective effort, cooperation, and trust between all the people working in it; and with helping the enterprise to meet its legal obligations and its social responsibilities toward its employees with regard to the conditions of work and quality of life provided for them." (Armstrong and Lorentzen, 1982, p. 3)
HRD is organized learning activities arranged within an organization to improve performance and/or personal growth for the purpose of improving the job, the individual and/or the organization (Gilley & Eggland, 1989).	By the early 1980s, the focus becomes one of "strategic management of human resources and the design of "strong" organizational cultures" (Bamberger and Meshoulam, 2000, p. 2). Storey (1992): "Human resource management is a distinctive approach to employment management which seeks to obtain competitive advantage through the strategic deployment of a highly committed and skilled workforce, using an array of cultural, structural and personnel techniques." (p. 3)
HRD is the study and practice of increasing the learning capacity of individuals, groups, collectives and organizations through the development and application of learning-based interventions for the purpose of optimizing human and organizational growth and effectiveness (Chalofsky, 1992).	Anthony, Kacmar and Perrewe (1996) state "the strategic human resource approach is involved in strategic planning and decision making and coordinates all human resource functions for all employees." (p. 15)
Human resource development is any process or activity that, either initially or over the long term, has the potential to develop adults' work-based knowledge, expertise, productivity and satisfaction, whether for personal or group/team gain, or for the benefit of an organization, community, nation or, ultimately, the whole of humanity (McLean & McLean, 2001, p. 322).	"Human resource management (HRM) can be defined as a strategic and coherent approach to the management of an organization's most valued assets: the people working there who individually and collectively contribute to the achievement of its objectives" (Armstrong, 2001, p. 4).

But even with these repudiations, many different definitions have indeed been published since 1970, when Len Nadler first coined HRD as a series of organized activities conducted within a specific time and designed to produce behavioral changes. Its definition remains contentious and subject to many heated debates among scholars (practitioners do not seem to have the same obsession to define what they do). It should be noted that with few exceptions these definitions are U.S. developed and based.

It is beyond the scope of this chapter to offer a complete inventory of the many and varied definitions of HRD and HRM. A scan of the several common and widely published definitions of HRD and HRM reveals that in their early histories both reflected their evolution from related fields (See Table 5.1, Definitions of HRD and HRM for a illustration of this evolution). HRM has in most cases been defined within the organization and its economic conditions. Until recently, the large majority of definitions of HRD have also been focused on the organization and much of its definitional language has had an economic tone. It was not until the late 1980s and early 1990s, did a rift open between definitions of HRM and HRD.

HRM as "personnel management retitled" was a common theme in the late 1980s. As the fields matured definitions changed to reflect the sophistication of the skills and knowledge of professionals and the complexity of the organizational contexts in which they were applied. This is noticeable in how some definitions changed. For example, while the changes in definitions of HRM from the 1980s and 1990s until today were not significant, some definitions of HRD have made an important conceptual shift away from the *process* of training or organization development more toward a focus on *outcomes* in terms of HRD's impact on people, organizations, communities and society. McLean & McLean (2001) defined HRD as any process or activity that develops people's "knowledge, expertise, productivity and satisfaction...for the benefit of an organization, community, nation or, ultimately, the whole of humanity" (p. 322).

HRM has been defined as managing the people-side of enterprise, and leveraging human capital, while HRD develops individuals through training and education skills and knowledge in people associated with work-related systems. And while a portion of management has recently shifted its rhetoric to one that views people as an asset versus a liability, it is still true that in many organizations people are seen as a resource that requires controlling and manipulating in much the same way as physical resources. "To call a person a resource is already to tread dangerously close to placing that human in the same category with office furniture and computers" (Greenwood, 2002, p. 261). Casse (1994) added that it is ethically wrong to equate people with resources; that defining humans as resources is obsolete, demeaning and out of line with our sociological evolution. And some research (Tampoe, 1993) implies that the increase in knowledge workers who "would most likely be inclined to develop and exploit their own potential, and would resent the idea of being a resource to be used as management sees fit. "Ever since the term came into currency it has come in for much criticism, because it is generally felt that to treat human beings like any other resource is derogatory and demeaning" (Kalra, 1997). "In the absence of any other alternate and appropriate terminology, the terms HRM and HRD are still in vogue and have, in fact, become much more popular than ever before (Kalra, 1997). Legge (1996) said that HRM has been "depicted as wearing the emperor's new clothes, and even as being a wolf in sheep's clothing" (p. 25).

Marciano (1995) identified three "families" of HRM definitions:

1. A management philosophy that employees are "valuable organizational resources, rather than expenses"
2. "A new synonym for personnel management," and
3. A "manageralist/unitarist resurgence in Britain during the Thatcher years...HRM is essentially a sophisticated form of union avoidance, and a camouflaged method of managerial control" (p. 226).

A noteworthy distinction between the concepts of HRD and HRM is the "hard/soft" definitions of HRM. The former "hard" model of HRM emphasizes integrating human resources with business strategy. It also regards employees as resources to be managed, controlled and exploited by management. In contrast, "soft" HRM views employees not as resources but as assets that through training and development are a source of organizational competitive advantage. Watson has eloquently said that the initial distinction between hard and soft was Storey's (1987) way of distinguishing between intellectual/academic points of view originated either in the "hard" Michigan or "soft" Harvard approaches. He also pointed out that this was simply a misinterpreted distinction between *writing about* and *practicing* HRM. Scholars and practitioners have suggested that this distinction is a fallacy and that "soft" HRM is in reality "hard."

> When we examine the practices followed in organizations following allegedly "caring" or "soft" practices, it soon becomes apparent that their behaving this way happens alongside, and indeed supports, a "hard" and calculative use of labor resources to further business ends. (Watson, 2004, p. 455)

It should also be noted that HRM is a term that originated in and was primarily limited to the United States. Prior to the 1980s, human resource management was a term little used in Britain (Harley & Hardy, 2004). It is interesting to observe that unlike the U.S. where HRM originated and has been supported by academics, in the UK the importation of the concept was "management led, and most academics remain skeptical, if not critical, of its view points" (Marciano, 1995, p. 226). The UK has led both critical management studies and the critical HRM movement and today is leading the genesis of critical HRD.

Contemporary definitions of HRD have shifted towards addressing the context in which it is applied. HRD scholars and even some enlightened practitioners are beginning to be aware of the ethics and social responsibility of HRD. A number of current yet not widely disseminated definitions reflect this change. Sleezer, Conti & Nolan (2004) made the point that definitions of HRD had expanded our understanding of HRD.

Definitions of HRD and HRM are in many ways simply intellectual exercises. The extent that any of the many and varied definitions of the two disciplines have been validated by practitioners or the extent they were developed with input from practice remains unclear, yet likely inadequate.

A relatively prudent yet empirically unproven conclusion to the differences in definitions discussed here is that concepts of HRD and HRM are moving further apart. Evidence of this separation can be found in the *Human Resource Management* journal where only 20% of the published articles from 1994–2005 were primarily about training, with the majority of training related articles published in the mid-1990s. At the same time, several new HRD-specific journals emerged in the U.S. and in Europe, namely the *Human Resource Development Quarterly, Human Resource Development International, Human Resource Development Review, Advances in Developing Human Resources,* and the *Journal of International Training & Development.*

This brief discussion of the definitions of HRM and HRD brought to light five pertinent issues:

1. Neither discipline has "fixed" prescriptive definitions.
2. HRD has continued to question and debate how it defines itself and questions the extent that definitions should be sought.
3. HRM has maintained a somewhat less fluid evolution of definitions as compared with HRD and thus may posses less variance in practice (assuming a relationship between definition and practice exists).
4. Current HRD definitions are beginning to address outcomes in terms of ethics and social responsibility.
5. From a critical studies analysis of HRM, definitions and theories questions can be raised about the ethicality of HRM.

These two disciplines can be viewed through very different lenses, and as workplaces become more global, technological, and complex, what they are being asked to do is widening the content gap between them. But simple definitions do not a discipline make. The central capacity, the "heart and soul" of the practice and scholarship of a profession, are the underlying theories that make up its conceptual framework. These theories as they become institutionalized within a discipline then become part of an overall belief system that professionals, practitioners and scholars either embrace or criticize, and accept or reject. Much like the philosophies of deontology and teleology in ethics, these concepts are beliefs through which people practice and evaluate HRD and HRM.

Theories

Both HRM and HRD are multidisciplinary with regard to their underlying theories. The problem for both disciplines is that neither has fully agreed upon concepts that are stable or uniformly applied; that fit all practice or research in each and every context or set of influencing variables. Nor do theories ensure or in most cases even address ethical practice and scholarship (See Table 5.2 for a comparison of HRD and HRM theoretical foundations).

Table 5.2.   A Comparison of HRD and HRD Theoretical Foundations

HRD Theoretical Foundations	*HRM Theoretical Foundations*
Adult learning (andragogy), the art and science of helping adults learn (Knowles, 1970, 1990).	The theoretical perspectives that help theorize strategic HRM are universalistic, contingency and configuarational (Delery & Doty, 1996).
System theories based primarily on the work of von Bertalanffy (1968), and more recently Capra (1996), and Senge (1990)	Lepak & Snell (1999) say that their HR architecture consists of 3 theoretical backgrounds: Transaction cost economics, human capital theory and resource-based view of the firm.
The foundation for a broad human resource philosophy includes economics (human capital theory), psychology (behaviorism), communications (mathematical and behavioral models), education (techniques, humanistic or behavioral), organization development (large system change over time), and management (human resources school & systems school) (Sredl & Rothwell, 1987).	Theory of the firm consists of a number of neoclassical economic theories such as transaction cost theory, managerial and behavioral theories, and more recently a shift to knowledge-based approaches to theories of the firm (see Crew, 1975; Foss, 1996; Grant, 1996. Theory of the firm has been discussed intensively in Germany. These theories have largely been imported from the USA and comprise partly legal, partly-microeconomic theories, the theory of property rights, agency theory, transaction cost theory and contract theories, in particular (Drumm, 1994).
HRD 's underlying theories include five major bodies of knowledge, education, systems theory, economics, psychology, and organizational behavior (Jacobs, 1990).	Mayrhofer (2004) said a 'grand theory' of social systems theory would contribute to theoretical foundation of HRM.
Watkins (1989) said there were five alternative theories: general systems, field and intervention theory, theory of work, design theory, critical theory, and human capital theory.	Weber & Kabst (2004) said HRM "needs to be theoretically grounded" and that the following have been used: systems theory, organizational psychology, behaviorism, personnel economics and rational choice.
Swanson (1999) identified the theoretical foundations of HRD as economic, systems theory and psychology.	Drumm (1994) said that theoretical and ethical foundations of HRM are embedded in a national context (in Germany), that no single theory exists so we must construct intelligent, but untested, HRM hypotheses. These hypotheses cause ethical problems.

Table 5.2.   A Comparison of HRD and HRD Theoretical Foundations

HRD Theoretical Foundations	HRM Theoretical Foundations
Hatcher (1999) empirically identified HRD theoretical foundations as economic, systems thinking, sociology, adult learning and psychology.	Stakeholder theory. Applicable more to corporate social responsibility theoretical foundations than to general business. However, stakeholder theory, or the theory that a firm has multiple stakeholders such as employees, communities, society and the environment that influence and is influenced by it, is an applicable theory when addressing HRM and organizational ethics.
Hatcher (2000) justified HRD theoretical foundations as economics, systems thinking, sociology, adult learning, psychology and ethics. Social responsibility and stakeholder theory were suggested as new foundational theories.	"Modern HR management is radically different from personnel management of decades ago. Since the turn of the century, the managerial philosophy that has defined the personnel function has undergone significant changes. In the last 80 years, both the scientific management approach and the human relations approach have appeared and declined; today what has popularly become known as the human resource approach has emerged." (Carrell, Elbert and Hatfield, 2000, p. 5). This includes human capital theory (Becker, 1976).
Hatcher (2004) made the case that ethics should be added to existing HRD theoretical frameworks.	Humanistic theories/concepts are concerned with the development of the whole person with an emphasis on individual traits such as personality and emotion.

While some theories of HRD and HRM are *prima facie* similar, they do differ and are at times conflicting. For example, basing HRD practice on the theoretical foundation of sociology may seriously conflict with HRM practices based on the theory of the firm. Conversely, economic-based HRD may result in less than humane treatment of employees while HRM practices that follow stakeholder theory may result in more equality when dealing with employees and the community. Given the diversity of views about theories, having to answer: "What is a definitive theory?," is difficult. However, it would be hard to argue that the *theory of the firm* is not a commonly held foundational concept for HRM and that *adult learning theory* is not foundational for HRD. Under the guise of various names, these general theories are indeed different. For example, the theory of the firm is actually a number of primarily neo-classical economic theories that describe organizational behavior and how a firm interacts with the market. It has a focus on economic outcomes. Adult learning theory or "andragogy," a common HRD theory, explains how adults learn within organizational contexts and is focused on individual and organizational learning and knowledge.

Applying these two theories to practice might involve making decisions based on a return on investment and margins or the extent that employees learn how to do their jobs. We might alter these outcomes by shifting our economic focus to include learning as a way to increase profit and view learning in terms of its utility. But when we face an ethical dilemma as a result of increasing margins or building learning capacity, these two theories seem inadequate. In neither case do the theories add much value in building ethical and responsible organizations. The theories that have potential to enhance ethics include systems theories and stakeholder theory. Although not a true theoretical foundation for either HRD or HRM, stakeholder theory is a conceptual foundation for corporate social responsibility and has been identified as a possible conceptual theory for HRM. It has potential to influence ethics if each stakeholder is analyzed in terms of potential ethical issues and outcomes.

Theoretical foundations also impact outcomes. HRM assumes people are in fact resources and not autonomous individuals. Storey (2001) said that "the human resource ought to be nurtured as a valuable asset" (p.6). HRM is "hard" or "soft" in writing, yet in practice even the soft side bears witness to strategic outcomes that are economic and often result in unethical behaviors (Kochan, 1999). Thus, the rhetoric of soft HRM as "caring for the development of people in organizations," has a decidedly underlying economic, instrumental and less than humanistic focus. Legge (1995) says "hard has supplanted soft."

According to Drumm (1994), "this impressive picture of HRM's theoretical fundamentals is, however, nothing more than a fascinating paper exercise" (p. 36). More than 25 years of such research into problems of mere subsections of the wide-ranging scope of HRM issues has created, as a consequence, only very modest advances towards restricted theories of HRM (Drumm, 1994).

A "theory pitfall" exists for scholars that seek to explain and design theoretical HRM models. "A high level of complexity in HRM theories reduces their testability. A low level of complexity allows easier testing, but reduces precision and therefore increases the risk of refutation" (Drumm, 1994, p.40). The existence of this theory pitfall in HRM therefore explains why, "even in a national context, general and complex theories are scarcely to be expected" (Drumm, 1994, p. 42). This "pitfall" forces scholars to develop untested theoretical foundations and theories of HRM. It is pertinent, therefore, to ask whether these theories could close the theory gap in HRM, by applying them to the solution of HR problems (Drumm, 1994).

It is axiomatic that sound theories would help explain the social, political, and psychological integration of personnel into what Drumm (1994) called the "conflictual social system of the enterprise." However, this view-point is one of sociology or social psychology, and is not so much found among apologists for the practices of business management (Drumm, 1994). This inability to address how people work together through conflict and other ethical dilemmas creates a void in the moral makeup of the firm. "The entire concept of HRM, whether it be so-called hard or soft, is devoid of morality; that as a species, we should behave towards our fellow humans with the overriding objective of extracting 'added value'" (Hart, 1993, p. 30). Greenwood (2002) concluded that "HRM is ethically deficient" (p. 262). Where social and moral issues such as equality of opportunity, fairness and justice are pursued, it is only with the objective to add value to the organization.

Over the past 20 or so years, HRD has sought to become its own discipline, with a unique set of competencies, standards of integrity, journals, and certifications. While still functionally a part of HRM in some organizations and the training component still accepted as an HRM responsibility, HRD has nevertheless expanded into leadership in OD, change initiatives, leadership development and enhancing the environmental compliance and ethics of organizations and many of their stakeholders. While some scholars still feel that HRD is a discipline in search of itself, others have sought to either solidify or question and expand upon its underlying theoretical foundations. Three of the most vocal have been Swanson, McLean and Hatcher. Swanson (1999) in particular has made the case that theories are needed to "stabilize" or otherwise professionalize the field while McLean (1998) has suggested that because of its multidisciplinary nature HRD must have a myriad of underlying theories that are malleable depending upon specific interventions and contexts. I have continued to question the validity of theoretical foundations of HRD such as economics that limit its ability and/or potential to address ethical issues on the job, enhance workplace democracy and assist in the social responsiveness of organizations in which it is practiced (Hatcher, 1999, 2000, 2002, 2004). I have also made the case that in order for HRD to address the myriad of ethical dilemmas in today's organizations ethics and, through stakeholder theory, the concept of social responsibility must be considered as "new" but compulsory theoretical foundations of HRD.

I agree with Greenwood (2002), Legge (1995) and others who doubt the kinds of questions that the disciplines have posed in research or the kinds of workplace dilemmas they choose to solve create more humane or ethical workplaces but seek rather to reinforce the status quo. HRD scholars continually discuss and question the theories that under gird practice and research as is evidenced in the many published editorials, articles and manuscripts on the subject over the past decade. This, I believe is a healthy and critical path for the evolution of HRD's theory base with potential to impact upon research, scholarship and practice that, compared to similar disciplines, can provide impetus for HRD as a leader in organizational ethics.

And to complicate the definition and theory landscapes of HRD and HRM, both practitioners and some scholars have said that they are simply "academic exercises" that fail to establish clear relationships between research, scholarship and practice. "HRM is a construct largely invented by academics and popularized by consultants" (Armstrong, 1999) and the "rhetoric of the HR academics who have been debating what HRM means, how different it is, whether or not it is a good thing, indeed, whether or not it exists, endlessly and unproductively," are seen, "as irrelevant to practitioners who have pressed on regardless, in the justified belief that what the academics were writing about had little relevance to their day to day lives as they wrestle with the realities of organizational life" (p. 586). Others have implied that HR is purely a "verbal revolution" introducing a new and ofttimes incomprehensible vocabulary, but making little difference in the "real" world of work. I have also made a similar case that interventions that do not consider ethical outcomes continue to support an economic status quo and fail to progress HRD towards an ethical or socially responsive discipline. "Practitioners have pressed on regardless in the justified belief that what the academics were writing about had little relevance to their day-to-day lives as they wrestled with the realities of organizational life. The true personnel or HR professional just kept on doing what they had always done but tried to do it better" (Kearns, 2002). Practitioners do not seem to respect scholars nor do they seek to have what they do legitimized by them. "HR academics have their place—but it is called a university rather than a workplace. Beware of ever letting them loose in the real world" (*Personnel Today*, June 04, 2002).

The processes and outcomes of learning, OD, change initiatives, personnel activities and employee relations have ethical implications and should be socially responsive. Both HRD and HRM must be aware of and assume responsibility for developing initiatives that have negative effects on people, organizations, communities and the environment; that there is an intimate relationship between HRD/HRM and ethics. HRD and HRM are complicit and have responsibilities in or for whatever their respective organizations do; both good and bad.

The definitions and theories of HRD and HRM discussed herein unfortunately illustrate little real potential as currently defined and used to address the complexity of ethical issues and environmental and human evils that occur in global, highly technical and increasingly bottom-line focused organizations. As companies seek more knowledge-based solutions and attempt large-scale change and diversity initiatives, disciplines with the competence and integrity to address these needs will likely gain power over those that do not. This power may afford opportunities to address ethics without jeopardizing what organizations require of the discipline. While HRD research addresses knowledge, change and diversity, I question whether it builds knowledge about effective ethical practice. We are typically marginalized when an organization faces crucial moral questions or seeks guidance when faced with an ethical dilemma. Revisions to definitions and theories may provide a solution to such limitations.

I tend to disagree with scholars who suggest that HRD and HRM are coalescing into an amorphous "hybrid" (Ruona & Gibson, 2004), because the evolution of and the underlying conceptual frameworks for each discipline are dissimilar enough to justify noteworthy differences and outcomes. I agree with Sambrook (2004) who said if HRD is part of HRM, then HRD serves the interest of organizations first, and individuals second. The evaluation of definitions indicated that HRM has not moved very far from economics and does not appear to be as "self-reflective" as HRD in terms of questioning its theories and definitions.

HRD has potential to move into a leadership position, offering analyses for and solutions to problems around organizational ethics, morals and social responsibility. Not only does HRD have a future potential but it is through research and practice currently addressing complex ethical dilemmas. The next section discusses some of these practices and a glimpse of the possible future directions of HRD that might sustain its promise to provide solutions to ethics and other morality-based problems in work-related contexts.

CURRENT PRACTICE AND FUTURE TRENDS IN HRD

The discipline of HRD has a pluralistic nature that can create both a positive and negative influence on the ethics of people in work-related settings and organizations. It has been viewed as a corporate handmaiden and complicit in many organizational wrong-doings including the now infamous behaviors of CEOs. "It is increasingly obvious that lapses in ethical judgment, well illustrated by Enron, resulted, in part or perhaps largely, from poorly designed or implemented people development systems" (Hatcher, 2003, p.45). Hammonds (2005) supported this idea by writing: "HR doesn't tend to hire a lot of independent thinkers or people who stand up as moral compasses" (p. 43). Conversely, HRD as a concept and practice has been the consciousness of the organization. Witness its role in the success of Interface, Inc. a large commercial floor covering maker in Atlanta. Interface decided through training and education of its workforce it would become an environmental "evangelist" and within 10 years became the industry's first zero waste manufacturer and winner of many environmental and social responsibility awards (and has been financially successful). An obvious question is: Why such a wide range? The opposing behaviors described here, while ostensibly schizophrenic, can be at least partly explained in terms of the environments in which HRD is practiced and its lack of professionalism and the loss of subsequent power that typically comes with a *bona fide* profession.

As for-profit organizations become more powerful, it becomes harder for emerging professions that rely on them to influence ethical leadership, achieve equality within the workforce, or establish workplace democracy. In uni-cultural settings it is much easier for a profession to influence a corporate culture or to normalize behaviors especially in highly regulated nationalistic work environments. It is much harder if not impossible for a relatively new profession such as HRD to accomplish the same results in multi-cultural settings with little or no nationalistic or regulatory constraints on the "use" or "misuse" of people.

Currently, there is a visceral yet often unacknowledged or ignored tension between the emerging profession of HRD and the ubiquitous bottom-line focused company and the growing power of the multi-national, global organization. For HRD professionals who choose to ignore this tension their role in these organizations remains one of unquestioned support for organizational strategic initiatives, no matter how unsustainable, unethical, irresponsive or unfriendly to local communities or indigenous groups. Fortunately, there is some evidence that organizations that fail in ethics and responsibility are subject to public scrutiny and financial consequences and thus may be unsuccessful in the long term. Unfortunately, there are also examples of very bad organizations that are also successful. HRD scholarly organizations such as the Academy of Human Resource Development are attempting to develop venues within their conferences and publications in which professionals can question their roles in organizations and learn to provide discipline-supported ethical guidance to organizational leaders/managers without significantly compromising their employment and/or professional status. As pointed out earlier, relatively new codes of ethics have the potential to provide guidance and support that takes care of people and the environment.

In addition to development and training on ethics codes, ethics is being taught in many HRD academic programs and in HRD-related conferences ethics and values are increasingly discussed. HRD has developed and implemented training that supports the recent Sarbanes Oxley Act in the U.S. that requires organizations to address the ethics of their accounting processes. HRD continues to offer leadership development training in many firms and has taken a recent interest in addressing the gap between research and practice and the ethics of practice.

HRD is being used in national-level strategies and public policy in Taiwan and Austria. In the UK, the National Vocational Qualification scheme to certify the skills of workers has national and EU implications. Large NGOs like the UN use HRD as policy and in interventions to stimulate workforce and economic development in developing and war-torn countries. There is a Korean Ministry of Education and HRD, and India has a National Human Resource Ministry. HRD is viewed as public policy in the Pacific Islands, and there are continuing country level HRD policies and initiatives in the EU through the European Training Foundation. These efforts are having a profound professional and economic impact on thousands of lives.

Examples of what HRD is currently doing in terms of its impact on people, organizations and societies are impressive. But we dare not rest on our laurels. For the future, we must begin to question what it is that HRD will become, what or whom it will be for, and what it will need to do to be a positive influence on humanity. Issues such as power, domination, manipulation, coercion, inequality, justice, conflict, and privilege have barely been touched upon in any significant way by HRD scholars or practitioners. This may be attributed to a lack of adequate theories that might address the entire scope of HRD in context. It may also be that we tend not to challenge the status quo of the "rationale" organization or seek to replace it with workplace democracy or emancipatory practices or even research. We fail to ask tough questions about the weaknesses of orthodoxy, questioning tradition, honestly addressing the inherent tensions in organizational life, or simply asking "is this the right thing to do?" According to Harley & Hardy (2004), HRM's benevolence, convergent thinking and ambiguous practices rationalized downsizing as an ideologically "good" thing. If we are to evolve as a discipline then taking a more critical view is necessary. Sambook (2004) pointed out that being critical conveys maturity within a discipline.

Especially in the U.S. and to a lesser degree in the UK and Europe, HRD has been dominated by a performance orientation and situated within a unitary versus pluralistic organizational perspective (Sambrook, 2004). However, with the advent of critical management studies in the UK and now critical HRD studies, research on workplace democracy, the meaning of work and emerging definitions that include humanism and ethics, the HRD landscape is changing. Significant themes include the role of HRD in ethics, corporate social responsibility and its more emancipatory role in helping individuals in their own aspirations and transforming the socio-political structures in which they work. "Being critical means recognizing the messiness, complexities and irrationality—rather than the sanitized reason and rationality—of organizational practices (Sambrook, 2004, p. 17).

We must approach critical HRD with some vigilance, since as Sambrook (2003), Fenwick (2005) and others have lamented that bringing critical discourses to bear among current predominant theories and models of HRD, must be done without privileging the critical iconoclast pitted against the HRD "other" (Fenwick, 2005), lest we alienate the majority by pressing uncommon points of view on others. We must also be careful not to undermine the scientific neutrality of the language of management and organizations by adopting evocative and emotive language (Harley & Hardy, 2004), while at the same time ensuring that "silenced" voices outside the mainstream are heard.

Research is needed on power relations in organizations and what role HRD plays in these power issues, gender and equity issues, and addressing the outcomes of the practice of HRD to all stakeholders including communities and the ecosystem. And our propensity to create what Fenwick (2005) called "cultural engineering with questionable ethics" through culture change and other HRD initiatives must be seriously and critically assessed.

SUMMARY AND CLOSING THOUGHTS

This chapter on HRD's potential to help create organizations where people act in responsible and ethical ways and to provide ethical guidance to organizations focused on three issues: a. definitions of contemporary HRM and HRD and the evolution of their conceptual frameworks and how the transformation of definitions may be attributing to ethical behaviors especially within HRD, b. a discussion of the outcomes of HRD research and practice on ethics, both positive and negative and, c. the future potential of HRD to help create ethical organizations, especially the potential of critical HRD. Table 5.3 provides a general overview of these comparisons.

The reality of our workplaces is change, speed, "moving our cheese," different paradigms and values, outsourcing, downsizing, workforce diversity, globalization and rapidly changing and omnipotent technologies. We can either choose to address these challenges as opportunities and take on the responsibility of coping with and mediating them with humanity and integrity or we can allow them to be exploited by others. If we choose not to make our intentions explicit in terms of ethics and social responsibility and then follow through on them we leave the results to those who may take advantage of this weakness. The choice is ours.

Table 5.3.   General Comparisons of HRM and HRD

	HRM	*HRD*
Philosophy	Instrumental/utilitarian/positivists	Humanistic/Developmental/constructivists
	Manage, control, performance, expense	Develop, learning, meaning, asset
Predominate theoretical and conceptual foundation(s)	Economics, organization strategy, theory of the firm, unitary, prescriptive, normative, managerial, "hard" vs. "soft," economic return on employment of labor	**Economics, systems theory, adult education, pluralism, prescriptive, social science**
Level of analysis	**organization**	**individual**
	quantitative	**qualitative**
Critical perspective(s)	Yes—maturing since Legge in 1970s	Yes—early adoption since 2000 a la Sambrook, et al.
Language	Efficiency, standardization, unitary, scientific and neutral language	Justice, democracy, emancipatory, diversity, equality, pluralistic, more evocative and polemic language
Includes ethics?	Yes—maturing	Yes—early adoption
Views of globalization	Positive	Neutral to negative
Future needs for research and practice	Self-reflection, duality of roles, more proactivity, coalescence of work and society (increase interest in SIM & CSR), power and politics	Political and power dimension, epistemology, welfare of people and nature, morality, spirituality, gap between espoused values and values in use. Managerial interpretation and reputation of HRD, empancipatory, workplace democracy, justice

Note: bold indicates a recent shift or changing perspective

REFERENCES

Anthony, W. P., Kacmar, K. M. & Perrewe, P. L. (1996). (2nd edition). *Strategic human resource management.* Fort Worth: The Dryden Press.

Armstrong, M. (1999). *A handbook of human resource management practice* (7th ed.). London: Kogan Page.

Armstrong, M. (2001). *A handbook of human resource management practice* (8th edition). London: Kogan Page.

Armstrong, M. & Lorentzen, J. F. (1982). *Handbook of personnel management practice: Procedures, guidelines, checklists, and model forms.* Englewood Cliffs, NJ: Prentice-Hall.

Bakke, E.W. (1958). *The human resources function.* New Haven: Yale Labor Management Center.

Bamberger, P. & Meshoulam, I. (2000). *Human resource strategy: Formulation, implementation, and impact.* Thousand Oaks: Sage.

Beach, D. S. (1975). *Personnel: The management of people at work* (3rd ed.). New York: Macmillan.

Becker, G.S. (1976). *The economic approach to human behavior.* Chicago: University of Chicago Press,

Capra, F. (1996) *The web of life: A new scientific understanding of living systems,* New York: Anchor Books.

Carrell, M. R. , Elbert, N. F. & Hatfield, R. D. (2000). *Human Resource Management: Strategies for managing a diverse and global workforce* (6th edition). Orlando: Dryden Press.

Casse, P. (1994). People are not resources. *Journal of European Industrial Training, 18*(5), 23–26.

Chalofsky, N. (1992). A unifying definition for the human resource development profession. *Human Resource Development Quarterly, 3,* 175–182.

Crew, M.A. (1975). *Theory of the firm.* London: Longman.

Delery, J.E., & Doty, D.H. (1996). Models of theorizing in strategic human resource management. *Academy of Management Journal, 39*(4), 802–833.

Desatnick, R.L. (1972). *Innovative human resource management.* New York: AMACOM.

Dessler, G. (1999). *Essentials of human resource management.* New Jersey: Prentice Hall.

Drucker, P. F. (1954). *The practice of management.* New York: Harper & Brothers.

Drumm, H.J. (1994). Theoretical and ethical foundations of human resource management: A German point of view. *Employee Relations, 16*(4), 35–48.

Fenwick, T. (2005). Conceptions of critical HRD: Dilemmas for theory and practice. *Human Resource Development International, 8*(2), 225–238.

Foote, D., & Robinson, I. (1999). The role of the human resources manager: Strategist or conscience of the organization? *Business Ethics: A European Review, 8*(2), 88–98.

Foss, N.J. (1996). Knowledge-based approaches to the theory of the firm. *Organization Science, 7,* 470–476.

Gilley, J.W., & Eggland, S.A. (1989). *Principles of human resource development.* Reading, MA: Addison-Wesley.

Grant, R.M. (1996). Toward a knowledge-based theory of the firm, *Strategic Management Journal, 17,* 109–122.

Greenwood, M.R. (2002). Ethics and HRM: A review and conceptual analysis. *Journal of Business Ethics, 36*(3), 261–278.

Hammonds, K.H. (2005). Why we hate HR. *Fast Company, 97,* 40–52.

Harley, B., & Hardy, C. (2004). Firing blanks? An analysis of discursive struggle in HRM. *Journal of Management Studies, 41*(3), 377–400.

Hart, T.J. (1993). Human resource management- time to exorcize the militant tendency. *Employee Relations, 15*(3), 29–37.

Hatcher, T. (1999). Reorienting the theoretical foundations of human resource development: Building a sustainable profession and society. In P. Kuchinke

(Ed.), *The Academy of Human Resource Development 1999 Research Conference Proceedings* (pp. 202–208). Academy of Human Resource Development, Arlington, VA.

Hatcher. T. (2000). A study of the influence of the yheoretical foundations of human resource development on research and practice. *Proceedings of the 2000 AHRD International Conference* (pp. 40–45). Research Triangle, N.C.

Hatcher, T. (2002). *Ethics and HRD: A new approach to leading responsible organizations.* Cambridge, MA: Perseus Books.

Hatcher, T. (2003). New world ethics. *Training & Development, 57*(8), 42–57.

Hatcher, T. (2004). A rationale for HRD-ethics and its inclusion as a theoretical foundation. *Academy of Human Resource Development International Research Conference Proceedings*, Austin, TX, Feb.29 –Mar 4, 2004. p. 272–286.

Jacobs, R.L. (1990). Human resource development as an interdisciplinary body of knowledge. *Human Resource Development Quarterly, 1*(1), 65–72.

Kalra, S.K. (1997). Human potential management: Time to move beyond the concept of human resource management? *Journal of European Industrial Training, 21,* 176–182.

Kearns, P. (June 04, 2002). Why do we clutch at academic musings? *Personnel Today,* June 04, 2002.

Knowles, M.S. (1970). *The modern practice of adult education: Andragogy versus pedagogy.* Chicago: Follett.

Knowles, M.S. (1990). *The adult learner: A neglected species.* Houston, TX: Gulf Publishing.

Kochan, T. A. (1999). Beyond myopia : Human resources and the changing social contract. In G. Ferris (Ed.) *Research in Personnel and Human Resource Management: Supplement 4,* 199-. 212. Stamford, CT: JAI Press.

Lee, M. (2001). A refusal to define HRD. *Human Resource Development International, 4,* 327–341.

Lepak, D.P., & Snell, S.A. (1999). The human resource architecture: Toward a theory of human capital allocation and development. *The Academy of Management Review, 24*(1), 31–48.

Legge, K. (1995). *Human resource management: Rhetorics and realities.* Basingstoke: Macmillan.

Legge, K. (1996). Morality bound. *People Management, 25*(2), 34–36.

Mahoney, T.A., & Deckop, J.R. (1986). Evolution of concept and practice in personnel administration/human resource management. *Journal of Management, 12*(2), 1986, pp. 223—41.

Marciano, V.M. (1995). The origins and development of human resource management. *Academy of Management Journal, Best Papers Proceedings 1995,* 223–227.

Mayrhofer, W. (2004). Social systems theory as theoretical framework for human resource management. *Management review, 15*(2), 178–191.

McLagan, P. (1989). Models for HRD practice. *Training & Development, 43*(9), 49–59.

McLean, G.N. (1998). HRD: A three-legged stool, an octopus, or a centipede? *Human Resource Development International, 1*(4), 375–377.

McLean, G.N., & McLean, L. (2001). If we can't define HRD in one country, how can we define it in an international context? *Human Resource Development International, 4*(3), 313–326.

Nadler, L. (1970). *Developing human resources.* Houston, TX: Gulf Publishing.

Nadler, L., & Nadler, Z. (1989). *Developing human resources.* San Francisco: Jossey-Bass.

Personnel Today (June 04, 2002). The evolution of HRM. *Personnel Today,* June 04, 2002.

Ruona, W.E. (2001). The foundational impact if the training within industry project on the human resource development profession. *Advances in Developing Human Resources, 3*(2), 119–126.

Sambrook, S.A. (2004). A "critical" time for HRD? *Critical Management Studies 2004 Conference Proceedings, Stream 25: A critical turn in HRD,* pp. 1–15.

Senge, P. (1990). *The fifth discipline: The art and practice of the learning organization.* New York: Doubleday.

Sleezer, C.M., Conti, G.J., & Nolan, R.E. (2004). Comparing CPE and HRD programs: Definitions, theoretical foundations, outcomes and measures of quality. *Advances in Developing Human Resources, 6*(1), 20–34.

Sredl, H.J., & Rothwell, W.J. (1987). *Professional training roles & competencies* (Vol. 1). Amherst, MA: HRD Press.

Storey, J. (1987). Developments in the management of human resources: An interim report. *Warwick Papers in Industrial Relations, 15.* Warwick, U.K.: University of Warwick.

Storey, J. (1992). *Developments in the management of human resources.* London: Blackwell.

Storey, J. (2001). *Human resource management: A critical text* (2nd. Ed). London, Thomson Learning.

Swanson, R (1999) Foundations of performance improvement and implications for practice. In R.J. Torraco (Ed.), *Performance Improvement Theory and Practice* (pp. 1–25). The Academy of Human Resource Development: Baton Rouge, LA.

Tampoe, M. (1993). Motivating knowledge workers. *Long Range Planning, 26,* 49–55.

Watkins, K. (1989). Five metaphors: Alternative theories for human resource development. In Gradous, G. (Ed.), *Systems Theory Applied to Human Resource Development,* pp. 167–184, Alexandria, VA: University of Minnesota & American Society for Training & Development.

Watson, T.J. (2004). HRM and critical social science analysis. *Journal of Management Studies, 41*(3), 447–467.

Weber, W., & Kabst, R. (2004). Human resource management: The need for theory and diversity. *Management Review, 15*(2), 171–176.

CHAPTER 6

THE ROLE OF MORAL DEVELOPMENT IN MOTIVATING ETHICAL BEHAVIOR BY EMPLOYEES

Paul L. Schumann
Minnesota State University–Mankato

INTRODUCTION

There are lots of possible examples of employee behaviors that raise ethical issues. A retail store employee steals merchandise from the store. Hourly production workers collude to falsify their timecards to hide unexcused early departures from work. A salesperson falsifies expense claims in order to inflate reimbursements. A manager sexually harasses a subordinate. Top executives collude to falsify the accounting reports of the business to inflate the company's reported profits. Why do some employees engage in these kinds of unethical behaviors, while other employees, who work in the same situations and under the same conditions, do not? What can managers do to motivate ethical behavior by employees? In this chapter, I examine how managers can use an understanding of moral development to create human resource management policies, practices, and procedures that motivate employees to act ethically.

Human Resource Management Ethics, pages 111–128
Copyright © 2006 by Information Age Publishing
All rights of reproduction in any form reserved.

To understand what can motivate ethical behavior, it is first useful to understand what is meant by ethics and by ethical behavior. *Ethics* is study of how individuals use moral principles to make moral judgments (Pojman, 1989; Velasquez, 2002). Thus, an action is said to be *ethical* if people judge the action to be consistent with moral principles. *Business ethics* is the subfield of ethics that examines how moral principles can be used to analyze ethical issues in business (Velasquez, 2002). Similarly, *human resource management ethics* is the subfield of business ethics that is concerned with applying moral principles to human resource management issues (Schumann, 2001).

If an action is judged as being ethical when it is consistent with moral principles, then the next issue is to understand what moral principles can be used to make moral judgments. Philosophers and ethicists have advocated a set of five complementary moral principles for three primary reasons (Pojman, 1989; Rachels, 1999; Schumann, 2001; Velasquez, 2002). First, the five principles are supported by a well-developed ethics literature. Second, the principles are commonly used in practice to make moral judgments. Third, each of the five principles emphasizes a different relevant factor in making moral judgments while no single principle captures the full range of relevant factors. Since Schumann (2001) examines the five moral principles in the context of human resource management ethics, here I only provide a brief summary of the principles:

- *Utilitarian Principle:* the morally correct action is the one that does the most good and the least harm for everyone who might be affected.
- *Rights Principle:* the morally correct action is the one that the decision-maker has a moral right to do, that does not infringe on the moral rights of others, and that furthers the moral rights of others; furthermore, when deciding moral rights issues, decision-makers should be willing to have the action done to them if the roles were reversed (reversibility, also commonly known as the "Golden Rule"), decision-makers should be able to imagine a world in which everyone performed the action all the time (universalizability), and decision-makers should be treating the people who are affected by the action with respect and in ways that these people have consented to be treated (respect and free consent).
- *Distributive Justice Principle:* the morally correct action is the one that produces a fair distribution of good and harm for everyone who might be affected.
- *Ethics of Care Principle:* the morally correct action is the one that appropriately cares for the individuals involved.

- *Virtue Ethics Principle:* the morally correct action is the one that displays good character virtues (such as courage, generosity, honesty, and loyalty), not bad character vices (such as cowardice, selfishness, dishonesty, and disloyalty).

Note that each of the five moral principles focus in some way on how the decision-maker's actions affects others. Unlike the five principles, *ethical egoism* maintains that the morally correct action is the one that is in the decision-maker's own personal, self-interest (Pojman, 1989; Rachels, 1999). Thus, for example, retail store employees who steal merchandise from the store are acting ethically according to ethical egoism as long as the thefts are in the best interests of the employees who are doing the stealing. While some philosophers have defended ethical egoism, others have rejected it as being an inadequate moral principle (Pojman, 1989). For example, Rachels (1999: 95) concludes that "It is this realization, that we are on a par with one another, that is the deepest recognition why our morality must include some recognition of the needs of others, and why, then, Ethical Egoism fails as a moral theory."

If ethics involves looking beyond one's self-interest by applying moral principles that ask us to consider the effects of our actions on others, then how do individuals develop these moral reasoning abilities? How can managers use an understanding of moral development to motivate employees to behave ethically? To answer these questions requires an examination of the relevant literature on moral development.

MORAL DEVELOPMENT

Beginning with Kohlberg (1958), moral development has been extensively studied from both theoretical and empirical perspectives. An instrument commonly used in the empirical literature to measure moral development is the Defining Issues Test (DIT), which was originally developed in 1972 by Rest (1986a) and subsequently revised to create the DIT-2 (Bebeau & Thoma, 2003). The moral development and DIT literature is large, spanning more than one thousand articles (Bebeau & Thoma, 2003; Rest, 1986a). Since reviews of the moral development and DIT literatures already exist (e.g., Rest, 1986b; Rest, Narvaez, Bebeau, & Thoma, 1999), in this chapter I focus on the conclusions from the literature that are relevant in guiding managers who desire to motivate their employees to behave ethically.

Kohlberg (1976) originally proposed six stages of moral development. There has been some debate in the literature whether all six stages actually occur in practice and whether there might be a seventh stage (Kohlberg,

1976; Lickona, 1976; Reed, 1997; Rest et al., 1999). Another complexity in the literature is that the DIT, which is the commonly used empirical measure of moral development, does not conceptualize moral development as a series of stair-step stages as does Kohlberg, but rather as a continuous construct along a continuum of schemas (Rest et al., 1999). Nevertheless, the DIT measure of moral development does "... keep Kohlberg's notion that moral judgment structures ... follow a developmental sequence" (Rest et al., 1999:135).

These debates in the moral development literature are not central to the purpose of this chapter. What is important are some of the primary conclusions from the literature that cut across a large number of researchers and methods:

- Moral development is not just a theoretical concept; it is linked to actual, real-life behavior (Bebeau & Thoma, 2003; Lickona, 1976; Reed, 1997; Rest, 1986a; Rest et al., 1999).
- People progress through the stages (Kohlberg, 1976) or schemas (Rest et al., 1999) of moral development in sequence, from the lowest stage of moral development to higher stages (Bebeau & Thoma, 2003; Lickona, 1976; Reed, 1997; Rest, 1986a; Rest et al., 1999; Velasquez, 2002).
- Not everyone progresses through all the stages; some individuals remain in one of the lower stages of moral development throughout their lives (Bebeau & Thoma, 2003; Lickona, 1976; Reed, 1997; Rest, 1986a; Rest et al., 1999; Velasquez, 2002).
- While there has been some debate about whether there are gender differences in moral development (Gilligan, 1982; Reed, 1997), the empirical research suggests that men and women do not differ in fundamental ways in their moral development (Bebeau & Thoma, 2003; Derry, 1987; Eisenberg, Fabes, & Shea, 1989; Friedman, Robinson, & Friedman, 1987; Kittay & Meyers, 1987; Rest et al., 1999; Sprinthall & Sprinthall, 1987; Velasquez, 2002).
- While it is difficult to find estimates in the literature of the percentages of the population in each of the stages, empirical evidence suggests that the full range of moral development occurs, including the lower and higher stages of moral development (Bebeau & Thoma, 2003; Lickona, 1976; Reed, 1997; Rest, 1986a; Rest et al., 1999; Velasquez, 2002).
- Life experiences, education in general, and specific education in ethics, all influence a person's moral development (Bebeau & Thoma, 2003; Lickona, 1976; Parks, 1993; Piper, Gentile, & Parks, 1993; Reed, 1997; Rest, 1986a; Rest, 1988; Rest et al., 1999; Velasquez, 2002).

- Moral development does not stop at any particular young age; instead, dramatic and extensive increases in moral development occur when individuals are in their 20s and 30s (Bebeau & Thoma, 2003; Lickona, 1976; Parks, 1993; Reed, 1997; Rest, 1986a; Rest, 1988; Rest et al., 1999; Velasquez, 2002).

Thus, based on the literature on moral development, managers are likely to have employees at any or all of the stages of moral development. Furthermore, what motivates an employee who is at one particular stage of moral development may not motivate employees at other stages of moral development. Therefore, managers who want to use human resource management policies, practices, and procedures to motivate employees to behave ethically will need to tailor those policies, practices, and procedures to all of the possible stages of moral development.

Stage 1: Heteronomous Morality

At the lowest stage of moral development, individuals take an egocentric point of view (Kohlberg, 1976). What motivates a person to act is his or her self-interest. They want to know, "What is in it for me?" Furthermore, individuals at Stage 1 do not consider the interests of others. The rules and expectations of society are external to the individual and are perceived as being imposed on them by others who have the power to do so. What motivates individuals at Stage 1 to follow rules and expectations is the fear of being caught and punished for failing to follow the rules. An employee who is at Stage 1 might say, "The only crime is getting caught."

Thus, for example, Stage 1 employees will steal merchandise from the retail stores in which they work. They will falsify their timecards to hide unexcused early departures from work. They will falsify their expense claims to inflate reimbursements. They will sexually harass co-workers and subordinates. They will falsify accounting reports to inflate the company's reported profits. In each case, Stage 1 employees engage in unethical behavior if they believe the behavior will benefit them and if they believe they will get away with it. They are not concerned with the interests of others. They do not care if their actions harm others. They act as if the only crime is getting caught.

So what can stop Stage 1 employees from committing unethical actions? Since their only motivation not to lie, cheat, steal, or engage in other unethical behaviors is the fear of being caught and punished, managers must make real the threat of being caught and punished. Managers can motivate their Stage 1 employees to behave ethically by increasing the probability of being caught and by increasing the sanctions imposed on employees when they are caught.

The literature on employee disciple systems describes how managers can create and enforce discipline in the workplace (Arvey & Jones, 1985; Ball, Trevino, & Sims, 1994; Falcone, 2000; Guffey & Helms, 2001; Imundo, 1985; Klass & Feldman, 1993; Mitchell & O'Reilly, 1983; Osigweh & Hutchinson, 1991; Segal, 1992; Trevino, 1992). Managers need to create a clear set of rules and expectations for employees to follow. Managers need to communicate the rules and expectations to employees. Managers need to create policies and practices to monitor and to enforce the rules and expectations. The policies and practices need to identify the sanctions that will be used in cases where the rules and expectations have been violated. As Cardy and Selvarajan (Chapter 4) emphasize in this volume, while compliance-based rules and procedures have limitations, the rules and procedures nevertheless provide a useful starting point in motivating ethical behavior by employees.

Thus, to motivate Stage 1 employees to behave ethically, managers have two tactics to use in tandem: (1) increase the probability of unethical behavior being caught and punished and (2) increase the cost to the unethical employees of their unethical behavior by making the punishments severe enough that employees choose to behave ethically to avoid the punishments. The specific control mechanisms need to be tailored to the needs of the organization and to the nature of the jobs. The challenge for managers of Stage 1 employees is to try to anticipate all the ways in which employees might engage in undesirable behaviors on each job (Cardy & Selvarajan, Chapter 4 in this volume). Managers can use brainstorming, their own experiences, and the experiences of other managers in trying to identify possible undesirable employee behaviors and the specific methods to catch and punish those employees who engage in unethical behavior. Managers can also use the critical incident technique to identify examples of unethical conduct that resulted in poor performance or other harm to the organization (Cardy & Selvarajan, Chapter 4 in this volume). Managers can then use the examples identified in the critical incidents to develop rules and policies to enforce the rules.

Furthermore, with Stage 1 employees it is important to catch and punish undesirable behaviors consistently. By consistently catching and punishing unethical behaviors, managers not only punish the wrongdoers, managers also send a message to the other Stage 1 employees about the probability of being caught and about the costs to the employees of unethical behavior.

While fear of punishment motivates Stage 1 employees to behave ethically, positive incentives for ethical behaviors would tend to be ineffective with Stage 1 employees. Stage 1 employees each focus on their own self-interest and their desire to avoid punishment. They would tend to view with suspicion a manager who promises incentives; they would suspect the manager is a liar who will find a way to cheat them out of the promised incentives, thus weakening the motivational force of the incentives.

Stage 2: Individualism, Instrumental Purpose, and Exchange

As in Stage 1, the person in Stage 2 is still motivated to act based on self-interest (Kohlberg, 1976). They still want to know, "What is in it for me?" However, unlike the Stage 1 person who does not realize that other people have their own interests, as individuals develop from Stage 1 to Stage 2, they come to realize that everyone has their own interests to pursue. This realization opens the door to exchanges that are mutually beneficial. That is, Stage 2 employees see others as instruments to their own self-satisfaction. The Stage 2 employee is the prototypical *Homo Economicus* (Ghoshal, 2005). Stage 2 employees would tend to see their employer and their jobs merely as tools to be used to achieve their own self-satisfactions. They will be willing to work hard and behave ethically if there is something in it for them. The employee who is at Stage 2 might say, "I will scratch your back if you scratch mine."

Thus, Stage 2 employees are motivated by incentives, including incentives to get them to behave ethically. In creating the incentives, the goal for managers is to create a work environment in which employees have a stake in ethical behavior. Some of the incentives might be negative and some might be positive.

For example, consider punishing an employee for unethical behavior by firing the employee. The threat of being fired when an employee engages in unethical behavior motivates the Stage 2 employee to behave ethically for a different reason than the Stage 1 employee. The Stage 1 employee fears being fired because he or she wishes to avoid the pain of the punishment. The Stage 2 employee fears being fired because it would terminate the employment relationship that is in the employee's self-interest. That is, at Stage 2 it is not the punishment itself that motivates ethical behavior, but rather that the punishment interferes with the employee's pursuit of their self-interest. Unlike the Stage 1 employee, the Stage 2 employee realizes that the organization has its own interests to protect. While the underlying cause for why punishments motivate Stage 2 employees to behave ethically are different than for Stage 1 employees, the result is the same for both — the threat of punishment can motivate both Stage 1 and Stage 2 employees to behave ethically. Thus, the disciplinary policies, practices, and procedures that I described in the section on Stage 1 can also be used to motivate Stage 2 employees to behave ethically.

In addition to disciplinary procedures that punish unethical behavior, negative reinforcements can also be effective with Stage 2 employees. The idea is to withhold benefits valued by the employee whenever they engage in unethical behaviors. For example, an attendance bonus can be withheld from employees who have had unexcused absences.

Furthermore, positive incentives for ethical behavior can also be created. Agency theory is helpful in finding ways to create effective incentives (Eisenhardt, 1989; Jensen & Meckling, 1976). Agency theory emphasizes that an organization's owners, managers, employees, and other stakeholders have divergent interests and goals. What is best for the managers of a business may not be what is best for the owners. Similarly, what is best for the employees may not be what is best for managers or owners. Agency theory suggests that incentives be created in ways that align the otherwise divergent interests.

Thus, for example, agency theory suggests that executive compensation systems be created that align the interests of executives with the interests of the owners of the business (Gomez-Mejia, Tosi, & Hinkin, 1987; Lambert & Larcker, 1989; Tosi & Gomez-Mejia, 1989). One mechanism by which the interests of owners and the interests of managers can be brought into alignment is to have the managers of a business have an ownership stake in the business. Managers can obtain an ownership stake through methods such as stock options and other stock plans.

When creating incentive systems, care should be taken to ensure that there are not inadvertent incentives for unethical behavior. For example, consider the following scenario. Suppose the top executives of a company receive a significant part of their compensation in the form of stock (or stock substitutes such as stock options). By the executives having an ownership stake in the company, the theory is that the interests of executives and the interests of owners have been aligned. Further suppose that Wall Street has come to expect particular profit numbers from the company. Now suppose the executives know that the company will not achieve Wall Street's profit expectations. If the company fails to achieve Wall Street's expectations, then the company's stock price will plummet. To avoid the personal losses in the value of the stock owned by the executives, they would be tempted to use their positions in the company to falsify the company's accounting reports so that the company appears to meet or exceed Wall Street's expectations. Thus, in this example, the executive compensation system that was designed to align the interests of owners and executives has actually operated to create incentives for the executives to lie to the owners of the business about the profitability of the business. This example is not to suggest that stock ownership by executives is a bad idea. Rather, this example illustrates the importance of considering the full range of incentives created by any incentive-based reward system to ensure that it does not inadvertently create incentives for unethical behavior.

In addition to creating incentives that align the interests of owners and executives, agency theory can also be used to create incentives that align the interests of employees with the interests of the managers and the owners of a business. For example, consider the potential of some employees to shirk their work. Stage 1 employees will not shirk their work responsibilities if they think they would be caught and punished whenever they shirk. Stage 2 employees will not shirk their work responsibilities if they are rewarded for not shirking. Thus, Stage 2 employees would be willing to work hard if there are incentives and rewards for working hard. For example, a merit pay system that ties an employee's pay to that employee's job performance will motivate a Stage 2 employee to try to improve his or her job performance. Similarly, a sales commission pay system will motivate salespeople to try to increase their sales.

Thus, in general, Stage 2 employees will need incentives for ethical behavior. For example, Stage 2 employees might choose not to steal from the company if they are to receive bonuses that are tied to reductions in the amount of employee theft. Similarly, a profit sharing plan might motivate Stage 2 employees to work hard for the goals of the business, including motivating them to avoid unethical behaviors that might tend to reduce the profits of the business and thus reduce the amount of profit sharing that they receive. Elsewhere in this volume, Orlitzky and Swanson (Chapter 1) suggest that employee performance appraisals should incorporate a balanced scorecard in which employee job performance is measured in terms of both financial and social objectives so that managers can create rewards for employees to be attuned to societal expectations and to ethical behavior. Also elsewhere in this volume, Cardy and Selvarajan (Chapter 4) describe how critical incidents can be used to invent behaviorally anchored rating scales to measure the extent of ethical behavior by individual employees; the rating scales can then be made part of the organization's merit pay system, thus creating rewards for ethical behavior.

The challenge, then, for managers of Stage 2 employees is to create reward systems that provide incentives for ethical behavior. The incentives might take the form of money (such as merit pay or bonuses) when employees engage in ethical behavior themselves or when employees report unethical behavior by others. Alternatively, the incentives might take the form of any kind of reward that is valued by the employees (such as an increased chance for promotions).

Stage 3: Mutual Interpersonal Expectations, Relationships, and Conformity

In Stage 3 of moral development, the person becomes aware of shared feelings, agreements, and expectations with others that take primacy over the person's individual interests (Kohlberg, 1976). As a result, the person is able to put themselves into the shoes of others. They can see things from the perspective of others. They develop empathy. Furthermore, Stage 3 individuals are motivated by the need to be seen as a good person, not only in their own eyes, but also in the eyes of others with whom they have close relationships — their families, their friends, their co-workers, and their direct supervisors. In order to be seen in the eyes of others as a good person, individuals at Stage 3 are motivated to live up to the expectations of others. That is, the person is motivated by a desire to be seen by relevant others as a good son or daughter, a good brother or sister, a good friend, a good co-worker, and a good employee. To Stage 3 employees, merit pay increases motivate them to work hard not because of the increased pay itself, but rather because of the desire to be recognized by their direct supervisors as good employees. An employee who is at Stage 3 might say, "It is my duty as a good employee to work hard and not engage in unethical behaviors."

Unlike the moral development literature with its stages of moral development and a variety of possible motivations, agency theory assumes that everyone is motivated exclusively by the pursuit of their own self-interest. Ghoshal (2005) warns us that if we assume that everyone is motivated exclusively by their self-interest that it becomes a self-fulfilling prophecy — that if managers always treat employees as liars, cheats, thieves, and shirkers, then employees will begin to act in those ways. The moral development literature can be used to understand what else can motivate ethical behavior in addition to the incentives that are so important in agency theory and at Stage 2 of moral development.

What can managers do to motivate Stage 3 employees to behave ethically? To motivate Stage 3 employees, who are concerned with the opinions of the people immediately around them, managers need to focus their efforts on direct supervisors and co-workers. At Stage 3, group norms and expectations are important. As a result, it is important for managers to take steps to ensure that employee groups have the desired norms and expectations. For example, suppose a group of employees in a retail store believe that stealing from the store is okay. In this instance, a Stage 3 employee will be conflicted between the desire to live up to the expectations of his or her co-workers to participate in the thefts and the desire to live up to the expectations of the store manager to be a good, loyal, hard-working employee. The lesson from this example is that managers need to be aware of the norms and expectations among the workgroups of the organization and need to work to create the desired norms and expectations.

Elsewhere in this volume, Orlitzky and Swanson (Chapter 1) suggest screening applicants for employment based on their moral development, personality traits associated with normative receptivity (such as agreeableness), and workforce diversity. Similarly, Cardy and Selvarajan (Chapter 4) suggest that managers try to assess the ethics of job applicants by the use of tests and interviews. For example, managers can include behavioral interview questions that deal with ethical issues (Janz, Hellervik, & Gilmore, 1986). Thus, through careful recruiting and selection, managers can hire applicants who have the desired norms and expectations.

Once applicants are hired, managers can use formal socialization and orientation sessions to inseminate the culture, norms, and expectations of the organization in the employees (Adkins, 1995; Feldman, 1976; Feldman, 1980; Fisher, 1986; Klein & Weaver, 2000; Louis, Posner, & Powell, 1983; Morrison, 1993; Wanous, Reichers, & Malik, 1984). Elsewhere in this volume, Orlitzky and Swanson (Chapter 1) suggest that training also deal with how to engage and balance a multitude of stakeholder interests and issues by developing employees' skills in working with a variety of stakeholder groups.

Furthermore, the literature on moral development concludes that ethics can be taught and that one is never too old to learn ethics (Bebeau & Thoma, 2003; Lickona, 1976; Parks, 1993; Piper, Gentile, & Parks, 1993; Reed, 1997; Rest, 1986a; Rest, 1988; Rest et al., 1999; Velasquez, 2002). Thus, the literature on moral development supports Cardy and Selvarajan's (Chapter 4) suggestion elsewhere in this volume that managers create training programs in ethics.

Managers can create work teams and then coach the teams to instill the desired norms and expectations. Managers can use self-managed teams that self-enforce team norms (Banker, Field, Schroeder, & Sinha, 1996; Macy & Izumi, 1993). Managers can praise employees for ethical behavior and express disappointment when employees fall short. Managers can create formal recognition systems at the local or departmental level that officially and publicly praise employees. For example, a district sales manager can create a Salesperson of the Month award that recognizes the top salesperson in the district. Similarly, managers can create recognition for a wide variety of ethical behaviors. For example, a district manager in a retail store chain can create a monthly award that recognizes the district store with the lowest theft rate. Stage 3 employees in this example would be motivated to take steps to reduce theft because they want to win the recognition and praise of their district manager for being good employees. For another example, a manager can praise an accountant who uncovers an accounting fraud. Such recognition by a supervisor not only motivates the accountant who discovered the fraud and who directly receives the recognition, it also sends a message to all employees that supervisors will appreciate and recognize good performance and good ethics, thus motivating Stage 3 employees to improve their performance and to behave ethically in order that they too receive the praise of their supervisors.

Stage 4: Social System and Conscience

As individuals develop from Stage 3 to Stage 4, they begin to broaden the groups that are relevant to them from the smaller, more immediate groups of Stage 3, such as family, friends, co-workers, and supervisors, to entire institutions and to society at large at Stage 4 (Kohlberg, 1976). The person not only has empathy for specific individuals with whom he or she interacts, the person also values institutions and the social system as a whole. Compare Stage 3 to Stage 4 in a business context: the Stage 3 employee is motivated to be seen as a good co-worker and a good employee by living up to the expectations of co-workers and direct supervisors; the Stage 4 employee is motivated by a desire to see the business succeed for its own sake. At Stage 4, the person is motivated by a desire to keep entire institutions and the integrated social system of institutions working well. The person is motivated by a desire to do his or her duty to institutions and to society at large. They want to be a good citizen and to do their duty as a good citizen. Furthermore, the person's conscience drives the person to avoid behaviors that would threaten a breakdown in institutions or in the entire social system. The employee who is at Stage 4 might say, "Unethical behavior threatens the business" or "If everyone engaged in unethical behavior, then the entire social system would break down."

Thus, Stage 4 employees are unlikely to engage in unethical behavior that would threaten the business in which they work, threaten other institutions that might be affected, threaten the business system as a whole, or threaten society at large. While Stage 4 employees are unlikely to engage in unethical behaviors, managers can still take steps to help Stage 4 employees. For example, a corporation could create company-wide awards and recognitions in addition to departmental awards. The company newsletter and website could also publicize examples of employees who engaged in ethical behavior or who uncovered unethical behavior. Elsewhere in this volume, Orlitzky and Swanson (Chapter 1) endorse non-monetary rewards, such as awards for good citizenship, as an effective tool to motivate employees who are at higher levels of moral development than those who respond mostly to financial incentives. Furthermore, the awards and publicity are more than incentives for ethical behavior that are received by the recipients; the awards also send a message to all Stage 4 employees of examples of good corporate citizenship that they will want to emulate so that they too can be seen as a good corporate citizen in their own eyes as well as in the eyes of others.

Stage 5: Social Contract or Utility and Individual Rights

At Stage 5 of moral development, individuals are aware of fundamental values and rights that are independent of any particular attachment or institution (Kohlberg, 1976). Stage 5 individuals consider moral and legal points of view that cut across the beliefs, principles, and laws of particular societies. They recognize that individuals can disagree. They value formal mechanisms by which disagreements can be resolved, such as majority rule. They value impartial due process procedures. They desire to develop and enforce rules that have impartially been decided to be to everyone's joint best interest. They are willing to make personal sacrifices if the sacrifices will produce benefits for others. The employee who is at Stage 5 might say, "We should do whatever will impartially produce the greatest good for the greatest number."

Stage 5 employees are unlikely to engage in unethical behaviors. Managers can help Stage 5 employees by creating and using impartial due process procedures that are so important to Stage 5 employees (Pennock & Chapman, 1977). Furthermore, Stage 5 employees will want to participate in decision making (Adizes & Borgese, 1975; Locke, Schweiger, & Latham, 1986; Sashkin, 1984). For example, Stage 5 employees would be motivated to participate on task forces charged with the creation of due process procedures. Similarly, Stage 5 employees would be motivated to serve on administrative review committees that handle issues requiring due process. By creating and using due process procedures and by participative management techniques, Stage 5 employees are able to help establish ethical behavior within the organization and thus put into practice the factors that motivate them.

Stage 6: Universal Ethical Principles

At the highest stage of moral development, individuals have chosen to live their lives according to universal moral principles (Kohlberg, 1976). Examples of universal moral principles might include the utilitarian, rights, distributive justice, ethics of care, and virtue ethics principles that were described previously in this chapter. Stage 6 individuals respect the dignity of human beings as individual persons and the equality of human rights. They believe in the rational validity of the universal moral principles and are personally committed to living their lives in accordance with the principles, even if to do so requires sacrifice.

Stage 6 employees are unlikely to engage in unethical behaviors no matter what the pressure. If Stage 6 employees are ordered by their supervisor to commit an action that violates their moral principles, then they would tend to follow their principles and refuse to follow the order even if it meant that they suffered personal losses, such as being fired for insubordination. This example suggests that managers should establish formal mechanisms of appeal and review for employees who feel they are being pressured to take actions that violate their moral principles. For example, a company could create a formal procedure in which employees who feel that their supervisors are issuing unethical orders can go over their supervisor's head for review without fear of retaliation. A company could create an ethics hotline that employees could call to report suspected legal or ethical violations. Similarly, a company could create a special webpage that employee could use to report illegal or unethical behavior.

A company could create an office of ombudsmen. The ombudsoffice would investigate complaints, report findings, and work to achieve appropriate resolution of employee complaints of illegal or unethical behavior. The ombudsoffice serves as an important part of the company's conscience, seeking to resolve issues guided by independence, confidentiality, objectivity, and ethics. The ombudsoffice would be responsible to ensure that employees are protected from abuse, improper treatment, or pressures to behave illegally or unethically. The ombudsoffice might report directly to the CEO or, if the CEO is involved in the alleged wrongdoing, to a committee made up of the independent directors on the board of directors. Employees who feel that the company is taking unethical actions could take their case to the ombudsoffice for review. By creating an ombudsoffice and ombudsprocess within the company, Stage 6 employees are not placed in the position of external whistleblowing being their only option to address unethical corporate conduct (DeGeorge, 1985).

CONCLUSIONS

Why do some people lie, cheat, and steal while others in the same situation do not? Why do some employees engage in unethical behaviors, while other employees, who work in the same situations and under the same conditions, do not? The research on moral development concludes that individuals go through a developmental sequence of stages of moral development (Kohlberg, 1976).

Furthermore, individuals are motivated to behave ethically for different reasons depending on their stage of moral development. Stage 1 employees are motivated to behave ethically by the fear of being caught and punished if they behave unethically. Stage 2 employees are motivated to behave ethically by the rewards they will receive as incentives for ethical behavior. Stage 3 employees are motivated to behave ethically by a desire to be seen as a good co-worker and a good employee. Stage 4 employees are motivated by a desire to be a good corporate citizen. Stage 5 employees are motivated by a desire to uphold the social contract, to follow due process procedures, and to do what is best for everyone overall. Finally, Stage 6 employees are motivated by a desire to live up to the requirements of universal moral principles.

The empirical research on moral development concludes that the full range of moral development occurs (including the lower and higher stages of moral development); that life experiences, education in general, and specific education in ethics, all influence a person's moral development; that moral development does not stop at any particular young age; and that dramatic and extensive increases in moral development occur when individuals are in their 20s and 30s (Bebeau & Thoma, 2003; Lickona, 1976; Parks, 1993; Reed, 1997; Rest, 1986a; Rest, 1988; Rest et al., 1999; Velasquez, 2002). Thus, managers are likely to have employees at all of the stages of moral development.

The nearly 50 years of research on moral development has produced a cognitive-developmental theory that can be used to create human resource management policies, practices, and procedures that are designed to motivate employees to behave ethically. The moral development literature emphasizes that managers need to do more than rely on one thing, such as incentives, to motivate behavior. Instead, managers need to develop an array of policies, practices, and procedures that are tailored to all of the stages of moral development. Managers need to use control mechanisms and disciplinary procedures that will catch and punish unethical behavior. Managers need to create incentives that reward ethical behavior. Managers need to create norms of ethical behavior among workgroups as well as recognize and praise ethical behavior. Managers need to publicize examples of good corporate citizenship. Managers need to use participatory management techniques that allow employees to participate in creating and using administrative procedures, including due process procedures. And managers need to create effective formal mechanisms of review for employees to report illegal or unethical behavior. By doing all of these things, managers create a comprehensive mosaic of management methods designed to motivate employees to behave ethically no matter what their stage of moral development.

Furthermore, by using all of the methods together, managers are creating an integrated management system that will encourage employees to develop to higher stages of moral development. For example, the availability of incentives for ethical behavior will encourage the Stage 1 employee to develop to Stage 2. Similarly, the recognition and praise of co-workers and supervisors will encourage the Stage 2 employee to develop to Stage 3. Conversely, the consistent punishment of employees for their unethical actions will help to prevent Stage 2 employees from back-sliding down to Stage 1. In these ways, managers motivate all employees to behave ethically no matter what may be the underlying motivating factors of the employees. Through these human resource management policies, procedures, and practices, managers can motivate all employees, no matter what their stage of moral development, to behave ethically.

REFERENCES

Adizes, I., & Borgese, E.M. (1975). *Self-Management: New Dimensions to Democracy.* Santa Barbara, CA: Clio Books.

Adkins, C.L. (1995). Previous Work Experience and Organizational Socialization: A Longitudinal Examination. *Academy of Management Journal,* 38, 839–862.

Arvey, R., & Jones, A. (1985). The Use of Discipline in Organizational Settings: A Framework for Future Research. In Cummings, L., & Shaw, B. (Eds.), *Research in Organizational Behavior, 7,* 367–408.

Ball, G., Trevino, L., & Sims Jr., H. (1994). Just and Unjust Punishment: Influence on Subordinate Performance and Citizenship. *Academy of Management Journal, 37,* 299–322.

Bebeau, M.J., & Thoma, S.J. (2003). *Guide for DIT-2.* Minneapolis: Center for the Study of Ethical Development, University of Minnesota.

Banker, R.D., Field, J.M., Schroeder, R.G., & Sinha, K.K. (1996). Impact of Work Teams on Manufacturing Performance: A Longitudinal Study. *Academy of Management Journal, 39,* 867–890.

Cardy, R.L., & Selvarajan, T.T. (2006). Beyond Rhetoric and Bureaucracy: Using HRM to Add Ethical Value. In Deckop, J.R. (Ed.), *Human Resource Management Ethics.* Information Age.

DeGeorge, R.T. (1985). Whistleblowing: Permitted, Prohibited, Required. In Elliston, F.A. (Ed.), *Conflicting Loyalties in the Workplace.* Notre Dame, IN: University of Notre Dame Press.

Derry, R. (1987). Moral Reasoning in Work Related Conflicts. In Frederick, W. (Ed.), *Research in Corporate Social Performance and Policy, 9,* 25–49.

Eisenberg, N., Fabes, R., & Shea, C. (1989). Gender Differences in Empathy and Prosocial Moral Reasoning: Empirical Investigations. In Brabeck, M.M. (Ed.), *Who Cares? Theory, Research, and Educational Implications of the Ethic of Care.* NY: Praeger.

Eisenhardt, K.M. (1989). Agency Theory: An Assessment and Review. *Academy of Management Review, 14,* 57–74.

Falcone, P. (2000). A Blueprint for Progressive Discipline and Terminations. *HR Focus,* August, 3–5.

Feldman, D.C. (1976). A Contingency Theory of Socialization. *Administrative Science Quarterly, 21,* 433–452.

Feldman, D.C. (1980). A Socialization Process that Helps New Recruits Succeed. *Personnel, 57,* 11–23.

Fisher, C.D. (1986). Organizational Socialization: An Integrative Review. *Research in Personnel and Human Resources Management, 4,* 101–145.

Friedman, W.J., Robinson, A.B., & Friedman, B.L. (1987). Sex Differences in Moral Judgments? A Test of Gilligan's Theory. *Psychology of Women Quarterly, 11,* 37–46.

Ghoshal, S. (2005). Bad Management Theories Are Destroying Good Management Practices. *Academy of Management Learning & Education, 4,* 75–91.

Gilligan, C. (1982). *In a Different Voice: Psychological Theory and Women's Development.* Cambridge, MA: Harvard University Press.

Gomez-Mejia, L.R., Tosi, H., & Hinkin, T. (1987). Managerial Control, Performance, and Executive Compensation. *Academy of Management Journal, 30,* 51–70.

Guffey, C.J., & Helms, M.M. (2001). Effective Employee Discipline: A Case of the Internal Revenue Service. *Public Personnel Management,* Spring, 111–127.

Imundo, L. (1985). *Employee Discipline: How to Do It Right.* Belmont, CA: Wadsworth.

Janz, T., Hellervik, L., & Gilmore, D.C. (1986). *Behavior Description Interviewing: New, Accurate, Cost Effective.* Newton, MA: Allyn & Bacon.

Jensen, M., & Meckling, W. (1976). Theory of the Firm: Managerial Behavior, Agency Costs, and Ownership Structure. *Journal of Financial Economics, 3,* 305–360.

Kittay, E.F., & Meyers, D.T. (1987). *Women and Moral Theory.* Totowa, NJ: Rowman and Littlefield.

Klass, B., & Feldman, D. (1993). The Evaluation of Disciplinary Appeals in Non-Union Organizations. *Human Resource Management Review, 3,* 49–81.

Klein, H.J., & Weaver, N.A. (2000). The Effectiveness of an Organizational-Level Orientation Training Program in the Socialization of New Hires. *Personnel Psychology,* Spring, 47–66.

Kohlberg, L. (1958). The Development of Modes of Moral Thinking and Choice in the Years 10 to 16. Ph.D. dissertation, University of Chicago.

Kohlberg, L. (1976). Moral Stages and Moralization: The Cognitive-Developmental Approach. In Lickona, T. (Ed.), *Moral Development and Behavior: Theory, Research, and Social Issues* (pp. 31–53). NY: Holt, Rinehart, and Winston.

Lambert, R.A., & Larcker, D.F. (1989). Executive Compensation, Corporate Decision Making, and Shareholder Wealth. In Foulkes, F. (Ed.), *Executive Compensation* (pp. 287–309). Boston: Harvard Business School Press.

Lickona, T. (1976). *Moral Development and Behavior: Theory, Research, and Social Issues.* NY: Holt, Rinehart, and Winston.

Locke, E.A., Schweiger, D.M., & Latham, G.P. (1986). Participation in Decision Making: When Should It Be Used? *Organizational Dynamics, 14,* 58–72.

Louis, M.R., Posner, B.Z., & Powell, G.N. (1983). The Availability and Helpfulness of Socialization Practices. *Personnel Psychology,* Winter, 857–866.

Macy, B., & Izumi, H. (1993). Organizational Change, Design, and Work Innovation: A Meta-Analysis of 131 North American Field Studies. *Research in Organizational Change and Development, 7,* 235–313.

Mitchell, T., & O'Reilly III, C. (1983). Managing Poor Performance and Productivity in Organizations. *Research in Organizational Behavior, 1,* 201–234.

Morrison, E.W. (1993). Longitudinal Study of the Effects of Information Seeking on Newcomer Socialization. *Journal of Applied Psychology, 78,* 173–183.

Orlitzky, M., & Swanson, D.L. (2006). Socially Responsible Human Resource Management: Charting New Territory. In Deckop, J.R (Ed.), *Human Resource Management Ethics.* Information Age.

Osigweh, C., & Hutchinson, W. (1991). Positive Discipline. *Human Resource Management, 28,* 367–383.

Parks, S.D. (1993). Is It Too Late? Young Adults and the Formation of Professional Ethics. In Piper, T.R., Gentile, M.C. & Parks, S.D. (Eds.). *Can Ethics Be Taught?* (pp. 13–72). Boston: Harvard Business School.

Pennock, J.R., & Chapman, J.W. (1977). *Due Process.* NY: New York University Press.

Piper, T.R., Gentile, M.C. & Parks, S.D. (1993). *Can Ethics Be Taught?* Boston: Harvard Business School.

Pojman, L.P. (1989). *Ethical Theory: Classical and Contemporary Readings.* Belmont, CA: Wadsworth Publishing.

Rachels, J. (1999). *The Elements of Moral Philosophy* (3rd ed.). Boston: McGraw-Hill.

Reed, D.R.C. (1997). *Following Kohlberg: Liberalism and the Practice of Democratic Community.* Notre Dame, IN: University of Notre Dame Press.

Rest, J.R. (1986a). *DIT Manual: Manual for the Defining Issues Test* (3rd ed.). Minneapolis: Center for the Study of Ethical Development, University of Minnesota.

Rest, J.R. (1986b). *Moral Development: Advances in Research and Theory.* NY: Praeger.

Rest, J.R. (1988). Can Ethics Be Taught in Professional Schools? The Psychological Research. *Ethics: Easier Said Than Done, 1,* 22–26.

Rest, J.R., Narvaez, D., Bebeau, M.J., & Thoma, S.J. (1999). *Postconventional Moral Thinking: A Neo-Kohlbergian Approach.* Mahwah, NJ: LEA, Inc.

Sashkin, M. (1984). Participative Management Is an Ethical Imperative. *Organizational Dynamics, 12,* 4–22.

Schumann, P.L. (2001). A Moral Principles Framework for Human Resource Management Ethics. *Human Resource Management Review, 11,* 93–111.

Segal, J. (1992). Firing Without Fear. *HR Magazine,* June, 125–130.

Sprinthall, N., & Sprinthall, R. (1987). *Educational Psychology* (4th ed.). NY: Random House, pp. 157–177.

Tosi Jr., H.L., & Gomez-Mejia, L.R. (1989). The Decoupling of CEO Pay and Performance: An Agency Theory Perspective. *Administrative Science Quarterly, 34,* 169–189.

Trevino, L. (1992). The Social Effects of Punishment in Organizations: A Justice Perspective. *Academy of Management Review, 17,* 647–676.

Velasquez, M.G. (2002). *Business Ethics: Concepts and Cases* (5th ed.). Upper Saddle River, NJ: Prentice Hall.

Wanous, J.P., Reichers, A.E., & Malik, S.D. (1984). Organizational Socialization and Group Development: Toward an Integrative Perspective. *Academy of Management Review, 9,* 670–683.

CHAPTER 7

CARING FOR WORKERS, CARING FOR CLIENTS

Everyday Ethics in Assisted Living

Carol C. Cirka
Ursinus College

Carla M. Messikomer
The Acadia Institute

> *I am in a concentration camp for the old, a place where people dump their parents or relatives exactly as though it were an ash can.*
>
> —Caro Spencer,
> the narrator in May Sarton's, *As We Are Now* (1973, p. 3)

The image of American nursing homes as "places to die" or the "last stop on the train" persists despite efforts by regulators and providers to change how care is delivered to frail elders in skilled nursing facilities. Americans, nearly universally, want to "age in place," that is, grow old and die in a residential setting, where care needs are met in one place, even as they change. It is the rare individual who willingly relocates to an institutional setting to receive needed care. Not surprisingly, as people age, they and their families are concerned about where they will be cared for if they can-

Human Resource Management Ethics, pages 129–158

not live independently. The assisted living industry has positioned itself in the larger market for long term care services as a desirable answer to that question; however, two additional questions, "Who will care for us?" and "What quality of care will we receive?" are equally important.

Answering these questions, regardless of where care is delivered, requires close examination of the long term care workforce since these are the workers—described by a variety of terms including "direct care workers," "frontline workers," or "paraprofessionals"—who provide day-to-day care to elders. Despite their importance, we know little about frontline workers. What research exists has largely been conducted in nursing homes or home health care settings, with little attention to assisted living, a segment of the industry that employs a distinct and growing subset of the long term care workforce. To date, the bulk of research on workforce issues in long term care concerns identification of "best practices" aimed at successful recruitment and retention of frontline workers in nursing homes. Practices related to staff training, supervision, and career development have significant ethical implications for recruitment and retention, worker competence, continuity of care, and client quality of life. In addition, the quality of care that is marketed to residents and their families is compromised when organizations overlook critical elements in the human resource management process. When analyzed through an ethical lens, this situation raises questions about how providers implement their mission to provide care to older persons and their moral obligation to treat workers in ways that enhance that mission.

The study of everyday ethics in assisted living, the results of which will be reported here, was the first, to our knowledge, to look at the ethical challenges that arise in this residential arrangement. Our main purpose was to identify the range, type, and severity of ethical challenges in assisted living, the sources from which they arise, and how they are managed. Since our work was exploratory, our sole hypothesis was that ethical issues are present in this industry since all human organizations breed problems and issues of an ethical nature.

Content analysis of our data revealed four general findings: 1) Ethical issues arose at every assisted living facility, at all staffing levels, and across all functional areas; 2) generally, there were no formal policies or mechanisms in place to manage and resolve ethical dilemmas in these organizations; 3) where mechanisms existed, staff were, by and large, unfamiliar with their process and function; and 4) staff distrusted internal policy makers whom they believe are insufficiently educated about the concept and practice of assisted living, thereby limiting their ability to deal appropriately with questions of ethics in this setting. The ethical problems that we identified can be traced to a number of roots, among them the culture of the organization, its business strategy, mission and values, regulatory influence and control, financial goals, ideology of care, and its particular approach to human resource management.

From a human resource management point of view, and specifically the perspective that an organization's human resources are its most important competitive asset, an analysis of care staff in assisted living settings using the framework of everyday ethics should help to guide providers as they work towards development of an ethical culture. We argue that a sustainable ethical culture built on shared moral beliefs, norms and practices fosters delivery of the highest quality of care in assisted living settings, and ultimately leads to competitive advantage; however, failure to develop an ethical culture will lead to unintended and unwanted consequences. Therefore, in the ensuing pages, we focus on those ethical issues that directly impact frontline workers, and through them, the care provided to residents.

ETHICS AND LONG-TERM CARE

Conversations about ethics in the context of long term care rely heavily on bioethics and focus nearly exclusively on clinical decisions related to the "patient" (Carter, 2002). Despite growing interest in organizational ethics, scholars have only recently begun to integrate the two fields (e.g., Boyle, DuBose, Ellingson, Guinn, & McCurdy, 2001; Fisher, 2001; Gallagher & Goodstein, 2002; McCurdy, 2001; Spencer, Mills, Rorty, & Werhane, 2000), and research about ethics and frontline workers in long term care is sparse (see Kane, 1994 and Stone & Yamada, 1998). The topic of ethics is noticeably absent from the assisted living literature. Only two recent conceptual papers focus on ethics. One of these (Powers, 2005) looks exclusively at the ethics of resident care; the other (Redmond & Chafetz, 2001) adopts a legal perspective in its discussion of risk management in AL.

As social actors responsible for the behavior of employees, organizations develop an ethical climate that informs employees as to what one can do, and what one "ought" to do when faced with choices related to organizational practices or policies that have an ethical dimension (Victor & Cullen, 1988). There is debate in the literature as to whether ethical climate and ethical culture are interchangeable constructs (e.g., Key, 1999; Trevino, Butterfield, & McCabe, 1995) and whether they are descriptive or normative. We rely on Victor & Cullen's (1988) operational definition of ethical climate as "perceptions of how the members of their respective organizations typically make decisions concerning various 'events, practices, and procedures' requiring ethical criteria" (p. 109). As such, ethical climate is a descriptive, rather than a normative construct, and varies across and within organizations. For example, the decision whether or not to provide training in death and dying or to offer bereavement support to front-line workers in assisted living would be guided by the organization's ethical climate. Some providers would choose to offer such training while others might not. We define ethical culture as a type of ethical climate where employees and managers exercise moral imagination (Werhane, 1999), are able to recognize actual and potential moral issues and dilemmas, can develop creative alternative courses of action, and evaluate them from a moral point of view, and make ethically appropriate decisions (MacIagan, 2003; Werhane, 1999). Though all organizations have an ethical climate, not all ethical climates lead to ethically appropriate decisions. Continuing with our example, an organization with an ethical culture would anticipate and recognize that to uphold its commitments to value employees and deliver quality care, it must provide bereavement support for its frontline workers. By doing so, the organization would also increase worker productivity, avoid a decline in the quality of care delivered, and fulfill its moral obligation to care for workers as well as clients—the residents.

In 1990, Caplan defined "everyday ethics" as "...the small decisions about the content and order of one's daily life that, when added together, determine something of fundamental ethical importance...the quality of life" (p. 38). Some management scholars also call for heightened attention to the "ongoing moral dimension of managerial life" (Waters, Bird, & Chant, 1986, p. 383) because the majority of ethically charged situations in organizations are "everyday" rather than the dramatic events that attract media attention (e.g., MacIagan, 2003; Waters et al., 1986; Werhane, 1999). Everyday moral decision making does not occur in a vacuum, however, and therefore organizations, as well as individuals, must "think more imaginatively and to [sic] engage in integrating moral decision making into ordinary business decisions" (Werhane, 2002, p. 33). Unfortunately, these calls remain largely unanswered in the bioethics, management, and long-term care literature.

THE ASSISTED LIVING INDUSTRY

The type of residential facility that is currently labeled as an assisted living residence (ALR) appeared in the market during the 1980s in response to strong consumer preferences to age in place, a desire for alternatives to nursing homes, and changing demographics—tremendous growth in the population of older adults and changes in family structure that limit the ability or willingness of families to care for older relatives. As demand for alternatives to nursing home care increased, the nascent assisted living industry expanded, and in some areas, supply now exceeds demand. Over one million older people now live in an estimated 40,000 assisted living residences nationwide, and projections are for the supply of beds to reach 1.9 million by 2030 (National Center for Assisted Living [NCAL], 2001), and for ALRs to serve more elders than nursing homes by 2010 (Meyer, 1998). There is a clear preference for the more homelike environment (where residents often live in private apartments yet receive housekeeping services, meals and assistance with one or more ADLs or activities of daily living—dressing, bathing, grooming, toileting, and eating/feeding), and lower cost of ALRs over skilled nursing facilities, even if the older person is clinically ready for a higher level of care (Namazi & Chafetz, 2001). The AL population is diverse with a range of care needs that varies both across and within facilities (Gurnik & Hollis-Sawyer, 2003). Unfortunately, there is not a clear, precise definition for AL, even 20 years after the emergence of the current "corporate style" (Namazi & Chafetz, 2001) form, and it is often difficult for consumers to compare one facility to another. The Joint Commission on Accreditation of Healthcare Organizations (2005) uses the definition adopted by the Assisted Living Quality Coalition:

> A congregate residential setting that provides or coordinates personal services, 24-hour supervision and assistance (scheduled and unscheduled), activities and health-related services. It is designed to minimize the need to move, accommodate individual residents' changing needs and preferences, maximize residents' dignity, autonomy, privacy, independence, choice and safety, and encourage family and community involvement.

This definition is only one of many found in state regulations and published literature. Across facilities, there is enormous variation with regard to size, auspice, fees, services, affiliation, regulations, governmental oversight, and values and philosophical underpinnings. For example, the average monthly cost for AL nationally, for a basic level of service in 2003, was $2,524 and ranged from $550 to $6,550 (MetLife Mature Market Institute [MMMI], 2004). Consolidation of brands, differentiated products and services (Gelhaus, 2001), intensified competition, and overbuilding in some areas describe the industry as it moves from growth toward maturity. As demand for assisted living grows, so does the need for frontline care staff to provide direct day-to-day care to residents (Gurnik & Hollis-Sawyer, 2003).

FRONTLINE WORKERS IN ASSISTED LIVING

There are currently 2.5 million frontline workers employed in all sectors of the long-term care industry, and more than 800,000 additional direct care positions are projected by 2012, a 34% increase over the number of positions in 2002 (National Clearinghouse on the Direct Care Workforce [NCDCW], 2005). These workers, who provide nearly 80% of paid hands-on long-term care and personal assistance to elderly and disabled Americans, are typically unskilled, uncertified, receive minimal training, and their average median hourly wage in 2003 was $9.50 (NCDCW, 2005). Nearly all direct care workers are female; about half are non-white, and they are more likely to be unmarried with children at home than the general workforce. Demographics of the direct care workforce have changed since the 1980s: current workers are younger, more educated and more likely to have children, and less likely to be native-born U.S. citizens. Nearly 30% have at least some college education (Harris-Kojetin, Lipson, Fielding, Kiefer, & Stone, 2004).

After building costs, labor represents the largest budget item for AL providers, and most AL employees are direct care staff. Across the long-term care industry, attracting and retaining workers who perform at consistently high levels is a constant challenge, especially as the available pool of labor shrinks, and turnover rates remain unacceptably high—71% for Certified Nursing Assistants in 2002 (NCDCW, 2005). In addition, care workers lack respect—they are typically poorly trained, poorly educated, and poorly paid women who perform unpleasant work. The absence of a career ladder, poor wages and benefits, and the cultural gap between aides and other employees and residents (which can lead to conflict) discourage workers from entering the field, and contribute to high turnover (Eaton, 2003; Stone, 2004). Research on frontline worker retention argues for development and testing of "best practices" (Stone, 2004); however, this work is largely drawn from the nursing home and home health care sectors, and does not focus on the relationship between staff turnover and quality outcomes. Further, since so little research examines paid care staff in AL, it is unclear whether these findings apply to AL (see Gurnik & Hollis-Sawyer, 2003; Konetzka, Stearns, Konrad, Magaziner, & Zimmerman, 2005; and Sikorska-Simmons, 2005 for three recent articles on this topic). Research that addresses other AL problems, such as medication under-treatment and mismanagement (Mollica, 2002; Sloane et al., 2004) under-recognition of cognitive impairment in AL (Magsi & Malloy, 2005), quality problems (Fallis, 2004; GAO, 1999; McCoy & Appleby, 2004; Mollica, 2002) limiting negative outcomes and employing AL as an alternative to delay or avoid more costly entry into SNFs (Morgan, Eckert, Gruber-Baldini, & Zimmerman, 2004), affordability (Wright, 2004), and marketing (Carder, 2002; Carder & Hernandez, 2004; O'Bryan, Clow, O'Bryan, & Kurtz, 1996; Sykes, 2000) typically does not highlight the role of direct care staff. When issues related to AL staff quality and qualifications are examined (GAO, 1999; McCoy & Appleby, 2004; Mollica, 2002; O'Keeffe, O'Keefe & Bernard, 2003), the significance of ethical culture as an important explanatory lens is not acknowledged.

Only two published articles that we know of explicitly examine ethics in ALRs. Redmond and Chafetz (2001) adopt a legal perspective in their discussion of risk management, although they acknowledge the ethical and legal minefield that surrounds AL terminology (e.g., "personal care" and "assistance" (170)), staff-to-staff relations, hiring, scheduling, and firing staff, staff-family relationships, end-of-life care for clients, and the potential for elder abuse. Powers' (2005) taxonomy on everyday ethical decision making in AL is an initial step; however, her research was conducted in nursing homes and limited to the organization's responsibilities to the AL client/resident. As employees who have much responsibility but little authority, frontline caregivers make decisions that require moral imagination and application of ethical principles, yet they are not trained to make decisions that involve choices between personal and organizational values.

METHOD

The study was conducted over a two-year period, from January 2003 through December 2004. All five sites chosen for this study are located in Chester County, Pennsylvania, one of the counties in southeastern Pennsylvania and the greater Philadelphia metropolitan area. The county has historical significance in the field of long term care as one of the first areas in the country to have developed both assisted living facilities and continuing care retirement communities. The Quaker influence in this regard has been substantial. The sample of ALRs was a purposive one, and our deliberate selection of sites provided a broad brush stroke of the organizational types currently operating in the assisted living industry across the U.S. The sites varied on a number of dimensions, including auspice (for profit vs. not-for-profit), affiliation (religiously affiliated vs. secular), age, and levels of care (e.g., free standing assisted living vs. part of a multi-level care organization including Continuing Care Retirement Communities [CCRCs]). The five assisted living facilities that participated in the study included: a private, not-for-profit, religiously affiliated organization that offered both apartments for independent older adults, and those requiring assisted living services; a private, religiously affiliated facility that is part of a regional non-profit corporation and that offers both assisted living and skilled nursing on its campus; a private, stand-alone, religiously affiliated non profit facility that offers assisted living services exclusively; a free standing facility exclusively offering assisted living services, that is part of a publicly-held, for profit, national company; and one facility within a CCRC, operated by a publicly-held, for profit, national long term care company. Respondents ($\underline{n}$=45) included the administrators, resident care coordinators, directors of marketing, selected direct care workers from each facility, and several local "experts" in the field of long term care who had established an ethics committee in a CCRC.

Focused interviews lasted between one and eight hours, though most fell somewhere between these two extremes. Similar to the methodological approach described by Waters et al. (1986) in their study of everyday moral issues experienced by managers, we asked respondents (all of whom signed an Informed Consent Form) to recall specific situations that they personally experienced or observed that presented ethical challenges. We did not define ethics nor did we describe what might or might not be an ethical dilemma. In addition to questions about the respondent's work history and/or professional background, we asked each person to define an ethical dilemma. In addition, we observed selected meetings of resident committees, where they existed, and reviewed sets of organizational documents for each participating site. In return for their participation in the study, we offered each facility a written and/or oral presentation to a constituency of their choice at the conclusion of the research project.

FINDINGS

> Recruiting and selection of frontline workers are frequently driven by the need to fill positions rather than by a strategy that matches jobs to applicant experience, skills and abilities. Hiring standards for caregivers are often minimal and vary widely.

There is little research related to the recruiting (or development) of a paraprofessional workforce (Stone, 2001). While the practitioner literature increasingly focuses on "best practices"—purportedly designed to improve recruiting and retention—it, in fact, largely emphasizes strategies to increase retention. A shortcoming in the long term care literature is the apparent assumption that retention is a bigger problem than recruiting.

Although the traditional supply of direct care recruits comes from the female civilian workforce between the ages of 25 and 44, this population will decline dramatically during the next ten years. As demand for these workers grows, AL providers compete with other employers of direct care labor. These and other structural changes require employers to rethink their approach to recruiting and hiring. In particular, assumptions about frontline workers may need to be re-examined. Despite sparse research about their characteristics in assisted living, the assumption that seems to drive current recruiting practices is "you've seen one direct care worker, you've seen them all." Our research seems to suggest otherwise.

Data from our study demonstrate that at least a subset of direct care workers expressed a strong preference to work in assisted living as opposed to either acute care or nursing homes. Although the skill sets required to perform effectively in both settings are similar, if not equivalent, the variation in the functional level of the AL population creates a different working environment. A care coordinator with an RN described her preference to hire direct care workers without experience in a skilled setting:

> I see a big difference in how they look at staff-resident interaction (when compared to care assistants who do not come from the skilled care industry). They (workers with a skilled nursing background) don't think too much about resident choice and tend to be very authoritative...treating residents in a childlike fashion... I don't really like to hire CNAs who have worked in a nursing home...They (nursing homes) are much more regulated and they (the CNAs with experience in SNFs) carry that over.

Similar to other long term care providers, ALRs need workers who are competent, compassionate, and willing to provide personal care to an increasingly frail and older population. In addition, the physical surroundings, the model of care, the commitment to a homelike atmosphere, staffing requirements, less stringent supervision, and looser regulatory oversight were identified as distinguishing features that account for the preferences of AL workers we interviewed. To the extent that our findings are representative of the population of frontline workers, AL providers who strive to become employers of choice are likely to benefit from recruiting strategies that target the subset of workers who have a preference for AL as well as necessary knowledge, skills and abilities to perform effectively. While recruiting and hiring an employee who matches the job requirements does not guarantee performance or retention, hiring someone who does not have the necessary skills dramatically increases the likelihood of performance problems and turnover—either voluntary or involuntary.

Staff vacancies affect quality and continuity of care and ultimately force clients to be turned away (Dawson & Surpin, 2001). An abundant supply of labor, and pressure to fill vacancies lead employers to develop recruiting strategies that focus first on hiring "warm bodies" and only secondarily on hiring competent and compassionate workers (Stone, 2004). While Stone's review is limited to nursing homes and home health care workers, our findings suggest that AL providers also concentrate primarily on recruiting "warm bodies" rather than identifying people whose skills match position requirements.

Filling vacancies with warm bodies has both ethical and economic implications. Ethically, unless a provider is willing and able to train an employee who lacks basic experience and skills in direct care, questions of competence arise. Economically, quality of workers impacts quality of life for residents and other employees; thus, dissatisfied workers and residents will be more likely to leave, or at a minimum, say and do things that contradict the stated values and desired market position of the organization, leading ultimately to a competitive disadvantage. Although there is little empirical evidence to support a causal link between quality of care and quality of life, ample anecdotal and qualitative data (including the findings reported here) suggest that the quality of the frontline worker influences the quality of resident life.

A fundamental problem in hiring frontline workers is that the job itself is unattractive to many—the work is hard and unpleasant (though as discussed later, there is a fairly common misperception that direct care tasks in AL are less demanding than those in nursing homes), physically and emotionally challenging, wages are low, benefits are often minimal or nonexistent, and clients can be confused, resist care, and sometimes act abusively. In addition, advancement is limited—becoming even a licensed practical nurse (LPN) requires additional education (and many of these workers lack a high school degree and do not speak English as a first language), time and money. In addition, upward mobility within AL organizations is also restricted.

When asked to identify the major challenges facing the AL industry, one executive director ranked "the kind of people you hire" as one of two critical issues (the other was "reimbursement for care"). Despite her espoused belief that hiring the "right" people is one of the most critical challenges facing the industry, data from this facility suggest that turnover of direct care workers is consistently high, in part because of unrealistic expectations of what the job entails. Reflecting on her initial expectations as a new hire, a direct care worker at this facility stated:

> I thought of it as a nursing home, but the residents would be more 'with it' … they would be able to do more of their own ADLs. I didn't know there was a (dementia) unit and I didn't know I would be with stage 3 and 4 dementia patients. I thought I would be serving meals and housecleaning…

In contrast to the "warm body" approach to recruiting, this care coordinator acknowledged the importance of hiring as she described her reality.

> We attract all kinds of people through advertising…we don't necessarily attract excellent people…The interview process has to be extensive…I need to make them what I need them to be…in 90 days [after they are hired], I'll know.

She had no trouble articulating the qualities she looks for in a prospective employee:

> Someone who is compassionate, caring, patient…is able to be creative about a situation, a team player, can accept constructive criticism, and they can't mind being touched by a resident. I watch their body language and how they

interact with the residents at the interview. If I don't get a good feeling, they are not for hire. If they ask how much the pay is coming in the door—if that's the first question out of their mouth, they are not for hire. If their cell phone rings during the interview—it's the little things that make me think they are not interested in the job. Like, if they cancel twice, they're out.

When discussing how she assesses applicants for the specific tasks required on the job, she said "I take applicants up the steps and down the elevator. Some are poor readers. Some read but don't comprehend. [She made it clear, however, that lacking literacy will not be cause for rejection.] I want to know what I'm dealing with." In regard to the pay, she said that "If you can't give them the dollar, I can care for them on a personal level by concerning myself with schedules and its [sic] effect on their family life. Are the hours (here) working out with your kids?" Besides her uncommon approach to assessing applicants, she hires on a part-time basis as a strategy for limiting her investment until the worker demonstrates motivation to learn and performs at a satisfactory level. At that point, the employee is offered a full-time position when one opens. This approach reduces worries about vacancies, since she has an active pipeline of part-time employees. Her comments reflect that this care coordinator is not typical of others in our study, nor is her success in attracting and retaining a stable, well trained workforce.

In every facility, respondents who are frontline workers were able to describe the qualities of a good caregiver and their descriptions parallel that given by the care coordinator quoted above. Applicants who fail to demonstrate that they want the job because they "care about the residents" and not because of the money inevitably turn out to be performance problems and usually leave—either voluntarily or involuntarily—creating even more problems in delivery of care and workload pressure on remaining staff. Despite the presence of knowledgeable employees, they are rarely consulted in the hiring process. We will discuss this point in more detail later in this chapter.

Most of the ALRs in our study relied on a "friends and family" model for recruiting workers. At one facility, three of the direct care workers were related and the care coordinator began as an aide to her mother, since retired, who had also worked there for many years. At another facility, the care coordinator's daughter and son were employed by the organization, and at a third, which was heavily staffed by local college students, management routinely relied on referrals from current employees.

Location of the ALR impacts recruiting practices as well. For example, two of the facilities were geographically close to local universities and many, though not all, of the frontline workers were students, some with an interest in health care careers. The marketing director for one of these facilities emphasized that employing college students has worked to their advantage in the marketplace. At the second facility, the care coordinator has a reputation for mentoring direct care workers as they prepare for higher education in the health professions. At both facilities, part-time workers qualify for benefits, including tuition reimbursement, and can schedule shifts around their classes.

Traditional approaches to recruiting direct care workers leave much to chance. In particular, measuring recruiting effectiveness on the basis of "numbers of people" hired rather than on qualifications is likely to lead to problems with training and job performance, and will do little to reduce turnover. In addition, providers leave to chance the possibility of finding direct care workers who feel called to helping older persons.

An explicit emphasis on competence must occur along the employment continuum—and must be a priority in hiring in order for organizations to be faithful to the value of providing quality care, which all the organizations in our study espoused. Quality care cannot be delivered by untrained or under-trained staff, particularly when the population served is vulnerable, often with functional health problems, and with an ever-increasing need for competent care. In addition, organizations have a moral responsibility to make certain that personnel are not put in positions that compromise the health and functioning of these residents. Untrained and under-trained direct care workers unfairly carry this risk when the organization does not properly prepare them for their roles in the organization. By recruiting "warm bodies," the organization not only puts its residents at risk, thereby being unfaithful to its mission, but also devalues the employees they profess to respect and, just as importantly, hope to retain.

Turnover is a Problem at All Levels—Frontline Workers, Mid-Level Administrators, and Executive Directors

Understanding why frontline workers leave their jobs is important—especially when one considers that the average rate of turnover in AL is 40% (NCAL, 2001). Analysis of turnover requires examination of its causes as well as its costs—both direct and indirect. Policy makers and providers have focused on identifying causes of turnover among direct care workers; however, less attention focuses on its costs. Direct costs result from productivity losses, and can be quantified—a conservative estimate is $2,500 per frontline worker (Seavey, 2004). Indirect costs are less easily measured because they are not "out-of-pocket" and are incurred at the service delivery level by residents and consumers who may receive lower quality of care due to disruptions in its continuity, the lack of experience of new hires, and by the workers themselves who are more stressed and at greater risk of injury (Seavey, 2004).

When "care" is the "product" and the client is a vulnerable, frail elder, concern about both quantity and quality of staff is necessary. When quality care is not delivered—either because there is insufficient staff or because staff are new and inexperienced—an ethical violation occurs. Quality care is universally marketed, but not consistently delivered. Unlike other settings, the AL client cannot always wait for someone to be available without harm being done. Excessive turnover—especially among frontline workers—is likely to have negative consequences including increased costs; disruptions in continuity of care; obstruction of organizational learning; interference with efforts to build or sustain an ethical culture; and disruptions in stability of the environment (less homelike, more institutional). There is, however, little to no empirical evidence that supports these negative outcomes.

Despite the fact that the mean annual wage for direct care workers who are employed year-round and full-time (many work less than 40 hours a week) ranged from $16,750 and $20,760 in 2003 (Wright, 2005), there is no consensus about the impact of wages and benefits on turnover of frontline workers (Konetzka et al., 2005; Noelker & Ejaz, 2001); and, like other published work in long-term care, what research exists has been done in nursing homes and home health care agencies. There is evidence that other factors—including the worker's relationship with the supervisor, the worth attached to the position, autonomy, responsibility, and involvement in care planning and other decisions (Banaszak-Holl & Hines, 1996; Eaton, 2003; Harris-Kojetin et al., 2004; Stone & Wiener, 2001)—are important.

We found that turnover rates are indeed high in the five assisted living communities that participated in this study. What was most interesting, though, is our finding that turnover occurred at every level—from frontline worker to activities directors to care coordinators to marketing directors to executive directors. While the circumstances surrounding each change varied, every ALR in the study experienced personnel changes that caused disruptions within the organization. In several facilities, the same position was held by three different people during the course of the two-year data collection period.

Changes at the executive level occurred in three of the five facilities. Directors of Marketing turned over at all five facilities, sometimes more than once. In two facilities, the entire management team changed during the study period. In one facility, the AL care coordinator—the person charged with supervising direct care workers—changed three times during the course of the fieldwork. Every facility reported high rates of direct care worker turnover; however, in the two oldest ALRs, we found employees who had been enthusiastically providing care for decades.

Victor and Cullen (1988) argue that a lack of fit between an employee's level of moral development and the organization's ethical climate will lead to stress, dissatisfaction, and turnover. Some who are not satisfied with the ethical climate may not leave; however, they may operate in a "zone of indifference" (Barnard, 1938; Victor & Cullen, 1988). One cause of high turnover among frontline workers is that they are not prepared for the nature and difficulty of the work (Eaton, 2003). Consistent with Eaton's claim, a primary reason for why direct care workers left their jobs in our study was because they became "disillusioned" by the levels of assistance they must provide and the levels of disability in AL residents. People leave quickly because "...it's not what they expected [the work] ... Most know this in a week or two and then they're gone", and one worker told us that aides don't understand that AL is the resident's home and "[to them] helping residents is drudgery." A realistic portrait of what AL entails and the sometimes noxious tasks that are required of care managers must be clearly described to prospective employees. As one frontline employee put it:

> Someone who can't tolerate bodily fluids! ...You will smell it, you will see it, and nine out of ten times, you will probably wipe it. But, what did you expect? If you can't do it, there is no point in being here.

The problem stems, in part, from the tension between the stated criteria for admission to and retention in assisted living, and the care staff's determined efforts to keep the resident in assisted living no matter what.

Although some frontline workers came to AL with experience in nursing homes, this background did not necessarily reduce the chance that they would leave. Several respondents told us that workers with nursing home experience came to AL because they were looking for an "easier job"—and were stunned when they discovered that AL residents need more help than they expected. In fact, nearly all our respondents identified a significant minority of AL residents who mirrored the functional profile of nursing home residents. They voice a strong preference for working in an environment that is less medical, and one care coordinator said she would seriously consider leaving her job if there were "too many changes toward the way they are doing things in skilled care." Caring for residents with dementia also proved problematic, and even if aides were not assigned to secure dementia units (which are not available in every AL facility), the fact that more than half of AL residents have some form of dementia means that aides who are uncomfortable or unprepared to deal with these individuals are more likely to leave for other employment.

Evident from our research is the discomfort that many workers feel around the death and dying process. In addition to being surprised that death occurs in ALRs, not having personal experience with death, and then developing intimate relationships with people who die, presents challenges that are different from the hard and often unpleasant daily work of personal care. As one care worker put it: "I'm getting better with death…I'm still getting used to bodies." She described how hard it can be for workers who have no personal experience with death to cope with residents who die. Her memory of the first time she experienced death (during her third week on the job) illustrates the uneasiness, and sometimes distress, expressed by many of the respondents: "…It was the first time I saw someone actively dying…and I was scared to death." For workers who develop an intimate relationship with a resident, the loss is acute and personal. This same care worker described how two of her peers avoided the hallway where this resident lived and died because of their grief over her death.

Several respondents cited poor worker attitudes and performance as reasons why aides leave (or should leave), but it is difficult to replace these workers when they do. One worker said that "People don't get fired here when they probably should… They come in late, leave early, or [are in] violation of the dress code," she said, and that medicated lotions are left "unlocked" instead of in a secure cabinet as is the rule. Despite raising these issues with administration, she reported, action has not been taken and she is concerned that resident safety will be compromised. This respondent also told us that in three years (during which she left and was later rehired by this ALR), she has worked for four different supervisors, and during one year there was a complete turnover of staff (supervisors and frontline workers) in the secure dementia unit to which she is assigned. A nurse at another facility described an employee whose performance was questionable, and offered this explanation for why the employee has not been terminated: "First, no one wants to go through the discipline process.…" Second, "when you're (a facility) so short on staff, you just hope she'll get better."

Wages and benefits were not typically cited as a cause of turnover. In fact, a care coordinator and a direct care worker at two different facilities emphatically argued that if money is what a prospective employee is most concerned about, they should "stay away" because "you'll [the aide] be unhappy and God help the residents!" Some aides in our study also voiced concern that they are not appreciated—within the organization and society more generally—despite the fact that without their efforts, the mission of the organization could not be accomplished. One told us that when she applied for the job [in AL], her mother was against it because her mother believed she "deserved to work in an office." Another bristled at her supervisor's insinuation that she was "just an aide."

At one ALR, "aides" (this ALR's job title for direct care workers) are regularly asked to fill in for the LPN when she is absent. One respondent, a five-year employee at this facility, regularly subbed for the LPN. She explained that her employer requires a "witness" to be present when aides are "written up" for a violation; the supervisor, she added, normally depends on the LPN for corroboration in such cases. But, while recently subbing for the LPN, our respondent told us, "I was good enough to be a witness when someone got wrote up [sic]," but on the occasion of another incident—which occurred shortly thereafter—she was asked to leave the room because the LPN was present. When the respondent quizzed her supervisor about the reason she was asked to leave, she was told that the LPN would act as the witness because "(name of LPN) is higher than you." "That made me feel that I was nothing," she admitted to us, but she mustered the courage to challenge her supervisor: "You said," just minutes ago at a staff meeting, "that 'we are all equals, we just have different roles.'" With that, our respondent left the room.

Although turnover cannot be entirely avoided, when it occurs at a rapid rate and at all staff levels, it is difficult to develop and sustain an ethical culture. Providers must consider the impact that management turnover has on the motivation and ability of frontline employees to deliver high quality care and to make ethical choices on an everyday basis. Constant staffing changes at the administrative and supervisory level lead to instability in organizational structure and policies, and in functional relationships. Turnover at the management level raises the spectre that ethical challenges are likely to be resolved by individuals working on the front lines. In addition to this person-based approach to ethical decision making, high turnover among managers almost guarantees a type of ethical drift in the organization. The absence of written policies coupled with frequent departures of managers, some of whom may have provided ethical leadership, erodes ethical culture, if it exists, and prevents its formation, if it does not.

Human resources are often overlooked and undervalued. The organization does not capitalize on the informal training and experience that workers bring to the job; nor does the organization provide sufficient orientation, training, and development to frontline workers. Many employees—those in our study and others—who choose to work in health care bring to their work a strong internal sense of morality, and providers can take advantage of this by building on the moral resources that already exist (Boyle et al., 2001). Our fieldwork suggests that the assisted living industry may be overlooking the "value added" of experienced direct care workers in the areas of human resource management, including hiring, orientation and training, continuing education, and employee development.

Despite the fact that many direct care workers in AL come without any formal training, and frequently, with no experience in health or long term care, some, nonetheless, are well equipped to provide care. As care providers to members of their families and members of their communities, they informally have acquired a skill and knowledge base that is transferable to a formal care setting, including assisted living and nursing home care. Several of these "un"trained but highly skilled women came to our attention during the course of the study. Although they were not recruited for their significant experience, their knowledge and skills were valued but only in the narrow domain of direct caregiving. Their employers did not tap them for assistance with other human resource management activities, including the hiring process, formal training, and staff evaluation and development. Two cases are highlighted here.

A 24 year old, black, single parent told us that she "grew up (living) with her grandparents," which she viewed very positively, and, that as a young adult, she was trained by a hospice nurse "…to provide hospice care for my mother" who "was dying of breast cancer." Although she claimed to "…know nothing" before working in assisted living, she came to her position with experiential training, albeit informal, that involved living with and caring for her grandparents. We heard a similar refrain from a young, white, college student at another facility whose initial attraction to geriatric care stemmed, in part, she told us, from a close relationship to her grandparents.

The accumulated informal experience of a white, middle-aged caregiver at a third site extended over a lifetime, beginning more than 30 years ago when she gave birth to a son diagnosed with mental retardation, who required "one on one" care into early adulthood. For nine months she also ministered to her dying father-in-law while he was on hospice service—monitoring the feeding tube, administering oxygen, caring for the ostomy bag and providing emotional support. Before her mother was placed in a public, county-supported nursing home as a result of a fall that left her unable to walk, she lived with her daughter for four years because an aneurysm left her with residual disability. For the past 11 years she has also been "caregiving at a distance"—calling for periodic meetings with nursing home staff to advocate for her mother's physical, emotional, and social needs.

The recruitment efforts of assisted living facilities do not generally target informally trained care workers, but perhaps they should. These employees arrive, minimally, with poise and confidence derived from living with and/or caring for an older adult, with a commitment to the concept of "caritas," and with an understanding of the art and practice of caregiving. Employees such as the three described above are capable of identifying training needs, of taking an active role in developing and delivering training programs, and of informally coaching less experienced workers. To the extent that quality of care is marketed and promised, and to the extent that these frontline workers can deliver competent care, the organization will benefit from their ability to help create or strengthen the building of an ethical culture.

As stated earlier, recruitment and retention of direct care workers is a challenge for the long term care industry, and has been the subject of both numerous conferences and lively debates in the professional literature. Data from our study indicated that long term workers were not involved in either the hiring process or training program, despite their expressed confidence in their ability to identify behavioral characteristics associated with success or failure in direct care work. Caregivers with long tenures in assisted living seemed to have a good sense of what it takes to be successful.

For example, in the context of the initial hiring interview, one college-aged worker said:

> [Y]ou can tell by their (the applicant's) responses if they are here for the money or if they really care ...(someone) who is caring, willing to be a universal care manager" who does not quibble about "whether or not a person is (or is not) on my list of assignments...." You have to be patient and have flexibility...and a sense of humor.

This respondent "sat in on interviews" with a few applicants and several other direct care workers from other facilities, and had been "shadowed" by new employees during initial training. This, however, was the extent of their participation in the vetting processes and training programs.

The perspective of another worker suggested that employers should assess work ethic and attitudes about older persons during the hiring process. Without exception, frontline workers reported that management had never solicited their ideas on orientation and training needs, on the wisdom of providing continuing education and its content, or on identifying the behavioral characteristics that would likely lead to effective performance and worker retention.

In terms of effectively building an ethical culture, our data seem to confirm Jackson's (1991) contention that lower level employees are a vital source of knowledge that should be tapped by higher management as the organization confronts ethical dilemmas. Not only can such knowledge aid in making ethically appropriate decisions, but organizations must also recognize that as decision makers in everyday care delivery, frontline workers are also moral agents (Kane, 1994) who take their cues for behavior from both their personal value systems and the organization's ethical climate. To the extent that an organization fails to acknowledge and value the knowledge and skills of its direct care workers, and, at the same time, does not strive to build an ethical culture that supports and guides ethical decision making by these workers on an everyday basis, the likelihood of ethical violations increases.

Person-dependent approaches to ethical decision making versus process-based approaches encourage choices that are based on individual rather than organizational values, and may hinder organizational learning.

All organizations have a culture, but the extent to which ethics is emphasized in it varies. The study of organizational ethics is a relatively new area of inquiry, and thus the accumulated literature is sparse relative to that in business ethics, more generally, and in clinical and professional ethics. "Business ethics focuses on the choices of the individual *in* [sic] an organization, whereas organizational ethics focuses on the choices of the individual *and* [sic] the organization" (Boyle et al., 2001, p. 16). The bioethics literature is centered primarily around extraordinary issues at the beginning and end of life, many of which occur in crisis situations and grab media headlines. Up until recently, the ethical concerns of bioethicists have arisen primarily in acute care settings. In contrast, our focus here is on everyday ethical decisions made by long term care organizations and the individuals within them.

Our findings show that staff often made local, frequently individual, decisions because few formal policies or structures were in place to help employees recognize or manage ethical dilemmas. Formal attention to ethics was absent at all of the facilities in this study. No facility dealt with the topic of ethics during orientation and formal training of frontline workers, including discussion of how to recognize or manage ethical dilemmas. When the topic was discussed, it was only because an individual supervisor or executive director was personally committed to doing so. Although every site publicly stated and displayed its values—often in prominent locations in the building, on the back of their corporate business card, and in print advertising—when asked to describe the decision making process used to resolve a situation where two or more of these values were in conflict, respondents fell back on personal value systems. To the extent that employees' personal values are aligned with those of the organization, all parties involved are likely to accept the decision as ethical. However, without a formal process to assist ethical decision making, inconsistencies between them are likely, and decisions are potentially open to debate.

When organizational mechanisms exist to support resolution of ethical dilemmas, they were rarely, if ever, used or understood. Two of the five facilities had access to an Ethics Committee (at the parent organization in one case, and in the other through a relationship with a nearby hospital). No issue arising in AL had ever been considered by an Ethics Committee because, according to our respondents, AL staff did not know of its existence, did not view its members as being knowledgeable about AL, or viewed the "domain" of the committee as outside of AL. That is, the Ethics Committee was perceived as a group that made decisions on extraordinary, clinical, end-of-life questions. Yet, when asked, respondents readily agreed that there are problems in AL that would benefit from a "hearing" by a larger group who could bring a variety of perspectives to bear on the issue.

Our perspective on organizational ethics in assisted living is one that considers both the client (resident) and employee populations. Publicly stated values underscore an organization's commitment to serve the senior population. However, developing an ethical culture in any organization requires conscious effort beyond values statements or codes of ethics, and, in our view, an equal commitment to clients and employees. Therefore, as values are translated into everyday practice, action steps and behaviors should reflect the organization's obligation to both groups. However, the traditional view in long-term care is to emphasize quality of life (via quality of care) for the care recipient, i.e., the resident. Staff, especially direct care workers, are often viewed as the means to that end. Often, providers fail to conceptualize quality of life as including *both* residents and employees. To this end, we describe how the organizations in our study tended to adhere to their values in client-centered ways that at times, disregarded their obligation to the employees.

Our findings confirm that residents of AL are primarily white women in their mid-eighties who have the economic means to pay privately for AL services. AL direct care workers are primarily women of color, often single, and usually with children at home, living near or below the poverty level, poorly educated (though in some instances, have some college and/or are pursuing a college degree), and of varied religious and ethnic backgrounds. Similar to the other findings discussed in this chapter, there is little in the literature about the ethical challenges that arise in AL settings as a result of diversity within the workforce, although some research acknowledges indirectly that differences between direct care workers and residents may give rise to conflicts.

One young, black worker recalled an incident when a white, male resident "said things that were wrong and disrespectful" about one of his tablemates. "Everyone could hear what he said, including the person who was the object of his words," the direct care worker told us. "Can you please stop? It's disrespectful," she recalled asking him. His response, she remembered, included words to the effect that "he wouldn't take sass from a colored girl."

> I had to control my temper…I remember what I said to him. I felt very disrespected…I didn't want to give him any service…I told him it (his behavior) might have been acceptable when he was coming up…but, I didn't appreciate it, and I felt disrespected…I still do *some* [her emphasis] things for him…but his behavior hasn't changed…. He still makes comments…. I hear him when you're passing by…about other residents and about race.

How did she handle this situation? She said that she went to her supervisor who empathized with her: "…(She) was very understanding and didn't have a problem" with the worker's decision to have "no interaction with him (the resident) even in the dining room." The employee said that to her knowledge, no organizational policy existed to guide decisions in situations like this, before or after this incident occurred.

A second instance involving employee discipline at a faith-based facility illustrates a gross violation of best practices in human resource management, which clearly has an ethical component. The care coordinator at this site told us that a department head was caught twice with alcohol on his breath at work. All department heads were asked to attend a meeting with this person to establish a list of behavioral expectations for him. With raised eyebrows, the care coordinator rhetorically asked:

> What happened? He started drinking again... He had to go to the EAP (Employee Assistance Program) which set up the meeting and the meeting was hostile... No one else should have been involved. I don't know about you, but I think it was wrong.... Do you think it's wrong?

This example illustrated her belief that "...we are not practicing what we preach" referring to the stated values that are printed, framed, and hang in the lobby, and to which she directed our attention.

Regarding the service package a resident should receive and be billed for, our data suggest that decision making rests with the AL care coordinator, but the direct care worker, who is most intimately involved with the resident, usually initiates the process to consider a change in service level. At times, employees involved in care delivery act in ways that they believe benefit the resident despite the fact that these decisions go against policy. Every facility has public pricing lists that enumerate the costs associated with different levels of care and the variety of "add on" services, such as medication management. The organization prefers that every service, even the most minor one, generates revenue. However, whether or not to bill for actual care delivered is a question that faces every care coordinator, and each has developed her own localized method for managing this complex billing process.

Recognizing that added care can lead to increased dependency, and frustrated with the complicated record keeping associated with actual care delivered, our data show that care delivered is not always billed. One care coordinator described her own strategy in this regard, though other respondents echoed her approach. She said that she "makes a conscious decision not to clock the time" spent providing care to new residents as they transition from their previous home to AL, even though she feels pressure from the financial office to do so. For established residents who have intermittent increases in care requirements, she does not upgrade the care level because, she claims, "there's too much paperwork." However, if a resident has been declining for several months, she directs her staff to provide necessary care while documenting the changes in function. At the same time, she involves the family, and eventually they agree to formally change the level of care and with it, the billing level. This respondent was comfortable with this approach to managing care. She was vehement in her belief that overcharging for services is "an ethical violation" and at times, she has fought to have a resident who had been upgraded to a higher level of care changed back to the basic level when the resident no longer needed the additional services. Interestingly, this care coordinator did not view her practice of providing care to residents (and families—to help them with the transition of their relative from home to AL) that was not billed as unethical. She did say that the practice of "parsing" billing for services (a practice that all facilities regularly engage in where individual services are priced on an a la carte basis) is unethical to begin with. She also made it clear that, in her view, a major ethical challenge is expanding access to AL since Pennsylvania does not permit Medicaid waivers for assisted living.

The philosophy of assisted living emphasizes maintaining the independence of residents so that they can age in place, with dignity, until death. Interview data confirmed that the respondents in this study completely internalized this philosophy of care, to the extent that they resisted relocating residents to skilled care, even when they recognized that the residents' health and functional needs warranted a transfer. A telling example involved a resident whose functional health needs were increasing, but who had no cognitive deficiencies. Reflecting her commitment to the philosophy that AL is the resident's home, a care coordinator emphatically stated: "If I have someone who is independent of mind, I'll do *anything...anything* to keep them there [in AL as opposed to moving them to a nursing home]." In this facility, staff felt pressure from the administration to move AL residents to the higher priced nursing unit even when, in their view, the residents' needs could be adequately met without a move. In several facilities we encountered staff who expressed a similar sentiment. Part of the reason for their resistance seemed to be associated with the stigma of nursing homes. Our data, combined with the literature, indicate that staff, residents and families across the board view nursing homes as "the last stop on the train." In fact, our results suggest that for the most part they oppose moving their residents into skilled facilities, and they resist any changes that will cause assisted living to be regarded as a nursing home. The emergence of AL as an option on the long-term care continuum has further stigmatized nursing homes.

The underlying assumption in any ethically laden situation is that the stakeholders define the problem as an ethical one. Publicly stated values emphasize the importance of quality of life for AL residents; however, whether and how ethical dilemmas are recognized and managed directly influences quality of life—for residents, family members, and staff. Our data show that respondents were unable to define ethical dilemmas conceptually. When asked to define what constitutes an ethical problem, they had difficulty responding. Instead, they gave specific, empirical examples of past or ongoing situations that caused them to experience anxiety or other physiological symptoms (e.g., staying awake at night, worry, upset stomach, etc.). When a problem was resolved—satisfactorily or not—respondents told us that although they learned from the experience, organizational policy to guide decision making in a future similar situation rarely followed. Without written guidelines based on experience, in the absence of ethics committees that reach out to and educate AL staff, and with the high degree of turnover at all occupational levels, the opportunity for organizational learning—particularly in the area of ethics—is almost non-existent.

DISCUSSION

Our findings suggest that not only is ethical decision making occurring on an everyday basis, but decisions are made at the individual level and any learning that occurs is not incorporated into the organization's memory so that it can benefit others. Moreover, high turnover of management exacerbates the problem. When workers cannot rely on formal policies to guide their ethical decision making, they often look to unwritten guidelines that have evolved under current leadership. If leaders come and go frequently, as was the case in our study, workers are uncertain about how to proceed in a changing environment. Too much change creates ambiguity and mitigates against the development of a stable ethical culture. When people leave, they take their ethical learning with them.

A recent report for the *Better Jobs/Better Care* initiative of the Robert Wood Johnson (RWJ) Foundation concludes that "frontline turnover in long-term care can be expensive, and when it does become costly, it becomes a business problem, a quality-of-care problem, and a public resource problem" (Seavey, 2004, p. 7). The RWJ report makes no mention of leadership turnover, nor does it acknowledge the potential ethical consequences of turnover. Not doing so, we believe, is a major omission that could create significant business and quality-of-care problems in the future. Development of an ethical culture that fosters delivery of quality care must consider all choices made by individual workers, choices made by residents and their families, and choices made by the organization as a whole—especially ethical ones.

Research generally brings a negative conceptual framework to questions of turnover and retention. That is, reducing turnover is necessary to avoid additional costs. It is rarely argued that reducing turnover can have positive implications for the organization. For instance, a low rate of turnover allows the organization to retain the special talents of its frontline workers, thereby building its resource base, and stabilizes and strengthens the existing ethical culture. AL organizations, like society in general, devalue care workers and, therefore, the very product that they are selling (and expecting to profit from). In our research direct care workers whom we interviewed were surprised and touched that we included them in the study, and that we valued their perspective. Both research and practitioner literature underscore the fact that the direct care worker establishes the most intimate relationship with residents in long term care settings. While they are often consulted by management around particular issues affecting residents, their input is sought, for the most part, on a situational basis. Management's failure to recognize these workers as valuable resources, limits both what they can contribute to the organization and the residents, and what they, in turn, receive as a result of being respected. Among the resources direct care workers bring to their organizations is the ability to act as a moral agent.

Kane (1994) argues that frontline workers are moral agents because they continually make decisions that affect clients. Our findings confirm that this is true. As Haddad puts it, "In the daily lives of frontline care workers...there is little or no time for quiet discourse on theory. Ethical problems are usually pressing, and although they may be subtle, they are unmistakably real" (1994, p. 75). The ethical soul searching that occurred among our respondents was not confined to a particular position or occupational category. Although the frontline workers we interviewed had all encountered ethical dilemmas, they were not recognized as doing so, supported by superiors, or given guidance in how to recognize and resolve them in ways that were consistent with the organization's desires. Acknowledging and supporting the frontline worker as a moral agent is essential if the organization's goal is to provide the highest quality of care. As Kane (1994) argues, organizations have an ethical obligation to frontline workers to provide them with the necessary structure and tools to make competent ethical choices, to provide working conditions that foster self-respect and dignity and allay questions about the morality of "balancing the budget at the expense of the frontline worker" (p, 72). Despite the persuasive arguments offered by Kane (1994), Stone & Yamada (1998), and Haddad (1994), their focus is on frontline workers in nursing homes; there is virtually no empirical research on the topic of everyday ethics in assisted living. What little attention has appeared to date is conceptual and focuses on ethical responsibilities to the resident (Powers, 2005) or risk management (Redmond & Chafetz, 2001). In addition, no work adopts our twin-pronged perspective that considers both the workers' responsibilities to the client and the organization's responsibilities to the worker.

The traditional focus on the problems associated with the direct care workforce clouds the recognition of a subset of direct care workers who view and live care giving as a calling (Weber, 1976). Such workers are a valuable asset, but undervalued in practice, for the industry as a whole, the organization, their peers, and the residents. All of the long term frontline workers we interviewed had been informal caregivers to family or friends, and all felt a calling to help the elderly. Each brought a strong internal sense of personal morality to the role of caregiver. The organization and the AL industry can build on these moral resources by recognizing and cultivating their moral sense (Boyle et al., 2001, p. 91). Providers can only benefit by tapping these employees who bring increased skills, a well-developed cognitive approach to care, and a capacity to act as role models for other employees. If the status of carework and direct care workers is to improve at a societal level, the impetus for change must come from within organizations whose core business is care and whose core workers are those who deliver that care. When carework is valued from within, it will eventually become valued by others; however, if care work is devalued by employers, it is not likely to be seen as valuable by either the individual workers or society, more generally.

As market and demographic forces evolve, and as the stigma of nursing homes persists, nursing homes and assisted living appear to compete for many of the same people. Direct care workers in AL acknowledge that at least a portion of their resident population is nursing home eligible. Management respondents also saw a significant minority of their residents as the functional equivalent of nursing home residents. In particular, marketing directors consistently identified nursing homes as among their direct competitors. As people age, a decline in ability to care for themselves is predictable, existing chronic conditions are often exacerbated, and new ones are frequently diagnosed. Longer term residents of AL do tend to look more like nursing home residents; however, admissions officers repeatedly told us that applicants routinely arrive in a more debilitated state than either their family or primary care physician had reported. As one care coordinator put it, "The picture painted by the family (about the resident's needs and capabilities) and the physician is always different than the package that arrives." And once they are residents, they, their families, and AL staff resist their relocation to a nursing home, even though their decline is recognized and documented.

Our data reflect the stigma attached to nursing homes not only by the resident, but by family and staff, many of whom state a clear preference for AL. Based on our interview and observational data, it appears that the market preference for assisted living as an option for long term care has further stigmatized nursing homes. Frontline workers react to this stigma by emphasizing the value underlying the social model of care and, therefore, resisting the relocation of residents to a nursing home setting, even when a higher level of care is appropriate. Resistance intensifies when the front-line worker develops an intimate caring relationship with their residents. We describe this situation as a crisis of success: workers have completely internalized the philosophy of assisted living and their objectivity is clouded by the personal relationships they develop with the people they care for and about.

IMPLICATIONS FOR PRACTICE

The value of examining assisted living through the lens of ethics helps to reveal moral problems in the following areas: organizational learning, fail-ure to value carework and careworkers, and organizational mission. How can the industry begin to address some of the issues identified here? First, creative strategies that attract and retain more qualified applicants to direct care positions are essential. Our data suggest a few. Targeting infor-mally trained workers who have garnered their experience by caring for family and friends represent a potential source of employees who have pride in this work, and who are motivated, skilled, and reliable. Proactive recruiting of these individuals may help providers achieve a more stable and productive workforce. Those facilities located in or near colleges or universities could recruit students with an interest in the health profes-sions. For all direct care workers, attention to job design and benefit pack-ages can enhance interest and increase the applicant pool. Enriching the frontline worker's job by, for example, tapping them for assistance in training, care planning, and recruitment, will communicate that the orga-nization values them, their skills, and their knowledge. Employers might also consider targeting local part-time labor. Doing so provides an oppor-tunity to assess the person-organization match before making the commit-ment to a full time position. Moreover, this strategy benefits the worker economically.

Second, a substantial literature has grown up around the assisted living industry. Most of these publications, whether academic or practitioner, focus on facility planning, operational strategies, and marketing in an increasingly competitive environment. What is absent is attention to the development of an ethical culture. Why ethics? The pragmatic answer to this question is that "ethics is good business." The fundamental ethical question facing all long-term care providers concerns the proper relation-ship between delivery of care and profitability. To provide quality care, organizations must concern themselves both with caring for older people, and the people who care for them. To fulfill their ethical obligation to pro-vide quality care to clients, ALRs must insure competence of their direct care employees. As the AL population ages and their needs increase, insuring competence requires ongoing training and attention to job design and supervisory support. Training and support must include discussions of how to identify and respond to ethical dilemmas that arise everyday in the workplace, but it need not be costly. It can be included as an agenda item for a staff meeting, or in-service session, or can be addressed in an ad hoc way as situations arise.

CONCLUSION

When ethics is discussed in organizations, it is viewed often as a strategic tool to enhance competitive advantage; however, a sustainable ethical culture requires that the moral reasons for behavior are agreed upon by all members so that they can become a part of the lived experience of organizational life. Without such a moral basis, the pragmatic benefits of ethical culture—improved market position, avoidance of unintended and unwanted consequences—are more likely to be short-lived. We urge providers and scholars to adopt a broad view of ethical culture in AL—and all of long-term care. Unless the "sub" disciplines of clinical/professional ethics, business ethics, bioethics, and organizational ethics are integrated, and unless providers conceptualize "quality of life" as it applies to residents, families and employees, and the relationships between and among them, it will be difficult to build a sustainable ethical culture that fosters delivery of the highest quality of care.

REFERENCES

Banaszak-Holl, J., & Hines, M. (1996). Factors associated with nursing home staff turnover. *The Gerontologist, 36,* 512–517.

Barnard, C. (1938). *The functions of the executive.* Cambridge, MA: Harvard University Press.

Boyle, P.J., DuBose, E.R., Ellingson, S.J., Guinn, D.E., & McCurdy, D.B. (2001). *Organizational ethics in health care: Principles, cases, and practical solutions.* San Francisco: Jossey-Bass.

Caplan, A.L. (1990). The morality of the mundane: Ethical issues in the daily lives of nursing home residents. In R.A. Kane & A.L. Caplan (Eds.), *Everyday ethics: Resolving dilemmas in nursing home life* (pp. 37–50). New York: Springer.

Carder, P. (2002). Promoting independence: An analysis of assisted living facility marketing materials. *Research on Aging, 24*(1), 106–123.

Carder, P.C., & Hernandez, M. (2004). Consumer discourse in assisted living. *Journal of Gerontology, 59B*(2), S58–S67.

Carter, M.W. (2002). Advancing an ethical framework for long-term care. *Journal of Aging Studies, 16,* 57–71.

Dawson, S.L., & Surpin, R. (2001). Direct-care healthcare workers: You get what you pay for. *Generations, 25*(1), 23–29.

Eaton, S.C. (2003). Frontline caregivers in nursing facilities: Can policy help in the recruitment and retention crisis? *Public Policy and Aging Report, 13*(2), 8–11.

Fallis, D. (2004, June 27). VA. Records show more problems in assisted living. *The Washington Post,* p. C1.

Fisher, J. (2001). Lessons for business ethics from bioethics. *Journal of Business Ethics, 34,* 15–24.

Gallagher, J.A., & Goodstein, J. (2002). Fulfilling institutional responsibilities in healthcare: Organizational ethics and the role of mission discernment. *Business Ethics Quarterly, 12,* 433–450.

Gelhaus, L. (2001, August). More reasons to stay. *Provider,* 19–28.

General Accountability Office (GAO). (1999, April 26). *Assisted living quality of care and consumer protection issues.* (GAO/T-HEHS-99-111).

Gurnik, M., & Hollis-Sawyer, L. (2003). Empowering assisted living front-line care staffs to better care for Alzheimer's and dementia residents. *Ageing International,* Winter, *28*(1), 82–97.

Haddad, A.M. (1994). Reaching a right and good decision: Ethical decision-making and the frontline worker. *Generations, 18*(3), 75–77.

Harris-Kojetin, L., Lipson, D., Fielding, J., Kiefer, K., & Stone, R. (2004). *Recent findings on frontline long-term care workers: A research synthesis 1999–2003.* Office of Disability, Aging, and Long-Term Care Policy, U.S. Department ofHealth and Human Services. Available: http://aspe.hhs.gov/daltcp/reports/insight.htm

Jackson, N. (1991). Case material in an ethics workshop: A reply to Patrick MacIagan. *Management Education and Development, 22*(2), 97–100.

Joint Commission on Accreditation of Healthcare Organizations. (2005). Available: http://www.jcaho.org/accredited+organizations/assisted+living/faqs/#G1

Kane, R. (1994). Ethics and the frontline care worker: Mapping the subject. *Generations, 18*(3), 71–74.

Key, S. (1999). Organizational ethical culture: Real or imagined? *Journal of Business Ethics, 20,* 217–225.

Konetzka, R.T., Stearns, S.C., Konrad, T.R., Magaziner, J., & Zimmerman, S. (2005). Personal care aide turnover in residential care settings: An assessment of ownership, economic, and environmental factors. *The Journal of Applied Gerontology, 24,* 87–107.

MacIagan, P. (2003). Varieties of moral issue and dilemma: A framework for the analysis of case material in business ethics education. *Journal of Business Ethics, 48,* 21–32.

Magsi, H., & Malloy, T. (2005). Underrecognition of cognitive impairment in assisted living facilities. *Journal of the American Geriatrics Society, 53,* 295–298.

McCoy, K., & Appleby, J. (2004, May 27). Many facilities accept people who are too ill; Effort to provide maximum choice means elderly sometimes don't get proper level of health care. *USA Today,* p. A6.

McCurdy, D.B. (2001). Creating an ethical organization. In M.B. Holstein & P.B. Mitzen (Eds), *Ethics in community-based care* (pp. 79–93). New York: Springer Publishing Company.

MetLife Mature Market Institute. (2004). *The MetLife market survey of assisted living costs: October 2004.* Available: http://www.metlife.com/WPSAssets/1419079602 1098449460V1F2004%20Assisted%20Living%20Survey.pdf

Meyer, H. (1998). The bottom line on assisted living. *Hospitals and Health Networks, 72*(14), 22–25.

Mollica, R. (2002). *State assisted living policy 2002.* Princeton, New Jersey: Robert Wood Johnson Foundation.

Morgan, L.A., Eckert, J.K., Gruber-Baldini, A.L., & Zimmerman, S. (2004). Policy and research issues for small assisted living facilities. *Journal of Aging and Social Policy, 16*(4), 1–16.

Namazi, K.H., & Chafetz, P.K. (2001). The concept, the terminology, and the occupants. In K.H. Namazi and P.K. Chafetz (Eds.) *Assisted living: Current issues in facility management and resident care* (pp. 1–14). Westport, CT: Auburn House.

National Center for Assisted Living. (2001). *Facts and trends: The assisted living sourcebook.* Washington, DC: American Health Care Association. Available: http://www.ahca.org/research/alsourcebook2001.pdf

National Clearinghouse on the Direct Care Workforce. (2005). Direct care worker information center. Available: http://www.directcareclearinghouse.org/s_state _det.jsp?res_id=52&x=11&y=3

Noelker, L., & Ejaz, F. (2001). *Final report: Improving work settings and job outcomes for nursing assistants in skilled care facilities.* The Margaret Blenkner Research Center, The Benjamin Rose Institute.

O'Bryan, D., Clow, K.E., O'Bryan, J., & Kurtz, D. (1996). An empirical study of the influence of demographic variables on the choice criteria for ALFs. *Health Marketing Quarterly, 14*(2), 3–19.

O'Keeffe, J., O'Keeffe, C., & Bernard, S. (2003). *Using Medicaid to cover services for elderly persons in residential care settings: State policy market and stakeholder views in six states.* Washington, DC: U.S. Department of Health and Human Services, Assistant Secretary for Planning and Evaluation, Office of Disability, Aging and Long-Term Care Policy, December.

Powers, B.A. (2005). Everyday ethics in assisted living facilities: A framework for assessing resident-focused issues. *Journal of Gerontological Nursing, 31,* 31–37.

Redmond, R., & Chafetz, P.K. (2001). Legal and ethical issues for assisted living facility operators: Managing risk by doing the right thing. In K.H. Namazi and P.K. Chafetz (Eds.) *Assisted living: Current issues in facility management and resident care* (pp. 167–181). Westport, CT: Auburn House.

Sarton, M. (1973). *As we are now.* New York: W.W. Norton & Company.

Seavey, D. (2004). The cost of frontline turnover in long-term care. *Better jobs better care: Institute for the future of aging services.* Available: http://www.bjbc.org/content/ docs/TOCostExecutiveSummary.pdf

Sikorska-Simmons, E. (2005). Predictors of organizational commitment among staff in assisted living. *The Gerontologist, 45,* 196–205.

Sloane, P.D., Gruber-Baldini, A.L., Zimmerman, S., Roth, M., Watson, L., Boustani, M., Magaziner, J., & Hebel, J.R. (2004). Medication undertreatment in assisted living settings. *Archives of Internal Medicine, 164,* 2031–2037.

Spencer, E.M., Mills, A.E., Rorty, M.V., & Werhane, P.H. (2000). *Organization ethics in health care.* New York: Oxford University Press.

Stone, R. (2001). Research on frontline workers in long-term care. *Generations, 25*(1), 49–57.

Stone, R. (2004). The direct care worker: The third rail of home care policy. *Annual Review of Public Health, 25,* 521–537.

Stone, R., & Yamada, Y. (1998). Ethics and the frontline long-term care worker: A challenge for the 21st century. *Generations, 22*(3), 45–51.

Stone, R., & Wiener, J. (2001). *Who will care for us? Addressing the LTC workforce crisis.* The Urban Institute and the American Association of Homes and Services for the Aging. Available: http://aspe.hhs.gov/daltcp/reports/ltcwf.pdf.

Sykes, J.T. (2000). Marketing promises, managing realities: Assisted living approaches maturity. *The Gerontologist, 40*(1), 118–122.

Trevino, L.K., Butterfield, K.D., & McCabe, D.L. (1995, August). *Contextual influences on ethics-related outcomes in organizations: Rethinking ethical climate and ethical culture.* Paper presented at the Annual Academy of Management Meeting, Vancouver, BC.

Victor, B., & Cullen, J.B. (1988). The organizational bases of ethical work climates. *Administrative Science Quarterly, 33,* 101–125.

Waters, J.A., Bird, F., & Chant, P.D. (1986). Everyday moral issues experienced by managers. *Journal of Business Ethics, 5,* 373–384.

Weber, M. (1976). *The Protestant ethic and the spirit of capitalism.* New York: Charles Scribner's Sons.

Werhane, P.H. (1999). *Moral imagination and management decision making.* New York: Oxford University Press.

Werhane, P.H. (2002). Moral imagination and systems thinking. *Journal of Business Ethics, 38,* 33–42.

Wright, B. (2004). *An overview of assisted living 2004.* AARP Public Policy Institute (October) Available: http://www.aarp.org/research/housing-mobility/assisted-living/ Articles/assisted_living_in_the_united_states.html

Wright, B. (2005). *Direct-care workers in long-term care research report.* AARP Public Policy Institute. Available: http://assets.aarp.org/rgcenter/il/dd117_workers.pdf

PART II

FOCUSED PERSPECTIVES

CHAPTER 8

REEVALUATING DRUG TESTING

Questions of Moral and Symbolic Control

Michelle R. Greenwood, Peter Holland, and Karen Choong
Monash University

INTRODUCTION

In recent years, new techniques and improved technology related to monitoring and surveillance in the workplace have advanced dramatically (Hartman, 2005; Holland, 2003; Moore, 2000; Persson & Hansson, 2003). With costs steadily reducing, this technology is now within the reach of most organizations. At the forefront of these developments is workplace drug testing which is viewed as a measure designed to enhance efficiency and productivity through fewer workplace accidents and the elimination of problem employees. Despite arguments that justify drug testing under the rubric of occupational health and safety, these developments are increasingly seen in the context of the rights of the individual (Holland & Wickham, 2002).

The debate over workplace drug testing can be depicted as a question of competing interests between the provision of a safe and productive work-

Human Resource Management Ethics, pages 161–180
Copyright © 2006 by Information Age Publishing
All rights of reproduction in any form reserved.

place and the individual's right to privacy (Cranford, 1998). Yet, these contrasting perspectives are not as clearly delineated as they may initially appear, due to the issue being blurred by a number of factors. These factors include the notion that drug testing may provide the employer with information that is not job-related; the inaccuracy and unreliability of current drug testing techniques; and the availability of more appropriate testing alternatives to assess fitness for duty.

This chapter addresses the question of why employers continue to use drug testing in the workplace despite the moral and practical evidence against it. The chapter begins with a brief overview of the extent and nature of drug use and drug testing in U.S. organizations. This is followed by an outline of traditional arguments for and against workplace drug testing. Both practical and moral issues are considered. The review suggests that, on balance, the arguments against drug testing outweigh the arguments in favor of drug testing. The chapter then explores other potential explanations for the continued use of drug testing in the workplace. Two major ideas are posited: first, that drug testing is used to focus on employees' illegitimate and wrongful behavior in order to distract from systemic and work related conditions that may have brought about the employees' drug use in the beginning; second, that drug testing is used by employers as a form of symbolic control of the workplace, a way of asserting moral superiority and demanding employee compliance—management's right to manage. These two propositions are not mutually exclusive, and, in fact, share commonality in the idea that employers use drug testing to claim the moral high ground over employees.

DRUGS AND DRUG TESTING IN THE WORKPLACE

Substance abuse and potential dangers it poses in the workplace are well documented (Allsop & Pidd, 2001; Greenburg & Greenburg, 1995; Wall, 1992), as are the substantial costs in human and economic terms. Whilst levels of drug use are difficult to quantify various studies in the field do indicate similar findings. Normand, Lempert and O'Brien (1994) for example, identified that 7% of the U.S. workforce reported taking illicit drugs in the previous month and 6 %reported having drunk heavily. They also estimated that slightly less than 10% of workers used marijuana in the past 12 months, with less than 3% identified in the study as regular users, and less than 3% of workers could be described as heavy drinkers over the previous 12 months. Hoffman and Larison (1998) in their study found that slightly less than 10% of workers had used marijuana in the past 12 months with 3% being regular users. However Normand et al, (1994) did find that many the workers frequently using drugs were poly-drug users often taking a cocktail of drugs simultaneously. Despite these relatively low figures, the concern regarding drug use in the workplace has increased over the last two decades fuelled by assessments of the on-going cost to the workplace which Hartford Insurance Company loss control department (HCLD, 1999) classified in terms of the average drug user to be:

- 2.5 times more likely to use 8 or more days of sick leave per year;
- absent about 40% more than non-users
- 3.6 times likely to be involved in an accident;
- 5 time as likely to file a compensation claim;
- one-third less productive and
- likely to incur 300% higher medical costs

These results are supported by Normand et al. (1994), and Hoffman and Larison (1998, p. 169) who note that:

> Field studies have consistently linked alcohol and drug abuse to higher rates of absenteeism; they also provide evidence of an association between alcohol and perhaps other drug use and increased rates of accidents.

One tacit outcome of these findings has been an increase in drug testing in the workplace in the U.S. by an estimated 277% in the period 1987–2002 (ACLU, 2002), with 98% of the Fortune 200 companies employing some form of drug testing. The industry sectors of utilities (80%) and manufacturing (64%) have been leading the drive. It is also estimated that 69% of medium sized companies conduct drug-testing on job applicants (HLCD, 1999). However, as Hoffman and Larison (1998, p. 9) point out:

> The findings indicate that drug use among the U.S. workforces was rare. Although there were many former users of marijuana and cocaine in the workforce, few were currently using and fewer still using frequently. For instance, weekly use of marijuana and cocaine was very uncommon among workers.

PRACTICAL ARGUMENTS FOR AND AGAINST DRUG TESTING

In addition to economic costs, drug abuse has significant human costs for which management is ultimately responsible (Richmond, Heather, Holt, & Hu, 1992). Under Occupational Health and Safety legislation employers are obligated to provide a safe workplace for all employees and visitors to their sites. Employers subject to liability under the law and face significant penalties if found to be in breach. Employer liability extends to their employees' actions and/or omissions, regardless of their state of mind.

This responsibility can be regarded as a catalyst for drug testing in the workplace as it reflects management taking responsible steps to reduce harm stemming form drug related negligence.

This prima facie evidence illustrates why drug testing is commonplace in the U.S. and is supported by research which indicates that the use of drug testing programs in both employment and pre-employment testing has been a major factor in the reduction of absenteeism and accidents (Flynn, 1999; Hartwell, Steele, French, & Rodman, 1996). It is therefore, identified as the most popular method of removing the issue of substance abuse in the workplace and potential litigation and reputation damage associated with these issues (Flynn, 1999; Greenburg & Greenburg, 1995; Hartwell et al., 1996; Osterloh & Becker, 1990). Hence, it can be argued that drug testing in the workplace to ensure that first, the employee is meeting their contractual obligations to a satisfactory standard, and second, to meet the employer's requirements of duty of care under occupational health and safety legislation (DesJardins & McCall, 1990). Implicit in these points is the potential that employers who do not have drug testing policies and programs are maintaining an unsafe workplace (Redeker & Segal, 1989). This perceived onus is extended by the increasing availability and low cost of the technology to undertake drug-testing, putting it within the range of small to medium sized operations, and is reflected in increases in drug-testing over the last two decades notes above (ACLU, 2002).

However, the cost-effectiveness and overall value of drug testing is questionable. The American Civil Liberties Union (ACLU) argues, based on an analysis by a committee of the National Academy of Sciences (NAS), that "most workers who use illicit drugs never use them at work, and when they use drugs on their own time, they do so in a way that does not affect work performance" (ACLU, 1999, p. 16). In addition they note that "lost productivity' studies claiming that drug users cost industry up to $100 billion each year are based on dubious comparisons of household drug use and income, with no analysis of actual productivity data.

Within the scope of a contract of employment, the issue of productivity raises an important consideration in the drug testing debate. As DesJardine and McCall (1990) question: to what level of performance are employers entitled? If an employees' productivity is satisfactory, they are meeting contractual obligations. Under these circumstances knowledge of the employees' drug use on the grounds of productivity is not pertinent. In addition, whilst the issue of duty of care is important, not every job has the potential to do harm. Evidence shows that hard core drug users are usually not in the workforce but are often chronically unemployed (Maltby, 1999). Thus, it is argued that "to say that employers can use drug testing to prevent harm is not to say that every employer has the right to know about the drug use of every employee" (DesJardine and McCall, 1990, p. 204).

Important and often overlooked is the nature of work and the work environment. Within the larger context of the employment relationship, work culture and the social environment are critical and complex factors in the drug-testing debate. For example, a culture of drug use, both legal and illicit drugs, has been linked to geographically isolated locations (Allsop, Phillips, & Calogero, 2001). As Allsop and Pidd (2001, p. 5) note:

> In a variety of cultures, formal and informal pressures still encourage weekly after work team building and relaxation based on alcohol consumption. Sanctioned drugs such as caffeine and tobacco have been embraced in ritualised breaks in work time.

A burgeoning body of research has focused upon the relationship between the nature of work and associated drug use. Issues of control, alienation and stress, linked with individuals' perceptions of their powerlessness, have been identified as factors related to drug use in the workplace and to a certain extent are in the control of the employer (Ames, 1999; Greenburg & Greenburg, 1995; Seeman & Seeman, 1992; Trice & Sonnenstuhl, 1990). As Midford (2001, p. 46) argues: "to gain an understanding of workplace drug problems, one must look at a full range of factors that influence patterns of drug use."

The nature of drug-testing is also a contentious issue which causes tension because of its invasive and humiliating nature in the test require a body sample such as urine, blood or hair. In a study of 63 Silicon Valley companies, Shepard and Clifton (1998) identified that undertaking urine testing actually reduced productivity. This occurrence may result from to a perceived lack of trust the employer has in their workforce, and may explain the finding by the U.S. government that the real or explicit cost to find one drug user is on average $77,000 (Maltby, 1999). In addition there is also the issue of error in testing and the consequences for both false positive and false negative results, on morale, trust and safety. Indeed, the ACLU (2002) argue that in 1992, an estimated 22 million tests were administered and, using a conservative estimate of 5% positive results, approximately 1.1 million people could have been sacked or denied employment because of mistakes. Further, it is suggested that setting up such mistrust in the employment relationship can deter high quality workers from joining such an organization on the grounds of unjustified intrusion (Maltby, 1999). It is also important to note that such testing does not identify actual impairment which is the real on-the-job issue. Alternate approaches for measuring impairment, such as the use of computer based performance tests, are available. These tests measure hand-eye coordination and response times which are very effective in determining whether an employee is fit for duty. Fitness for duty is supposedly the key issue of concern in the debate on drug testing and as such it would seem logically to test it directly. Doing so takes into account a wider perspective of impairment causes, including fatigue or illness, and certainly is less invasive. In summary, when drug abuse may not be negatively related to productivity, when so few organization (as little as 8% of U.S. firms in 1996) evaluate their programs (Maltby, 1999), and when there is an alternative practice available, this leads to obvious questions about the real worth of drug-testing programs.

MORAL ARGUMENTS FOR AND AGAINST DRUG TESTING

Traditionally the debate about the moral issues involved in workplace drug testing have been posed as a balance between the rights of individual employees to protect their privacy and the obligations of the employer to provide a safe workplace and to ensure the organizations profitability. These arguments are reviewed in the following sections.

Individual Rights to Privacy

The right of a person to privacy is considered to be a fundamental human right. Oliver (2002) describes individual privacy as the preservation of the confidentiality of information about individuals, which is essential in the protection of personal autonomy and democracy. Before assuming the existence of a moral duty to uphold privacy rights it is necessary to consider particular conditions of workplace drug testing. First there is the question of whether the employment contact mitigates the employee's right to privacy to any extent. Second there is the consideration of how the actual nature of drug testing, that it is physically invasive and that it is subject to inaccuracy, affects employees' privacy rights. Finally, there is the possibility that information gathered by drug testing may be used by the employee for purposes other than stated. To infringe upon moral imperatives such as the protection of individual privacy has inherent moral risks and, as such, must be balanced against other moral imperatives or possible benefits.

Employment as a Special Case

It is recognized that when an individual is at work, he or she is no longer on "private time." It is generally accepted that employees give up considerable expectations to privacy upon entering the "public arena" of the workplace to perform paid work, and should expect to be observed by their superiors (Oliver 2002). This argument is often cited in favor of workplace surveillance and monitoring. Employers are entitled to know about employee drug use on the grounds that "such knowledge is relevant to assessing an employee's capability to perform according to the terms of the (employment) agreement" (Cranford, 1998, p. 1807). However, despite employees being to a large extent under management control whilst at work, it cannot be assumed that they completely abandon their basic right to privacy upon entering the workplace. Whilst some erosion of privacy may be accepted, employees retain an expectation to be treated with dignity and respect, evident in a degree of 'private space' in the workplace, such as toilets, change rooms, locker areas and lunch rooms (Coleman & SaratChandran, 2004, p. 3.54).

It is possible that employees could test positive to drug use having used illicit substances outside of work hours. A drug test may yield a positive result as drug metabolites can appear in a person's urine long after the drug has ceased to affect their behavior. Under such circumstances the prohibited substance may have no effect on an individual's work performance and therefore be of no regard to the employer (Comer, 1994). The employment relationship only extends to the selling of one's work, not the selling of oneself such as in slavery (Persson & Hansson, 2003); hence drug testing is an intrusion into an employee's private life which wrongly appropriates time which was not purchased (Caste in Comer, 1994). Drug testing surpasses the employer's legitimate sphere of control by dictating the behavior of employees on their own time (Maltby, 1987). Certainly information about an employee's personal life is their own concern and an employer has no right to violate this privacy and intrude into their employees' private lives (DesJardine & Duska, 2001; Moore, 1989).

A counter argument for the testing for drugs used in private time is that such testing acts as deterrent against drug use and as such is of benefit to the drug-using employees themselves (Comer, 1994; Cranford, 1998). This action, however, could be viewed as management taking upon itself the role to which it is not entitled, that of de-facto parents or police. Such an overly paternalistic standpoint risks undermining employees' autonomy and dignity in addition to their fundamental rights.

Given the potential to invade the privacy rights of employees, it is imperative that drug testing and other forms of monitoring be undertaken only with the voluntary consent of employees (DesJardine & Duska, 2001; Moore, 2000). DesJardins and Duska (2001) view the purpose of the employment relationship purely as the means to satisfy the economic interests of the contracting parties and any obligations incurred by each party are only those that it takes on voluntarily. However, Moore (2001) introduces the concept of 'thin consent' whereby consent has been obtained with some degree of coercion. Thin consent is "thinner" in environments where jobs are threatened and employment is precarious (Moore 2000, p. 701) and in organizations where there is low trust and job security. Consent may be particularly thin for the less employable—less skilled, less mobile and older workers. Employees with such limited options employees may relinquish their privacy rights for fear of the consequences if they do not. Further, the employment relationship is inherently marked by such a power imbalance as to undermine the notion of *entirely* free or voluntary consent (Coleman & SaratChandran, 2004). The questionable nature of the voluntary consent given by employees in some circumstances further jeopardizes the moral foundation of workplace drug testing.

Invasive and Inaccurate Techniques

The techniques involved in collecting the samples for drug testing are both highly invasive and intrusive. A blood test involves puncturing the skin, whilst a urinalysis compels an employee to provide a urine sample on demand (Nolan, 2000). This sample must be acquired under direct observation to guard against substitution and falsification of results (Wagner DeCew, 1994). These practices involve significant imposition on individuals not only in a physical manner, but also in a psycho-social sense as they require an individual to expose themselves, or submit themselves, to other. Such impositions may be particularly injurious for individuals from certain religious or ethic backgrounds, individuals with psychological problems or previous experiences of trauma, and physically disabled or older employees.

Furthermore the accuracy of drug testing is questionable as the test procedures are far from foolproof and there is a high incidence of error. Although there are many types of testing instruments available, the accuracy, validity and reliability vary considerably (MacDonald, Wells, & Fry, 1993). Some opponents of drug testing claim that tests yield inaccurate results as often as 60% of the time (Wagner DeCew, 1994). More conservative estimates suggest that error rate is much lower yet still significant (as noted earlier, 5% of positive results may be inaccurate). . A false positive result, whereby a person is wrongly accused of drug use when there has been none, may lead to moral and legal issues such as defamation due to damage to their reputation, discrimination and wrongful dismissal (MacDonald et al., 1993). Additionally, false negative test results may cause the failure to prevent employees under the influence of drugs from conducting safety sensitive tasks whilst impaired, thus placing their own safety and the safety of the workplace at risk. Given the likelihood of inaccurate results and gravity of the consequences such results, it is doubtful that drug testing is an appropriate means of testing for on the job impairment to prevent harm.

Information May Be Used for Other Purposes

Another possible intrusion into an employee's right to privacy involves the use of drug testing to obtain information other than drug usage. The individual's interest in safeguarding the confidentiality of the information contained in the sample taken (Wagner DeCew, 1994). Analysis of blood or urine samples can be used to obtain information about personal medical conditions, such as the use of contraceptives, pregnancy, epilepsy, manic depression, diabetes, schizophrenia or heart trouble (Wagner DeCew, 1994) that is not relevant to job performance and therefore not the employer's business (Khan, Chawla, & Cianciolo, 1995). An employee's right to privacy is violated whenever personal information is requested, collected or used by an employer in a way for any purpose that is irrelevant to the contractual relationship that exists in employment (Persson & Hansson, 2003). Hence the use of bodily samples obtained under the pretext of drug testing to obtain information other than that clearly stated represent such a violation. Indeed, the acquisition of information in this manner would be deceitful and illegal and therefore present moral risks over and above the invasion of privacy rights.

Employer Obligations

Maximizing Performance and Profit

Drug or alcohol abuse accounts for up to 25% of workplace accidents, according to the World Health Organization; whilst the International Labour Organization attributes 15% of workplace fatalities to drugs and alcohol (Buckley, 2000). It is not surprising that an employee's performance would be impaired, as these substances alter a person's body functions, behavior and personality. Consequently, on the job motor skills, reaction time, sensory and perceptual ability, attention, concentration, motivation and learning ability are all likely to be impaired (Jardine-Tweedie & Wright, 1998). Butler (1993 in Jardine-Tweedie & Wright, 1998) suggests that such a chemically dependent employee is less than 75% effective. Further expenses borne by the organization could include absenteeism, lost productivity, quality control problems, increased health insurance costs, increased worker's compensation costs, turnover costs and employee theft (Wagner DeCew, 1994). Whilst this argument is most often depicted as purely an economic argument, it is also potentially a moral argument. From the classical and neo-classical perspective managers, as agents of the shareholders, have a moral responsibility to allocate company resources in a manner that will protect and maximize the shareholders' investment (Friedman, 1970; Sternberg, 1997). As agents of the owners, the managers are morally bound to safeguard the interest of the owners. It follows that it is in an employer's best interests to reduce and eliminate the use of drugs by its employees in the pursuit of profit maximization. Further, it can be argued that others involved in contractual arrangements with the company, whether they be employees, customers or suppliers will have their best interests served by the organization being left to its own devices, as the market will ensure that self-interested profit-seeking behavior results in optimal outcomes for all parties.

Preventing Potential Harm

Persson and Hansson (2003) further advance the moral argument by suggesting that organizations do not have only an economic interest in preventing harm to employees, but also a moral responsibility established through the relationship created by the contract of employment. This relationship places the onus on the employer for the employee's work-related interests, primarily the provision of a safe work environment. Hence, as the employer would be held morally responsible for any injury sustained by the employee at work, and is held financially accountable for compensating any third party injured by their employees in the course of performing their duties, then they must have the means to prevent such harm from happening (Persson & Hansson, 2003). Moore (1989) describes this assertion as the "ought implies can" argument.

Proponents of drug testing claim regular or random testing programs inhibit use and serves as a deterrent for fear of the ramifications of a positive result (DesJardine & Duska, 2001). Random drug testing has been likened to breath testing for blood alcohol concentration of road users, which has proven to be a very effective deterrent that has resulted in a significant decrease drunk driving (Knott, 2003). Knot (2003) takes the "prevention is better than cure" stance, claiming that testing after an incident is pointless other than to find fault. Prevention is particularly salient in workplaces which are safety sensitive and operate heavy plants, machinery and equipment, such as mines, airlines and heavy manufacturing require zero tolerance for such impairment.

This safety-first argument is supported by Occupational Health and Safety (OHS) legislation and, as such, OHS is frequently identified as a key driver for employing workplace drug testing programs. The key principle of OHS legislation is the duty of care responsibility which requires everything reasonably practicable to be done to protect the health and safety of the workplace and an obligation to avoid the risk of injury (Coleman & SaratChandran, 2004; DeCieri, Kramer, Noe, Hollenbeck, Gerhart, & Wright, 2003). Accordingly, it can be argued that as employers have the responsibility to prevent harm from occurring (DesJardine & Duska, 2001), drug testing falls under management prerogative and thus employers should have the right to manage and control their workplace to protect themselves against potential legal liability (Coleman & SaratChandran, 2004). Such measures may be considered to be consistent with employee expectations, who do indeed expect the employer to provide them with a safe workplace (Coleman & SaratChandran, 2004), which would include managing the potentially unsafe behavior of other employees.

In summary, an employer's knowledge of an employee's drug use may be considered vital as a person who is in an impaired state poses an immediate threat to the safety of themselves and others, particularly in potentially dangerous industries. Accordingly, drug testing is justified by utilitarianism argument that it prevents harm and ensures a safer work environment for the many.

An Unnecessary Moral Risk

Drug testing of employees poses the moral risk of violating individuals' human rights. However, Moore (1989) recognizes that whilst fundamental human rights are universal, not all rights are absolute. Whilst overriding an individual's rights should be avoided where possible, such action may be justified if, in doing so, a fundamental good is served. Under these conditions drug-testing is only permissible if it is essential for the protection of public safety. Furthermore, it is argued that if employers are held legally and morally responsible for public safety, then it is only right that they should be permitted to be allowed to use the means necessary to fulfill such responsibilities. This "ought implies can argument" however has one additional caveat, and that is, that no other more morally acceptable way exists to achieve this goal (Moore, 1989).

Fitness for duty testing (also known as performance, behavior or skills testing) is a more accurate assessment of work performance including safety and impairment issues that screening for illicit drugs. Fitness for duty tests an individual's physical and mental dexterity through eye-hand coordination, balance, reflexes, reasoning ability, alertness and reaction time (DesJardines & Duska, 1987; Moore 1989; Comer, 1994). Such tests are less intrusive, are more easily administered and give instant results (DesJardines & Duska, 1987). These tests are more informative about an employee's job ability and are more effective in preventing harm than drug testing. Such tests also take into consideration impairment caused by illness, sleep deprivation or emotional preoccupation, which are also important factors in an employee's performance in safety sensitive industries (Comer, 1994). Fitness for duty testing holds far fewer potential moral risks than drug testing and as such, is considered morally preferable.

Consequently overriding individual privacy rights by drug testing is unjustified, and drug testing represents an unnecessary moral risk, as there are more morally appropriate means to protect public safety. It also focuses on the broader issue of occupational health and safety rather than the employee's private life.

ALTERNATIVE EXPLANATIONS FOR DRUG TESTING

Blaming the Individual

Thus far this chapter has presented the traditional arguments for and against drug testing in the workplace. In doing so, it has been argued that workplace drug testing serves neither the interests of the employees nor the employers, and that fitness for duty testing offers employers a viable alternative. Given that such an alternative is available, why do employers continue to employ workplace drug testing? One possible explanation advanced here is that employers pursue drug testing in order to place the onus and responsibility for any drug abuse in the workplace solely on the individual employees. Blaming the employee has the added feature of being a means of diverting attention away from their own role in creating working conditions that may induce employees to use drugs to cope:

> Holding the view that drug use is a problem for the individual worker is functional from the employer's point of view because it avoids any exploration of how the workplace, and management's support of such an environment, may contribute to the problem. (Midford 2001, p. 46)

Focusing on fitness for duty would have the opposite effect. By testing for actual work performance, fitness for duty assessment would not exclude impairment caused by work related factors. As such, work conditions which are under the control of the company such as overtime, stressful work conditions, and poor training could be identified through such testing.

Ironically, these very work conditions may be complicit in employee drug use. It has been argued that drug use may be symptomatic of issues of control, alienation and stress due to underlying structural problems such as hazardous work, a poor work environment, unrealistic deadlines, lack of job satisfaction, lack of participation and control, perceptions of powerlessness, inadequate training and supervision, shift work and the culture of the industry (Holland, 2003; Holland & Wickham, 2002). Charlton (1994 in Jardine-Tweedie & Wright, 1998) acknowledges that problems in the workplace that lead to stress and fatigue should be eliminated where possible, as these contribute directly to drug use. He suggests such problems include excessive overtime, boring repetitive tasks and poorly planned shift work. Evidence also suggests that fatigue, rather than impairment from drug abuse, leads to the majority of workplace accidents (Nolan, 2000). Maltby (1987) thus dismissed drug testing as fundamentally flawed as it tests for the wrong thing. He claims that to be effective in detecting employees whose impairment present potential harm, the initiative would test for the underlying conditions that actually creates the danger rather than merely identification of the symptoms.

Drug testing is becoming increasingly prevalent in a time of decreasing union control and the increasing use of casual and contract employees (and the simultaneous reduction of management responsibility to these employees). Understandably, employees and unions have questioned why drug testing has assumed such priority in an industrial climate where increasing demands have been placed upon workers (Nolan, 2000). These endless pressures of working longer and harder are rarely linked to illicit drug use that may be sustaining these work patterns (Holland, 2003). Thus by focusing on drug use as the individual's problem, it absolves management from any responsibility and ignores their contributing role in creating stressful and unsustainable working conditions.

Symbolic and Moral Control

Another explanation for the practice of drug testing is that the employer undertakes this activity as a way of enforcing a form of indirect or symbolic control over employees. Drug taking tends to be seen in our society as an irrational and anarchistic activity pursued by deviants. In modern organizations, drug use and the presence of drug using employees threatens to undermine organizational rationality by introducing elements of disorder and deviance. More than endangering productivity and performance, drug use threatens the fundamental "rational" foundations of organizations by undermining the work ethic and promoting an immoral disregard for the collective well being of the organization (Cavanaugh & Prasad, 1994). Such irrationality cannot be controlled through the use of traditional managerial techniques (Cavanaugh & Prasad, 1994) but requires control through the management of more abstract and emotional elements of the organization. Cavanaugh and Prasad (1994) posit that drug testing offers three interrelated "symbolic" functions for employers: as means for restoring or creating the image of managerial control; as providing management a scientific and rational response to an irrational and chaotic situation; and, as providing management moral legitimation in the eyes of its constituents and stakeholders.

Creating the Image of Control

In the perceived volatile and chaotic environment created by drug use, management is symbolically demonstrating through workplace drug testing that they are nevertheless in control and taking action. Otherwise, in failing to act, management may be perceived as being passive and futile, and the situation as being out of their control, leading to their authority being undermined (Cavanaugh & Prasad, 1994). Hence despite the controversy surrounding drug testing, the existence of such testing programs focuses attention on the fact that at least something is being done to combat the drug problem in the workplace.

Pfeffer (1981) has suggested that persistent management behavior that is ineffective in pursuing stated organizational goals is best understood as "symbolic" behavior. Such behavior, rather than being aimed at achieving organization goals, is aimed at reinforcing power and control relationships in the organization. Because of our focus on the rational and the analytic, we tend to downplay the potency of symbolic action (Pfeffer, 1981). Language, ceremonies, and settings are important in the exercise of influence because we are rarely conscious of their effects on us. Indeed, "the effectiveness of this symbolic action is enhanced by the confusion of all involved between substantive and symbolic results" (Pfeffer, 1981, p. 47).

Trade unions often see the introduction of activities such as drug testing as management exercising control under the guise of its 'right' to manage (Holland & Wickham, 2002). Such actions are also seen as strategies to marginalize the countervailing power of unions, limiting their effectiveness while significantly increasing managerial control, particularly where there has been no consultation (Holland & Wickham, 2002). This view is particularly salient as many policy issues associated with employer directed substance testing can result in employee-union conflict.

The continued use of workplace drug testing suggests that privacy rights do not seem to be included in the negotiated terms of employment. This omission may be due to the acceptance of the invasion of information privacy rights as being less intuitively "wrong" than invasions of other rights (Oliver, 2002). However, the fundamental issue underlying such disregard of individual privacy rights is the reluctance for employers to sacrifice their management prerogative to run their workplace in order to protect these rights. It is argued that when employers are prevented from performing monitoring such as drug testing, they are effectively being prevented from controlling their own workplace (Oliver, 2002). Thus retaining management control may be considered an underlying motivation for the overriding of employee privacy rights. The changing nature of the employment relationship, and consequent increasing support of management prerogative, may provide some indication as to why drug testing is continuing.

Scientific Response

Drug testing further can demonstrate that a neutral, scientific response is being employed (Cavanaugh & Prasad, 1994). Sonnenstuhl (1980 in

Cavanaugh & Prasad, 1994) observes that historically management has often introduced a number of policies designed to set work standards, motivate workers and control deviants under the guise of science. Modern day drug testing is historically and ideologically consistent with previous managerial responses to lack of order and rule adherence. It is intended to strengthen management's symbolic control over employees by responding rationally and scientifically.

American sociologist Robert Merton argued in 1947, that science and technology was not benign and neutral as it is often represented (Buchanan & Huczynski, 1985). He argued that the use technology in corporations has significant social implications and, as such, should be regarded as a political tool. The scientific management of Taylorism has been identified as an ideological effort to establish managerial legitimacy and control over the workforce (Littler & Salaman, 1982). The ideology of technocracy with "its attendant insistence on neutrality and inevitability of modern, scientific, rational technologies and social structures" is said to have significantly influenced employees' attitudes (Littler & Salaman, 1982, p. 258). The notion that management uses calculated and ordered activities to "technologize," and thus "prematurely colonize," potentially sensitive activities has been explored in alternate contexts (see Power, 1991 on auditing and Livesey, 2002 on sustainable development).

Scientific and rational language is used in organizational discourse in order to form arguments in a manner as to make it hard them rebut or undermine by presenting them as "objective" or "fact" and, by inference, fair and rational (Livesey, 2002; Potter & Wetherell, 1994). Managers may be able to manipulate employees through the use of science and technology by appealing to the technological determinist argument "We have to do this because the technology demands it." Consequently, technological determinism is often used to justify unpopular management decisions (Buchanan & Huczynski, 1985, p. 243).

Moral Legitimation

The prevalence of drug testing has further been strengthened out of concern for maintaining the organization's reputation, as no organization wants to be perceived as being "soft on drugs" (Rothman, 1988). The moral legitimacy of an organization is understood as the acceptability of the organization, the product it supplies and the manner in which the product is created, as to whether its activities promote social welfare. Moral legitimacy "reflects the positive normative evaluation of an organization and its activities" based on "judgments about whether the activity is "the right thing to do'" (Suchman, 1995, p. 589). Hence, the moral legitimacy of an organization is based to a large extent on the projected image or reputation of that organization. Legitimacy is not considered a characteristic of the organization per se but rather a measure of societal perceptions of the adequacy of corporate behavior compared to societal expectation of corporate activity (Nasi, Nasi, Phillips, & Zyglidopoulos, 1997).

Organizations seek to influence stakeholders' behavior by demonstrating that they are morally legitimate. Organizational activities such as drug testing are undertaken to legitimate the organization in the eyes of its constituents and stakeholders (Cavanaugh & Prasad, 1994). Organizational responsiveness to social problems such as drug use can be understood as strategically appealing to stakeholders to further the interests of the company (Goodpaster, 1991). In this pursuit of maximizing shareholder value, community perceptions of zero tolerance against drugs are incorporated into the organization's own stance, translated into drug testing practices. The organization is seen to be reflecting and supporting the community's values.

There is corporate peer pressure to be perceived as responsive to drug issues (Rothman, 1988). This sense of corporate peer pressure echoes Aldrich (1979, p. 265 in DiMaggio & Powell, 1983) who argued that among "the major factors that organizations must take into account are other organizations." Organizations compete not just for resources and customers, but also on the basis of political power and institutional legitimacy and social acceptance.

Furthermore, when one organization publicly takes this stance many others are likely to follow. This process of homogenization is consistent with DiMaggio and Powell's (1983) concept of institutional isomorphism. Hawley (1968 in DiMaggio & Powell, 1983) describes isomorphism as a constraining process which forces one unit in a population to resemble other units that face the same set of environmental conditions. DiMaggio and Powell's (1983) description of mimetic isomorphic processes is consistent with the conditions surrounding drug testing. They claim uncertainty is a powerful force that encourages imitation. When the environment creates symbolic uncertainty, organizations tend to model themselves on other organizations. Isomorphism may explain why so many organizations continue to adopt drug testing procedures.

CONCLUSION

This chapter has addressed the question of why drug testing continues to be used in workplaces. Following a review of the traditional arguments it is concluded that the moral arguments against drug testing outweigh those in favor of drug testing. We concur with Moore's argument (1989), that the moral considerations regarding drug testing render the economic considerations irrelevant. Despite this, as she argues, drug testing is still not able to be morally justified. It is unnecessary and wrong to impinge on the privacy rights of individuals if doing so will not necessarily ensure the health and safety of others and, indeed, if there exists morally less hazardous alternatives.

What then is the attraction for employers to drug test? Two related alternatives have been posited. One explanation is that by focusing blame on individual employees for socially unacceptable drug use, the spotlight is drawn away from the contributing role of the employer which may in fact cause and sustain such deviant behavior. These might include the imposition of intense rosters and long hours, alienation, high pressure, the stress of job insecurity, poor working conditions, and the lack of adequate training and supervision. Indeed, these factors may have been complicit in creating a problem for the employee in the first place. The second explanation is that in an environment where traditional forms of control may not be effective, managers may seek more abstract and symbolic forms of control. Drug testing may provide symbolic control through a number of mechanisms. A common theme in these alternative explanations is that drug testing allows management to "seize the moral high ground" (Moore, 2000, p. 701).

REFERENCES

ACLU. 2002. Drug Testing: An Overview: American Council of Civil Liberties. http://www.aclu.org/DrugPolicy/DrugPolicy.cfm?ID=10997&c=79.

Allsop, S., Phillips, M., & Calogero, C. (Eds.). 2001. *Drugs and Work: Responding to Alcohol and Other Drug Problems in Australian Workplaces*. Melbourne: IP Communications Pty Ltd.

Allsop, S., & Pidd, K. 2001. The Nature of Drug-Related Harm in the Workplace. In S. Allsop, M. Phillips, & C. Calogero (Eds.), *Drugs and Work: Responding to Alcohol and Other Drug Problems in Australian Workplaces*. Melbourne: IP Communications Pty Ltd.

Ames, G. G., J.W. 1999. Alcohol Availability and Workplace Drinking: Mixed Method Analysis. *Journal of Studies of Alcohol, 60*(3), 383–393.

Buchanan, D. A., & Huczynski, A. A. 1985. *Organisational Behaviour.* London: Prentice Hall.

Buckley, S. 2000. *Drugs and alcohol—An issue for the coal industry.* Paper presented at the Queensland Mining Industry Health and Safety Conference.

Cavanaugh, J. M., & Prasad, P. 1994. Drug testing as symbolic managerial action: In response to "A case against workplace drug testing". *Organization Science, 5*(2), 267–271.

Coleman, S., & SaratChandran, P. 2004. Workplace Privacy Options Paper. Melbourne: Victorian Law Reform Commission.

Comer, D. 1994. A case against workplace drug testing. *Organization Science, 5*(2), 259–266.

Cranford, M. 1998. Drug testing and the right to privacy: Arguing the ethics of workplace drug testing. *Journal of Business Ethics, 17*(16), 1805–1815.

DeCieri, H., Kramer, R., Noe, R., Hollenbeck, H. R., Gerhart, B., & Wright, P. M. 2003. *Human Resource Management in Australia.* Sydney: McGraw Hill.

DesJardine, J. R., & Duska, R. F. 2001. Drug testing in employment. In T. L. Beauchamp, & N. E. Bowie (Eds.), *Ethical Theory and Business,* 6th ed. New Jersey: Prentice Hall.

DesJardins, J. R., & McCall, J. J. 1990. *Contemporary issues in business ethics.* Belmont, CA: Wadsworth Publishing Company.

DiMaggio, P. J., & Powell, W. W. 1983. The iron cage revisited: Institutional isomorphism and collective rationality in organizational fields. *American Sociological Review, 48*(2), 147–160.

Flynn, G. 1999. How to Prescribe Drug Testing. *Workforce, 78*(1), 107.

Friedman, M. 1970. The social responsibility of business is to increase profit, *The New York Times Magazine.*

Goodpaster, K. E. 1991. Business Ethics and Stakeholder Analysis. *Business Ethics Quarterly, 1*(1), 53–73.

Greenburg, E., & Greenburg, S. 1995. Work Alienation and Problem Alcohol Behavior. *Journal of Health and Social Behavior, 36*(1), 83–102.

Hartman, L. P. 2005. Technology and ethics: Privacy in the workplace. In A. Gini (Ed.), *Case Studies in Business Ethics.* Upper Saddle River, NJ, USA: Pearsons Education.

Hartwell, T. D., Steele, P. D., French, M. T., & Rodman, N. E. 1996. Prevalence of drug testing in the workplace. *Monthly Labour Review, 19*(11), 35–42.

HCLD. 1999. Drug screening in the workplace: Rationale and guidelines. Hartford CT: Hartford Company Loss Control Department.

Hoffman, J., & Larison, C. 1998. Drugs and the Workplace Report. Chicago: National Opinion Research Center University of Chicago.

Holland, P. 2003. Case-study: Drug testing in the Australian mining industry. *Surveillance and Society, 1*(2), 204–209.

Holland, P., & Wickham, M. 2002. Drug testing in the workplace: Unravelling the issues. *Journal of Occupational Health Safety—Australia New Zealand, 18*(1), 55–59.

Jardine-Tweedie, L., & Wright, P. C. 1998. Workplace drug testing: avoid the testing addiction. *Journal of Managerial Psychology, 13*(8), 534–543.

Khan, Z. U., Chawla, S. K., & Cianciolo, S. T. A. 1995. Ethics of drug testing: What are workers attitudes? *Business Forum,* Summer/Fall, 17–20.

Knott, S. 2003. Shorten out of touch with current approach to drug and alcohol issues in the workplace, *Media Release.* Melbourne: Australian Mines and Metals Association. http://www.amma.org.au/publications/Shorten's%20opposition %20to%20random%20drug%20and%20alcohol%20testing_DRAFT.pdf.

Littler, C. R., & Salaman, G. 1982. Bravermania and beyond: Recent theories of labour process. *Sociology, 16*(2), 251–269.

Livesey, S. M. 2002. The discourse of the middle ground. *Management Communications Quarterly, 15*(3), 313–349.

MacDonald, S., Wells, S., & Fry, R. 1993. The limitations of drug screening in the workplace. *International Labour Review, 132*(1), 92–113.

Maltby, L. 1987. Why drug testing is a bad idea, *Inc.*, 152.

Maltby, L. L. 1999. Drug Testing—A Bad Investment, 1–27. New York: American Civil Liberties Union.

Midford, R. 2001. The Nature and Extent of Drug-Related Harm in the Workplace. In S. Allsop, M. Phillips, & C. Calogero (Eds.), *Drugs and Work: Responding to Alcohol and Other Drug Problems in Australian Workplaces.* Melbourne: IP Communications Pty Ltd.

Moore, A. 2000. Employee monitoring and computer technology: Evaluative surveillance v. privacy. *Business Ethics Quarterly, 10*(3), 697–709.

Moore, J. 1989. Drug testing and corporate responsibility: The "ought implies can" argument. *Journal of Business Ethics, 8*(4), 279–287.

Nasi, J., Nasi, S., Phillips, N., & Zyglidopoulos, S. 1997. The evolution of corporate social responsiveness. *Business and Society, 36*(3), 296–321.

Nolan, J. 2000. Stuffed or stoned, *Workers Online.* Sydney: Labour Council of NSW. <http://workers.labor.net.au/71/c_historicalfeature_drugs.html>.

Normand, J., Lempert, R. O., & O'Brien, C. P. 1994. *Under the Influence? Drugs and the American Work Force.* Washington D.C: National Academy Press.

Oliver, H. 2002. Email and internet monitoring in the workplace: Information privacy and contracting out. *The Industrial Law Journal, 31*(4), 321–352.

Osterloh, J., & Becker, C. 1990. Chemical Dependency and Drug Testing in the Workplace. *Western Journal of Medicine, 152*(2), 506–513.

Persson, A. J., & Hansson, S. O. 2003. Privacy at work—Ethical criteria. *Journal of Business Ethics, 42*(1), 59–70.

Pfeffer, J. 1981. Management as Symbolic Action: The Creation and Maintenance of Organizational Paradigms. In L. L. Cummings, & B.A.Straw (Eds.), *Research in Organizational Behavior, 3*, 1–52. Greenwich: JAI Press.

Potter, J., & Wetherell, M. 1994. Analyzing Discourse. In A. Bryman, & R. G. Burgess (Eds.), *Analyzing Qualitative Data*: Routledge.

Power, M. 1991. Auditing and environmental expertise: Between protest and professionalisation. *Accounting, Auditing and Accountability Journal, 4*(3), 30–42.

Redeker, J., & Segal, J. 1989. Profits Low? Your Employees May Be High! *Personnel, 66*(6), 72–77.

Richmond, R., Heather, N., Holt, P., & Hu, W. 1992. Workplace policies and programs for tobacco, alcohol and other drugs in Australia. Canberra: AGPS.

Rothman, M. 1988. Random drug testing in the workplace: Implications for human resource management. *Business Horizons*, March/April, 23–27.

Seeman, M., & Seeman, A. Z. 1992. Life Strains, Alienation and Drinking Behaviour. Alcoholism. *Clinical and Experimental Research, 16,* 199–205.

Shepard, E., & Clifton, T. 1998. Drug Testing: Does it really improve labor productivity? *Working USA,* 76.

Sternberg, E. 1997. The defects of stakeholder theory. *Corporate Governance: An International Review, 5*(1), 3–10.

Suchman, M. C. 1995. Managing legitimacy: Strategic and institutional approaches. *Academy of Management Review, 20*(3), 571–610.

Trice, H. M., & Sonnenstuhl, W. J. 1990. On the Construction of Drinking Norms in Work Organisations. *Journal of Studies in Alcohol, 51*(3).

Wagner DeCew, J. 1994. Drug testing: Balancing privacy and public safety. *Hastings Center Report, 24*(2), 17–23.

Wall, P. S. 1992. Drug Testing in the Workplace: An Update. *Journal of Applied Business Research, 8*(2), 127–132.

CHAPTER 9

THE PERSISTENCE
OF SEXUAL HARASSMENT

Nancy Hauserman
University of Iowa

INTRODUCTION

In 1984, I served as chairperson for a University panel charged with investigating claims of sexual harassment brought by a professor, Dr. Jean Jew. Our committee was to determine whether the series of incidents described by Dr. Jew over several years had in fact taken place and, if so, to suggest a remedy. After weeks of investigation, and hearing testimony from dozens of witnesses both on and off campus, our committee was unanimous in its findings. We found the events Dr. Jew described had occurred. These incidents included: denigrating graffiti around campus, faculty and students spreading rumors around the world about an alleged sexual relationship between Dr. Jew and the then-chairperson of her department, dozens of anonymous letters to Dr. Jew and other University administrators, stalking by various faculty and Dr. Jew having been called "a whore" in front of hundreds of students in her large lecture class.

Over a period of years, Dr. Jew had complained to various University administrators about her mistreatment. Eventually, at the threat of litigation, the University convened the committee I chaired. In spite of our unequivo-

Human Resource Management Ethics, pages 181–194
Copyright © 2006 by Information Age Publishing
All rights of reproduction in any form reserved.

cal findings and our support for Dr. Jew's allegations, The University chose to ignore our report and our relatively uncomplicated and inexpensive suggestions for remedying the situation. In response to the University's continued inaction, Dr. Jew brought a lawsuit against the University.

In finding for Dr. Jew, the judge issued a strongly worded decision, criticizing the University for its failure to respond to the sexual harassment claims (*Jew v. University of Iowa*, 1990). Astoundingly, the University announced it would appeal the decision until a public outcry by University faculty and staff caused them to withdraw the appeal.

At the time, as we conducted our investigation, I remember being amazed and appalled by the University's apparent inaction over a period of years. (see Chamallas 1994 for a similar inquiry). I wondered then why our top management did not respond to the complaints of ongoing, obvious, and egregious sexual harassment. Aside from the obvious personal costs, physically and emotionally, to Dr. Jew and some of her colleagues, hundreds of hours were spent by people either creating or exacerbating the hostile environment or responding to it; hours that were not being spent in productive teaching, learning, and research. What could possibly explain the tolerance for such bad behavior?

In the ensuing years, I have worked as an expert witness on court cases, helped write the sexual harassment policy for my University and advised many other campuses and business about their sexual harassment policies. I do sexual harassment training and have served as our University's Ombudsperson, handling conflicts including sexual harassment for students, staff, and faculty. In sum, I have spent a great deal of time working in, and thinking about, sexual harassment and, frankly, I remain puzzled. I am puzzled about why sexual harassment continues to be such a persistent problem in the workplace—despite federal and state laws, the proliferation of corporate policies, thousands of lawsuits, many of which are successful, and a fair amount of research suggesting enormous costs to businesses that allow sexual harassment.

That sexual harassment is a persistent problem seems clear. In fiscal year 2004, there were 13,136 charges of sexual harassment filed with the EEOC, and state and local Fair Employment Practices agencies. Although this figure is down from 15,889 in fiscal year 1997 and 15, 836 in fiscal year 2000, it nonetheless suggests a substantial problem (EEOC, 2005).

Simply put, my thesis is this: sexual harassment persists either (1) because people really do not care about it or, (2) as a marginally less depressing explanation, they care more about other things. Both of these explanations are likely compounded or confounded by our insistence on thinking about sexual harassment as something done only by individuals (e.g., bad boys) in isolated situations in the organization rather than thinking about this as a systemic problem of the corporation—a deep and enduring corporate culture. For purposes of this chapter, I focus on men harassing women since that is overwhelmingly the most prevalent form of harassment in the United States today. I also focus on corporations that tolerate sexual harassment, though I am aware of a number of corporations that have taken steps to eradicate the same. My conclusion is that only if corporations decide to prioritize the value of respecting employees and seriously work to create and maintain a culture that reflects that value, can we then reduce if not eradicate sexual harassment in the workplace.

I begin with a brief overview of several important U.S. Supreme Court cases. These developments are particularly relevant as they underscore the need to pay attention to the reduction of sexual harassment. I will then posit an explanation for the persistence of sexual harassment. Finally, I offer some suggestions for minimizing the occurrence of sexual harassment and maximizing a respectful workplace in a healthy corporate culture.

A VIEW FROM THE TOP

In 1998, in a series of decisions, the U.S. Supreme Court offered employers an opportunity to successfully defend themselves in many sexual harassment cases. In *Burlington Industries, Inc. v. Kimberly Ellerth (1998)* and *Beth Ann Faragher v. City of Boca Raton (1998)* the Court determined that, absent a claim of sexual harassment by a supervisor where the harassment resulted in a tangible negative employment action (*Ellerth*, 1998, p.765), employers could offer an affirmative defense to the claim of sexual harassment. The Court held that where no tangible job action is taken against the victim of sexual harassment (e.g., the victim was not fired or denied a job or promotion), an employer may prove by a preponderance of evidence that it had taken reasonable steps to prevent and correct the harassment, and that the victim-employee did not avail him or herself of any preventive or corrective opportunities provided by the employer or that the employee did not try to avoid harm by some other method. In essence, the Court ruled that most victims of sexual harassment must at least give the employer a chance to remedy the situation before seeking refuge in the courts.

The 1998 decisions of the U.S. Supreme Court allowed employers to raise an affirmative defense to liability or damages. Again, the defense has two requisite elements: (1) the employer must show it "exercised reasonable care to prevent and correct promptly any sexually harassing behavior" (*Ellerth*, 1998, p. 765), and (2) that the victim employee "unreasonably failed to take advantage of any preventive or corrective opportunities provided by the employer" or to otherwise avoid harm (*Ellerth*, 1998, p.765). The Court added that while it was not absolutely necessary that an employer show that it had a sexual harassment policy in place, the existence or absence of such a policy would go to the employer's ability to prove the first prong of the affirmative defense. The Court stated that, assuming the supervisor's harassment did not result in a tangible negative employment action for the employee, the existence of an adequate complaint procedure coupled with a complaining employee's failure to use the same, would normally be sufficient to prove the second prong of the defense.

For employers, these decisions significantly broadened the means of defending a sexual harassment case. Prior to 1998, defenses to sexual harassment largely turned around employers attempting to show either that the behaviors had not in fact occurred or, if they did, they were welcomed by the alleged victim. The fact that an employee did not complain about the behavior to the employer might be introduced to suggest the welcomeness of the behavior, i.e. if she really minded the comments about her body or her sex life, she would have done everything she could to get the behavior to stop including reporting it to the employer. Similarly, a showing by the employer that it tried to stop sexual harassment in its workplace by creating a sexual harassment policy, and conducting sexual harassment training for employees might have had little bearing on a judge or jury finding on a particular claim of sexual harassment. With the announcement of the decisions in *Ellerth* and *Faragher*, the Court recognized that employers may be making a good faith effort to deal with sexual harassment and that employees seeking relief in the courts must show that they availed themselves of their employer's remedies.

Of course, not all employers do make good faith efforts to at least minimize if not eradicate sexual harassment. Many employers still do not have effective policies and procedures in place to deal with complaints of sexual harassment. Many employers still do not take claims of sexual harassment seriously. Indeed, in the *Faragher* case, the Court found that, although the City of Boca Raton had a sexual harassment policy, they failed to disseminate it. The Court also said the City had a poor record of addressing complaints: they kept no records of the complaints nor did they assure victims that they could by-pass their supervisors to file a complaint when necessary. The Court said this would not constitute reasonable care taken by the employer; again, the first prong of the affirmative defense available to the City.

While these two cases dealt with sexual harassment by a supervisor toward his or her employee, it is possible for an employer to be held liable for co-worker harassment if the determination is that the negligence of the company permitted the harassment to occur. If an employer does not have a written anti-harassment policy and a formal procedure for enforcement, it may be negligent.

But avoiding liability using the affirmative defense is not only possible but fairly straightforward. Courts have found in favor of companies that had, and used, grievances processes and where the policies and procedures were widely distributed and well-known to employees. Again, the test for the Court seems based on an inquiry about whether policy and procedures exist, are known to employees, and are actually followed in a timely manner.

I use these decisions from the U.S. Supreme Court to highlight the legal importance of employers responding affirmatively to sexual harassment by aggressively developing and implementing policies and programs to minimize its occurrence and respond effectively to complaints. In light of the increased legal incentive for businesses to respond to sexual harassment, it is especially curious that sexual harassment remains so prevalent. I use these cases to raise the critical underlying issue: why does sexual harassment continue to persist at the level it does?

EXPLANATION OF PERSISTENCE

Again, I suggest two reasons for the persistence of sexual harassment: (1) people simply fail to see sexual harassment as a serious ethical issue or (2) the cost or importance of stopping such misbehavior competes with other values, and ultimately, stopping sexual harassment simply does not emerge as the dominant priority.

Sexual Harassment as an Ethical Issue

Clearly, sexual harassment does not seem to be an issue, ethical or otherwise, for some people. As I shared my thoughts for this chapter with colleagues, several people commented that I was, perhaps, making a big deal out of a simple question: why does sexual harassment persist? One colleague, a male attorney, suggested that sexual harassment simply is not an issue that most men and some women care about. Instead, they think most of it is only natural and acceptable behavior. This "natural behavior" is probably what Sandra Tangri describes as a possible theoretical model for sexual harassment, a

> ..."*natural/biological model*" [that] interprets sexual harassment as a consequence of sexual interactions between people, either attributing a stronger sex drive to men than to women (i.e., men need to engage in aggressive sexual behavior) or describing sexual harassment as part of the "game" between sexual equals. (Levy & Paludi, 1997, p. 56)

Levy and Paludi suggest that men's need to engage in aggressive sexual behavior

...is one of the major ways of proving their masculinity, especially among those men who feel some sense of powerlessness in their lives...Sexualizing a professional relationship may be the one way that such a man can still prove his masculinity...Thus, sexual harassment is not so much a deviant act as an overconforming act of the masculine role in this culture." (Levy & Paludi, 1997, p. 54)

But sexual harassment is not just about men being interested in women (or women being interested in men, or same sex interest). Instead, it is about the misuse of power. My sense is that when someone says that sexual harassment is "natural," at best they are referring to a physical attraction between people, which is qualitatively different than sexual harassment.

Certainly sexual harassment usually involves actions between the sexes. And it is usually is done by men towards women. In this way, sexual harassment reflects a dominant sexist attitude in U.S. society and in most of the world. Several studies support the conclusion that the biggest factor in sexual harassment is men's sexist attitudes (Saal, 1996). Sexist attitudes should not be confused with flirting or sexual interest. Even men who may misperceive women's actions and wrongly interpret them as sexually provocative do not necessarily sexually harass. Indeed, research suggests, that as many of us have long suspected, it is a specific kind of sexist person who engages in sexual harassment.

Perhaps the reference to "natural behavior" is really meant to refer to what one writer suggests is historically and socially embedded misbehavior.

It is shaped by social motivations in the broadest sense. People bring with them into the organization expectations about work or various gender, class and other identities that predispose them to behave or misbehave in particular ways. For example, those who sexually harass their fellow employees have been affected by a wider social construction of masculinity and femininity. But it still requires a *context* [italics added] to create opportunities or shape the form and content of action."(Ackroyd, et al. 1999, p. 129)

The "context" referred to here is the corporate culture. I will address that culture later in this chapter.

The sanctioned misbehavior, sexism, is linked with power, and in our society, men still have the power. "Even in supposedly 'desexualized' organizations, the rules are still made by men" (Ackroyd, et al. 1999, p.124). Barbara Gutek argues that expectations arising from the female role of subordinate sex object and male role of dominant aggressor are carried into work (Gutek as cited in Ackroyd & Thompson, 1999, p. 125). Cockburn writes that "Men's power in the extra-organizational world, in the family, the state and civil society, enters the workplace with them and gives even the most junior man a degree of sexual authority relative even to senior women" (Cockburn as cited in Ackroyd & Thompson, 1999, p. 124).

Once we recognize that power concepts are carried from one world into the other–from home and the extra-organizational society into the corporation, "it becomes impossible to operate with the concept of separate public and private spheres" (Ackroyd & Thompson, 1999, p. 125). In other words, there is no basis for believing that people will leave their sexist attitudes outside the corporate door.

In addition to the effects of sexism, most employees do not see workplace sexuality as a serious problem unless it clearly disrupts of threatens them (Gutek as cited in Ackroyd & Thompson, 1999, p. 138). And although it might seem clear to some of us that we are all threatened by the lack of respect shown to any employee, such indirect harm may not move most people to action. If sexual harassment does not happen to them, their family, or a member of their work team, it remains too distant to really be a pressing ethical concern.

In particular, since most managers are male, sexual harassment may be too personally distant for them to take action. They may tolerate or trivialize misbehavior by other men; especially what is often considered to be homosocial behavior—horseplay, jokes between same sex individuals–behavior that may well constitute hostile environment. Managers may see this kind of sexually harassing activity as localized behaviors and not so disruptive or important to deal with (Ackroyd & Thompson, 1999). In sum, sexual harassment may persist because it is not considered an ethical issue that requires attention. It is simply not viewed as particularly important.

Competing Values

A second explanation for the persistence of sexual harassment focuses on competing values. To the extent that there are competing values in the workplace, the elimination of sexual harassment is largely given short shrift.

I will consider three competing values: (1) economics, (2) status quo, and (3) loyalty. This is not an extensive list of competing values. The point is this: other values dominate or receive priority over the elimination of sexual harassment. These three values, economics, status quo, and loyalty, seem to me to be dominant corporate values generally.

The Value of Economics

Some people would assert that maintaining bottom line profitability (or however it is phrased, e.g., shareholders' interest) is a more crucial value than addressing sexual harassment. But of course, profitability is not unrelated to sexual harassment. Sexual harassment is very costly. Even ten years ago, sexual harassment was estimated to cost the federal government at least $267.3 million a year (Knapp, 1996). The economic costs of sexual harassment include lost work time of the harasser, the victim, and co-workers; various insurance costs and, especially, employee turnover [Minnesota Advocates, 2003]. Essentially, even if one maintains that economic issues should take priority, and maybe *especially* if economics ranks high, eliminating sexual harassment should be of critical importance (Raver & Gelfand, 2005, p. 395). Moreover, if one argues that certain kinds of economic issues should be prioritized, given that costs of sexual harassment directly or indirectly affect all economic issues, valuing the eradication of sexual harassment should be integral to increasing bottom line results. Francis Achampong writes, "Prevention of sexual harassment losses involves preventing sexual harassment from taking place and taking prompt and effective remedial action upon becoming aware of harassment" (Achampong, 1999).

Maintaining the Status Quo

A second value competing with the reduction and eradication of sexual harassment is the maintenance of the status quo and resistance to change. It is in many ways similar to the first reason I suggested for the persistence of sexual harassment—sexism. While we might resist setting up status quo as an ethical value, it certainly appears that many people work very hard to hold on to "the way things have always done," even if they have not been done well. Many people place great value on continuity. So, if they have always behaved in certain ways, e.g., certain ways of treating women, they persist in those behaviors even when those behaviors are defined as illegal activities that constitute sexual harassment. Of course, it must be noted that ethical values do not necessarily flow from legal issues. For example, simply categorizing an activity or behavior as illegal will not always make people see the action as an ethical issue. Indeed, if people respond only to the legal duty they are unlikely to rank the behavior as an ethical issue and will not place it as a high priority when competing ethical issues are at stake. Even if sexual harassment is considered to be a problem, people must value the cessation of the behavior and take action. Bowes-Sperry and Powell note that "Labeling an incident of social-sexual behavior as sexual harassment...does not in itself constitute an act of ethical behavior. Individuals must next make a judgment regarding the behavior that places moral concerns above all others and establish moral intentions" (Bowes-Sperry & Powell, 1999, p. 107). Of course, law may be used to try to force priorities by making people behave certain ways regardless of whether they classify the action as ethical, but, at least in the case of sexual harassment, the law alone has not been successful in changing behavior. Even with federal and state laws, many corporate policies and many lawsuits, sexual harassment clearly persists.

Loyalty

The third value that competes with stopping sexual harassment is loyalty. Here, loyalty is often interpreted as perpetuating a stigma against tattling. To the extent that people see tattling as bad and see stopping sexual harassment as tattling, they will value silence above action. Collegiality is a highly valued component part of loyalty. Acting to stop sexual harassment may disrupt or destroy support at least support of certain colleagues. Although in a different and more respectful company culture, loyalty should include protecting other employees and the corporation by stopping sexual harassment.

SUGGESTIONS FOR CHANGE

None of this prioritization takes place in a vacuum. It is not just a matter of how an individual prioritizes ethical values. Individual employees act within in a culture. Here I am specifically concerned with the culture of the organization. Organizational culture and climate is defined as "shared perceptions, among members of a relevant group, department, or organizations, of contingencies between specific behaviors and their consequences, both private and public, positive and negative" (Hulin, et al., 1999, p. 133). "For sexual exploitation to occur repeatedly, facilitative local norms *must* exist" (Pryor, et al., 1997, cited in Hulin, et al., 1999, p. 131).

Assuming there are competing values, it seems fair to ask whether the elimination of sexual harassment should take priority. But is it appropriate or sufficient to label the value at issue here as "the elimination of sexual harassment?" Are we not really considering the value of respect for people, with sexual harassment as a subset of that larger value? The question then would be whether respect for employees should be the dominant value. Would we really permit corporate culture to be so sanguine about relegating respect for people to a lower rung? I certainly do not mean that by renaming and reframing the value, the problem of sexual harassment would necessarily go away. Nor does it mean that respect for people would necessarily become the dominant value. Nonetheless, I think that as a society, we would be less casual about tolerating let alone accepting the behaviors if they were subsumed under the umbrella value of respect.

In the last few years, I have incorporated this broader value, respect for people, into my training on sexual harassment. Indeed, although I cover the basics of sexual harassment law, the crux of my sessions involves the use of various hypothetical situations that are designed to push the audience beyond simply considering whether or not something constitutes sexual harassment. My goal is to encourage participants to think about whether the behavior is of a respectful nature and how, as managers, they can respond respectfully. This approach successfully minimizes both the defensive reactions often immediately apparent when sexual harassment is considered and the anxiety producing need to categorize the situation as sexual harassment or not and then ignore behaviors which do not appear to constitute unlawful behavior. Instead, participants can easily and comfortably label behavior as disrespectful and understand the need for some appropriate response without bogging down in the legalities of the situation. Obviously, I do not mean to imply that it is not important for people to understand what constitutes prohibited behavior, but frankly, such a focus misses the larger issue and avoids important underlying ethical issues about treating people with respect.

It is this treating people with respect that differentiates many businesses. Let me return to one of my opening caveats—that while I focused on corporations that appear to permit or tolerate sexual harassment, some corporations actually take the eradication of sexual harassment seriously. Why is this? Because in their corporate culture, the primary value is respect for individuals and concern about the responsible use of power. It is unlikely that these corporations are less concerned with the bottom line. Rather, these are the "holistic thinkers," people who can appreciate the complete impact and myriad costs involved with tolerating sexual harassment.

If corporate culture is the key, then the challenge is how to go about changing the culture. Some changes seem obvious; if culture is determined by observing how others around us behave, then, for Corporate America, this translates into how employees see their leaders behave. It means that the ways in which expectations are communicated and the extent to which people are held accountable will establish the cultural norms. Linda Trevino says that for better or worse, most managers reason at conventional levels of cognitive moral development. Much like children, they engage in social referencing: they look to others for cues about what is right and wrong behavior (Trevino, 1986, cited in Bowes-Sperry & Powell, 1999, p. 114). Cardy and Selvarajan suggest that "People need to see examples of good and bad levels of ethical performance and develop an operational understanding of ethical conduct in the organization" (Cardy & Selvarajan, Chapter 4 in this volume). As with our children, setting clear standards about appropriate and inappropriate behavior is critical.

Another key to ensuring or modeling good behavior is to be sure that we are choosing principled people as managers. Principled people are ones guided by their own beliefs and moral integrity, and they are more likely to take the perspective of target of sexual harassment (Bowes-Sperry & Powell, 1999, p. 114). They have a lower threshold for defining the severity of consequences, thus increasing the perceived magnitude of consequences of sexual harassment and foreseeing future consequences arising from behavior.

To the extent that the tolerance of sexual harassment results from what might be, at best, immature ethical development, business would be well-served to establish and strong rules with enforced consequences. If sexual harassment is not to be tolerated, say so clearly. Be sure all employees know well what is meant by sexual harassment, and what will occur should they engage in this prohibited behavior. Business must be sure as well that behavior they want to see from employees is modeled for them consistently at all levels.

And while clear consequences are important, punishing people for bad behavior is not enough. "[C]ontrolling or adapting to misbehaviour involves an essentially passive attitude to the phenomenon itself, while using sanctions, rewards and rules to set the parameters of acceptability"(Ackroyd, 1999, p.96). Businesses could have real incentives for positive behavior, e.g., reward managers who stop sexual harassment in their units.

Certainly there is a need to be clear about what constitutes sexual harassment, or as I suggested earlier, a need to get people to focus on whether behavior reflects respect for people. I believe that the latter is generally less fraught with ambiguity and so is more easily a shared perception. Clarity about what behavior is acceptable is critical, particularly if, as Bowes-Sperry and O'Leary-Kelly suggest, observers are less likely to get involved, for example, report or tell someone to stop behavior that is ambiguous (Bowes-Sperry & O'Leary-Kelly, 2005).

We need to "...shift from thinking about sexual harassment as involving a group of bad men doing bad things to weak women, to the modification of features of the organization that shape behavior and contribute to denigrating, abusive workplace" (Cleveland & McNamara, 1996, p.228). Sexual harassment is not an interpersonal problem It is not about sex. It is not private behavior. It is a cultural problem. The eradication of sexual harassment must be viewed as a question of organizational culture, organizational effectiveness, and organizational behavior.

Finally, a change from a corporate culture that tolerates or supports sexual harassment to one in which such behaviors are clearly not the norm or tolerated, will encourage employees to consider issues beyond the specific targets of sexual harassment; to step up and stop the behavior. As Bowes-Sperry and O'Leary-Kelly suggest, organizations that regard reporting or otherwise intervening to stop sexual harassment "as a positive action on behalf of the organization, rather an as an act of dissent," are more likely to have third party observers intervene to stop unwanted behavior and so, necessarily, have less unwanted behavior in the workplace (Bowes-Sperry & O'Leary-Kelly, 2005, p.300). Moreover, they caution that in organizations where a culture of nonintervention prevails, "this can be a perilous condition" (Bowes-Sperry & O'Leary-Kelly, 2005, p.303) that in fact, "…may create an environment that encourages sexual harassment" (Bowes-Sperry & O'Leary-Kelly, 2005, p.304).

CONCLUSION

Perhaps as human resource professionals, consultants, trainers and teachers, we can consider our responses to the frequent lament of people who say they do not know how to behave anymore, that they do not know what is right or even what they can and cannot do. We can interpret what they really mean is that they are confused by the absence of an integrated message between what appears to be an ethical value established by regulation and a tolerance of behavior allowed by corporate culture.

Last year, I flew to Sweden on a flight with several senior U.S. managers. As soon as the plane left Chicago, they began harassing the stewardesses, making comments, grabbing them and engaging in sexually harassing behavior. Many of us were appalled and asked them whether they behaved this way in their own companies. Of course not, they told us, but up here in the air, they could be themselves.

Corporations can help with this confusion—they can begin by clearly stating priorities and prioritizing or ranking the values. It sounds good to say values co-exist but values often can exist in conflict with each other. Which value takes priority? How will that decision be made? There is no point in simply stating corporate values. People will come to see sexual harassment as an ethical issue if they understand that there is a high degree of social agreement that the act is evil (Jones, 1991 cited in Bowes-Sperry, et al., 1999).

Sometimes as I read sexual harassment cases or media accounts of sexual harassment, I wonder what would happen if sexual harassment stopped altogether. To a certain degree, I suppose some people would see the end of sexual harassment as a tragic loss of power. In reality, it would really mean that power is used appropriately and that, consistent with the purpose of Title VII, all people would have the potential to succeed in the workplace, free from various forms of discriminatory treatment.

If businesses that assign their human resources departments or hire external consultants to help them write policies and do training were to first establish respect for employees as the top the priority, and create and maintain a corporate culture reflecting that priority, then perhaps instead of wondering about the persistence of sexual harassment, we will begin to see healthy and more profitable businesses.

REFERENCES

Achampong, F. 1999. *Workplace Sexual Harassment Law.* Westport, CT: Quorum Books.

Ackroyd, S. & Thompson, P. 1999. *Organizational Misbehaviour.* London, U.K.: Sage.

Burlington Industries, Inc. v. Kimberly Ellerth, 524 U.S. 742 (1998).

Beth Ann Faragher v. City of Boca Raton, 524 U.S. 775 (1998).

Bowes-Sperry, L. & O'Leary-Kelly, A. 2005. "To act or not to act: The dilemma faced by sexual harassment observers." *The Academy of Management Review.* 30, 288–306.

Bowes-Sperry, L., & Powell, G.N. 1996. Sexual harassment as a moral issue: An ethical decision-making perspective. In M.S. Stockdale (Ed.), *Sexual harassment in the workplace,* vol. 5, (pp. 105–124). Thousand Oaks, CA: Sage.

Cardy, R., & Selvarajan, T.T. 2006. "Beyond Rhetoric and Bureaucracy: Using HRM to Add Ethical Value." In J.R. Deckop (Ed.), *Human resource management ethics,* Information Age.

Chamallas, M. 1994. "Jean Jew's case: Resisting sexual harassment in the academy." *Yale Journal of Law and Feminism, 6,* 71–90.

Cleveland, J. N. & McNamara, K. 1996. Understanding sexual harassment: Contributions from research on domestic violence and organizational change. In M.S. Stockdale. (Ed.), *Sexual Harassment in the Workplace.* Vol. 5, (pp. 217–240). Thousand Oaks, CA: Sage Publications.

Equal Employment Opportunity Commission. (March 2, 2005). Sexual Harassment. Retrieved May 1, 2005, from http://www.eeoc.gov/types/sexual_harassment.html

Hulin, C. L., Fitzgerald, L. F., & Drasgow, F. 1996. Organizational influences on sexual harassment. In Stockdale, Margaret S. (Ed.), *Sexual Harassment in the Workplace.* Vol. 5, (pp. 127–150). Thousand Oaks, CA: Sage Publications.

Jean Y. Jew, M.D. v. The University of Iowa and the Board of Regents of the University of Iowa, 749 F. Supp. 946 (S.D. Iowa, 1990).

Knapp, E. & Kustis, G. A. 1996. "Sexual Harassment and the Bottom Line." In Stockdale, Margaret S. (Ed.), *Sexual Harassment in the Workplace.* Vol. 5, (pp. 199–216). Thousand Oaks, CA: Sage Publications.

Levy, A. C. & Paludi, M. A. 1997. *Workplace Sexual Harassment.* Upper Saddle River, N.J.: Prentice Hall.

Minnesota Advocates for Human Rights (2003, November 1). Effects of sexual harassment. Retrieved May 1, 2005 from http://www.stopvaw.org/Effects_of _Sexual_Harassment.html

Raver, J. & Gelfand, M. (2005). Beyond the individual victim: linking sexual harassment, team processes, and team performance. *The Academy of Management Journal, 48,* 387–400.

Saal, F. E. 1996. Men's misperceptions of women's interpersonal behaviors and sexual harassment. In Stockdale, Margaret S. (Ed.), *Sexual Harassment in the Workplace*. Vol. 5, (pp. 67–84). Thousand Oaks, CA: Sage Publications.

Stockdale, M. S. (Ed.) 1999. *Sexual Harassment in the Workplace.* Vol. 5 Thousand Oaks, CA: Sage Publications.

Trevino, L.K. 1996. Ethical decision making in organizations: A person-situation interactionist model. *Academy of Management Review, 11,* 601–617.

CHAPTER 10

FAIRNESS AND RECIPROCITY

Norms to Enhance the Ethical Quality of Compensation Scholarship and Practice

Edilberto F. Montemayor
Michigan State University

The Ethics literature considers an ethical problem exists whenever one's decisions result in harm for persons who are not involved in making such decisions (Morris, 2004). Accordingly, ethical problems are intrinsic to Compensation strategy and policy decisions, which usually involve changes to the scope and/or the level of financial resources allocated to pay and benefit programs. For example, the decision to increase employee contributions to the cost of health benefits (premiums, deductibles and/or co-pays) results in larger employee expenditures for health-related contingencies that counter pay raises reducing the purchasing power associated with the employees' compensation package.

However, the Compensation literature has been mostly silent regarding the ethical dimension of Compensation strategy and policy decisions. This chapter seeks to motivate a conversation on the ethical aspect of such decisions by taking a rather critical approach arguing the neo-classic Econom-

Human Resource Management Ethics, pages 195–216
Copyright © 2006 by Information Age Publishing
All rights of reproduction in any form reserved.

ics paradigm (called Competitive Markets Economics from here on) dominating Compensation scholarship and practice is ethically deficient. I will use phenomena well established in Competitive Markets Economics to argue the conceptual foundations for Compensation scholarship and practice may result in the expropriation or destruction of financial investments employees made in the firm, and may also result in breaching critical terms in the implicit contract between the firm and its employees.

ORGANIZATIONAL COMPENSATION ETHICS

The ideas in this chapter are based on the general Business Ethics literature and on the growing literatures on Management Ethics and on Human Resource Management Ethics because the literature published to this date has not addressed directly the specific nature and scope of Compensation Ethics.

Ethics concerns identifying what human conduct ought to be by assessing whether, or the degree to which, specific acts or decisions are (morally) right or wrong—see for example Shaw and Barry (2001) and Velasquez (1997). Ethics is important because it provides philosophical criteria for evaluating the degree to which prevailing scholarship and practice are (morally) right or wrong (Beauchamp & Bowie, 2001). Moreover, an Ethics perspective should surface unexamined assumptions that have a critical influence on the ethical quality of scholarship and practice (Treviño & Weaver, 1998; Weaver & Treviño, 1994).

Ethics is essential to good Management scholarship and practice. As Schumann (2001) noted recently, even the most influential scholars in Management and Economics assumed Ethics provides fundamental guidance for managerial decision-making. For example, Peter Drucker argued managers must consider the impact their actions and decisions have on societal well-being (including of course employee well-being). Likewise, Milton Friedman, the much-cited defender of Competitive Markets Economics, stated managers must seek to maximize profits *"while conforming to... ethical custom"* (1970, p. 126).

It is important to recognize there are three distinct but related Ethics levels—Personal, Professional, and Organizational Ethics (Wooten, 2001)—each having its own domain. Personal Compensation Ethics concerns norms for the behavior of Compensation managers and specialists when dealing with other individuals. The so-called "golden rule" (treat others as you wish to be treated) is a very clear example of a relevant Personal Ethics principle with implications for Compensation scholarship and practice. Professional Compensation Ethics concerns behavioral and technical norms applicable to the specialized functions involved in Compensation.

Among others, behavioral norms in Compensation Professional Ethics include the obligation to protect the confidentiality of information entrusted someone because of her participation in Compensation matters (Wiley, 2000). Among others, technical norms in Compensation Professional Ethics include the mandate to ensure that all Compensation policies and their application comply with relevant legislation (Milkovich & Newman, 2005). The third level, Organizational Compensation Ethics concerns norms for Compensation strategy and policy decisions. Unfortunately, there is a serious vacuum in the literature concerning this third Ethics level whose standards could help answer questions such as: "Is it ethical (right) to discontinue retiree health benefits in order to protect the firm's financial performance?", and "Is it ethical (right) to freeze or even cut employee pay in order to secure dividend payouts for the firm's shareholders during high-inflation periods?"

Ethical principles (derived mostly from moral philosophy) are difficult to apply in a practical way to situations and decisions in organizational life (Quinn & Jones, 1995). Classical Ethics theory involves concepts and principles intended to assess whether the conduct of human beings is right or wrong (Phillips & Margolis, 1999), but organizational systems, processes, and behavior generally "defy attempts to apply traditional [Ethical] theory and detached philosophical wisdom" (Barker, 2002, p. 1099). The literature on Business Ethics, including Human Resource Management and Compensation Ethics, is characterized by vague, general guidelines. For example Buckley et al. (2001) recommend that "individuals must be treated equitably with respect to compensation, this includes ensuring perceptions of distributive and procedural *justice* (and) evaluating the *fairness* of the reward system" (p. 20, emphasis added). This sort of guidelines has little value for people making strategy and policy decisions in organizations (Bagley, 2003; Stark, 1993).

Quinn and Jones (1995) suggested Ethics can become as important as the core social science fields of Economics and Psychology, which have considerable influence on Management scholarship, provided ethical analyses are related to concepts and models already used in the Management literature. Thus, a symbiotic blend of Ethics and Management scholarship should promote substantial progress in Management Ethics including Compensation Ethics (Schminke, 1998). As Barker (2002) and Phillips and Margolis (1999) explain, ethical issues in business organizations require an Organizational Ethics theory that acknowledges business organizations exist within a "non-ideal" world (which in our case means that the idealized concept of perfectly competitive spot labor markets seldom applies), recognizes the unique phenomena that occur within business organizations (which in our case would include the contractual nature of employment relationships), and incorporates relevant Ethics norms.

The purpose of this chapter is to motivate a conversation towards an explicit Organizational Ethics for Compensation. The next section presents a summary of my argument for a more ethical framework to guide Compensation scholarship and practice. Each of the two sections that follow concern issues that have been neglected but have major implications for the ethical quality of Compensation scholarship and practice: the dual (trade and investment) economic relationship between the firm and its long-term dedicated employees, and the contractual nature of the relationship between the firm and its long-term dedicated employees. The last two sections present, respectively, a normative framework for improving the ethical quality of Compensation strategy and policy decisions, and a discussion of the framework's implications for Compensation scholars and practitioners.

ARGUMENT SUMMARY

The business firm is a system of economic relationships connecting various types of resource contributors[1] including capital investors, employees, top managers, customers, and suppliers. In order to address Organizational Compensation Ethics, this chapter focuses on three types of resource contributors: capital investors (those whose contribution to the firm is limited to financial resources), long-term dedicated employees (those who have a significant level of seniority in the firm), and top managers (those ultimately responsible for strategic and policy decisions within the firm).

One may distinguish two types of economic relationships between the firm and specific resource contributors: (spot market) trade relationships and investment relationships. The distinction between trade and investment has ethical relevance. Sellers in a (spot market) trade relationship expect to receive a price that reflects the full economic value of their contribution. Therefore, trade exchanges in competitive spot markets are regarded as self-contained in the sense that the parties meet their respective obligations while completing their transaction. In contrast, and because it involves significant risk, investors expect their investment will grow in value and produce a stream of income over time that is consistent with the risk incurred (Haksever, Chaganti & Cook, 2004; Hill & Jones, 1992). Therefore, investment relationships are regarded as open-ended in the sense that the risk inherent in investment relationships creates ownership privileges for investors and fiduciary obligations for those managing such investment (Boatright, 2000b).

As indicated above, the contribution capital investors make to the firm is limited to financial resources. In contrast, and as will be explained below, dedicated employees contribute labor resources but also invest implicitly financial resources in the firm. Both capital investors and dedicated employees establish a repeated-exchange economic relationship with the firm. Repeated-exchange relationships create a "contract" between the parties (Macneil, 1980), a contract that may have explicit and implicit components. These contracts also have ethical relevance because they serve to protect investments made in the firm and establish how various resource contributors will be compensated (Boatright, 2002a).

Top managers have a more complex relationship with the firm. First, top managers are employees. Second, top managers may be (or at least may be treated as) capital investors. Third, top managers serve as agents for those investing in the firm through their strategic decision and policy-making roles. Fourth, top managers serve as financial adjudicators between dedicated employees, capital investors, and themselves. I will ignore the first two elements in the relationship between top managers and the firm for the sake of argument simplicity and to focus on Organizational Compensation Ethics. Top managers serve as agents for those investing in the firm because investors entrust top managers with their respective contributions and because top managers decisions affect the use and value appreciation (or depreciation) of the various resources invested in the firm (Haksever, Chaganti & Cook, 2004; Hill & Jones, 1992). Also, and to the extent that increases in Compensation costs are assumed to reduce firm profits (which is a common assumption in Compensation practice), top managers making Compensation strategy and policy decisions adjudicate financial gains and losses between dedicated employees, capital investors, and themselves. Therefore, top managers are responsible for the ethical consequences of Compensation strategy and policy decisions.

Compensation strategy and policy decisions have an important ethical dimension. These decisions are mostly about changes—changes to the level of financial resources allocated to employee compensation and changes to compensation policies and programs. For example, Compensation strategy includes changes to the employee pay rates, changes to the degree of variability (risk) in employee pay, changes to the scope of employee benefits, changes to employees' contribution to pay for the cost of benefits, and so on. These changes often have significant consequences for employees' lives such as reduced purchasing power, need to dedicate time to a second job, need for other family (household) members to work, and so on. That is, these changes have an ethical dimension because they affect employees who do not have any say in the matter (Hosmer, 1987).

Unfortunately, Compensation scholarship has failed to provide ethical guidance for top managers making Compensation strategy and policy decisions. Compensation scholarship and the resulting practice are ethically deficient because they are based on a spot market transactional view of employment relationships that makes qualitative and unrealistic distinctions concerning the relationship the firm has with its dedicated employees and the relationship the firm has with capital investors. Employees are viewed as "spot market traders" receiving compensation in exchange for work while capital investors are viewed as "investors." This spot market transactional view of employment relationships is ethically deficient because it leads to the expropriation or destruction of significant financial investments that dedicated employees made in the firm and may lead to breaching critical terms in the tacit contract established between the firm and its dedicated employees through their repeated-exchange relationship.

An ethical orientation means intentionally avoiding harm and unfairness to those affected by one's decisions because it is wrong and regardless of the consequences that such approach may have for one's material welfare (Goodpaster, 1991). Accordingly, an ethically-oriented framework for Compensation scholarship and practice should acknowledge dedicated employees make financial investments in the firm, should consider the tacit contract between the firm and its dedicated employees, and should incorporate ethical norms into the process for making decisions about Compensation strategy and policy. The following sections discuss in more detail each of these three issues.

DUAL RELATIONSHIP BETWEEN THE FIRM
AND ITS DEDICATED EMPLOYEES

Competitive Markets Economics dominates Compensation scholarship and practice. The influence of this paradigm on Compensation practice is clear. Compensation professionals often defend questionable actions and decisions on the grounds that these actions and decisions are constrained, even dictated by "the market" (Gerhart & Rynes, 2003). Consider the following ideas from a recent dialogue on Ethics among compensation professionals (WorldatWork, 2002):

> Giving executives much better benefits and compensation packages than those for other employees "is not unethical if it can be shown that it is in fact competitive."

> Ceasing to pay overtime premiums to exempt professional employees, which was a major factor attracting them to the firm, is not unethical if "the market conditions have changed."

As stated above, Compensation scholarship and practice regards employees as spot market traders exchanging labor for compensation while capital investors are regarded as investors. This distinction has major implications for the inherent ethicality of Compensation scholarship and practice.

Spot-market trade does not create any privileges or obligations for the parties involved. It is considered to be short-term and to entail no risk, or at most negligible risk, for the parties involved. Trade exchanges in competitive spot markets are regarded as self-contained in the sense that the parties meet their respective obligations while completing their transaction. Theoretically, spot market trade occurring within competitive markets results in "marginal productivity justice" (c.f. McClelland, 1990), the widespread belief that competitive spot markets produce fair outcomes because the parties trade voluntarily, are well-informed, have equal (or at least comparable) bargaining power, and are paid according to the economic value of their contribution.

In contrast, investment relationships create privileges and obligations for the parties involved. These relationships are considered to be long-term and to entail substantial risks because the resources invested are "locked in" the firm and cannot be withdrawn easily, because there is considerable uncertainty due to an unpredictable future, and because the ultimate value of such investments will depend on the firm's future performance (Boatright, 2002b). Thus, investment relationships are regarded as open-ended in the sense that risk, assumed to be intrinsic to investment relationships, creates ownership privileges for investors and fiduciary obligations for those managing such investment.

In reality, the economic relationship between any individual employee or shareholder and the firm may involve trade and investment. Some individuals—like stock speculators, temporary employees, and contingent employees—only have a spot-market trade relationship with the firm. These individuals are not true investors in the sense ascribed to the term because their short-term relationship with the firm entails minimal (or at most negligible) risk for them. In contrast, others have a dedicated relationship involving a substantial engagement with the firm and the consequent risk. Individuals or institutions that place a substantial portion of their equity in the firm, or own a substantial portion of the firm's accounting capital, are true capital investors. In addition, and to the extent that they accept compensation that is less than the economic value of their contribution, dedicated employees[2] are implicit financial investors in the firm (Etzioni, 1998).

Competitive Markets Economics asserts the price in competitive spot markets equals the economic value of what is traded. Consequently, sellers who accept a lower price than their contribution is economically worth are making a financial investment in the relationship and should expect future benefits. Therefore, dedicated employees make significant, but implicit financial investments in the firm, because they often work for less than the economic value of their contribution (their so-called Marginal Revenue Product). This conclusion is based on two convincing Competitive Markets

Economics explanations for the relationship between pay and seniority that is very common across all sorts of firms and jobs: dedicated employees work under a delayed compensation agreement with the firm and/or dedicated employees invest in firm-specific human capital[3] (Ehrenberg & Smith, 2003).

According to distinguished economist Edward P. Lazear (1995, 1998), many employees work under a delayed compensation scheme in which employees are paid less than they are economically worth early in their career with the firm expecting that they will be paid more than they are economically worth later in their career. Lazear argues such delayed compensation scheme motivates employees to put forth their best effort throughout their careers. More importantly, there is a substantial body of research that supports the existence of this delayed compensation scheme in various occupations and across countries (see for example Barth, 1997; Hutchens, 1989; James & Johnson, 2000).

Additionally, dedicated employees invest in firm-specific human capital. Within Competitive Markets Economics, the theory of human capital provides the best explanation for individual pay differences (Milkovich & Newman, 2005). This theory asserts that a person's stock of work-relevant knowledge, skills, and abilities determines to a great extent the economic value of the individual's contribution. The literature distinguishes two components of a person's human capital: general human capital (such as knowledge and skills acquired through formal education) and firm-specific human capital (such as in-depth knowledge of the firm's products, markets, and customers). Building firm-specific human capital benefits both the firm and its dedicated employees because the firm will have a more productive workforce over time while employees' economic worth (and their deserved compensation) will also increase over time. However, expenditures on firm-specific human capital would be wasted if employees left the firm.[4] Consequently, Competitive Markets Economics asserts employees and profit-seeking firms must share in bearing the costs of building firm-specific human capital. Employees share in the cost of their firm-specific human capital by working for less than the economic value of their contributions to the firm (Reynolds, Masters & Moser, 1998). Arguably, employee investments in firm-specific human capital have become as important, if not more important, for firm performance and survival than the (purely financial) contributions of capital investors (Blair & Kruse, 1999; Etzioni, 1998).

In sum, dedicated employees make substantial investments in the firm by agreeing to work under a delayed compensation scheme and by investing in firm-specific human capital. Unfortunately for employees, Compensation scholarship and practice has failed to acknowledge these two phenomena mean dedicated employees are unrecognized financial investors whose contributions to the firm's financial capital are not recorded in the firm's accounting system. Compensation scholarship and practice has also neglected the contractual nature of employment relationships and, consequently, has failed to consider explicitly the obligations the firm acquires as a result of establishing an ongoing repeated-exchange relationship with its dedicated employees.

THE CONTRACTUAL NATURE OF EMPLOYMENT RELATIONSHIPS

The notion of a contract, whether explicit or implicit, represents a promising bridge concept for a symbiotic integration of Ethics and Management scholarship because contracts pervade business relationships and help define standards for business conduct (Donaldson, 1994). The contract metaphor has proven quite useful in the study of Compensation. One needs to consider existing informal contracts between the firm and its managers and/or employees in order to understand Compensation processes in organizations (Baker, Gibbons, & Murphy, 2002). Moreover, changes to the compensation portion of the (explicit or implicit) contract between the firm and its employees are more critical than actual compensation levels for understanding the impact employees have on firm performance (Milkovich & Newman, 2005).

The contract metaphor has also helped multiple disciplines in the study of employment relationships. The contractual view of employment relationships is fundamental to Employment Law scholarship. More importantly, developments in the legal conception of contracts have been incorporated, although incompletely and imperfectly, in Economics, Management, and Ethics scholarship (Roehling, 2004). Economists have written about implicit contracts between the firm and its employees that provide mechanisms to foster employee commitment and motivation (see for example Ehrenberg & Smith, 2003; Mitchell, 1989; and Reynolds, Masters, & Moser, 1998). More recently, Baker, Gibbons and Murphy (2002) have suggested properly developed informal contracts between the firm and its employees allow firms to obtain better results than those that would attain under market competition processes. Management scholars led by Denise Rousseau and colleagues (see Rousseau, 2004) have used the psychological contract construct to specify and explain mechanisms and processes within the employment relationship that have a strong effect on employee attitudes and behaviors. Business Ethics scholars have also applied the contract metaphor. Donaldson and Dunfee (1999) developed Integrative Social Contracts Theory that proposes a hierarchy of contracts (at societal, community and firm levels) who's content provide standards regarding the ethical quality of business acts and actors. More recently, Van Buren (2000) blended psychological and social contract notions to develop an ethical framework for judging workforce downsizing decisions.

As Roehling (2004) noted recently, legal scholars' thinking about contracts has evolved from an original view, known as Classical Contract Theory, that contracts represent bilateral agreements consisting of bargained-for promises to a post-modern view, known as Relational Contracting Theory (cf. Macneil, 1980), that contracts include not only the promises (again, whether explicit or implicit) the parties make but also the expectations the parties have when engaging in a repeated-exchange relationship. Arguably, Relational Contracting Theory is the development in legal scholarship that has had the strongest impact on the recent use of the contract metaphor for the study of employment relationships. In essence, Relational Contracting Theory notes that most exchanges are embedded in ongoing relationships and argues that a complete understanding of exchange processes requires consideration of both their "transactional" and "relational" aspects (Roehling, 2004). The transactional-relational distinction has been applied to the types of psychological contracts associated with various Compensation strategies (e.g., Rousseau & Ho, 2000), to Human Resource Management systems (e.g., Lepak & Snell, 1999; Tsui, Pearce, Porter & Tripoli, 1997), and even to the analysis of organizational governance systems (e.g., Baker, Gibbons & Murphy, 2002).

Transactional elements in an exchange relationship are concrete, verifiable and independent from past or future dealings between the parties. Transactional elements are concrete in the sense that the parties define precisely and completely their intended contributions before the exchange takes place. For example, when a person gets a car washed, the service provider explicitly states the service components depending on the price the buyer is willing to pay. Transactional elements are verifiable in the sense that the parties can evaluate actual contributions during or shortly after the exchange takes place. Following our car wash example, one can easily judge whether the car was properly washed. Finally, transactional elements are independent from any past or future dealings between the parties. In terms of our example, the current exchange does not create any expectation that a similar exchange between the parties will take in the future. Moreover, buyers and sellers seldom expect that car wash services offered today will be the same in content and/or price as they were last time, or as they will be in the future.

Purely transactional agreements are very difficult, if not impossible, to create in the case of employment relationships for several reasons. First, the parties (the firm and its employees) know they will enter into a repeated exchange relationship and, therefore, do not have to "even the score" during each transaction. For example, employees are willing to work for less than the (labor market) value of their services provided they expect to recover such investment in the future (Lazear, 1998). Second, the parties (the firm and its employees) cannot define precisely and completely the contributions they need or expect from the other side. For example, future changes in technology or competitive strategy may require new competencies from employees and may call for qualitative changes to the firm's compensation package such as the introduction of incentive pay and/or equity-based compensation (Heneman, Ledford & Gresham, 2000). Third, the parties (the firm and its employees) cannot anticipate future events and developments that may change the need for, or the value of, specific contributions the parties make to the exchange relationship. For example, the much-discussed future of Medicare and Social Security implies that employees cannot judge the extent to which the retirement income and insurance benefits currently offered by the firm will suffice for their post-retirement needs.

Thus, the implicit and/or explicit contract between the firm and its dedicated employees contains transactional and relational elements. As stated above, transactional contract elements are concrete, verifiable, and independent from past or future dealings between the parties. In contrast, relational contract elements are vague or at least have not been specified yet, are difficult to verify, or depend on past or future dealings between the parties.

The literature generally treats Compensation as purely transactional. For example, the leading textbook states: "an organization is a network of returns including total compensation *and* relational returns... [such as] recognition and status ... challenging work, and opportunities to learn" (Milkovich & Newman, 2005, p. 11, emphasis added). It should be noted that, contrary to the view prevailing in the literature, compensation elements of the employment contract are not always transactional (Roehling, 2004). For example, the statement "we offer competitive pay and benefits" (which is common when recruiting employees) is vague, implies not-yet-specified future changes to employee compensation levels, and is very difficult for employees to verify. Likewise, the common linkage between seniority and some items in the Compensation package, such as pension vesting and paid vacation time, implies that future compensation will depend on prior dealings between the firm and its long-term employees.

By treating its subject as purely transactional, Compensation scholarship and practice has ignored critical relational elements in the tacit contract established between the firm and its dedicated employees through their repeated-exchange relationship. Further, there are two qualitatively different types of employee expectations regarding the firm's relational obligations: comprehensive obligations, which provide general guidance for all strategy and policy decisions, and decision- specific obligations, which set limits to particular policies and strategic actions. Comprehensive obligations derive from basic ethical norms but decision-specific obligations derive from the firm's tacit endorsement of norms implicit in relevant legislation, in judicial interpretations of such legislation, in common practices across firms, and/or in the firm's past practices (Boatright, 2002a, Macneil, 1980).

The next section focuses on some of the firm's comprehensive relational obligations that have been neglected, for the most part, in Compensation scholarship and practice. A thorough discussion of the firm's decision-specific relational obligations is beyond the scope of this chapter. However, and for illustrative purposes, the following list provides a partial sample of decision-specific relational expectations that relate to Compensation strategy and policy decisions and may be common among American employees.

1. Employees expect their pay will not decline in the future (Reynolds, Masters & Moser, 1998; Rousseau & Ho, 2000).

2. In return for their commitment and loyalty, employees expect long-term gains from their investments in firm-specific human capital reflected in regular pay increases as long as their performance is satisfactory (Mitchell, 1989; Rousseau & Greller, 1994; Tsui et al., 1997).

3. When offered a good benefits package, employees expect the firm will protect them financially in return for their loyalty and commitment (Rousseau & Ho, 2000).

4. Benefit obligations continue even after the employment relationship ends. The Consolidated Omnibus Budget Reconciliation Act of 1984 obliges firms to help terminated employees maintain health insurance for a time period considered sufficient to regain employment. Likewise, the Employee Retirement Income Security Act of 1974 establishes fiduciary obligations for firms with defined benefits plans towards current and retired employees.

5. A "dismissal only for just cause" expectation is prevalent among American workers who expect to keep their job as long as they want and perform satisfactorily (Roehling, 2002).

FAIRNESS AND RECIPROCITY NORMS FOR COMPENSATION STRATEGY AND POLICY DECISIONS

Compensation strategy is an ongoing zero-sum process for dedicated employees and capital investors if one assumes that increases to Compensation costs imply a reduction in firm profits. Although it may be questionable because it ignores the reciprocal relationship between Compensation strategy and the firm's financial performance, this assumption pervades Compensation strategy in practice. For example, pay raises are reduced, delayed, even cancelled when the firm is not expected to achieve its financial targets (Milkovich & Newman, 2005). Likewise, increases to the cost of health benefits are frequently blamed for the poor financial performance of major U.S. corporations (Hawkins, 2004; Pfeffer, 2004). Under this assumption, each Compensation strategy (budget) round represents a zero-sum distribution because gains for dedicated employees represent losses for capital investors. More importantly, from this point of view, top managers serve as financial adjudicators (between dedicated employees, capital investors, and themselves) when deciding on Compensation strategy and policy.

Top managers making business decisions are not exempt from the basic Personal Ethics obligations we all have (Quinn & Jones, 1995). Further, comprehensive relational obligations that arise in any repeated-exchange relationship derive from basic Personal Ethics principles (Macneil, 2000; Boatright, 2002a). Furthermore, economic relationships are sustained by obligations concerning fairness and reciprocity (Oosterhout, Wempe & Willigenburg, 2004). Fairness, the obligation to seek an adequate distribution of gains and losses among those affected by any act or decision, provides the core for much of Ethics[5] (Solomon & Martin, 2004). Arguably, fairness is one of the strongest influences on the stability and effectiveness of employment relationships (Folger, 1998; Milkovich & Newman, 2005). Reciprocity, the obligation one has towards others on the basis of past exchanges, is also one of the few universally accepted requirements for the establishment and continuance of any sort of human relationship (Gouldner, 1960). Reciprocity is particularly critical to the survival of repeated-exchange relationships (Macneil, 2000).

Thus, some of the firm's comprehensive relational obligations derive from basic ethical norms concerning fairness and reciprocity. These obligations provide a normative framework to improve the ethical quality of Compensation strategy and policy decisions for several reasons. First, distributive fairness is a central issue when questioning the ethical quality of Compensation strategy. Second, the notion of a relational contract between the firm and its dedicated employees raises the issue of contractual fairness. Third, reciprocity is an essential requisite for distributive fairness in investment relationships (Etzioni, 1998).

Distributive fairness, which refers to the proper distribution of financial gains and/or losses among those affected (Beauchamp & Bowie, 2001), is a central concern in Compensation decision-making (Milkovich & Newman, 2005). It should be noted this chapter is concerned with a distributive issue different from that considered in the Organizational Behavior and Human Resource Management literatures. These literatures examine fairness in the distribution of rewards and/or punishments among (otherwise compa-rable) employees. In contrast, the notion of distributive fairness in this chapter refers to the distribution of financial gains and/or losses between qualitatively different parties: employees, capital investors, and top manag-ers. This distinction is important because, in the case of the Organizational Behavior and Human Resource Management literatures, all employees make a comparable contribution to, and have a similar relationship with the firm. In contrast, in the case of this chapter, dedicated employees, capi-tal investors, and top managers differ importantly in terms of their invest-ment in the firm and their contractual relationship with the firm.

As stated above, the contractual relationship between the firm and its dedicated employees raises the issue of contractual fairness. Ensuring fair-ness in the extent to which various parties share in the firm's financial gains and losses is a particularly important contracting problem. The Eth-ics literature includes a gamut of statements about fairness, most of which propose a single distribution criterion such as need, equality, or contribu-tion (Velasquez, 1997). In contrast, John Rawls proposed a theory of "jus-tice as fairness" that is based on the notion of contractual relationships among those affected and, therefore, is quite applicable for the purposes of this chapter. Rawls theory has received the most attention of any mod-ern philosophical thinking about fairness[6] (Raphael, 2001), is considered as "the single most influential work of the post-World War II period in social and political philosophy" (Shaw & Barry, 2001, p. 114), and provides a comprehensive perspective that integrates into a logical whole most (if not all) other Ethics thinking about fairness (Velasquez, 1997).

Noting that all persons are morally equal and that social systems require a sort of contract that induces collaboration, Rawls argued that participants should find acceptable any advantages given others and should feel they will fare as well as they can reasonably hope to do (Raphael, 2001). Based on these considerations, Rawls argued any process for distributing gains and losses is fair if, and only if, the process would be acceptable to all ratio-nal persons who considered the situation with absolute impartiality. Because human judgments tend to be biased by self-interest, Rawls pro-posed a "veil of ignorance" as a rhetorical device to help judge the fairness of any given distribution process. In plain words, Rawls suggested that, in order to be fair, any distribution process should elicit an affirmative answer to the question: "Knowing that persons will be categorized and each cate-gory will be treated differently, would I prefer the rules and criteria in this distribution process to any other alternatives, even if I could not tell in advance how I would be categorized (and hence treated)?"

In the context of this chapter, Rawls theory means that to be fair the process for making Compensation strategy and policy decisions (which de facto distribute financial gains and losses between capital investors, employees and top managers) should be preferred by most rational individuals even if they do not know whether they will be treated as a capital investor, as a rank-and-file employee, or as a top manager. This seems almost impossible because the unrealistic spot market transactional view of employment relationships that dominates Compensation scholarship and practice is frequently used to justify sharp differences in how these three parties are treated (Peterson, 2004). Rawls' theory supports two norms that can help enhance the ethical quality of Compensation strategy and policy decisions: fairness as equal consideration and fairness as MAXMIN distribution.

(1) The norm of fairness as equal consideration stipulates that parties to a fair distribution contract should be willing to be treated like other parties to the same contract are treated.[7] For purposes of this chapter, this norm may be stated as: "Compensation strategy and policy decisions should apply the same criteria, reasoning and rules for all employee groups including the top management group." For example, this norm was clearly violated by top managers in a now defunct airline who asked unionized employees to accept a ten percent pay cut while, at the same time, granted an eleven percent average raise to the company's managers (Solomon, 1997). A suggestion consistent with this norm would be that firms should not install nonqualified pension plans that give preferential treatment to some but not all employee groups.

(2) The norm of fairness as MAXMIN distribution.[8] The term MAXMIN is used in Decision Science and related disciplines to indicate a decision criterion that gives preference to the alternative associated with the best results under the worst case scenario. The political philosophy and ethics literatures adopted this term to indicate the best possible results (MAX) for those who will fare the worst, which is for those who will receive the least (MIN). For purposes of this chapter, this norm may be stated as: "To the extent they are affected, Compensation strategy and policy decisions should seek the best possible results for the least compensated employees." A suggestion consistent with this norm would be that all employees contribute to the cost of health benefits in proportion to their pay levels in order to alleviate the negative effects on lesser-paid employees. After all, it is normal practice to distribute pay increases in the same fashion, as a percentage of current pay.

In addition to contractual fairness, reciprocity expectations are also essential for investment relationships (such as the relationship between the firm and its dedicated employees) because investors provide valuable resources expecting future gains. The notion of reciprocity calls to mind obligations one has towards others as a consequence of past exchanges. Further, reciprocity is an essential requisite for distributive fairness in economic systems (De George, 2001; White, 2003). Reciprocity is a multifaceted notion that encompasses a diverse collection of widely held ethical beliefs. The literature on economic justice recognizes three distinct facets for the notion of reciprocity: reciprocity as indebtedness, reciprocity as "fair play,"[9] and reciprocity as long-term balance. These three reciprocity dimensions suggest norms that can help enhance the ethical quality of Compensation strategy and policy decisions.

(3) The norm of reciprocity as indebtedness is reflected in a set of widely held ethical beliefs that includes the following: (a) one should help (and one should not harm) those who have helped one; (b) one can expect to get something back for something given; (c) one owes others who have suffered losses for one's gain; and (d) one should exercise gratitude for gains received and provide reparation for losses caused within any exchange relationship with others (Gouldner, 1960; Macneil, 2000; Ross, 1930). For purposes of this chapter, this norm may be stated as: "Compensation strategy and policy decisions *should* acknowledge the investments dedicated employees have made in the firm." Establishing a substantive severance policy for dedicated employees is consistent with this norm. Another suggestion consistent with this norm would be that employees whose work has changed drastically (through re-engineering, establishment of lean manufacturing or other high-performance work systems, and the like) should receive a noticeable pay increase in recognition of their investment in firm-specific human capital. Such pay increases would lend more credence to common claims of a partner-like relationship with these employees.

(4) The norm of reciprocity as "fair play" is reflected in a set of widely held ethical beliefs that include the following: (a) one has the obligation to contribute to an ongoing relationship as much as one can; (b) one acquires the obligation to reciprocate whenever one accepts the gains from a cooperative scheme with others; and (c) the strength of one's reciprocity obligation depends on the intensity of the loss incurred by other parties and/or on the size of the gains one enjoyed (Coyle-Shapiro & Conway, 2004; Gouldner, 1960; Phillips, 1997; White, 2003). For purposes of this chapter, this norm may be stated as: "Strategy and policy decisions that increase employee compensation *should* redress any financial losses (in real income terms) endured by dedicated employees in the recent past. Conversely decisions that reduce employee compensation *should* consider the history of financial gains (in real income terms) enjoyed by dedicated employees in the recent past." A suggestion consistent with this norm would be that a firm experiencing a financial turnaround should redress the negative effects of any pay cuts or freezes previously imposed on various employee groups. Another suggestion consistent with this norm would be that a firm planning to curtail compensation due to anticipated financial pressures should cut and/or freeze pay among the best paid employee

groups before the least paid employee groups are asked to sacrifice for the sake of the firm's financial viability.

(5) The norm of reciprocity as long-term balance is reflected in a set of widely held ethical beliefs that includes the following: (a) no one party to an exchange relationship should get "too good a deal"; (b) gains and losses should be divided fairly between the parties; and (c) while the allocation of gains and losses for a specific exchange may not be strictly fair, the accumulation of gains and losses should balance over time (Macneil, 2000; Gouldner, 1960). For purposes of this chapter, this norm may be stated as: "Compensation strategy and policy decisions *should* seek a balanced cumulative allocation of financial gains and losses between capital investors and dedicated employees acknowledging their corresponding history of investments in, and contributions to, the firm." A suggestion consistent with this norm would be that firms having a history of exceptional shareholder returns should refrain from curtailing employee compensation at the first sign of financial difficulties. In this case, the notion of long-term balance implies shareholders should endure not-so-good returns (again, after a "good times" period) before dedicated employees are asked to sacrifice for shareholders' sake.

CONCLUSION

This chapter argues five norms can help enhance the ethical quality of Compensation scholarship and practice. These norms, explained above, were labeled: (1) fairness as equal consideration; (2) fairness as MAXMIN distribution; (3) reciprocity as indebtedness; (4) reciprocity as fair play; and (5) reciprocity as long-term balance.

This chapter started with the distinction between three levels (Personal, Professional, and Organizational) for Compensation Ethics and the choice to focus on the Organizational level. I suggested Organizational Compensation Ethics could help answer critical questions such as: "is it ethical (right) to discontinue retiree health benefits in order to protect the firm's financial performance?" and "is it ethical (right) to freeze or even cut employee pay in order to secure dividend payouts for the firm's shareholders during high-inflation periods?" The five norms proposed here suggest the answer is: "Probably not."

As the reader has probably realized, the five norms proposed here oppose strategy and policy actions regarding employee Compensation that are common in practice. These norms also run against the foundational knowledge (Competitive Markets Economics) that supports those decisions. I would like to remind the reader that I also argued such foundation is deficient from an ethical point of view because it is based on an unrealistic spot market transactional view of employment relationships. It leads to the expropriation or destruction of significant financial investments that dedicated employees made in the firm and may lead to breaching critical terms in the tacit contract established between the firm and its dedicated employees.

The five norms proposed here do not represent a complete theory of Organizational Compensation Ethics. The norms proposed here are intended to motivate a conversation that may lead to a more formal articulation of such theory. Missing from this chapter are other important ethical principles such as fidelity, the obligation to tell the truth and to honor one's agreements (Ross, 1930), that may suggest additional comprehensive norms or may suggest changes to the norms presented here. Additionally, this chapter neglects a thorough treatment of another fruitful avenue for the analysis of Organizational Compensation Ethics: decision-specific relational norms. Decision-specific relational norms correspond to employee expectations derived from the firm's tacit endorsement of norms implicit in relevant legislation, in judicial interpretations of such legislation, in common practices across firms, and/or in the firm's past practices.

Practitioners may consider the norms proposed here (and/or other ethical norms they find appropriate) when making Compensation strategy and policy decisions that will have a significant impact on employees' standard of living. Of course, running a company into the ground for the sake of ethicality also has negative consequences for employees. Therefore, the norms proposed here may be best applied as a sort of "check and balance" to the single-minded pursuit of maximum returns for shareholders through Compensation strategy and policy decisions. After all, investor surveys show that most shareholders seek good returns (in comparison with their investment alternatives) and do not necessarily seek "maximum shareholder value."

I hope this chapter motivates a fruitful conversation (or debate) about the substance and scope of Organizational Compensation Ethics that involves practitioners and scholars. In addition to the premises and conclusions in this chapter, possible lines for further scholarly inquiry may include: (a) the financial consequences of these norms for the financial performance of firms at various financial health stages and/or across various industries; (b) the extent to which various participants (employees, capital investors, and top managers) agree with these norms; and (c) what other norms may be developed from the point of view of various mainstream schools of thought in Ethics including Virtue Ethics, Care (or Feminist) Ethics, and Rights Ethics.

NOTES

1. Because of its multiple definitions and interpretations, I will not use the term "stakeholders" in this chapter, a term that is often used when referring to parties (like the "resource contributors" listed above) that are involved with, or affected by, the firm.

2. For the sake of simplicity/readability, I will use the term "dedicated employees" to designate those who have had a significantly long employment relationship with the firm in the remainder of this chapter.

3. A third theoretically possible, but improbable, explanation for the relationship between pay and seniority would be that workers' economic value (Marginal Revenue Product) increases constantly throughout their entire careers.

4. It is worth noting that termination of the relationship between the firm and an employee who made investments in firm-specific human capital would be costly not only to the individual but also to society as a whole because such productive capacity is lost when the employment relationship ends (Lazear, 1998).

5. Consistent with the bulk of the Ethics, HR and Compensation literatures, "fairness" and "justice" are treated as synonyms here although more sophisticated Philosophy and Ethics literatures attempt to differentiate between them (see for example Raphael, 2001).

6. Even Rawls' strongest critic, Brian Barry, has come around and proposed similar contractual views on fairness (Raphael, 2001).

7. This norm is very similar to the Kantian principle of reversibility.

8. The label MAXMIN is often used in the literature although Rawls used the label "the difference principle" for this norm.

9. Some, for example White (2003), use the term "fair dues" to refer to this norm.

REFERENCES

Bagley, C. E. (2003). The ethical leader's decision tree. *Harvard Business Review, 81*(2), 18–19.

Baker, G., Gibbons, R., & Murphy, K. J. (2002). Relational contracts and the theory of the firm. *Quarterly Journal of Economics, 117,* 39–84.

Barker, R.A. (2002). An examination of organizational ethics. *Human Relations, 55,* 1097–1116.

Barth, E. (1997). Firm specific seniority and wages. *Journal of Labor Economics, 15,* 495–506.

Beauchamp, T. L., & Bowie, N. E. (Eds.) (2001). *Ethical theory and business* (Sixth Edition). Upper Saddle River, NJ: Prentice-Hall.

Blair, M. M. & Kruse, D. L. (1999). Worker capitalists? Giving employees an ownership stake. *The Brookings Review, 17*(4), 23–26.

Boatright, J. R. (2002a). Contractors as stakeholders: Reconciling stakeholder theory and the nexus-of-contracts firm. *Journal of Banking & Finance, 26,* 1837–1852.

Boatright, J. R. (2002b). Ethics and corporate governance: Justifying the role of shareholder. In N. E. Bowie (Ed.), *The Blackwell Guide to Business Ethics* (pp. 38–60). Malden, MA: Blackwell.

Buckley, M. R., Beu, D. S., Frink, D. D., Howard, J. L., Berkson, H., Mobbs, T. A., & Ferris, G. R. (2001). Ethical issues in human resource systems. *Human Resource Management Review, 11,* 11–29.

Coyle-Shapiro, J. A-M. & Conway, N. (2004). The employment relationship through the lens of social exchange. In J. A-M Coyle-Shapiro, L. M. Shore, M. S. Taylor, & L. E. Tetrick (Eds.), *The employment relationship: Examining psychological and contextual perspectives* (pp. 5–28). Oxford: Oxford University Press.

De George, R. T. (2001). Negotiating Justice. In T. L. Beauchamp, & N. E. Bowie (Eds.), *Ethical Theory and Business* (Sixth Edition) (pp. 675–680). Upper Saddle River, NJ: Prentice-Hall.

Donaldson, T. (1994). When integration fails: The logic of prescription and description in Business Ethics. *Business Ethics Quarterly, 4,* 157–169.

Donaldson, T. & Dunfee, T. W. (1999). *Ties that bind: A social contracts approach to business ethics.* Boston, MA: Harvard Business School Press.

Ehrenberg, R. G. & Smith, R. S. (2003). *Modern labor economics and public policy* (Eighth Edition). Boston, MA: Addison-Wesley.

Etzioni, A. (1998). A communitarian note on stakeholder theory. *Business Ethics Quarterly, 8,* 679–691.

Folger, R. (1999). Fairness as moral virtue. In M. Schminke (Ed.), *Managerial ethics: Moral management of people and processes* (pp. 13–34). Mahwah, NJ: Erlbaum.

Friedman, M. (1970, September 13). The social responsibility of business is to increase its profits. *New York Times Magazine,* p. 126.

Gerhart, B. & Rynes, S. L. (2003). *Compensation: Theory, evidence, and strategic implications.* Thousand Oaks, CA: Sage.

Goodpaster, K. E. (1991). Business ethics and stakeholder analysis. *Business Ethics Quarterly, 1,* 53–73.

Gouldner, A. W. (1960). The norm of reciprocity: A preliminary statement. *American Sociological Review, 25,* 161–178.

Haksever, C.; Chaganti, R. & Cook, R. G. (2004). A model of value creation: A strategic view. *Journal of Business Ethics, 49,* 291–305.

Hawkins, L. Jr. (2004, October 15). GM cuts forecasts over health costs, earnings rise by only 3.5% and car maker's woes lead S&P to lower debt rating. *Wall Street Journal,* A3.

Heneman, R. L., Ledford, G. E. Jr., & Gresham, M. T. (2000). The changing nature of work and its effects on compensation design and delivery. In S. L. Rynes and B. Gerhart (Eds.), *Compensation in organizations: Current research and practice* (pp. 195–240). San Francisco: Jossey-Bass.

Hill, C. W. L. & Jones, T. M. (1992). Stakeholder-Agency theory. *Journal of Management Studies, 29,* 131–154.

Hosmer, L. T. (1987). Ethical analysis and Human Resource Management. *Human Resource Management, 26,* 313–330.

Hutchens, R. M. (1989). Seniority, wages and productivity: A turbulent decade. *Journal of Economic Perspectives, 3*(4), 49–64.

James, H. S. Jr. & Johnson, D. M. (2000). Just cause provisions, severance pay, and the efficiency wage hypothesis. *Managerial and Decision Economics, 21,* 83–88.

Lazear, E. P. (1995). *Personnel Economics.* Cambridge, MA: MIT Press.

Lazear, E. P. (1998). *Personnel Economics for Managers.* New York: Wiley.

Lepak, D. P. & Snell, S. S. (1999). The human resource architecture: Toward a theory of human capital and development. *Academy of Management Review, 24,* 31–48.

Macneil, I. R. (1980). *The new social contract: An inquiry into modern contractual relations.* New Haven, CT: Yale University Press.

Macneil, I. R. (2000). Relational contract theory: Challenges and queries. *Northwestern university Law Review, 94,* 877–907.

McClelland, P. D. (1990). *The American search for economic justice.* Cambridge, MA: Bassil Blackwell.

Milkovich, G. T. & Newman, J. M. (2005). *Compensation* (Eighth Edition). Boston, MA: McGraw-Hill Irwin.

Mitchell, D. J. B. (1989). *Human resource management: An economic approach.* Boston, MA: PWS-Kent.

Morris, D. (2004). Defining a moral problem in business ethics. *Journal of Business Ethics, 49,* 347–357.

Oosterhout, J. (Hans) van, Wempe, B., & Willigenburg, T. van (2004). Rethinking organizational ethics: A plea for pluralism. *Journal of Business Ethics, 25,* 387–395.

Peterson, R. B. (2004). A call for testing our assumptions: Human resource management today. *Journal of Management Inquiry, 13,* 192–202.

Pfeffer, J. (2004). The confidence game to boost profits, companies are slashing benefits and backing out of costly pension commitments. *Business 2.0, 5*(10), 94.

Phillips, R. A. (1997). Stakeholder theory and a principle of fairness. *Business Ethics Quarterly, 7,* 51–66.

Phillips, R. A. & Margolis, J. D. (1999). Towards an ethics of organizations. *Business Ethics Quarterly, 9,* 619–638.

Quinn, D. P. & Jones, T. M. (1995). An agent morality view of business policy. *Academy of Management Review, 20,* 21–42.

Raphael, D. D. (2001). *Concepts of Justice.* Oxford: Clarendon Press.

Reynolds, L. G., Masters, S. H., & Moser, C. H. (1998). *Labor Economics and labor relations* (Eleventh Edition). Upper Saddle River, NJ: Prentice-Hall.

Roehling, M. V. (2002). The "good cause norm" in employment relations: Empirical evidence and policy implications. *Employee Responsibilities and Rights Journal, 14,* 91–104.

Roehling, M. V. (2004). Legal theory: Contemporary contract law perspectives and insights for employment relationships theory. In J. A-M Coyle-Shapiro, L. M. Shore, M. S. Taylor, & L. E. Tetrick (Eds.), *The employment relationship: Examining psychological and contextual perspectives* (pp. 65–93). Oxford: Oxford University Press.

Ross, W. D. (1930). *The right and the good.* Oxford: Clarendon Press.

Rousseau, D. M. (2004). Psychological contracts in the workplace: Understanding the ties that motivate. *Academy of Management Executive, 18,* 120–127.

Rousseau, D.M., & Greller, M. M. (1994). Human resource practices: Administrative contract makers. *Human Resource Management, 33,* 385–401.

Rousseau, D.M. & Ho, V. T. (2000). Psychological contract issues in compensation. In S. L. Rynes and B. Gerhart (Eds.), *Compensation in organizations: Current research and practice* (pp. 273–310). San Francisco: Jossey-Bass.

Schminke, M. (1998). Management and ethics: Distant neighbors in theory and research. In M. Schminke (Ed.), Managerial ethics: Moral management of people and processes (pp. 1–11). Mahwah, NJ: Erlbaum.

Schumann, P. L. (2001). A moral principles framework for human resource management ethics. *Human Resource Management Review, 11,* 93–111.

Shaw, W. H. & Barry, V. (2001). *Moral issues in business* (Eighth Edition). Belmont, CA: Wadsworth.

Solomon, R. C. (1997*). It's good business: Ethics and the free enterprise for the new millennium.* Lanham, MD: Rowan & Littlefield.

Solomon, R. C. & Martin, C. (2004). *Above the bottom line: An introduction to business ethics.* Belmont, CA: Wadsworth/Thomson.

Stark, A. (1993). What's the matter with business ethics? *Harvard Business Review, 71*(3), 38–44.

Treviño, L. K., and Weaver, G. R. (1998). Punishment in organizations: Descriptive and normative perspectives. In M. Schminke (Ed.), Managerial ethics: Moral management of people and processes (pp. 99–114). Mahwah, NJ: Erlbaum.

Tsui, A. S., Pearce, J. L., Porter, L. W., & Tripoli, A. M. (1997). Alternative approaches to the employee-organization relationship: Does investment in employees pay off? *Academy of Management Journal, 40,* 1089–1121.

Van Buren, H. J. III (2000). The bindingness of social and psychological contracts: Toward a theory of social responsibility in downsizing. *Journal of Business Ethics, 25,* 205–219.

Velasquez, M. G. (1997). *Business ethics: Concepts and cases* (Fourth Edition) Upper Saddle River, NJ: Prentice Hall.

Weaver, G. R. & Treviño, L. K. (1994). Normative and empirical business ethics: Separation, marriage of convenience, or marriage of necessity? *Business Ethics Quarterly, 4,* 129–144.

White, S. (2003). *The civic minimum: On the rights and obligations of economic citizenship.* Oxford: Oxford University Press.

Wiley, C. (2000). Ethical standards for human resource management professionals: A comparative analysis of five major codes. *Journal of Business Ethics, 25,* 93–114.

Wooten, K. C. (2001). Ethical dilemmas in human resource management: Application of a multidimensional framework, a unifying taxonomy, and applicable codes. *Human Resource Management Review, 11,* 159–175.

WorldatWork (2002). Ethics panel in the Total Rewards Profession. [On-Line, 4–5-2005] Available: http://resourcepro.worldatwork.org/levelink/livelink/fetch/2000/2657/46405/269699/Ethics_chat_...

CHAPTER 11

RELIGION AND PAY

Implications for Compensation

Nancy E. Day
University of Missouri–Kansas City

I initially began considering the relationship between religion and pay at the end of an academic symposium on spirituality. One of the panelists, an expert in executive compensation, discussed the implications of American CEOs' hefty pay packages which are sometimes uncorrelated with firm performance, or negatively correlated with the rewards of the average workers. The discussion concluded that a spiritual, or a religious, person would have concerns with the fairness of this. But there is no evidence in the popular media that our highly religious society is much concerned with this issue, or any issues regarding how we pay people. Is this media bias or oversight, or is pay not relevant to spiritual or religious issues? Certainly pay has extraordinary significance for individuals; it is emotionally laden and correlated with feelings of overall well-being (Mitchell & Mickel, 1999). So is religion. What are the implications of considering the two together?

The juxtaposition of two divergent topics, pay and religion, was intriguing, and several questions arose. Most prominent was, if we considered and

Human Resource Management Ethics, pages 217–237
Copyright © 2006 by Information Age Publishing
All rights of reproduction in any form reserved.

incorporated religious perspectives into our compensation policies, would organizations pay differently?

While this is an interesting question, very little scholarly literature currently exists that directly links religion and pay. Thus, the purpose of this chapter is to tease out some relationships in current management literature that might enlighten how we understand religion and how we pay people. First, I will review the religious principles and teachings of three of the major U.S. religions, Christianity, Judaism, and Islam, that may relate to economic transactions among people. Then I will discuss what the appropriate response of religiously motivated managers might be regarding the design and implementation of pay plans. Relevant to this discussion will be contemporary issues such as the "just," or "living" wage, as well as executive pay.

RELIGIOUS PRINCIPLES RELATED TO PAY

The world's major religions seem to agree on certain overarching principles, such as treating others as you would be treated, and the prohibition of antisocial or destructive behaviors, such as stealing, killing, lying, and sexual immorality. Thus, human resource management conducted from a religiously motivated perspective would seek to treat all employees fairly, provide safe and healthy working conditions, allow for procedural justice, and care for workers' well-being. Part of these prescriptions includes fair compensation (Koys, 2001).

What do the major U.S. religions have to say related to pay practices? This section will briefly review relevant beliefs and constructs from Catholicism, Protestantism, Judaism, and Islam.

Catholic Teachings

While contemporary Catholic teaching clearly supports capitalism over socialism, it puts the well-being of the individual and society at the center of its theology (Gunther, 2004; Naughton & Laczniak, 1993). Two recent documents affirm these teachings: a pastoral letter from U.S. bishops, called *Economic Justice for All: Catholic Social Teaching and the U.S. Economy* (published in 1986), and an encyclical by John Paul II called *Centesimus Annus* (published in 1991), which reflects the dictates of an 1891 encyclical (Sethi & Steidlmeier, 1993). The arguments found in these documents call for several things: freedom for all people to participate in a fair economy; a system that allows for egalitarian distribution of pay; priority of labor over capital; a concern for the poor that supercedes profit maximization. *Centesimus Annus* declares that a political economy should be merely a means to the end of personal development and that the individual should be the moral and ethical foundation of any organization. It sets out a market-oriented vision for a moral economy in which human beings are the basis for decisions rather than the market itself. An organization exists not only to make a profit, but to provide for the well-being of persons within the community (Sethi & Steidlmeier, 1993).

Catholic economic teaching is also concerned with encouraging a "just" or "living" wage. The market itself will not produce a just wage (Sethi & Steidlmeier, 1993). Since the market exists for the purpose of human development, mechanisms must be introduced to ensure that all workers who work full time and produce sufficiently are adequately compensated.

Ironically, the proportion of lower paid workers in the U.S. is increasing. In 1996, 30% of American workers were paid $7.28 per hour or less, a percentage that increased from 23.5% in 1973 (Yang, 1996). The poverty level for a family of four in 1996 was $7.50 per hour (U.S. Department of Health and Human Services, 2005).

A living wage is defined by (Waltman, 2004) as "a wage that would provide someone who works full time year-round with a decent standard of living as measured by the criteria of the society in which he/she lives" (p. 86). The just price of labor, as described by Aquinas and other Catholic theologians, is that which is set in market transactions, mutually agreed upon by buyer and seller who are in equal bargaining positions, and free of coercion or threats of violence (Waltman, 2004), conditions that are not always present in economic markets. The living wage should be set at the level necessary for all citizens of the republic to fully participate. A living wage, its proponents suggest, is necessary not only for humanitarian reasons, but for the good of the democratic process. A people with extremely divergent standards of living results in unequal participation in the democracy, creating difficulties in the functioning of government institutions necessary to serve the public good (Waltman, 2004).

The Protestant Work Ethic

Max Weber's landmark essay, *The Protestant Work Ethic and the "Spirit" of Capitalism* (1905), started a wellspring of discourse on whether or not the rise and development of Protestantism, particularly Calvinism, encouraged a work ethic that raised labor to the level of a "calling." Such an ethic would make working and one's dedication to it evidence of religious devotion and moral commitment (Baehr & Wells, 2002; Jones, 1997), and the accumulation of material goods would be an indication of God's grace (Waltman, 2004). Calvinism's doctrine of predestination, that only a portion of humanity are members of the elect, created a psychological distancing from God that dedication to work alleviated. Not only did hard work provide a rigorous discipline that God was believed to appreciate, the fruits of financial prosperity were indications that a worker was indeed among the elite group of God's chosen people (Baehr & Wells, 2002), a belief shared by some of today's evangelicals (Roels, 1997).

One of the major tenets of Weber's theory is that work, since it is activity sanctified by God, represents a calling. For example, studies have found that a high percentage of American workers (65 to 95%), when asked if they would continue working even when it was no longer financially necessary, answer in the affirmative (Furnham, 1990).

Immediately after its publication, Weber's essay caused controversy and disagreement. Some believed that he overestimated the role of religion; others argued that other religious traditions also generated individuals who were highly dedicated to their duties (Baehr & Wells, 2002); others argued that the Protestant work ethic (PWE) is a myth that never really existed (Furnham, 1990). Indeed, Weber did not claim that the Protestants of his day were higher in this work ethic than others, but merely that their historical development had catalyzed the phenomenon (Furnham, 1990; Weber, 1905).

Some evidence exists, however, that Protestants tend to score higher than other Christians on measures of the PWE (usually measured using multi-dimensional scales including the components that Weber described: hard work, profitable use of time, emphasis on the importance of savings and innovation, and honesty; Jones, 1997). Some research shows that Protestants are more likely to have attitudes similar to the PWE than Catholics. They are more likely to give more importance to work, reject the welfare state, and develop their own human capital by moving away from family to improve their education or jobs (Furnham, 1990). Protestants who are more actively involved in their churches are also more likely to exhibit PWE characteristics, drawing some to conclude that the values instilled by at least some Protestant affiliations encourage a commitment to work and effort (Furnham, 1990).

However, other research also shows that Protestants do not have a corner on the work ethic market (Furnham, 1990). For example, while some studies have found differences in PWE between Protestants and Catholics, most have found no differences (Furnham, 1990). Indeed, some scholars have proposed that Catholic social teaching created its own "Catholic work ethic" (McCann, 1997), and, as will be discussed below, research has been conducted on an "Islamic work ethic" (Ali, 1988; Yousef, 2000, 2001). Further, other researchers have found similarities between the "Protestant" work ethic and Zoroastrian Parsis in India (Kennedy, 1962), traditional Japanese society (Bellah, 1963; Howard, Shudo, & Umeshima, 1983), Confucian value systems (Furnham, 1990), Muslims' belief in the centrality of work (Hafsi, 1987), and East African natives (although they were Christians converted by

Protestant missionaries; Munroe & Munroe, 1986). Notably, Arslan (2001) found that although Protestants were slightly higher in PWE than were Catholics, Muslims ranked highest of all three groups. Similarly, Niles (1999) found that Sri-Lankan Buddhists were higher in PWE than Australian Christians. Taiwanese workers were higher than British and United States workers, although U.S. workers were a close second (Tang, Furnham, & Davis, 2003). The PWE seems to be highest in countries having large discrepancies between their wealthiest and poorest citizens (Furnham, 1990), perhaps indicating a psychological mechanism on the part of the upper income levels to justify their good fortune (success is a measure of God's grace), and a device on the part of lower levels to work hard to improve their lot.

Thus, while some believe that modern America has in large part rejected the PWE in favor of relentless consumerism and immediate gratification (Buchholz & Rosenthal, 2003), there is evidence that at least in some people and cultures, this ethic about work is alive and well, regardless of whether or not it can be truly considered "Protestant" or not.

The living wage. The Catholic definition of just price of labor as one mutually, equally, and freely determined, was simplified in the advent of Protestantism to that determined by individual transactions alone (Waltman, 2004). However, Protestants as well as Catholics have wrestled with market economics, questioning that the value of labor can be determined merely by its market price, apart from the worker's value as human being (Waltman, 2004). Calvin himself stated that God was displeased with "the cruelty of the rich who employ poor people in their service and yet do not sufficiently compensate them for their labor" (in Waltman, 2004, page 37). Thus while valuing the market economy, early Protestant teaching saw the importance of structuring the business world to respond fairly and ethically (Childs, 1997), including paying a just wage.

Some Protestant groups have supported the idea of the living wage. The Christian social gospel movement of the 19th century stressed the presence of Christ in every person, and required Christians to recognize this and work to alleviate poverty (Waltman, 2004). American Evangelical Lutherans proposed it in their 1999 document, *Sufficient Sustainable Livelihood for All* (Waltman, 2004). Evangelical Christians, who have not been noted historically for entering into issues of economic inequality, have responded to wages issues, notably through Evangelicals for Social Action (Waltman, 2004).

Jewish Teachings

Jewish ethical tradition emphasizes the good of the community and God's commitment to it over individual rights (Dorff, 1997; Pava, 1998). It sees poverty as an evil that deprives its victims of dignity and their place in the community (Waltman, 2004, p. 139). Jewish law provides an "'operating manual' for living life" (Yanow, 2005) in just and ethical ways. The Biblical commandment that prohibits coveting others' property has implications to Jews in that all business transactions should be executed fairly, according to the norms of the relevant marketplace (Ali, Camp, & Gibbs, 2000).

Since wealth is received through divine ordination, it requires its owner to be aware of and act on his or her obligations to the larger community (Green, 1997; Tamari, 1997; Yanow, 2005). Employers must provide decent, non-hazardous work for fair wages, paid on a timely basis, regardless of the demographic or religious group to which the worker belongs (Koys, 2001). Workplace decisions must be made with the preservation and protection of human life in mind (Green, 1997). The Talmud prohibits paying wages lower than what the worker would have received in other circumstances; doing otherwise would equate to theft (Block, 1990). Employees also have a responsibility: They are to be independent, self-motivated, and hard-working, or they are in effect stealing from their employer (Schnall, 1993).

According to one Jewish ethical scholar (Green, 1993), the contemporary Catholic viewpoint as described in John Paul II's *Centesimus Annus* coincides with Jewish ethical standards in three ways: The right to private property must be balanced with the needs for the common good; the less fortunate of society must be provided for; the dignity of persons must be upheld in the social structure so that each individual has sufficient resources to live and participate in the broader community.

Islamic Teachings

Like other religions, Islam is based on holy writings and religious laws, developed over centuries. In addition to the Qur'an, the prophetic sayings or *hadith*, containing words and acts of the Prophet, the *Sunna*, prescribing ideal human behavior (Abassi, Hollman, & Murrey, 1989), and several other documents comprise the religious laws (Pomeranz, 2004).

Similar to Judaism, the practice of Islam encompasses the individual's entire life (Abassi et al., 1989; Ball & Haque, 2003; Pomeranz, 2004), with daily prayer requirements as well as annual fasting, modes of dress, dietary restrictions, and behavior. More so than the Bible, the Qur'an has precise and definite instructions for how one's economic life should be lived (Abassi et al., 1989; Rice, 1999).

Also similar to other religions, Islamic teaching upholds the value and sanctity of human labor and the importance of human rights (Abassi et al., 1989). In the Islamic tradition, work is an obligation (Koys, 2001), business should serve a moral good (Rice, 1999), and business owners have an obligation to employ others (Pomeranz, 2004). The Qur'an states that while individual work should be individually rewarded (Tayeb, 1997), financial relationships should be egalitarian. Among the values that Islam requires are prudent generosity, just and equitable dealings with others, and humbleness (Abassi et al., 1989; Rice, 1999).

Islam's approach to economic values is friendly to commerce, partly because Muhammad was a merchant himself (Abassi et al., 1989). The faith's economic ethic requires any transaction to pass a "moral filter" that judges its appropriateness in light of key Islamic values (Rice, 1999). These include avoidance of any transaction that results in harm or exploitation, a view of the individual as part of a social structure, and an emphasis on appropriate income levels and distribution of wealth. Greed is considered abhorrent (Abassi et al., 1989). Proper use of wealth contains a strong emphasis on stewardship, since everything on earth is truly owned by God (Abassi et al., 1989).

Individual rewards are considered appropriate if they are justifiably earned and received, and recipients should work hard for their employers. Differences in income and wealth are expected, since some are more favored by God than others in this regard. Charging or receiving interest (*riba*, or usury) is strictly forbidden (Abassi et al., 1989). Further, the "moral filter" of Islamic values prohibits the use of resources on luxuries until the needs of the community are sufficiently met (Rice, 1999).

Recently, scholars have studied an Islamic work ethic (e.g., Ali, 1988; Yousef, 2000 & 2001). While similar to the PWE, this construct includes the worker's duties to other individuals and society as a whole, and more than the PWE, considers intention more critical than results (Yousef, 2001). It is measured by a scale developed by Ali (1988), which shows patterns similar to those exhibited by the PWE in relationship to worker attitudes, particularly commitment to the organization, acceptance of organizational change (Yousef, 2000), and job satisfaction (Yousef, 2001).

RELIGIOUSLY MOTIVATED PAY PRINCIPLES

Organizational success if often defined by the accomplishment of goals, and on efficiency through pragmatic action. However, perhaps *how* organizations accomplish their activities should be considered as well. A Judeo-Christian perspective suggests that work serves moral purposes; it must be psychologically acceptable, allow workers to develop their skills, provide them with a degree of self-determination and the ability to influence their work environment, and prohibit the organization from being the sole judge of appropriate behavior (Golembiewski, 1992).

What are the implications of this more value-laden approach to how we pay people? Certainly the pay principles of internal, external, and individual equity are concerned with fairness. What more needs to be considered? What changes would compensation managers make if they attended more closely to these religious values?

The above discussion makes it possible to identify some "religious pay principles." First, all three traditions support the idea that people should be treated justly. This includes the mandate for fair pay, and equitable transactions of all kinds. Thus, our first religious pay principle is:

> Religious Pay Principle 1: Organizations should treat individuals fairly, in pay as well as in other transactions that have a financial or personal meaning for the worker. Workers who are loyal, honest, and diligent should be rewarded.

Second, these religious traditions seek to achieve a balance between the rights and benefits due to the individual, and the mandate to protect and nurture the good of the community. None reject the prerogative of the individual to work and thrive, as long as that work is justly done and does not harm others or the greater social network. Our second religious pay principle, then, is:

> Religious Pay Principle 2: The work done by individuals within the organization must not harm, but benefit, the broader community. The rewards or benefits garnered by the worker must not detract from the larger good.

Third, all belief systems include the need to provide for the less fortunate, whether through a just wage or other strategy. As Joan Pynes states in Chapter 12 in this volume, "Paying workers low salaries because you can is not consistent with economic justice." Although some distribution of wealth is to be expected, it is the person's responsibility to contribute to the good of all.

> Religious Pay Principle 3: Pay should be awarded and administered so that there is a sufficient amount for all workers to gain adequate or better compensation. No one should have so much it prevents others from having enough.

Fourth, particularly for Muslims and those high in the PWE, work is considered an important part of one's role on earth.

> Religious Pay Principle 4: Work is important for all. Organizations should do what they can to enhance the meaningfulness and satisfaction of work, through pay policies, job design, and other human resource practices.

Finally, there is broad agreement that market economies, while imperfect, are an appropriate means for supporting the society. However, a totally free market will not produce the social good necessary for all, thus regulation of some kind that ensures just transactions is needed. Further, as Edilberto Montemayor states in Chapter 10 in this volume, basing worker pay predominately on the market is "ethically deficient" because it ignores the fact that employees are investors in the firm through their commitment of time and talent, worthy of privileges that other long-term investors receive.

> Religious Pay Principle 5: The market economy should guide an organization's pay practices, but not dictate them. Organizations should support reasonable restrictions to the market so that it supports the first four religious pay principles.

THE ROLE OF PAY IN ORGANIZATIONS

Compensation's role in our economy is to motivate people to do certain things. The compensation level and mix should first be sufficient to attract potential employees to the organization. Second, it should be designed to motivate workers to perform the desired behaviors, at the level of performance necessary for the organization to survive and thrive. Third, it should motivate adequate or better employees to remain with the organization, and encourage those who do not meet expectations to exit.

To achieve these goals, traditional compensation theory says that employees must perceive that the pay package is equitable in three ways. The system must be internally equitable, meaning that jobs or work within the organization are paid according to the value they bring to that organization. The value for any one job across firms may differ, dependent on the values and goals of the organizations. Compensation packages must also be externally equitable, or competitive with the relevant labor market. To be externally equitable, the pay for a certain job at one organization should be relatively the same at another organization with which the first firm competes for labor.

It is important to note that these first two types of equity, internal and external, do not reflect differences between the performance of individuals, but rather in the jobs or work that exist in each organizational system. For example, an accountant job could be filled by a number of individual workers, but the fundamental nature and duties of that job would not change based on its incumbent.

The third type of equity does reflect the unique contributions of the individual. Individual equity requires that workers feels that they are equitably rewarded for the contributions made, be they effort, outcomes, loyalty, etc. The trick in achieving individual equity is designing and implementing a reward system that takes into account the needs and desires of the individuals within the workforce. Let us review how these principles might change in light of the proposed religious pay principles.

Internal Equity

Internal equity, which requires that jobs, as opposed to individuals, be compensated according to their contribution to the organization, must be established so that work of higher value receives higher remuneration (Koys, 2001). Internal equity suggests that the value of the work itself has some finite worth to the organization, and the jobs must be paid within the norms of the organization.

Several principles from the religious traditions cited above support this basic fairness issue: the value that the organization receives from the work should in some way be reflected in the wages that the individual receives (religious pay principle 1). Establishing internal equity creates a structure within the organization that supports the ideals of human development, providing the individual an avenue that allows him or her to continue building human capital and increase wages.

The pay structure in this religiously motivated framework would include elements of hierarchy and egalitarianism. The third religious pay principle, that there should be enough for all, would lead us to design pay systems that are egalitarian to the degree that no one gets so much that others cannot receive their just due. A religiously just pay system would also allow for hierarchy, since organizations should ensure that work is as meaningful as possible (principle 4). Thus pay bands or ranges would be fewer than in traditional hierarchical structures, and have significant overlap.

Internal equity and the living wage. The just or living wage concept can be supported by both the second and third religious pay principles, that the organization should benefit the individual as well as the greater community. The value of the job, or work, should be set high enough to support the reasonable needs of a worker, regardless of its current worth in the external market, or its place in the organization's job hierarchy. Not only would this help the individual, but since it allows workers full participation in the democratic process, the broader social system also benefits. All workers would receive enough to live on, as well as a safe workplace, access to health care, and paid time off for rejuvenation (Gunther, 2004). However, the mandate for these rewards must be balanced with the ability of the business to survive and compete.

The implications of the living wage standard for most organizations is that the job hierarchy resulting from job evaluation systems might have a higher floor, and wage dispersion at the lower levels may decrease. For example, if current jobs pay rates of $6.00, $7.00, and $8.00, and the living wage is determined to be $8.00, the organization could choose to combine all three jobs into the $8.00 rate, closing the distinctions between these jobs' values, and raising the floor of the hierarchy. Alternatively, the organization could increase the rates of the $8.00 jobs as well, in order to maintain the distinctions. Obviously, either strategy is potentially costly to the employer.

Not surprisingly, establishing "just wages" is not a popular idea. Not everyone agrees that a social benefit would result. The main objections are it would create wage compression, raise wages throughout the pay hierarchy, decrease the number of jobs added to the economy (Gaski, 2004), and lead employers to decrease overtime. Raising low wages may result in a decline in benefits offered, perhaps making the plight of the low wage workers actually worse than before (Brooks, 2001; Lee & McKenzie, 1987).

Currently, about 100 U.S. jurisdictions have living wage laws, meaning that the jurisdictions and their contractors are required to pay at levels that provide a reasonable standard of living. Research as to the outcomes of these ordinances is limited. Some research shows that, as feared, they tend to raise wage rates and reduce employment, particularly in geographic areas where many such laws exist (Adams & Neumark, 2005). However, other research finds that living wage laws do not reduce employment or the number of hours worked, but do create wage compression and perhaps result in lower profits for the organizations complying with them (Brenner, 2005).

Many California jurisdictions have these ordinances. A study in Los Angeles found that compared to non-living wage firms, turnover, absenteeism, overtime hours and job training decreased for the living wage firms (Fairris, 2005). Similarly, turnover of homecare workers in San Francisco ordinance significantly decreased (Howes, 2005). Airport workers in San Francisco also received significant pay increases, with reduced turnover, better morale and increased effort (Reich, Hall, & Jacobs, 2005). Thus, evidence shows that living wage laws may increase continuity of employment and productivity, but also increase wage compression and lower profitability.

Summary. What advice would we give to a religiously motivated compensation manager regarding internal equity? First, a religiously congruent and internally equitable pay structure would be a happy medium of egalitarianism and hierarchy, so that while jobs are paid according to their worth, no one receives so much that others go without. At its low end, the pay structure would provide sufficient wages so that any fully performing employee could adequately provide for himself or herself.

External Equity

Religious pay principle 5 accepts a reasonably regulated market economy. Thus, there is justification to establish external equity, which pays workers fairly as compared to the larger economic community (Koys, 2001). Unfortunately, external equity now encourages organizations to pay what their competitors are paying regardless of whether the rate supports the good of the larger community, or whether potential workers have free access to and equal treatment in transactions. It is likely that work which can benefit society may be undervalued, and that which has little value for the social good may be overvalued.

A popular example is child care workers; in 2002, the median hourly wage for this job, according to the U.S. Department of Labor's O*Net, was $7.86 (U.S. Department of Labor, 2004), or $16,349 per year, while the poverty rate for a family of four was $18,100 (U.S. Department of Health and Human Services, 2005). Certainly there is an argument that concerned and professional child care is a critical social good, both for our present and future. However, current market pressures keep pay for this job low.

Summary. The implications of this discussion in regard to external equity would be this: Religiously motivated compensation managers should endeavor to create pay structures that respond to the external market to the degree that they are fair to employees, and attract and retain workers appropriately. However, they should not be enslaved to the market to the degree that they violate the religious pay principles of upholding the common good and providing sufficiently for all workers.

Individual Equity

Our first religious pay principle encourages us to pay fairly. This is the heart of individual equity. The degree to which rewards are motivating depends on the culture and preferences of the workers. For example, norms of reward distribution (Kreitner & Kinicki, 2004) can vary based on culture or religious affiliation. The majority of American culture emphasizes the equity norm, or distribution of rewards based on performance. Some American workplaces continue to offer seniority pay, which in its strict application, favors an equality norm in which all workers share equally, with differences dependent only on years of service. Some religious managers, however, favor a norm based on need, often relying on the "head of household" principle to reward. However, unless such policies are designed so that women and men both have equal access to benefits, they are liable to meet legal challenges (Zigarelli, 1995).

Individual equity is established by identifying the behaviors the firm wants to motivate, and designing and awarding rewards that encourage these behaviors. However, in accordance with our third religious pay principle, rewards and incentives must be distributed according to merit, but so that everyone deserving of rewards can receive them. In other words, some people should not receive huge bonuses, stock options and other incentives when others receive small salary increases, or nothing at all.

Individual differences must also be taken into account in the design of systems that support individual equity. Such design supports our religious pay principle 4, which says that work should be meaningful. Thus, a reward system must be interesting and motivating to its recipients.

Executive pay. Executive pay is frequently accused of being exorbitant (Gupta, 2003; Moriarty, 2005; Nichols & Subramaniam, 2001), not related to firm performance (Lublin, 2005; Stanwick & Stanwick, 2003), designed to elicit improper behavior ("Special report: Fat cats feeding—executive pay; executive pay", 2003; Arya & Sun, 2004), based on inappropriate criteria (Ashley & Yang, 2004), guilty of contributing to an ever-increasing wage gap between the rich and the poor ("Executive excess [1]", 2003; Gupta, 2003), contributing to public skepticism and disdain for business ("Survey: Pigs and power", 2003; Anonymous, 2003), declining morale among the workforce (Wilhelm, 1993), and being poorly managed by their governing boards and compensation committees (Anonymous, 2003; Useem, 2003). Additionally, large severance packages awarded to poorly performing CEOs exiting their firms have been criticized as unethical, motivating the wrong behavior, and unsupportive of shareholders ("Special report: Fat cats feeding—executive pay; executive pay", 2003; Lublin, 2005; Useem, 2003).

The implications for modern business of the religious pay principles identified in this chapter are relatively clear. Over-inflated American CEO pay and the conspicuous consumerism that accompanies it may violate religious principle 3, if its magnitude restricts others in the firm from gaining rewards. While distinction in pay based on value to the organization and the economy is desirable, the dramatic differentials between our highest and lowest paid workers may be unacceptable, and may violate religious pay principle 1, that pay should be fair. However, few boards of directors see this as a moral, let alone a religious, issue (Gunther, 2004).

A further fairness implication is that all employees should have access to company ownership, for example, through stock options, since this would provide laborers access to capital. However, if companies granting stock options offset their cost with lower base pay, and the value of the stock declines so that workers do not realize any gain, then fairness is compromised (Gunther, 2004), particularly since most workers have little direct impact on stock price.

Summary. The implications for our religiously motivated compensation manager in regards to individual equity are that, first, individual rewards should be fairly distributed, based on the appropriate distribution norm for the culture. In the U.S., this norm is predominately one of equity: The better one performs, the more one should receive. Additionally, there should not be differences in rewards that are inappropriate in their magnitude. Rewards should be spread across all well-performing employees, not just the highly paid. Executive pay should be monitored so that, while it is motivational and properly responsive to the broader labor market, it is fair in relationship to the pay that others in the organization receive.

Performance Development and Management

Religious pay principle 4 states that work is important to individuals, and organizations have an obligation to make work meaningful. A reward system that is carefully designed in light of internal, external, and individual equities and aligned with the other religious pay principles will contribute to achieving this goal.

This pay principle also involves ensuring that workers' skills are not obsolete and the individual is able to earn a living (Sethi & Steidlmeier, 1993). Fair and accurate performance measurement supports not only the religious convictions to treat others fairly, but also requires employers to be truthful in assessing performance (Koys, 2001). Finally, the prescription to provide for a safe and healthy work environment should prompt employers to at least consider the provision of health care insurance (Koys, 2001), particular in societies such as the U.S. where access to health care is otherwise extremely expensive.

Organizations should assist their workers in developing the skills that they need to successfully compete in the labor market and will provide them wages that create self-sufficiency. For example, Marriott is well known for its efforts to assist low wage workers that also ensure the firm has a more stable workforce. By providing programs such as parenting education, child care subsidies and an Associate Response Line that offers toll-free referrals to relevant social service agencies, it helps maintain employment continuity for low-wage workers. It also attempts to create long-term employment through an accepting and welcoming work environment, providing opportunities for advancement, tuition reimbursement, and stock options (Yang, 1996). Other companies have similar policies (Greengard, 1995).

Summary. A religiously motivated compensation manager would ensure that performance management and measurement systems were fair, accurate, and consistently administered. She or he would also develop and implement a career management program, including career paths and promotional ladders so that workers can develop themselves. Jobs should be designed to be motivational and allow workers to improve their skill sets.

CONCLUSION

"Economic development means an increase in our ability to get what we want. Religion, however, raises the question of whether we want the right things." (Boulding, 2002, p. 128). American society in the early 21st century is among the most affluent in the history of the world. Given this impressive ability to manipulate and maximize our environment, it is essential for us to ensure that what we achieve results in the best possible outcomes (Boulding, 2002). Do we want the right things? Or, in the context of this chapter, are we paying for the right things? This investigation into the implications of incorporating religious principles into the design and implementation of our pay systems hopefully has shed some light on this question.

We have given our religiously motivated compensation manager several suggestions: First, internal equity should incorporate a blend of egalitarianism and hierarchy. Jobs should be rewarded according to their worth, but pay may be somewhat compressed so that all fully performing employees receive a living wage.

Second, pay structures should respond to the external market in order to be fair to employees, and attract and retain workers. However, the principles of fairness, balancing the welfare of the individual, the community, and the low wage workers should predominate over market forces.

Third, individual rewards are critical to making work meaningful, and should be allocated fairly. Differences between rewards should be appropriate, and available to all deserving employees. Executive pay should be monitored, and be motivational but fair to others in the organization.

Fourth, performance management systems should be fair, accurate, and consistently administered. An effective career management program should be in place in order that workers can learn new skills and develop themselves.

Certainly many of these recommendations are in place across many American companies. However, the motivation for doing them may reside in business efficiency or conformity rather than religious belief. In fact, it may be unlikely that religion will do much to change attitudes of how we pay ourselves. Religious beliefs seem to affect nonreligious realms of life only in limited domains, namely family, sexuality and personal honesty;

they seem to have little impact on economic values (Hoge & De Zulueta, 1985). However, the degree to which individuals hold religious identities, and those identities are salient, the more the religious beliefs may be likely to affect behavior at work (Weaver & Agle, 2002). Since religion seems to be taking up more and more of many Americans' life space (Cash & Gray, 2000; Conlin, 1999; Shorto, 2004), perhaps religious beliefs will begin to have an impact on policies and practices at work, pay being among them. To the degree that compensation decision makers, and those that approve their recommendations, believe that their work is a calling, perhaps it is more likely their organizations' pay systems will reflect religious values (Davidson & Caddell, 1994).

What is Not Covered in the Chapter

As I researched this area, it became clear that there are enough connections between religion and pay to fill practically every chapter in this book. Because of space, this particular chapter is limited to the implications that religious belief may have on compensation practices. What else is there to consider?

One area of interest is the effect of religion and religious affiliation on human capital development. Ample research exists that affiliation with religion, in one form or another, is related to social and psychological benefits. For example, religious people tend to be physically and mentally healthier and have better coping skills (for example, see Day, 2005). Religion may also add to human capital development through the encouragement of particular values, behaviors, and social contacts. Religious participation may encourage desirable workplace behaviors, such as honesty and discipline (Steen, 1996). Participation in religious activities themselves are likely to increase the value of one's human capital, through development of social networks, the propensity to live a conventional life that encourages studying, saving, and conservative lifestyles, and the provision of practical problem-solving skills through interaction with religious principles and social contacts (Keister, 2003). Further exploration into relationships between religious affiliation and human capital would be fruitful.

Second, I have not explored the potential of individual differences in reward motivation between religious versus nonreligious people. As noted, religious individuals have different characteristics from the nonreligious. Since they may be more likely to see their work as a calling, it may be that they would be more likely to find motivation in intrinsic versus extrinsic rewards. Thus, pay may not be as motivational for them as for their nonreligious counterparts. Further exploration into this is needed.

Third, I have not considered the broader social responsibility implied in the religious principles discussed here. What is the government's role, if any, in providing sufficient income for all workers? What is the role of religious organizations in promoting an economically just marketplace? What is the appropriate role of industry, and organizations, in enhancing the welfare of the broader community?

Fourth, the relationship of religion and pay is complicated by the proliferation of international business. Not only do religious values differ across borders, but cultural preferences for pay and sociopolitical and economic changes around the world create markedly different pressures for different pay systems within the same multinational corporation (Ioannau, 1994; Milkovich & Newman, 2002; Safranski & Kwon, 1988). Religious preferences are thus critical considerations in the global context (Kung, 1997).

However, the major religions of the U.S., Christianity, Judaism and Islam, share the call for managers, at all levels, to treat their workers equitably in all things, including pay (Ali et al., 2000). As the American business environment becomes more spiritual, or religious, it is yet to be seen whether this will translate into a sincere, value-motivated desire for establishing fairness, creating meaningful work, compassion for the less fortunate, and concern for the broader community.

REFERENCES

Abassi, S. M., Hollman, K., W., & Murrey, J. H. J. (1989). Islamic economics: Foundations and practices. *International Journal of Social Economics, 16*(5), 5–17.

Adams, S., & Neumark, D. (2005). When do living wages bite? *Industrial Relations, 44*(1), 164–192.

Ali, A. J. (1988). Scaling an Islamic work ethic. *The Journal of Social Psychology, 128*(5), 575–583.

Ali, A. J., Camp, R. C., & Gibbs, M. (2000). The ten commandments perspective on power and authority in organizations. *Journal of Business Ethics, 26*(4), 351–361.

Anonymous. (2003, July 15, 2003). Corporate governance: Corporate identity. *Vital Speeches of the Day, 69,* 596.

Arslan, M. (2001). The work ethic values of Protestant British, Catholic Irish and Muslim Turkish managers. *Journal of Business Ethics, 31*(4), 321–339.

Arya, A., & Sun, H.-L. (2004). Stock option repricing: Heads I win, tales you lose. *Journal of Business Ethics, 50*(4), 297–312.

Ashley, A. S., & Yang, S. S. (2004). Executive compensation and earnings persistence. *Journal of Business Ethics, 50*(4), 369–382.

Baehr, P., & Wells, G. C. (2002). The Protestant ethic and the "spirit" of capitalism: Editor's introduction. In P. Baehr & G. C. Wells (Eds.), *The Protestant ethic and the "spirit" of capitalism and other writings* (pp. ix-lxiii). London: Penguin Books.

Ball, C., & Haque, A. (2003). Diversity in religious practice: Implications of Islamic values in the public workplace. *Public Personnel Management, 32*(3), 315–330.

Bellah, R. (1963). Reflection on the Protestant ethic analogy in Asia. *Journal of Social Issues, 19*, 52–60.

Block, W. (1990). Jewish economics in the light of Maimonides. *International Journal of Social Economics, 17*(3), 60–68.

Boulding, K. E. (2002). What we want. *Harvard Business Review, 800*(1), 128.

Brenner, M. D. (2005). The economic impact of the Boston living wage ordinance. *Industrial Relations, 44*(1), 59–83.

Brooks, P. (2001). Compensation inequality. *The Quarterly Journal of Economics, 116*(4), 1493–1525.

Buchholz, R. A., & Rosenthal, S. B. (2003). Spirituality, consumption, and business. In R. A. Giacalone & C. L. Jurkiewicz (Eds.), *Handbook of workplace spirituality and organizational performance* (pp. 152–180). Armonk, New York: M.E. Sharpe.

Cash, K. C., & Gray, G. R. (2000). A framework for accommodating religion and spirituality in the workplace. *Academy of Management Executive, 14*(3), 124–134.

Childs, J. M. (1997). Business in an age of downsizing. *Business Ethics Quarterly, 44*(2), 123–131.

Conlin, M. (1999). Religion in the workplace. *Business Week, 3653,* 150–160.

Davidson, J. C., & Caddell, D. P. (1994). Religion and the meaning of work. *Journal for the Scientific Study of Religion, 33*(2), 135–147.

Day, N. E. (2005). Religion in the workplace: Correlates and consequences of individual behavior. *Journal of Management Spirituality and Religion, in press.*

Dorff, E. N. (1997). Judaism, business and privacy. *Business Ethics Quarterly, 44*(2), 31–44.

Executive excess [1]. (2003, September 2003). *Multinational Monitor,* p. 6.

Fairris, D. (2005). The impact of living wages on employers: A control group analysis of the Los Angeles ordinance. *Industrial Relations, 44*(1), 84–105.

Furnham, A. (1990). *The Protestant work ethic: The psychology of work-related beliefs and behaviors.* London: Routledge.

Gaski, J. G. (2004). Raising the minimum wage is unethical and immoral. *Business and Society Review, 109*(2), 209–224.

Golembiewski, R. T. (1992). Excerpts from "organization as a moral problem. *Public Administration Review, 52*(2), 95–98.

Green, R. M. (1993). *Centesimus Annus:* A critical Jewish perspective. *Journal of Business Ethics, 12*(12), 945–954.

Green, R. M. (1997). Guiding principles of Jewish business ethics. *Business Ethics Quarterly, 7*(2), 21.

Greengard, S. (1995, January). Leveraging a low-wage work force. *Personnel Journal, 74,* 90–97.

Gunther, M. (2004). *Faith and fortune.* New York: Crown Business.

Gupta, A. (2003). The death of shame. *Mid-American Journal Business, 18*(2), 3–4.

Hafsi, M. (1987). The effect of religious involvement on work centrality. *Psychologia, 30,* 258–266.

Hoge, D. R., & De Zulueta, E. (1985). Salience as a condition for various social consequences of religious commitment. *Journal for the Scientific Study of Religion, 24*(2), 21–38.

Howard, A., Shudo, K., & Umeshima, M. (1983). Motivation and values among Japanese and American managers. *Personnel Psychology*(36).

Howes, C. (2005). Living wages and retention of homecare workers in San Francisco. *Industrial Relations, 44*(1), 139–163.

Ioannau, L. (1994). Catching global managers. *International Business, 7*(3), 60–65.

Jones, H. B. (1997). The Protestant ethic: Weber's model and the empirical literature. *Human Relations, 50*(7), 757–778.

Keister, L. A. (2003). Religion and wealth: The role of religious affiliation and participation in early adult asset accumulation. *Social Forces, 82*(1), 175–207.

Kennedy, R. (1962). The Protestant work ethic and the Parsis. *American Journal of Psychology, 41,* 11–20.

Koys, D. J. (2001). Integrating religious principles and human resource management activities. *Teaching Business Ethics, 5*(2), 121–139.

Kreitner, R., & Kinicki, A. (2004). *Organizational behavior* (Sixth ed.). Boston: McGraw-Hill Irwin.

Kung, H. (1997). A global ethic in an age of globalization. *Business Ethics Quarterly, 7,* 17–31.

Lee, D., & McKenzie, R. B. (1987). Minimum wage: A weaker case both for and against. *Challenge, 30*(4), 55–56.

Lublin, J. S. (2005, April 11, 2005). CEO compensation survey (a special report); goodbye to pay for no performance. *Wall Street Journal,* p. 1.

McCann, D. P. (1997). Catholic social teaching in an era of economic globalization: A resource for business. *Business Ethics Quarterly, 44*(2), 57–70.

Milkovich, G. T., & Newman, J. M. (2002). *Compensation* (Seventh ed.). Boston: McGraw-Hill Irwin.

Mitchell, T. R., & Mickel, A. E. (1999). The meaning of money: An individual-difference perspective. *Academy of Management Review, 24*(3), 568–578.

Montemayor, E. F. (2006). Fairness and Reciprocity—Norms to Enhance the Ethical Quality of Compensation Scholarship and Practice. In Deckop, J.R. (Ed.), *Human Resource Management Ethics.* Information Age.

Moriarty, J. (2005). Do CEOs get paid too much? *Business Ethics Quarterly, 15*(2), 257.

Munroe, R., & Munroe, R. (1986). Weber's Protestant ethic revisited: An African case. *Journal of Psychology, 120,* 447–456.

Naughton, M., & Laczniak, G. R. (1993). A theological context of work from the Catholic social encyclical tradition. *Journal of Business Ethics, 12*(12), 981–994.

Nichols, D., & Subramaniam, C. (2001). Executive compensation: Excessive or equitable? *Journal of Business Ethics, 29*(4), 339–351.

Niles, F. S. (1999). Toward a cross-cultural understanding of work-related beliefs. *Human Relations, 52*(7), 855–867.

Pava, M. L. (1998). Developing a religiously grounded business ethics: A Jewish perspective. *Business Ethics Quarterly, 8,* 65–83.

Pomeranz, F. (2004). Ethics: Toward globalization. *Managerial Auditing Journal, 19*(1), 8–14.

Pynes, J. E. (2006). Ethics and Economic Justice in the Public Sector and Nonprofit Sectors. In Deckop, J.R. (Ed.), *Human Resource Management Ethics.* Information Age.

Reich, M., Hall, P., & Jacobs, K. (2005). Living wage policies at the San Francisco airport: Impacts on workers and business. *Industrial Relations, 44*(1), 106–138.

Rice, G. (1999). Islamic ethics and the implications for business. *Journal of Business Ethics, 18*(4), 345–358.

Roels, S. J. (1997). The business ethics of evangelicals. *Business Ethics Quarterly, 44*(2), 109–122.

Safranski, S. R., & Kwon, I.-W. (1988). Religious groups and management value systems. In R. N. F. E. G. McGoun (Ed.), *Advances in international comparative management* (Vol. 3, pp. 171–183). Greenwich, Connecticut: JAI Press Inc.

Schnall, D. J. (1993). Exploratory notes on employee productivity and accountability in classic Jewish sources. *Journal of Business Ethics, 12*(6), 485–491.

Sethi, S. P., & Steidlmeier, P. (1993). Religion's moral compass and a just economic order: Reflections on Pope John Paul II's encyclical *Centesimus Annus. Journal of Business Ethics, 12*(12), 901–917.

Shorto, R. (2004, October 31, 2004). Faith at work. *New York Times Magazine,* 40–69.

Special report: Fat cats feeding—executive pay; executive pay. (2003, October 11, 2003). *The Economist,* p. 84.

Stanwick, P. A., & Stanwick, S. D. (2003). CEO and ethical reputation: Visionary or mercenary? *Management Decision, 41*(10), 1050–1057.

Steen, T. P. (1996). Religion and earnings: Evidence from the NLS youth cohort. *International Journal of Social Economics, 23*(1), 47.

Survey: Pigs and power. (2003, June 28, 2003). *The Economist,* p. 7.

Tamari, M. (1997). The challenge of wealth: Jewish business ethics. *Business Ethics Quarterly, 44*(2), 45–56.

Tang, T. L.-P., Furnham, A., & Davis, G. M.-T. W. (2003). A cross-cultural comparison of the money ethic, the Protestant work ethic, and job satisfaction: Taiwan, the USA, and the UK. *International Journal of Organizational Theory and Behavior, 6,* 2.

Tayeb, M. (1997). Islamic revival in Asia and human resource management. *Employee Relations, 19*(4), 352.

U.S. Department of Labor (2004). Summary Report for: 39-9011.00—Child Care Workers. Retrieved May 24, 2005, from http://online.onetcenter.org/link/summary/39-9011.00.

U.S. Department of Health and Human Services (2005). Prior HHS poverty guidelines and *Federal Register* references. Retrieved May 25, 2005, from http://aspe.hhs.gov/poverty/figures-fed-reg.shmtl.

Useem, M. (2003, September 23, 2003). Behind closed doors. *Wall Street Journal,* p. 2.

Waltman, J. L. (2004). *The case for the living wage.* New York: Algora Publishing.

Weaver, G. R., & Agle, B. R. (2002). Religiosity and ethical behavior in organizations: A symbolic interactionist perspective. *Academy of Management Review, 27*(1), 77–97.

Weber, M. (1905). The Protestant ethic and the "spirit" of capitalism. In P. Baehr & G. C. Wells (Eds.), *The Protestant ethic and the "spirit" of capitalism and other writings* (pp. 1–392). London: Penguin Books.

Wilhelm, P. G. (1993). Application of distributive justice theory to the CEO pay problem: Recommendations for reform. *Journal of Business Ethics*(12), 6.

Yang, C. (1996, November 11, 1996). Low-wage lessons. *Business Week,* 108.

Yanow, D. (2005). Jewish administrative practice and a philosophy of public administration. *Administrative Theory and Praxis, 27*(1), 134–458.

Yousef, D. A. (2000). Organizational commitment as a mediator of the relationship between Islamic work ethic and attitudes toward organizational change. *Human Relations, 53*(4), 513–537.

Yousef, D. A. (2001). Islamic work ethic—a moderator between organization commitment and job satisfaction in a cross-cultural context. *Personnel Review, 30*(2), 152–169.

Zigarelli, M. A. (1995). The legal pitfalls in compensating employees based on their family need. *Journal of Church and State, 37*, 816–830.

CHAPTER 12

ETHICS AND ECONOMIC JUSTICE IN THE PUBLIC SECTOR AND NONPROFIT SECTORS

Joan E. Pynes
University of South Florida

Recent discussions about Social Security and Medicaid reforms have focused attention on ethics, economic justice and the responsibilities of government. In this context, economic justice refers to upholding what is economically just, in regard to the fair treatment of all workers, but especially the poor. Ethics relates to the body of obligations and duties that a particular society requires of its members.

The traditional political economy of the United States was based upon the following core values: Individualism and individual freedom; equality of opportunity; the sanctity of contract; market competition to satisfy consumer desires; and a limited role for the state. Over time a new political economy began to emerge and the core values began to change where community needs were recognized as being important; equality of results rather than opportunity were targeted; and citizens had the rights and duties of membership regardless of whether they owned property. Con-

Human Resource Management Ethics, pages 239–259
Copyright © 2006 by Information Age Publishing
All rights of reproduction in any form reserved.

cerns about the unintended consequences of the market system led to a more active role for the government (Lodge, 1984). Strengthening community and encouraging wider citizen participation are values emphasized by the communitarian school of sociology (Etzioni, 2003).

This chapter will discuss ethics and economic justice as it relates to minimum wages, living wages, the provision of the public good, and the responsibilities of public and nonprofit administrators.

INDEPENDENT SECTOR NONPROFITS

Modern public administration is a network of vertical and horizontal linkages between government, for-profit, nonprofit and voluntary organizations. Policymaking, program development, and policy implementation are shared among these organizations. This trend has resulted in a mixed economy in which the conventional differences between sectors have become blurred. Private organizations are being penetrated by government policy and public organizations are attracted to quasi-market approaches. The private organizations most infiltrated by government policy and that deliver a significant range of public services are nonprofits that fall under the banner of the Independent Sector. The Independent Sector is composed of 501(c)(3) public charities and 501(c)(4) social welfare organizations. Subsection 501(c)(3) affects the largest number of nonprofit organizations. These organizations are "organized and operated exclusively for religious, charitable, scientific, testing for pubic safety, literary, or educational purposes, or to foster national or international amateur sports competition or for the prevention of cruelty to children or animals." These organizations are referred to as *public charities*. Congress has from time to time made additions to the list. Permitting further additions to the 501(c)(3) takes into account the changing needs of society. Subsection 501(c)(4) *social welfare organizations* are composed mostly of civic and social welfare groups and local associations of employees that may lobby to promote community welfare and undertake charitable, educational, or recreational activities.

Nonprofits that fall under the Internal Revenue Code IRC 501(c)(3) or 501(c)(4) are private organizations that work for a public benefit. The major subsectors of the Independent Sector include health services; education and research; religious organizations; social and legal services; arts and culture; civic, social and fraternal organizations, and foundations. In 1998, there were 1.2 million independent sector nonprofits and 10.9 million individuals worked for them. The independents sector's share of total wages and salaries in the economy was $256 billion, with an annual average wage and salary estimate of $23,743, compared with $33,232 for all other non- agricultural employees. Seventy-one percent of the independent sector workforce is female and 14 percent is African American, both figures are higher than in the government and private sector (Weitzman, Jalandoni, Lampkin, Pollak, 2002, p. 31). Females were represented from 50 to 80 percent of all employees in all of the major sub sectors. Social and legal services, and health services had the highest rate of female and African-American employment, while social and legal services had the largest rate of Hispanic employment (Weitzman, Jalandoni, Lampkin, Pollak, 2002, pp. 45, 48).

WHY NONPROFITS

Because they operate under a non-distribution component, it is believed that they possess a greater moral authority and concern for the public interest than for-profit organizations. Nonprofits often perform pubic tasks that have been delegated to them by government or perform tasks for which there is a demand that neither government nor for-profit organizations provide. Among the examples are organizations established to prevent child abuse, domestic violence, or homelessness, or to assist the disabled, the elderly, the mentally ill, or to provide day care, counseling, vocational training and rehabilitation, or community/neighborhood centers, or advocacy and civic building activities (Lipsky & Smith 1989–90; Salamon,1999). Nonprofits are thought to be more flexible than government agencies. They can experiment with new programs and respond quicker to new social needs. Instead of government getting involved in new or controversial programs, it often gives money to nonprofit agencies to deal with the problem. Nonprofits get financial support and clients receive services. Government, through the conditions it places on agencies who receive public funds still has some influence, but can quickly disassociate itself from programs when things go wrong.

Public organizations and nonprofits are similar in that they define themselves according to their missions or the services they offer. These services are often intangible and difficult to measure. The clients receiving public or nonprofit services and the professionals delivering them make very different judgments about the quality of those services. Both sectors are responsible to multiple constituencies, nonprofits are responsible to supporters, sponsors, clients, and government sources that provide funding and impose regulations; and public agencies are responsible to their respective legislative and judicial branches, and to taxpayers, cognate agencies, political appointees, clients, the media, and other levels of government (Kanter & Summers, 1987; Starling, 1986). Lipsky and Smith (1989–1990) comment that public and private service organizations share many characteristics: the need to process clients through systems of eligibility and treatment, the need to maintain a competent staff to be effective, and the need to account for financial expenditures. These organizations are also expected to be fair (equitable), to accommodate likely and unanticipated complexities (responsive), to protect the interests of sponsors in minimizing costs (efficient), to be true to their mandated purposes (accountable), and to be honest (fiscally honorable) (pp. 630–631).

The Statement of Values and Codes of Ethics for Nonprofit and Philanthropic Organizations (http://www.independnetsector.org/members/code_main.html) goes even farther. It includes the following:

> Commitment of the public good; Accountability to the public; Commitment beyond the law; Respect for the worth and dignity of individuals; Inclusiveness and social justice; Respect for pluralism and diversity; Transparency, integrity, and honesty; Responsible stewardship of resources; and Commitment to excellence and to maintaining the public trust.

The values noted above could also be attributed to professional human resources management (HRM).

ECONOMIC JUSTICE

"The obligation to provide justice for all means that the poor have the single most urgent economic claim on the conscience of the nation." This is not a quote from left learning, anti-business organizations, but from the U. S. Catholic Bishops (1986) in *Economic Justice for All: Pastoral Letter on Catholic Social Teaching and the U. S. Economy*.

Employees are entitled to fair re-numeration for the services they perform. Compensation is affected by many factors: federal, state and local laws; competitive labor market wages, the expectations and perception of fairness by employees, the extent of other benefits provided to employees, and the organization's ability to pay.

The report, *Working Hard, Falling Short: America's Working Families and the Pursuit of Economic Security* funded by Annie E. Casey, Ford and Rockefeller Foundations documents that 9.2 million working families in the United States, one out of every four-earn wages that are so low they are barely able to survive financially. Seventy-one percent of low-income families work. More than half of these families are headed by married couples. One in five workers is employed in occupations where the median wage is less than $8.84 an hour. A full-time job at the federal minimum wage of $5.15 an hour is not sufficient to keep a family of three out of poverty.

Not only do these families suffer from low incomes, but they usually lack medical insurance, often spend more than a third of their income on a place to live, and do not received paid parental leave from their employers to deal with family issues and emergencies (Waldreon, Roberts, Reamer, Rab, Ressler, 2004). This report is consistent with U. S. Census data indicating that the number of Americans living in poverty and without health insurance continues to rise (U. S. Census Bureau, 2004).

The Federal Minimum Wage

Minimum wage, overtime pay, equal pay, and child labor rules are the major provisions of The Fair Labor Standards Act (FLSA), enacted in 1938. Its overtime provision requires that employers pay one and one-half the regular rate of hourly pay for each hour worked that exceeds forty hours per week. The minimum wage law applies to employees of companies with revenues of at least $500,000 a year. It also applies to employees of smaller firms if the employees are engaged in interstate commerce or in the production of goods for commerce. Also covered are employees of federal, state, or local government agencies, hospitals, and schools. The FLSA identifies job positions where exemptions to the law can lawfully be made. Minimum wage increases are passed at the will of Congress as amendments to the FLSA.

As of March 2005, the federal minimum wage is $5.15 an hour. Congress has not increased the minimum wage since 1997. An employee making $5.15 an hour, working full-time, 2,080 hours a year and earning $5.15 an hour would earn $10,712 a year.

Just recently, the U. S. Senate defeated a proposal to raise the minimum wage. Senator Edward Kennedy arguing to increase the minimum wage by $2.10 over the next 26 months stated "That anyone who works 40 hours a week, 52 weeks a year should not live in poverty in the richest country in the world" (Espo, 2005). Senate Republicans also proposed an increase to the minimum wage. Their proposal for an increase of $1.10 in two steps over 18 months was also defeated.

The federal minimum wage serves as the minimum hourly wage employees can earn. States can set a minimum wage higher that is higher than the federal minimum wage. As of March 2005, states with higher minimum wages include Alaska ($7.15), Connecticut ($7.10), California ($6.75), Delaware ($6.15), the District of Columbia ($6.60), Hawaii ($6.25), Illinois ($6.50), Maine ($6.35), Massachusetts ($6.75), Oregon ($7.25), Rhode Island ($6.75), Vermont ($7.00), and Washington ($7.35) (U. S. Department of Labor, Employment Standards Administration, March 13, 2005). Despite already having a state hourly minimum wage of $6.75, Massachusetts Governor Mitt Romney said he would support raising the state's minimum wage to $7.50 by January 1, 2006 and to $8.25 the next year (Atkins,

2005). This is despite its number one ranking (best) for the number of working families that are low income and its ranking of number two for children of working adults in low-income working families according to data compiled in *Working Hard, Falling Short* (Waldreon, Roberts, Reamer, Rab, Ressler, 2004).

On November 2, 2004, 71% of Florida voters passed Amendment 5 which raised the Florida minimum wage to $6.15 an hour. However, business lobbyists are urging the state legislature to step in with a law to minimize the measure's effects on restaurants, retailers, and other businesses that face paying the minimum wage workers an extra dollar an hour (Bosquet, 2005). The New Jersey Assembly voted 52–19 raise the state hourly minimum wage from $5.15 to $7.15 an hour. The Senate voted 26–10 in February to approve the bill. The bill calls for increasing the minimum wage to $6.15 an hour October 1 2005, followed by an increase to $7.15 an hour in October 2006 (Hester, 2005).

Living Wages

A living wage is a term often used by advocates to point out that the federal minimum wage is not high enough to support a family. Advocates have attempted to calculate a living wage based on income that would provide for family's basic needs. Living wages are also commonly referred to as wages set by local ordinances that cover a specific set of workers usually government workers or workers hired by businesses that have received a government contract, subsidy or grant. The justification behind living wage ordinances is to prevent city and county governments from encouraging the creation of jobs that pay wages so low that workers live in poverty. Without living wage laws, governments can inadvertently contribute to the creation of poverty-level jobs by hiring low-paying sub-contractors or giving business tax breaks or subsidies to create jobs without any guarantee that the new jobs will pay a fair wage. This creates additional demands on public services and benefits; because the responsibility of providing income supports and services to low-wage workers is passed on to the government and citizens pay for the services through increased taxes.

Living wage campaigns differ according to the objectives of community activists. Some local laws have been designed to address specific city or county contracts, while others have been planned to cover a variety of public expenditures that include increasing the hourly wages of public employees, or temporary employees working for public agencies, employees working for quasi-governmental agencies such as redevelopment authorities, school boards, hospital commissions, convention bureaus, or airports. In some cases, these employers are covered under separate ordinances, other times they are included in the definition of public employer. Other workers covered by living wages include employees working for contractors and subcontractors receiving public contracts, and tenants of firms that receive economic development assistance. For example, a developer that gets a tax break to build a shopping center is likely to rent space to tenants that employ low wage workers. The living wage must apply to those tenants and workers. Other ordinances have been extended to agencies or firms that lease city or county property such as businesses in or around airports and marinas where hotels, restaurants, and retail establishments are located. The businesses have been required to provide living wages. Concessionaires and the airlines that lease space from Los Angeles, CA & St. Louis, MO are included in the living wage city agreements. Presently, living wage ordinances exist in 123 cities and counties.

Living Wages and Nonprofits

The National Taxonomy of Exempt Entities–Core Codes (NTEE-CC) is a classification system used to identify the primary purpose of nonprofit organizations. It groups 629 codes into 26 major groups under 10 broad categories. Tables 12.1 and 12.2, respectively, present the 26 major groups and the 10 broad categories. The classification with the greatest number of nonprofits is *Human Services*, 14% of all nonprofits fall in this category, followed by *Public, Societal Benefit* with 7.9%, *Education* with 6.8%, *Religion* with 5.3, *Health* with 4.1%, and *Arts, Cultural and Humanities* with 4.6%, *Environment and Animals* with 1.8%, and *Mutual/Membership Benefit* with .4%. Fifty-four percent of nonprofits fall under the *Unknown, Unclassified* category.

Workers employed by nonprofit agencies provide critical services and are typically underpaid. The earnings of workers in the nonprofit industry adjusted for inflation fell by 5.2% between December 2002 through June 2004 (Irons and Bass, 2004). Declining wages and a reduction in the numbers of hours worked provide a partial explanation. There has also been a shift from full-time employment to contingent or part-time employment. Data from the U.S. Bureau of Labor Statistics reports that from February 1999 to February 2001 there 5.4 million contingent workers. Fifty-two percent of them would have preferred a permanent job. Contingent workers were more likely to be women, black or Hispanic. Over half the contingent workers were employed in the services industry. These workers are usually not provided with health or retirement benefits (U.S. Bureau of Labor Statistics, 2001). Contingent, part-time and temporary employees often work two jobs and still may be living in poverty (Weinbaum, 1999).

In many communities the workers that would benefit from a living wage ordinance are likely to work in the nonprofit human service sector.

Table 12.1.   Registered Nonprofit Organizations by Major Purpose or Activity (NTEE Code) December 2004

NTEE Major Group	Number of Registered Organizations	Percent of
A. Arts, Culture, and Humanities	64,157	4.6
B. Education	95,363	
C. Environemntal Quality, Protection, and Beautification	14,101	1.0
D. Animal-Related	11,434	
E. Health	31,914	0.9
F. Mental Health, Crisis Internvention	13,039	0.9
G. Diseases, Disorders, Medical Disciplines	8,251	0.6
H. Medical Research	4,033	0.5
I. Crime, Legal Related	10,894	0.8
J. Employment, Job Related	8,137	0.6
K. Food, Agriculture & Nutrition	5,441	0.4
L. Housing & Shelter	24,044	1.7
M. Public Safety, Disaster Preparedness & Relief	9,742	0.7
N. Recreation & Sports	45,232	3.2
O. Youth Development	17,247	1.2
P. Human Services	75,799	5.4
Q. International, Foreign Affairs & National Security	6,593	0.5
R. Civil Rights, Social Action & Advocacy	4,406	0.3
S. Community Improvement & Capacity Building	34,248	2.4
T. Philanthropy, Voluntarism & Grantmaking Foundations	61,758	4.4
U. Science & Technology	3,303	0.2
V. Social Science	1,395	0.1
W. Public & Societal Benefit	6,562	0.5
X. Religion-Related	74,262	5.3
Y. Mutual & Membership Benefit	5,088	0.4
Z. Unknown	765,065	54.6
Total	1,401,553	100.0

Source: IRS, Exempt Organiztions Business Master File (2004, Dec)
Available at: http://nccsdataweb.urban.org/NCCS/Public/index.php

These employees are typically paid low wages. In 1993, three out of four people worked for a service industry employer in offices, educational institutions, sweatshops, or health care facilities. Data from the U.S. Census

Table 12.2.   NTEE-CC Broad Categories

Major Group	Percent of Registered Nonprofits
I. Arts, Culture, and Humanities A	14.0
II. Education B	6.8
III. Envionrment and Animals C, D	1.8
IV. Health E, F, G, H	4.1
V. Human Services I, J, K, L, M, N, O, P	14.0
VI. International, Foreign Affairs Q	0.5
VII. Public, Societal Benefit R, S, T, U, V, W	7.9
VIII. Religion Related X	5.3
IX. Mutual/membership Benefit Y	0.4
X. Unknwon, Unclassified Z	54.6

Bureau shows the projections of employment by occupation between 1998 and 2008. Under largest job growth, the following positions are listed: registered nurses; personal care and home health aides; teacher assistants; nursing aides, orderlies, and attendants; child care workers, and social workers. With the exception of registered nurses, these positions have low hourly earnings. The data is presented in Table 12.3. Additional data shows the projections of employment by industry between 1998 and 2008. Under most rapid growth, many industries with a large presence in the nonprofit sector. Health services; residential care; museums, botanical and zoological gardens; research and testing services; child care services; job training and related services; and nursing and personal care facilities are some of the industries with the most projected growth. The data is presented in Table 12.4.

Concerns about low wages and diminishing benefits have been emphasized by union leaders when discussing the privatization of public services. In 1995, AFL-CIO President John Sweeney spoke to the California Association of Public Hospitals. At that time he expressed concern that an increasing number of public sector service workers such as technicians, nurse aides, and nurses working in hospitals, nursing homes, home health agencies, ambulatory clinics, blood banks, public health programs, and health maintenance organizations could lose their jobs as more health care services become privatized. Former public employees such as social workers, case managers, mental health therapists, psychologists, and juvenile justice workers are attractive targets for living wage campaigns. Workers in these positions often are responsible for case loads that exceed the recommended maximums stated in professional standards, confront stressful situations daily, are required to work overtime on a regular basis, and often do not have adequate health and retirement benefits.

Table 12.3. Employment Projections by Occupation: 1998 and 2008

	Employment		Change		Rank by	
Occupations	*1998*	*2008*	*# (1000)*	*%*	*Earnings*	*Education and training category*
Fastest Growing						
Computer engineers	299	622	323	108	1	Bachelor's degree
Computer support specialists	429	869	439	102	1	Associate degree
Systems analysts	617	1194	577	94	1	Bachelor's degree
Database administrators	87	155	67	77	1	Bachelor's degree
Desktop publishing specialists	26	44	19	73	2	Long-term on-the-job training
Paralegals and Legal assistants	136	220	84	62	2	Associate degree
Medical assistants	746	1179	433	58	4	Short-term on-the-job training
Social and human service assistants	252	398	146	58	3	Moderate-term on-the-job training
Personal care and home health aides	268	410	141	53	3	Moderate-term on-the-job training
Medical assistants	66	98	32	48	1	Bachelor's degree
Data processing equipment repairers	79	117	37	47	2	Postsecondary vocational training
Residential counselors	190	278	88	46	3	Bachelor's degree
Electronic semiconductor processors	63	92	29	45	2	Moderate-term on-the-job training
Medical records and health information technicians	92	133	41	44	3	Associate degree
Physical therapy assistants and aides	82	118	36	44	3	Associate degree
Engineering, natural science, and computer and information systems managers	326	468	142	43	1	Work experience plus bachelors or higher degree
Respiratory therapist	86	123	37	43	2	Associate degree
Dental assistants	229	325	97	42	3	Moderate-term on-the-job training
Surgical technologists	54	77	23	42	2	Postsecondary vocational training

Securities, commodities, and financial services sales agents	303	427	124	41	1	Bachelor's degree
Dental hygienists	143	201	58	41	1	Associate degree
Occupational therapy assistants and aides	19	26	7	40	2	Associate degree
Cardiovascular technologists and technicians	21	29	8	39	2	Associate degree
Correctional officers	383	532	148	39	2	Long-term on-the-job training
Speech-language pathologists and audiologists	105	145	40	38	1	Masters degree
Social workers	604	822	218	36	2	Bachelor's degree
Bill and account collectors	311	420	110	35	3	Short-term on-the-job training
Ambulance drivers and attendants except EMTs	19	26	7	35	3	Short-term on-the-job training
Biological scientists	18	109	28	35	1	Doctoral degree
Occupational therapists	73	98	25	34	1	Bachelor's degree
Largest Job Growth						
Systems analysts	617	1,194	577	94	1	Bachelor's degree
Retail salespersons	4,056	4,620	563	14	4	Short-term on-the-job training
Cashiers	3,198	3,754	556	17	4	Short-term on-the-job training
General managers and Top executives	3,362	3,913	551	16	1	Work experience plus bachelors or higher degree
Truck drivers light and heavy	2,970	3,463	493	17	2	Short-term on-the-job training
Office clerks, general	3,021	3,484	463	15	3	Short-term on-the-job training
Registered nurses	2,079	2,530	451	22	1	Associate degree
Computer support specialists	429	869	439	102	1	Associate degree
Personal care and home health aides	746	1,179	433	58	4	Short-term on-the-job training
Teacher assistants	1,192	1,567	375	31	4	Short-term on-the-job training

Table 12.3. Employment Projections by Occupation: 1998 and 2008 (continued)

| Occupations | Employment | | Change | | Rank by | Education and training category |
	1998	2008	# (1000)	%	Earnings	
Janitors and cleaners, including maids and housekeeping cleaners	3,184	3,549	365	11	4	Short-term on-the-job training
Nursing aides, orderlies, and attendants	1,367	1,692	325	24	4	Short-term on-the-job training
Computer engineers	299	622	323	108	1	Bachelor's degree
Teacher, secondary school	1,426	1,749	322	23	1	Bachelor's degree
Office and administrative support supervisors and managers	1,611	1,924	313	19	2	Work experience plus bachelors or higher degree
Receptionists and information clerks	1,293	1,599	305	24	3	Short-term on-the-job training
Waiters and waitresses	2,019	2,322	303	15	4	Short-term on-the-job training
Guards	1,027	1,321	294	29	4	Short-term on-the-job training
Marketing and sales worker supervisors	2,584	2,847	263	10	2	Work experience plus bachelors or higher degree
Food counter, fountain, and related workers	2,025	2,272	247	12	4	Short-term on-the-job training
Child care workers	905	1,141	236	26	4	Short-term on-the-job training
Laborers, landscaping and goundskeeping	1,130	1,364	234	21	3	Short-term on-the-job training
Social workers	604	822	218	36	2	Bachelor's degree
Hand packers and packagers	984	1,197	213	22	4	Short-term on-the-job training
Teachers, elementary school	1,754	1,959	205	12	1	Bachelor's degree
Blue-collar worker supervisors	2,198	2,394	196	9	1	Work experience plus bachelors or higher degree
College and university faculty	865	1,061	195	23	1	Doctoral degree

Source: U. S. Census Bureau, Statistical Abstract of the United States: 2001

Table 12.4. Employment Projections by Industry: 1998 and 2008

Industry	1987 SIC code	Employment (in 1,000)		Change 1998–2008 (in 1,000s)	Average annual rate of change 1998–2008
		1998	2008		
Total	(x)	140,515	160,795	20,281	1.4
Most Rapid Growth					
Computer and data processing services	737	1,599	3,472	1,872	8.1
Health services, n.e.c.	807–809	1,209	2,018	809	5.3
Residential care	836	747	1,171	424	4.6
Management and public relations	874	1,034	1,500	466	3.8
Personnel supply services	736	3,230	4,623	1,393	3.7
Miscellaneous equipment rental and leasing	735	258	369	111	3.6
Museums, botanical and zoological gardens	84	93	131	39	3.6
Research and testing services	873	614	861	247	3.4
Miscellaneous transportation services	473,474,478	236	329	94	3.4
Security and commodity brokers	62	645	900	255	3.4
Miscellaneous business services	732,733,738	2,278	3,172	893	3.4
Offices of health practitioners	801–804	2,949	4,098	1,150	3.3
Automobile parking, repair, and services	752–754	944	1,300	356	3.2
Amusement and recreation services, n.e.c.	791.9	1,217	1,653	436	3.1
Water and sanitation	494–497	196	263	67	3.0
Local and interurban passenger transit	41	468	622	154	2.9
Individual and miscellaneous social services	832,839	923	1,223	300	2.9
Child day care services	835	605	800	196	2.8

Table 12.4. Employment Projections by Industry: 1998 and 2008 (continued)

Industry	1987 SIC code	Employment (in 1,000)		Change 1998–2008 (in 1,000s)	Average annual rate of change 1998–2008
		1998	2008		
Job training and related services	833	369	484	114	2.7
Landscape and horticultural services	78	460	603	142	2.7
Veterinary services	74	196	255	59	2.7
Producers, orchestras, and entertainers	792	176	225	49	2.5
Cable and pay television services	484	181	230	49	2.4
Commercial sports	794	127	160	34	2.4
Engineering and architectural services	871	905	1140	235	2.3
Nondepository; holding and investment offices	61,67	906	1141	235	2.3
Miscellaneous transportation equipment	375,379	76	96	20	2.3
Nursing and personal care facilities	805	1762	2213	451	2.3
Automotive rentals, without drivers	751	200	250	50	2.3
Services to buildings	734	950	1187	237	2.3
Most Rapid Decline					
Crude petroleum, natural gas, and gas liquids	131,132	143	77	–66	–6.0
Apparel	231–238	547	350	–197	–4.4
Coal Mining	12	92	59	–32	–4.2
Footwear except rubber and plastic	313.4	38	25	–13	–4.1
Federal electric utilities	(x)	30	20	–10	–4.1
Metal cans and shipping containers	341	37	25	–12	–3.8
Watches, clocks and parts	387	7	5	–2	–3.7

Tobacco products	21	41	30	−11	−3.1
Metal mining	10	50	37	−13	−3.0
Luggage, handbags, and leather products, n.e.c	311,315–317,319	45	34	−11	−2.7
Blast furnaces and basic steel products	331	232	177	−55	−2.7
Petroleum refining	291	96	75	−21	−2.5
Weaving, finishing, yarn and thread mills	221–224, 226, 228	320	251	−69	−2.4
Private households	88	962	759	−203	−2.3
Forestry, fishing, hunting and trapping	08,09	48	38	−10	−2.3
Hydraulic cement	324	17	14	−4	−2.3
Electrical industrial apparatus	362	153	122	−31	−2.3
Railroad transportation	40	231	185	−46	−2.2
Knitting mills	225	159	128	−32	−2.2
Primary nonferrous smelting and refining	333	39	32	−8	−2.1
Service industries for the printing trade	279	50	41	−9	−2.0
Engines and turbines	351	84	69	−15	−1.9
Household appliances	363	117	96	−20	−1.9
Household audio and video equipment	365	82	67	−14	−1.9
Combined utilities	493	159	131	−27	−1.9
Jewelry, silverware, and plated ware	391	50	42	−8	−1.8
Ordnance and ammunition	348	41	34	−7	−1.8
Tires and inner tubes Electric distribution equipment	301	79	66	−13	−1.8
Electric distribution equipment	361	82	70	−13	−1.7
Photographic equipment and supplies	386	81	69	−12	−1.6

Source: U. S. Census Bureau, Statistical Abstract of the United States: 2001.

Teachers, assistant teachers, cooks and cleaners at 350 private nonprofit centers serving more than 30,000 low-income children went on strike in New York City in 2004 because they were without a contract since April 2000 and without a raise since December 2000 (Greenhouse, 2005; Kaufman, 2004). The day care teachers have comparable degrees and experience as teachers working for federally funded Head Start program ($45, 190) or New City Public School teachers (< $70,000) but make thousands of dollars less per year ($34,362) (Greenhouse, 2005).

Thousands of home health aides were also on a three day strike at the same time the day care personnel were. 1199/S.E.I.U. the union representing the home care aides was seeking to raise the hourly wage of the aides from $7.00 an hour to $10.00 (Greenhouse, 2004, June 8).

In Florida, the employees who guard and mentor juveniles in Florida's residential programs makes $17,398 or $8.36 an hour. This is less than juvenile officers in Mississippi, Alabama, South Carolina, and Louisiana. The low salaries encourage staff turnover. Low wages, poor training, a lack of experienced workers contributes to problems at the facilities. As a way to save money, Florida has privatized most of its wilderness programs vocational schools and teen detention facilities (Associated Press, 2005).

In Maryland, contract workers for Maryland's Medical Assistance Personal Care program that provides Medicaid patients with in-home care are paid $40 a day for eight hours work. The workers also have no health insurance, workers' compensation, sick leave, paid vacations or unemployment insurance. Last year the Governor of Maryland, Bob Ehrlich vetoed a $10.50 an hour living wage law, passed by both houses that would have required higher pay for those working on state contracts. In 2003, Gray Davis the Governor of California also vetoed a bill that would have required California and its contractors to pay a minimum of $10.00 an hour wage. Both governors said the bills would be too expensive for their states (Murphy, 2005).

The issue of increasing expenses for public employers and their contractors is a salient one. In 1996, social service nonprofits received approximately 43% of their revenues from fees and service charges or other commercial income, approximately 37% of their revenues from government grants, contracts and reimbursements; and approximately 20% of their revenues from private giving (Salamon, 1999, pp. 36–37). Shouldn't public entities be obligated to pay fair wages?

As a result some living wage campaigns have exempted nonprofit organizations from its provision. However, as the examples above indicate, employees at such agencies provide critical services and are often the most in need of a wage increase. Some local government campaigns have addressed nonprofits in different ways. Sometimes the law will set a threshold level to distinguish between nonprofits. The Boston living wage ordinance was amended to exempt nonprofits employing fewer than 25 workers; the previous threshold was 100 workers. Los Angeles exempted nonprofits if the compensation of their executive officer was less than eight times the lowest wage paid workers in the organization. Washtenaw County proposed a 3-year phase in and allowed nonprofits to petition local governments for either increased funding or special hardship exemptions if no new funds were provided.

The Dane County, WI campaign acknowledged the need for the county to increase funding to smaller nonprofits in the human service areas; and efforts in Allegheny County and Santa Cruz have won similar special funding pools. Multnomah County's law, while not covering nonprofit social service contracts, committed the county and the Living Wage Coalition to jointly lobby state and federal sources for increased funding for nonprofits to make living wage coverage eventually possible.

Elected officials and pro-business leaders typically raise concerns that living wage ordinances will cause job loss for business. This argument has also been used in the case of nonprofits as well. Opponents of living wage increases believe that public employers and nonprofits are unable to absorb the cost of increased wages through a reduction in their profits. Other opponents of increased wages assert that the government should not intervene in the marketplace. However, this position ignores the many ways in which governments intervenes to help businesses through subsidies, tax breaks, tax abatements, bond financing, tax increment financing, grants, tax credits, loans, and other assistance. Living wage laws typically only cover businesses that receive this type of assistance or have contracts with the government. It also overlooks how employers indirectly benefit from government programs to help the poor. They are able to pay low wages because some government programs exist to help low-income families meet their needs. This means that the burden of providing income supports and services to low-wage workers is passed on to the public, because these programs are paid for through taxes and charitable contributions. Dube and Jacobs (2004) found that low wage workers employed by Wal-Mart in California rely on food stamps, Medi-Cal, and subsidized housing to make ends meet. Specifically, reliance by Wal-Mart workers on public assistance programs cost California taxpayers an estimated $86 million annually, $32 million in health related expenses and $54 million in other assistance. The families of Wal-Mart employees use an estimated 38 percent more in food stamps, an estimated 40 percent more in taxpayer-funded health care, Earned Income Tax Credit, subsidized school lunches and subsidized housing (p. 1).

Other research on the minimum wage suggests that living wage ordinances will not cause job loss among less-skilled workers. A recent Economic Policy Institute study of the effects of the 1996–97 minimum wage increase, for example, found no evidence of job loss among teenagers and adult workers with less than a high-school education (two groups of workers that typically have lower skill levels) (Bernstein and Schmitt 1998).

In another chapter in this book, *Fairness and Reciprocity-Norms to Enhance the Ethical Quality of Compensation Scholarship and Practice,* Montemayor (Chapter 10) explains that Organizational Compensation Ethics concerns norms for Compensation strategy and policy. He notes that that the literature is lacking in regard to addressing questions such as: *is it ethical (right) to discontinue retiree health benefits in order to protect the firm's financial performance?,* and *is it ethical (right) to free or even cut employee pay in order to secure dividend payouts for the firm's shareholders during high-inflation periods?* Modifying those questions to fit the public and nonprofit sectors, *is it right for elected officials to oppose living wages for nonprofit employees, when businesses are helped through subsidies, tax breaks, tax abatements, bond financing, tax increment financing, grants, tax credits, loans, and other assistance; especially since low-wage workers depend on government programs to assist them?*

CONCLUSION

Wage stagnation, employment insecurity, and the growing economic inequality between workers and owners are issues that public, nonprofit, and HRM administrators need to be concerned about. Uncertain financial times place additional stress on public and nonprofit organizations. Increased unemployment often requires the expansion of financial assistance, medical aid, and job training or retraining services. These services are typically provided by public and nonprofit sectors, which must absorb an increase in demand for services without increasing their staffs and possibly facing layoffs themselves.

Employer responsibility, democracy in the workplace and worker rights, health care, and providing wages where families can support their families need to be addressed. Paying workers low salaries because you can is not consistent with economic justice. Executive salaries should not come at the expense of lower-level employees, and government entities that offer tax abatements, bond financing, tax increment financing, grants, tax credits, loans, and other assistance to organizations should insist that the recipient employers pay living wages. Public entities should lead by example, paying their employees and contractors fair wages. This is especially true when the contractor is a nonprofit organization providing a critical public service.

Another way of looking at the issue of fair wages is through John Rawls' *A Theory of Justice* (1971, 1999). In this theory, citizens should assume a veil of ignorance concerning their initial position in society. If one does not know ahead of time which positions in society would be yours, then Rawls suggests citizens would support a theory of justice that favors the least-advantaged within society.

REFERENCES

Associated Press (2005, February 8). Low pay for guards at juvenile lockups may endanger teens: Sen. Crist will fight for higher salaries. *The Tampa Tribune* , Metro, p. 4.

Atkins, K. (2005, March 9). Romney supports bids to hike state minimum wage. *Boston Herald.* Retrieved March 9, 2005 from bostonherald.com, http://news.bostonherald.com/localPolitics/view.bg?articleid=72336&formar=text

Bosquet Steve. Minimum pay fight resumes in Capitol, January 13, 2005. St. Petersburg Times, 1, 10.

Dube, A., & Jacobs, K. (2004, August 2). *Hidden cost of Wal-Mart jobs: Use of safety net programs by Wal-Mart workers in California.* Berkeley, CA: UC Berkeley labor Center.

Durr, E. (2002, October 4). New law stokes fires of union fight at Center for the Disabled. *Albany Business Review,* 29 (26) p. 6.

Espo, D. (2005, March 8). Senate rejects both minimum wage plans. *The Chicago Tribune.* Retrieved March 8, 2005 from Chicago Tribune.com. http://www.chicagotribune.com/news/nationworld/chi-0503080221mar08,1,1622449,printstory?co...

Etzioni, A. (2003). Communitarianism. In K. Christensen and Levinson, D. (Eds.), *Encyclopedia of community: From the village to the virtual world,* 1, A-D, pp. 224–228.

Gecan, M. (2000, Spring). A living wage for all American workers-Nonprofit workers too? *Neighborhood Funders Group* http://www.nfg.org/reports/71wage.htm

Greenhouse, S. (2003, April). Day to day, but making a living. *The New York Times.* Retrieved 2/14/2004, from nytimes.com. http://www.nytimes.com/2003/04/11/nyregion/14 care.html?ex=1077801830&ei=1&en

Greenhouse, S. (2004, February 14). Health aides who get sick days? *The New York Times.* Retrieved 2/14/2004, from nytimes.com. http://www.nytimes.com/2004/06/08/nyregion/08strike.html?ex=1087695830&ei=1&en=d56f1e3ef714a7aa.

Greenhouse, S. (2004, June). Thousands of home aides begin a strike. *The New York Times.* Retrieved 6/08/2004, from nytimes.com. http://www.nytimes.com/2003/04/11/nyregion/11LABO.html?th=pagewanted=print&pos

Greenhouse, S. (2005, January). After 4 years, day care workers await raise and contract. *The New York Times.* Retrieved 1/18/2005, from nytimes.com. http://www.nytimes.com/2005/01/18/education/18daycare.htm?ex=1107055151&ei=1&en=ae8f9a5698151c78

Hester, T. Jr. (2005, March 15). Minimum wage gets a boost in N. J. *The Times* Retrieved March 15 from nj.com; http://www.nj.com/printer/printer.ssf?base/news-2/111087766398060.xml

Independent Sector (2004). The Statement of Values and Codes of Ethics for Nonprofit and Philanthropic Organizations. http://www.independnetsector.org/members/code_main.html

Irons, J. S., & Bass, G. (2004, August). *Recent trends in nonprofit employment and earnings: 1990–2004. Tax and Budget Reports.* Washington, DC: OMB Watch

Kanter, R. M. & Summers, D. V. (1987). Doing will while doing good: Dilemmas of performance measurement in nonprofit organizations and the need for a multiple-constituency approach. In W. W. Powell (Ed.), *The nonprofit sector: A research handbook* (154–165). New Haven: Yale University Press.

Kaufman, L. (2004, June). Strike today to complicate day care for poor. *The New York Times.* Retrieved 6/09/2004, from nytimes.com. http://www.nytimes.com/2004/06/00/nyregion/09strike.html?ex=1087792993&ei=1&en=25c859634e4fdbb2

Leland, J. (2005, January 30). One more 'moral value': Fighting poverty. *The New York Times.* Retrieved 2/2/2005, from nytimes.com. http://www.nytimes.com/2005/01/30/politics/30poverty.html?ei=5070&en=9b40a db035c9b7ae&ex...

Lipsky, M., & Smith, S. R. (1989–90). Nonprofit organizations, government, and the welfare state. *Political Science Quarterly, 104,* 625–648.

Lodge, G. C. (1984). *The American Disease.* New York: Knopf.

Medina, J. (2003, February). Day care workers threaten one-day strike. *The New York Times.* Retrieved 2/10/2003, from nytimes.com. http://www.nytimes.com/2003/02/10/nyregion/10 CARE.html?pagewanted=print&position.

Montemayor, E. (2006). "Fairness and Reciprocity-Norms to Enhance the Ethical Quality of Compensation Scholarship and Practice." In J. Deckop (Ed.). *Human Resource Management Ethics* (pp. 195–216). Greenwich, CT: Information Age.

Murphy, K. (2005, March 10). State-paid aides to the elderly get $5 an hour. *Stateline.org.* Retrieved March 10, 2005 from, Stateline.org. http://www.stateline.org/live/ViewPage.action?siteNodeId=137&languageId=1&contentId=17569

Neighborhood Funders Group. *Working Group on Labor and Community.* http://www.nfg.org/labor/index.htm

Rawls, J. (1971, 1999). *A theory of justice.* (revised ed.).Cambridge: Harvard University Press.

Salamon, L. M. (1999). *America's nonprofit sector: A primer* (2nd ed.). NY: The Foundation Center.

Starling, G. (1986). *Managing the public sector* (3rd ed.). Chicago: The Dorsey Press.

Sweeney, John (public communication, Dec. 8, 1995, on-line: www.aflcio.org/press).

U.S. Catholic Bishops (1986). *Pastoral Economic Justice For All: Pastoral letter on Catholic social teaching and the U.S. Economy.*

U.S. Census Bureau, Statistical Abstract of the United States (2001). No. 594. Employment projections by occupations: 1998 to 2008. In *Monthly Labor Review,* November 1999.

U.S. Census Bureau, Statistical Abstract of the United States (2001). No. 597. Employment projections by industry: 1998 to 2008. In *Monthly Labor Review,* November 1999.

U.S. Census Bureau (2004). Income stable, poverty up, numbers of Americans with and without health insurance rise, Census Bureau reports. Retrieved March 14, 2005 http://www.census.gov/Press-Release/www/release/archives/income_wealth/002484.html.

Waldron, T., Roberts, B., Reamer, A., Rab, S., and Ressler, S. (2004, October). *Working Hard, Falling short: America's working families and the pursuit of economic security.* Annie E. Casey, Ford and Rockefeller Foundations. Available http://www.aecf.org/initiatives/jobinitiative/workingpoor.htm. Retrieved March 10, 2005.

Wetizman, M. S., Jalandoni, N. T., Lampkin, L. M., & Pollak, T. H. (2002). *The new nonprofit almanac and desk reference: The essential facts and figures for managers, researchers, and volunteers.* San Francisco: Jossey-Bass.

CHAPTER 13

THE CONSEQUENCES AND CHALLENGES OF UNION DECLINE

An Ethical Perspective

John McClendon
Temple University

Labor unions in the United States are in a crisis. Protracted union membership density loss and other indications of declining union strength suggest that the future viability of organized labor as an effective voice for workers is in doubt. Today, for example, union membership as a percentage of the U.S. workforce stands at only 13% (U.S. Bureau of Labor Statistics, 2005), a union density figure that is at its lowest point since the 1930s (Brofenbrenner, 1998). The situation is especially significant with respect to the U.S. private sector where union density has fallen to single digits, down from about 35% in the mid-fifties. In addition to membership, private sector union activities such as fewer strikes, concession bargaining, and declining political influence all point to organized labor's declining strength. The title of a 2004 New York Times Magazine article, *Is There a*

Human Resource Management Ethics, pages 261–281
Copyright © 2006 by Information Age Publishing
All rights of reproduction in any form reserved.

Place for Unions in the 21st Century Economy?, illustrates the degree to which the future of organized labor is being debated. In short, although there are exceptions to union decline in some areas, organized labor is in trouble.

The decline of U.S. unions suggests a number of questions. Why have private sector unions fallen on hard times? What are implications of labor's decline with respect to the modern workplace in an industrialized market economy? Should we care about the state of unions and, if so, what should be done about it? What role do managerial activities in the context of avoiding union formation play in labor's decline and how do these activities relate to managerial ethics?

The position taken here is that union decline and its impact on the contemporary American workplace is not only important, but involves numerous ethical dimensions. When performing their roles during a union organizing effort managers confront numerous ethical dilemmas, ranging from honesty in message content to disciplinary treatment of employees who are union activists. In contrast to many managerial responsibilities in which such behavior would be routinely considered unethical, the ethical dimensions of election conduct appear less salient than other managerial functions. Given that little attention has been devoted to viewing union avoidance behavior as a dilemma-laden ethical concern, there is a need to address the unionization process from such a perspective. While many ethical and social responsibility concerns relate to union decline, it is ultimately this concern—the ethical elements of managerial decision making and organizational strategy regarding private sector union avoidance—that is the principal focus of this chapter.

UNION DECLINE AND THE NEW MEMBERSHIP CHALLENGE

There has been extensive debate over the root causes for union density loss (e.g., Chaison and Rose, 1991). Among the explanations cited include changing economic conditions, a political climate less friendly to labor, and legal deficiencies (Bronfenbrenner, et al, 1998). The most widely accepted root cause of the decline is associated with the structural shift in the U.S. economy. Broad economic changes related to global competition, capital flight to low wage countries, technological change, and changes in work organization have contributed to a dramatic shift from a manufacturing to a service economy. While this and other structural forces have played a role in union decline, the economic shift explanation is only part of the story with some research (e.g., Chaison and Rose, 1991) concluding that less than one-third of union density loss is attributable to economic changes. Regardless of the impact of job loss in traditional union sectors, more than 300,000 new members must be organized each year to keep pace with labor force expansion and to replace displaced workers from the union ranks (Brofenbrenner, et al., 1998). This suggests it is imperative more successful organizing be accomplished if unions are to recover and regain viability.

The depth of the crisis and the enhanced awareness of the need to revitalize the union movement by recruiting new members, has led organized labor to place greater emphasis on organizing. In the mid-1990s John Sweeney was elected president of the AFL-CIO on a platform emphasizing efforts to increase membership. Nevertheless, with union density decline continuing unabated, Sweeney has now come under attack by dissident unions and leaders within the federation over calls to devote greater resources to membership expansion. The dissatisfaction with AFL-CIO organizing policies has recently culminated in the withdrawal of some of the largest U.S. unions from the federation and the creation of an alternative organization called "Change to Win." Included among these dissident unions are the Service Employees International Union, United Food and Commercial Workers, Teamsters, Unite-Here, Carpenters, Laborers International, and United Farm Workers of America. All combined, these unions represent over five million members. Only time will tell if the organizing efforts and strategies by these dissident unions will lead to union revitalization.

THE UNION ORGANIZING PROCESS

The anatomy of the typical private sector certification process is rooted in federal law and imposes rules on its participants. With respect to the official union certification campaign, the most common process begins when an election date is set under the auspices of the National Labor Relations Board (NLRB). However, in reality, the early card signing phase leading up to the NLRB petition for an election represents an important stage of the process. The process culminates in a secret ballot election where union certification is achieved only when a majority of the votes are cast in favor of unionization.

For an organizing attempt to result in an election, either employees must be highly dissatisfied about their workplaces and jobs or the national union successfully identifies an employer as ripe for organizing (Wheeler and McClendon, 1991). The campaign involves management and union campaign tactics designed to influence the voting. On the union side, the issues focus on being able to contact employees to convince them union representation is to their benefit. Tactics may include hand billing, letters to employees, and mass meetings.

Conversely, management tactics involve a communications effort designed to convince workers that unionization is not in their interest. Management attempts to alter the perception of union effectiveness and appropriateness by emphasizing that union leaders are outsiders, conditions may not improve as a result of unionization, and employees will be unable to deal with workplace issues individually. In doing so, management representatives or their consultants engage in communication activities such as mass meetings, small group meetings, written correspondence, and individual meetings.

Employer resistance plays a central role in the inability of unions to maintain membership density levels necessary to sustain a vibrant labor movement (Brofenbrenner, et al, 1998). Although employers never relished having unions organize their workplaces, beginning in the 1970s and 1980s employers became more aggressive and sophisticated at union avoidance. During this period a systematic and strategic-laden effort to avoid unionization created an industry of consultants who advise management on how to prevent union certification (Brofenbrenner, 1994). And even when unions win certification, employer opposition frequently continues, resulting in employers successfully preventing a first contract being achieved in about one-third of the cases where unions achieved an election victory (e.g., Cooke 1985; Pavy and Smith; 1996; Hurd, 1996).

Private sector union avoidance activities raise ethical and social responsibility concerns in two distinct ways. First, firm-level strategic effort to avoid unions can take many forms, ranging from progressive efforts to build pro-employer commitment by providing an array of high quality of work life programs to employment practices relying on intimidation, fear, and misleading communication. As a result, there are important ethical concerns regarding the nature and type of strategic-level union avoidance efforts undertaken. Second, when formal organizing efforts do occur, the competitive campaign by both the union and the company involves a high pressure context in which managers play an important role, a role that involves many potential ethical dilemmas. It is also a process in which participants are prohibited by federal law from committing unfair labor practices such as intimidating, spying, or punishing employees for exercising their right to form a union. These constraints involve many gray areas of election conduct which present additional decision making pressure for participants. As a result, union organizing creates a context in which ethical behavior is highly fragile and, as such, attention to the ethics of union avoidance behavior is needed.

The ethical concerns apply to all participants in the union organizing process, including the paid union professional staff employees who work to organize new members. While ethical issues abound for all participants, attention in this chapter is limited, however, to the management side. In

addition to practical space limitations, attention is restricted to the management role because our focus here is on union decline, a focus that naturally
directs attention toward management behavior and its role in this decline.

UNION DECLINE AND AVOIDANCE AS A SOCIAL CONCERN: BASIC PREMISES

The advocacy for enhanced sensitivity to ethical concerns when managing
in the union avoidance context emanates from four premises. These premises regard union function, the impact of labor's decline, the necessity of
organizing in arresting that decline, and the nature of management behavior that serves as a key determinant of union woes.

Premise 1:   *Unions represent an important institutional role in an industrialized
market economy and the consequences of its declining strength are deleterious for the
long-term interest of workers as well as society at large.*

The effects of unionization are important at numerous levels. At the
micro-level, through the process of union certification and, in turn, collective bargaining rights, unionization impacts union members by providing
contract based rights that impact all facets of their employment relationship, including all forms of compensation, voice mechanisms, due process,
and work rules. In addition to serving dues paying members, organized
labor also participates in the political process. In this role unions devote
considerable effort to influencing legislation that benefits not only its
members, but nonunion workers as well.

Premise 2:   *Only effective organizing of new membership will guarantee a future
viable union movement.*

There is considerable debate as to what ails organized labor with much
disagreement about the antecedents to labor's protracted decline. It is
clear, however, that a key determinant has been the inability to replace
membership loss through the certification of new bargaining units. As
such, no matter what the root causes of the decline—rather greater competition and its influence on wage pressures, structural economic shift, etc.—
it is only through more successful organizing that a revival of organized
labor can occur.

Premise 3:   *The failure to organize sufficiently is to a large extent a function of long-
term employer union avoidance strategies and practices, and these practices vary widely.*

Managerial efforts to avoid unionization represent basic HR management activities, some that are sophisticated state of the art best practices and some rooted in practices of a very different sort. On one hand, some approaches to avoiding unionization are consistent with progressive activities associated with high performance work systems and HR policies that engender positive employee reactions related to job satisfaction, morale, loyalty, and firm commitment. However, in contrast to progressive employers, many firms take a very different strategic approach to managing to avoid unionization. In treading very carefully along the edges of legal constraints, these organizations approach avoiding unions by relying on implied threats, intimidation, and manipulation. These contrasting strategies suggest that some employers meet the challenge of maintaining non-union operations in ways that yield very different outcomes in terms of employee treatment, outcomes that are closely related to ethical considerations regarding employee dignity, respect, and fair treatment.

Premise 4:   *Union organizing campaigns occur in a dynamic and stressful context that presents many ethical quandaries for managers.*

Union certification campaigns involve emotional charged activities that engender ethical dilemmas. Campaigns also represent a legalistic context in which a well defined set of legal constraints and rules regulate the process. Organizations have a choice when it comes to attempting to avoid certification by winning vote no campaigns. This choice involves either embracing the spirit as well as the letter of the law by conducting a legal campaign that respects employee rights or, alternatively, relying on intimidation, fear, distorted information, and other aggressive actions to win elections.

Using these four premises, it will be argued that what is needed is a more ethical approach in managing to avoid unions, both when formulating long-term human resource management strategies and practices and when conducting activities during specific union certification campaigns. It will also be argued that society in general benefits from having a vibrant union movement and, as a result, public policy changes are needed to facilitate a revitalization of unions.

BUSINESS ETHICAL FRAMEWORKS AND UNION AVOIDANCE

The business ethics literature presents many frameworks that are useful for our analysis. Among the widely used models that are relevant to ethical concerns associated with union avoidance include legal adherence, enlightened management, profit maximizing, utilitarian, and universal approaches to decision making (Hosmer, 2006). In outlining a call for a more ethical approach to managing nonunion, enlightened management and universal—as opposed to utilitarian and profit maximizing models—are advocated.

Concerning legal compliance, managerial behavior in avoiding union certification is regulated by rules produced through some seventy years of federal legislation, agency rulings, and federal court cases. Consistent with minimum standards for ethical managerial behavior, commitment to complying with the elaborate legal rules represent a basic responsibility. After all, even a profit maximizing model emphasizes adhering to legal requirements. However, the legal rules regarding union avoidance activities provide a great deal of gray area, a fact that permits considerable managerial leeway. It is the gray areas that facilitate many ethical challenges and, in contrast to many areas of business conduct, there has been little attention to managerial ethical considerations concerning union avoidance strategies and activities. In this sense the relative absence of ethical debate regarding union avoidance management is perhaps unique, a fact that reinforces the need for greater attention as to what constitutes appropriate managerial behavior. Consistent with this, a call for adherence to the legal rights of workers who consider union affiliation represents a most basic expectation, an expectation that is assumed to be the minimum necessary to begin a discussion of ethical behavior.

Ethical decision making is especially relevant to the HR management strategy formulation and execution when directed toward achieving the goal of maintaining non-union status. HR practices impact directly the human side of the business and there are two well established ethical models that serve as the basis for suggesting how firms should consider approaching managing non-union. These models are the enlightened management and universal approaches.

The enlightened management approach is consistent with and can be an effective device for guiding employers toward developing firm cultures and employer-employee relationships that are built upon trust, loyalty, respect, cooperation, and commitment (Hosmer, 2006), resulting in low propensity for employee desire for unionization. The assumption, therefore, is that an enlightened HR philosophy is more likely to engender progressive employee-centered approaches that are commensurate with building a high performance workplace. It is, in turn, such workplaces that are less likely to unionize (Wheeler and McClendon, 1991). In addition to an enlightened self-interest approach, a model of the principal of universal duties (Hosmer, 2006) to deciding a firm's general philosophy of HR can also be useful. Simply stated, a universal model emphasizes making decisions that are reflective of the right thing to do, independent of extenuating circumstances. As such, a universal model can help guide decision makers through the maze of ethical dilemma-laden HR issues and employ-ment related problems and can be instrumental to a higher level of employee treatment, treatment that can be consistent with a humane and productive non-union workplace.

With respect to the union organizing campaign, situations characteristic of the typical campaign are likely to invoke behaviors that fail to meet a high level of ethical standards. As with HR strategy, a universal framework can be most useful in helping managers navigate the many ethical mine-fields that commonly occur in the pressure cooker context of the union organizing campaign.

Like enlightened management and universal frameworks, utilitarian and profit maximizing are also relevant to union avoidance. A utilitarian approach (Hosmer, 2006) is based on the idea that opposing union forma-tion by aggressive means may be justified because management may per-ceive the long-term interest of many stakeholders—including employees—as best served by remaining non-union. Perhaps it is believed the divisive and conflicting nature of union-management relations, possible higher compensation costs, and/or the occurrence of labor disputes in the form of possible strikes may lead managers to calculate that unionization is not only not in the interest of managers, owners, and stockholders, but not in the long-term interest of the greatest number of employees, both in terms of material rewards as well as intangible aspects of work. Utilitarianism, however, fails to provide an appropriate model because of reasons unique to the unionization process. These relate primarily to the fact that manage-ment interest and other stakeholder pressure are too intense to allow objective assessment. In addition, hypothetically anticipating union effects in a specific workplace is also rife with great uncertainty, making utility assessment of impact a special challenge. Finally, the fervent ideological opposition to unions may distort any objective ability to make an assess-ment of the consequences very difficult, if not impossible.

In regard to a profit maximizing approach, it is perhaps widely used—implicitly—in much of the union avoidance activity. Given that unions are perceived as a threat to a firm's bottom line, this model arguably serves as the driving force behind many of the management actions undertaken in the non-union workplaces in which organizing occurs. As with utilitarian-ism, a profit maximizing approach is rejected here as a less than optimal model for guiding management. Although stockholders are principle stakeholders, workers and broader community interest are invested in the rights to form unions, rights that are not well served by the use of a profit maximizing approach.

THE EFFECTS OF UNIONS AND UNION DECLINE:
WHY PUBLIC POLICY CHANGE IS NEEDED

The importance of labor's decline is intricately linked to what unions do and how well they do it. It is well known that that much controversy abounds regarding the effects of unions on employees, the economy, and organizations. Business interests emphasize the adverse effects union representation has on productivity and the loss of employment in unionized sectors due to union wage effects, and some social critics emphasize the negative effects associated with union corruption and crime. Others, however, believe unions have beneficial effects, including positive impact, not only on union employees, but the economy and society in general. These contrasting views of organized labor have been classified as the two faces of unionism: the monopoly face and the voice/institutional response face (Freeman and Medoff, 1984).

This two faces dichotomy was promulgated by Freeman and Medoff (1984) and includes assessing unionization impact on the basis of efficiency, distribution of income, and the social nature of unions. With respect to efficiency, the monopoly perspective sees unionization as artificially raising wages above competitive levels and establishing work rules that constrain optimal work system design, factors that adversely impact productivity and, as a result, deleteriously impact firm performance and overall economic performance. The voice perspective, on the other hand, views unions as effectively reducing quit rates, inducing management to adopt more efficient methods via the greater investment made in compensation, adopting more HR practices, and improving employee morale as well as skill levels. These improvements, in turn, serve to improve efficiency at the firm and societal level.

In terms of effects on distribution of income, the monopoly perspective sees unions as increasing inequality by raising the wages of skill workers relative to less skilled workers and by creating greater differentiation of wages between union and non-union workers in comparable jobs. The voice perspective, on the other hand, views unions as reducing inequality and limiting arbitrary actions in promotions and layoffs.

In regards to social implications of labor, the monopoly view believes unions have adverse effects on society by limiting their political fights to their own interests and in creating corruption. The voice perspective, in contrast, sees unions not only as representing the interests of their members, but representing the political interests of lower-income, disadvantaged persons, and other segments of society other than the membership base.

The contrasting views are, of course, indigenous to the controversy and emotional-laden reactions that unions generate. These views are also, in part, manifestations of ideological differences that rest within various seg-ments of U.S. society. There is, however, empirical evidence on these mat-ters, especially with respect to the impact of unions on wages and benefits. The premium effect on bargaining unit members is well documented (e.g., Donohue and Heywood, 2000). In addition, studies also suggest that the economic impact of union decline extends across the workforce and is not limited to board certified union members. As such, union decline, at least in part, has played a role in the widening income dispersion of Amer-ican society (Bronfenbrenner, et al. 1998). Research has also demon-strated that unions raise wages overall, reduce wage inequality, and reduce gender, race, and age pay differences (Freeman, 1992, Spalter-Roth, et al, 1994). Although these findings are certainly not uniformly positive, much of this research, on balance, supports the position that will be taken here that the positive economic impact of unionization offsets the negative effects. In short, unions raise wages and reduce inequality, and not only for union members.

Union decline also results in declining political influence for workers in general, not just union members. Consistent with American "bread and butter" unionism, organized labor devotes considerable effort to influenc-ing legislation that benefits its members directly. However, organized labor also functions as the institutional voice for all of labor and has a long tradi-tion of contributing to the passage of wide-ranging legislation that benefits all workers across the spectrum. The recent decline in organized labor is manifested in many areas. Greater use of part-time/temporary workers, the demise of traditional pensions, forced arbitration in lieu of agreeing to give up one's right to sue under civil rights laws, declining real wages for the lower-middle strata, the failure of the federal minimum wage to be raised commensurate with inflation, and other changes in the American workforce can be linked to the declining influence of organized labor.

Overall, unions play an important role in several respects. First, through collective bargaining, organized labor has been a major force in providing improved pay, working conditions, and workplace voice/justice for its mem-bership. Second, by enacting forces that facilitate the union spillover effect, unions have indirectly produced many of the same improvements for non-union workers. This is especially the case in economic sectors in which the fear of union formation is strongest and, as a result, employers may be induced to provide better employment conditions in an effort to head off union certification. Third, as the principal representative voice for workers, unions play a crucial role in supporting and opposing legislation consistent with the interest of workers in general and society at large.

The right to secure collective bargaining as a means to determine the terms and conditions of one's employment is a basic right. It is a right that directly secures the means to better wages, work conditions, and workplace justice mechanisms for dues paying membership. It is also a right—due to its serving as the institutional voice for workers at large—that has broad implications for society in general. It is a right, it is contended here, that should be left up to the workers to decide free from extreme employer opposition. Because the history of union impact shows that unions do much good, the end of unions would be unfortunate. What is needed is legal reform that would better enable society to benefit from the positives of unionism while mitigating the negatives. Given the importance of "what organized labor does" and the crisis it faces, the first proposition is:

> The long-term health of U.S. society and, indeed, overall economic health, depends on a viable labor movement. That movement faces a crisis, a crisis that, if unabated, will render this institutional voice for workers impotent, resulting in deleterious implications for society's overall interest. It is imperative that U.S. public policy change to enhance the prospects of greater union density.

WHY EMPLOYERS WISH TO AVOID UNIONS

Some research at the firm-level provides evidence that unionization is not necessarily incompatible with productivity and firm performance (e.g., Freeman and Medoff, 1984). Such research also suggests that unionized employees can exhibit high levels of commitment to both the union and the employer (Roby, 1995). Nevertheless, unions, both in terms of effects and tactics, have long been controversial. Regardless of conflicting empirical evidence, there are several reasons managers are less than enthusiastic about having unions. Unions, after all, limit the authority and decision making discretion of management across a range of issues. The union may be viewed as an outsider who has no justified basis for legally required recognition as the exclusive representative of its employees and is likely seen as a troublemaker who undermines the employee's commitment and loyalty to the employer. And given union values such as seniority and the threat to managerial decision making autonomy that occurs with collective bargaining, it is not surprising that private sector firms vehemently oppose unionization.

Understanding employer incentives to resist unionization gives one better appreciation for the intensity and prevalence of union avoidance. And it is worth noting that by all accounts the opposition appears to have intensified in recent years as employers have honed the union avoidance models developed in the 1980s (Bronfenbrenner, 1998). This intensity can also enhance one's appreciation for the degree to which the context of union organizing is ripe for ethical dilemmas that may challenge the best intentioned manager. These ethical issues—which are rooted in the highly contentious and adversarial process of union avoidance– warrant much more attention in the field of business ethics, including how future and current business leaders receive training at American universities.

THE DECISION BY EMPLOYEES TO UNIONIZE

There is an extensive research literature on why workers unionize. Numerous studies have employed a wide-range of methodologies in examining causal determinants and outcome measures related to the unionization process (Wheeler and McClendon, 1991). One category of this voluminous literature consists of election-level studies that examine determinants of union success. It includes analysis of such factors as unit size, election location, voter turnout, use of management consultants, and time lapse between petition and actual election (e.g., Weikle, Wheeler, and McClendon, 1998). Other research has examined union campaign tactics (e.g., Brofenbrenner and Juravich, 1998).

While election-level studies have enhanced our understanding of the unionization process, as noted by Wheeler and McClendon (1991), the very heart of the collective action of unionization lies in the individual decision to support it. This decision occurs in the context of the workplace, and understanding why individual workers either support or oppose union formation requires consideration of many organizational factors (Fiorito and Young, 1998). It is this segment of the literature—the research on workplace determinants to an individual's decision to support a unionization effort—that is most relevant to the arguments promulgated here in support of a more ethical approach to union avoidance strategies and tactics.

Given that an extensive review of this literature is beyond the scope of this chapter, the discussion is limited to the two factors identified in research that have implications for ethical issues related to union avoidance. First, there are a number of employee attitudes about the job and the organization that have been consistently shown to correlate with union support. These include job satisfaction, the relations between management and workers, and organizational commitment (Wheeler and McClendon, 1991).

Most important regarding ethical issues of organizing, it is not simply the presence of these conditions and their inverse relationship to union support, but the managerial actions and programs that serve as the antecedents of these conditions that are of particular interest. Delaney and Huselid (1996) and Fiorito and Young (1998) identified several distinct HR practices that are key to influencing employee's attitudes and, in turn, the propensity to support or oppose union certification. These include such HR practices as reliance on internal promotions, hiring selectivity, an emphasis on training, employer sponsored grievance procedures, competitive benefits, incentive pay, and the absence of a history of pay cuts. In addition, employee involvement programs (Rundle, 1996) and job design characteristics such as level of autonomy and responsibility (Fiorito and Young, 1998) have also been identified. Wheeler and McClendon (1991; 1998) expanded on the role of workplace conditions as key by finding that it is not simply dissatisfaction, but strong emotional affect in the form of employee frustration and anger regarding employer treatment that drives unionization. Overall, employee attitudes are key determinants and, importantly, these attitudes are a manifestation of employer actions toward employees.

Second, the perception of union effectiveness has been shown to be a major factor in determining employee voting (e.g., Wheeler, Weikle, and McClendon, 1998). Consistent with this logic, it is not simply employee dissatisfaction, but the degree to which the union is viewed as having the capacity to produce desired results that is important. In other words, while dissatisfaction begins a search for ways to improve conditions, the union must be seen as a viable alternative before union support is achieved.

While union support is the result of an interaction of factors, research suggests that both employee attitudes and perceived union instrumentality are especially important. These two categories are also especially relevant to issues regarding ethical concerns. There are two reasons for this argument. First, employee reactions are a result of the various terms and conditions of employment provided by the employer. As such, given that managerial decision making regarding employee treatment, workplace conditions, and HR strategy are key root causes of employee reactions, one can, in fact should, view this as an issue of management ethics. Second, the employer's communication activities in the certification campaign focus on influencing employee perception of union effectiveness. This has implications for ethical guidelines to the extent to which employer behavior should be consistent with enlightened management and universal principles.

A MORE ETHICAL WAY TO MANAGE NONUNION: SUPPRESSION VERSUS ENLIGHTENED APPROACHES

In many private sector firms, union avoidance is associated with a strategic level goal to avoid unions. This strategic approach to union avoidance is distinguished by its long-term focus on activities devoted to an explicit goal of remaining non-union. However, apart from sharing in the objective of remaining non-union, the approaches to managing in the non-union environment take very divergent forms. And these divergent forms have profoundly contrasting implications for ethics.

The evidence suggests that many employers are willing to go to great lengths to avoid unions (Bronfenbrenner 1994; 1995), and one form of union avoidance can be called the union suppression approach. Eschewing the option of attempting to engender employee satisfaction and morale, this form of union avoidance relies primarily on intimidation and implied fear of retaliation. Consistent with this aggressive approach, a union suppression approach attempts to indoctrinate employees against the idea of unionization and it can even extend to using hiring practices designed to screen applicants who backgrounds may suggest a more favorable predisposition to unions. When official union organizing efforts occur, this type of private sector firm can go nuclear with its anti-union campaign tactics. By skirting along the edge of the legal constraints regarding unfair labor practices, the union suppressor shows few limits in the degree to which it attempts to prevent unionization, including conducting surveillance of employees for union activity, pursuing election delays, and searching for legally pre-textual reasons to discharge employees participating in pro-union activity (Bronfenbrenner et al., 1998).

A contrasting approach is the employer-substitution approach. Consistent with the research literature on union formation cited earlier, it is believed that employee dissatisfaction is the prime motivator that drives union organizing. The design and effective execution of a host of HR practices have been shown to impact employee satisfaction and other employee reactions to the job and organization. Improving employee attitudes, in turn, is associated with a reduced likelihood of union formation. Specifically, as discussed in a previous section, there are distinct HR programs that have been identified in the research literature that are instrumental to employee morale and, in turn, lower propensity to organize (e.g., Delany and Huselid, 1996.) These practices focus on fulfilling the psychological contracts of employees and relate to developing more positive employer-employee relationships.

By emphasizing programs that positively impact employee attitude, the employer substitution strategy involves preventing unionization through effective implementation of many HR best practices. A strategic approach designed to prevent unionization this way may be referred to as progressive or enlightened union avoidance (Fiorito and Young, 1998). Because it is designed preemptively to mimic polices provided in union contracts, this approach is also sometimes attributed to the union spillover effect (Fossum, 2002).

There are clearly important distinctions between the suppressor and enlightened self-interested approaches in terms of their ultimate impact on employee treatment. These approaches, however, are similar in that the impetus for their implementation is to prevent unionization. One, therefore, can further distinguish the approaches to non-union systems by what is called the philosophy-laden vs. the doctrinaire approaches (Fossum, 2002). Both of these approaches employ practices that resemble the employer-substitution emphasis of improving job satisfaction. They differ, however, in one important respect. While the primary motive for the doctrinaire approach is to prevent unionization, philosophy-laden firms focus on using progressive HR practices to build a high performance culture that is characterized by high morale, organization commitment, and employee involvement. In other words, management engages in progressive HR practices it believes are right and consistent with optimal organization health and performance, not simply to defeat the union. As a result, a philosophy-laden firm does not have unions as a natural result of its organizational climate, whereas the doctrinaire oriented firm may attempt a more positive approach because of fear and/or ideological opposition to unions.

This framing suggests that strategic HR approaches in non-union firms can be viewed on a continuum. First there is the suppressor firm that goes to virtually any length to prevent unionization. This approach violates many ethical principles regarding employee treatment and respect and violates the spirit, if not the letter, of the laws governing the right of workers to form a union. Second is the more progressive doctrinaire firm that uses more desirable HR practices designed to enhance employee motivation and morale. Although using many positive practices, firms employing this approach are driven primarily by the desire to prevent unionization. However, these firms likely use employer substitution practices, which is much preferable to the suppressor oriented firms. Nevertheless, this approach lacks the integrity imbedded in an approach predicated on a system devoted to building a high performance firm culture as its principal motive and which is based on management principles rooted in a moral imperative-laden model. In addition, this approach, although positive in many ways, also is fragile ethically. Because it perhaps emanates from utilitarian motives and is less rooted in basic moral principles of worker treatment, one can speculate that such a firm would be more susceptible to the pressures of an organizing campaign and, thus, is at some risk for compromising its approach to fair treatment.

In contrast, a philosophy-laden approach, as defined here, is more deeply rooted in core values of worker respect and dignity. It is also based on a management belief system that accepts the right of workers to form unions and is guided by ethical principles that are more resilient to the inevitable contextual pressures that impose ethical dilemmas, pressures that can result in compromises of otherwise well intentioned practices. It is this approach, the philosophy-laden approach that is most closely related to a universal approach to managing the workplace. This leads to the following proposition:

Support for unionization is closely linked to employee reactions and attitudes about the job, managers, and the organization. These attitudes are a result of management treatment and other terms and conditions of employment provided via the employer-employee exchange relationship. Consistent with ethical frameworks associated with enlightened management and universal models, an employer substitution approach to employment practices coupled with a philosophy-laden management philosophy—as opposed to a doctrinaire approach—is preferably. In fact, such an approach augments many HR activities associated with best practices in developing a high performance organization.

THE EMPLOYER ANTI-UNION CAMPAIGN: A CALL FOR A MORE ETHICAL APPROACH

It was pointed out in our review of determinants to unionization that perceived union effectiveness was a key determinant of union voting (e.g., Wheeler and McClendon, 1991). Consistent with this, both the union and management use an array of campaign tactics that are designed to alter the employees' perceptions of the union's ability to provide effective representation. This activity increases the importance of the campaign and represents the immediate context in which many important ethical issues arise.

One obvious ethical issue concerns employee fear of retribution for supporting unionization. Employee apprehension regarding possible management retaliation is a well documented inhibition to successful union certification (Cohen and Hurd, 1998), and exploiting the apprehension associated with fear of management reactions is fundamental to many management campaign tactics (e.g., Brofenbronner, 1994; Freeman, 1995). For example, one study of several union certification elections found that employee fear of employer retaliation for supporting the union was an important factor in suppressing pro-union activism (Wheeler et al, 1998). In today's workplace, employees attempting to organize confront legal delays, intimidation, and harassment. And given that aggressive employer opposition has become more commonplace in recent years (Bronfenbrenner, 1998), this fear appears justified.

Management actions that generate fear of retaliation can take many forms, ranging from the illegal discharge of employees who support the union to implied threats of the consequences of union formation. And research evidence suggests that some employers even go so far as to purposely commit unfair labor practices to blunt union organizing drives (Freeman and Kleiner, 1990). The equation of the costs vs. benefits for violating the law suggests that legal penalties for conviction of unfair labor practices are insufficient, a perception that has led many to calls for labor law reform.

In addition to fear, there are many activities, although legal, that represent serious ethical questions. For example, as a legal maneuver to delay the process, it is common for employers to challenge the union's claim of support via signed authorization cards. This challenge leads to lengthy NLRB sponsored hearings that serve to delay the time between the card signing stage and the secret ballot vote, delays which research has demonstrated are associated with union losses (Bronfenbrenner, et al. 1998). Such disingenuous legal machinations are unethical and subvert the concept of free employee choice.

Perhaps one of the more common ethical issues in the organizing campaign has to do with truthfulness of campaign information. Before 1977, the NLRB required that campaign information be truthful. Since that time the board has reversed itself three times and presently does not require truthfulness in campaign claims. The board reasons that because employees have experienced political campaigns they are not easily influenced by campaign rhetoric (Fossum, 2002). As a result, there is no legal accountability for knowingly distorting the truth when conducting campaigns, a fact that presents significant enticement for legal but nevertheless unethical behavior.

Finally, in many cases employer resistance continues even after the union secures victory. Employers may file objections based on voter eligibility, appropriateness of the bargaining unit, or other campaign irregularities in an effort to delay negotiating a first contract. Having gained a delay in the requirement of recognizing the union as the exclusive representative of its workers and, as a result, postponing the good faith bargaining requirement, management sometimes commits illegal actions such as discriminatory retaliation against union activists (Cooke, 1985). These activities send a message of employer intransigence and, if the company forestalls an agreement for one year, a decertification election may occur.

While workers continue to face greater risks for attempting to exercise their right to form a union (Bronfenbrenner, 1998), the pressure on management personnel to avoid unions is substantial. And for lower level supervisors—agents of the employer who are in the direct firing line of anti-union activities and who are expected to play a crucial role in delivering a victory for the employer—the pressure is especially acute. While a campaign operates with legal rules, it nevertheless provides tremendous opportunity for managers to act in ways inconsistent with optimal ethical conduct.

Using a utilitarian view of avoiding unions represents a slippery slope for management. A belief that union representation would not be in the interest of many stakeholders (including even the genuine perception that union representation is not in the interest of employees) can lead to a great deal of rationalization. This slippery slope can lead managers to commit a number of unethical acts, ranging from untruthful communications to discharging union activist on some unrelated pre-textual basis to more subtle forms of intimidation. The organizing process, why workers support or oppose unionization, and the role of management behavior provide an alchemy of factors that are ripe for unethical conduct. This leads to a third and final ethical proposition:

> Although employer anti-union campaign activities in the private sector are constrained by a federal regulatory agency and labor law, organizations and individual managers have considerable flexibility in how these campaign activities are conducted. And given that the context of the campaign represents a stressful situation in which great pressure may exist for avoiding unionization, the combination of flexibility and pressure is likely to lead to many ethical dilemmas for managers, dilemmas that can result in violations of spirit of the law, if not the letter. As such, is it important that organizations foster a management culture and code of conduct for campaign activities that respects the rights of workers to make an unfettered decision regarding union certification. This is consistent with ethical frameworks associated with universal and enlightened management approaches to managing non-union.

CONCLUSIONS

Private sector unionism faces many challenges and its future, as least as a major force in American society, is in question. Employers have become more aggressive and sophisticated in avoiding unions and any significant improvement in labor's situation may require public policy changes. It has been argued here that such policy changes would serve both workers and society well (Bronfenbrenner, 1994). However, the prospects of policy changes, given the current political climate, appear unlikely. In fact, previous efforts at labor law reform undertaken in more favorable political situations (1978 and in 1994) failed. Given the current context, advocates for a more vibrant labor movement should not hold out hope for help from a change in the rules, at least for the foreseeable future.

So what should labor do? Some scholars have argued that unions have the capacity to do better in spite of formidable obstacles. More sophisticated tactics in organizing have been advocated, some of which have been shown by empirical research to be effective in enhancing the possibility of union certification victories (Brofenbrenner, 1998). Most importantly, many labor leaders, including the leaders of several major unions, have advocated more resources be devoted to organizing new members. Building on the impressive successes of select unions at private sector organizing in recent years such as the Service Employees International Union (SEIU), these leaders believe that labor does indeed have the capacity to remain a viable force in representing 21st century workers.

The main focus in this chapter, however, has been on the ethical vulnerabilities confronting private sector managers. Whether formulating broad based firm-level strategies to avoid unions through HR systems or conducting management sponsored vote no campaigns in union certification elections, there are numerous ethical concerns that are indigenous to the process. Some of these issues relate to legal compliance and some do not. All, however, are important as they impact the lives and economic well being of employees and managers and impact the viability of business organizations and labor unions. In carrying out these activities it has been advocated here that all parties are best served when managers employ decision making models that reflect enlightened oriented approaches that show deference for the law as well as dignity and respect for workers. Moreover, because organizing campaigns represent pressure packed situations, it is argued here that managers are best guided by a moral imperative approach as opposed to utilitarian or profit maximizing models.

Finally, in recent years there has been greater emphasis on teaching business ethics in business schools, both at the undergraduate level as well as in MBA programs. What is likely missing from this positive trend is sufficient attention to the ethical challenges associated with managing to avoid unionization. There are, of course, many important ethical issues within the diverse portfolio of concerns related to business ethics issues that likely fall through the cracks. However, the ethical concerns related to union organizing are probably somewhat unique in two respects. First, there are many management behaviors that would almost certainly be viewed as unethical in most situations, but do not make it to the ethical radar screen when occurring in the context of a union campaign. For example, while overt dishonesty would almost universally be cited as unethical in most business dealings, managers can knowingly state inaccurate union campaign information as an institutionalized right. Second, not only does ethically questionable behavior occur on a wide scale in union campaigns, but such management actions appear widely accepted and, as a result, are frequently not even framed in ethical terms in much of contemporary American management culture. These concerns suggest that union avoidance is a topic that warrants much greater attention.

There are limitations of this chapter that warrant mention. First, the discussion here has dealt with private sector unionism in the U.S. only. As a result, it does not include review of public sector unionism in the U.S. or, additionally, discussion of issues regarding the state of unions in other industrialized market economies. Public sector unions have fared considerably better in the U.S. in some states and these unions operate in a legal context that varies from state to state, meaning that many of the organizing issues covered here have little to do with public sector employees. In addition, unions have been under pressure in many other industrialized countries in very recent years as well. However, given that U.S. law and its detailed union certification process are highly unique, the ethical issues discussed regarding the campaign are U.S. specific and not applicable to other situations.

Finally, it should be noted that only management behavior has been examined. Union organizers and their organizations also, of course, confront many ethical dilemmas when leading a certification election effort. The focus has been restricted to managers and their organizations because of the dire straits confronting unions today and the prospects of further declining status, a decline directly attributable to a great extent to management actions and polices. Future work should also be devoted to all actors in the unionization process, including the front-line professional union organizer.

REFERENCES

Brett, Jeanne M. (1980). Behavioral research on unions and union management systems. In *Research in Organizational Behavior*, pp. 31–70.

Brofenbrenner, Kate. (1994). Employer behavior in certification election and first-contract campaigns: Implications for labor law reform. In *Restoring the Promise of American Labor Law*, Ed. Sheldon Friedman, pp. 75–89.

Brofenbrenner, Kate, Sheldon Friedman, Richard W. Hurd, Rudolf A. Oswald, and Ronald Seeber, Eds. (1998). Introduction. In *Organizing to Win.*

Brofenbrenner, Kate and Tom Jurvavich. (1998). It takes more than house calls: Organizing to win with a comprehensive union-busting strategy. In *Organizing to Win*, Eds, Kate Brofenbrenner, Sheldon Friedman, Richard W. Hurd, Rudolf A. Oswald, and Ronald Seeber.

Bureau of Labor Statistics, United States Department of Labor. Washington D.C. 2005. www.bls.gov

Chaison, Gary N. and D.G. Dhavale (1990). A note on the severity of the decline in union organizing activity. *Industrial and Labor Relations Review, 43*(2), 366.

Chaison, Gary N. and Joseph B. Rose. (1991). In *The State of the Unions*, pp 3–46.

Cohen, Larry and Richard W. Hurd. (1998). Fear, conflict, and union organizing. In *Organizing to Win.*

Cooke, William N. (1985). Organizing and public policy: Failure to secure first contracts.

Delaney, John T. and Mark A. Huselid. (1996). The impact of human resource management practices on perceptions of organizational performance. *Academy of Management Journal, 33*, 949–969.

Donohue, Susan M and John S. Heywood. (2000). Unionization and nonunion wage patterns: Do low wage workers gain the most?" *Journal of Labor Research, 21*(3), 489–502.

Fossum, John A. (2002). *Labor Relations, Development, Structure, and Process*. 8th edition.

Fiorito, Jack, and Angela Young. (1998). Union voting intentions: Human resources policies, organizational characteristics, and attitudes. In *Organizing to Win*.

Freeman, Richard B. (1992). Is declining unionism of the U.S. good, bad, or irrelevant? In *Unions and Competitiveness*.

Freeman, Richard and Morris M. Kleiner, (1990). Employer behavior in the face of union organizing drives. *Industrial and Labor Relations Review, 43*(3), 351–365.

Freeman, Richard B. and James L. Medoff. (1984). *What do unions do?*

Hosmer, LaRur T. (2006). *The ethics of management*.

Hurd, Richard W. (1996). Union free bargaining strategies and first contract failures. In *Proceedings of the 48th Annual Meetings of the IRRA*.

Pavy, Gordon and Brett Smith. (1996). *A question of fairness: Employer opposition to negotiating a first contract*.

Roby, P.A. (1995). Becoming shop stewards: Perspectives on gender and race in ten trade unions. *Labor Studies Journal, 20*(3), 65–82.

Spalter-Roth, Roberta, Heidi Hartmann, and Nancy Collins. (1994). What do unions do for women?" In *Restoring the promise of American Labor Law*.

Weikle, Roger D., Hoyt N. Wheeler, and John A. McClendon. (1998). A comparative case study of union organizing and failure: implications for practical strategy. In *Organizing to Win*.

Wheeler, Hoyt and John A. McClendon. (1991). The individual decision to unionize. In *The State of the Unions*.

CHAPTER 14

THE ETHICAL PROBLEMS OF A MATERIALISTIC VALUE ORIENTATION FOR BUSINESSES

(And Some Suggestions for Alternatives)

Tim Kasser
Knox College

Maarten Vansteenkiste
University of Leuven

John R. Deckop
Temple University

The contemporary form of American capitalism does much to place the pursuit of money at the forefront of its aims. Consumers are continually bombarded by messages from the media suggesting that happiness and the good life can be attained if one has the money to purchase desirable products and services. Governmental policies attempt to maximize the eco-

Human Resource Management Ethics, pages 283–306
Copyright © 2006 by Information Age Publishing

nomic growth of the nation, in the belief that such indicators are the best marker of national "progress." And corporations strive to maximize quarterly profit reports and shareholder value. Regardless of the particular variation, a fundamental message comes through: Success equals the accumulation of money and possessions.

Although the pursuit of such materialistic aims may help improve certain indicators of progress or success, a growing body of literature suggests that a variety of costs occur when materialistic values become central to the aims of an individual. As we will review in more detail below, this body of research shows that a strong focus on materialistic values is associated with lower well-being, decrements in performance, and treating others in less caring ways. Each of these insalubrious outcomes can be viewed as "ethical problems" if one assumes that an ethical business tries to maximize the health, well-being and performance of its employees and to minimize the potential negative impacts of its business practices on customers, community members, and other species.

To better explicate how materialism is related to business ethics, we review relevant research on materialistic value orientations. Then we turn to theory and research that explains why some individuals come to emphasize materialistic pursuits in their value systems. Finally, we point out ways that some common business activities might be encouraging materialism, and thus working against ideal ethical practice.

THE ETHICAL PROBLEMS OF MATERIALISTIC VALUES

Unhappiness

Many businesses assume that the proper and best way to motivate their employees is by rewarding them with material wealth and possessions. Employees are lured to jobs by high salaries, excellent stock options, and company cars, and then rewarded with raises and other material benefits. Such common practices reflect the typical capitalistic belief that the pursuit of self-interest through financial success brings about happiness. Despite capitalism's promises that the "good life" is the "goods life," a growing body of research suggests that the more people "buy into" the belief that financial success and the accumulation of possessions are relatively important aims in life, the lower their well-being and happiness. As Kasser (2002) has recently reviewed, dozens of studies show that people's happiness diminishes as materialistic pursuits become more important to them. Importantly, as we will see in the brief review that follows, this conclusion has been documented with a variety of methodologies for measuring materialistic pursuits and personal well-being, and in samples with a wide range of characteristics.

A variety of strategies have been used to assess the strength of materialistic desires in individuals. The most straightforward involves surveys such as those developed by Belk (1985) and Richins and Dawson (1992) that ask participants how much they agree or disagree with statements like "I admire people who own expensive homes, cars, and clothes" or "I'd be happier if I could afford to buy more things." Another strategy asks individuals to rate the importance of a variety of types of aspirations, such as personal growth, spirituality, safety, popularity; then, statistical computations are used to assess the relative importance (Rokeach, 1973) that individuals place on materialistic goals such as "I will be financially successful" and "I will have a lot of expensive possessions" relative to the person's entire value system (Kasser & Ryan, 1993, 1996, 2001). Another, more "subject-centered" approach asks people to list their own strivings or goals and then to rate how much they are helpful in reaching a variety of possible futures, including financial success (Sheldon & Kasser, 1995, 1998, 2001). Finally, some recent studies have applied the reaction time methodologies popular in social-cognition research to measure how quickly individuals respond to the presentation of materialistic stimuli (Schmuck, 2001; Solberg, Diener, & Robinson, 2004).

Regardless of the way materialistic strivings are measured, these studies consistently yield the result that the more individuals' value-systems are colored by the pursuit of materialistic goals and pursuits, the lower their well-being. As Kasser (2002) has reviewed, a strong materialistic focus has been empirically associated with greater anxiety, depression, physical symptoms (e.g., backaches and headaches), alcohol and drug use, and narcissism, and with more frequent experiences of unpleasant emotions (e.g., being upset and angry). A stronger materialistic value orientation is also associated with lower happiness, life satisfaction, vitality, and self-actualization, and with fewer experiences of pleasant emotions (e.g., feeling happy and content). Importantly, such results have been reported with different methodologies for measuring well-being, including self-report surveys, interviewer ratings, and diary reports. Similar results have also been reported in the job context, as employees who primarily value their jobs for the status and financial success conveyed to others report more signs of emotional exhaustion, higher work-family conflict, and lower job well-being (Vansteenkiste, Neyrinck, Niemiec, Soenens, De Witte, & Van den Broeck, in press).

The negative associations of materialism and well-being have also been documented in a variety of samples, including middle and high school (Cohen & Cohen, 1996; Kasser, 2005; Schor, 2004), and college students (Kasser & Ryan, 1993, 1996), as well as in adult samples (Kasser & Ryan,

1996; Sheldon & Kasser, 2001). Parallel results have also been reported in many nations, including Australia (Saunders & Munro, 2000), Belgium (Vansteenkiste, Duriez, Simons, & Soenens, in press), Britain (Chan & Joseph, 2000), Germany (Schmuck, Kasser, & Ryan, 2000), Russia (Ryan, Chirkov, Little, Sheldon, Timoshina, & Deci, 1999), South Korea (Kim, Kasser & Lee, 2003), and Singapore (Kasser & Ahuvia, 2002), among others. Notably, even materialistic business students and entrepreneurs, who frequently experience social environments that strongly emphasize the attainment of materialistic goals, display lower well-being if they adopt a materialistic mindset (Kasser & Ahuvia, 2002; Srivastava, Locke, & Bartol, 2001; Vansteenkiste, et al., in press). In other words, the bulk of the evidence suggests that a match between individuals' personal materialistic values and the values encouraged in the social environment does not negate the negative effects associated with pursuing materialistic goals (although see Sagiv & Schwartz, 2000).

In sum, then, a growing and diverse literature suggests that people report diminished quality of life when they take on the values of capitalistic, consumer society, which claim that happiness comes from the pursuit of financial success and the accumulation of possessions. These findings are supported across various operationalizations of the key variables, as well as across samples varying in age, culture, and occupation. These results suggest that encouragement of materialistic values on the part of an organization is ethically problematic, as such practices will likely contribute to lower happiness on the part of employees. In sum, although many business agents seem to believe that well-being depends on creating a business culture that stimulates materialistic goal pursuits, scientific research indicates that the opposite is true.

Performance Deficits

Materialism may exact other costs that are also directly relevant to employees. Specifically, in addition to trying to maximize employees' happiness, an ethical business would also want its employees to perform at their optimal level of performance; however, when people engage in behaviors that are framed as serving materialistic goals, they often end up less deeply engaged in the activity than when the activity is framed as serving goals such as developing one's talents, contributing to society, or being physically healthy and fit (Vansteenkiste, Lens, & Deci, 2006; Vansteenkiste, Simons, Lens, Sheldon, & Deci, 2004). This conclusion is based on studies in which individuals are asked to engage in some activity, such as learning information, exercising, or eating healthily. The study participants are then told that such activities will help them move towards a goal such as financial success, more attractiveness, or higher status (e.g., a materialistic, extrinsic goal; Kasser & Ryan, 1996) or towards a goal such as personal growth, affiliation, benefiting the community, or physical health (or what we typically call "intrinsic" goals; Kasser & Ryan, 1996). Across these varied studies, the results demonstrate that when activities are framed in a more materialistic way, individuals perform at lower levels and do not persist as long. Notably, participants encouraged to adopt a materialistic frame on their activities had lower performance than people in a control-condition who were not provided with any particular goal to have in mind while performing the activity (Vansteenkiste, Simons, Soenens, & Lens, 2004).

These results are quite sensible when interpreted through the lens of self-determination theory (SDT; Deci & Ryan, 1985; 2000). Since the early 1970s, SDT researchers have been investigating the motivational outcomes associated with a focus on external rewards such as money, finding that such rewards, when administered in ways that control behavior and undermine intrinsic motivation for activities, lead to decrements in performance and persistence (see Deci & Ryan, 1985, 2002 for reviews, or Deci, Koestner, & Ryan, 1999 for a meta-analysis of over 100 studies investigating this topic). What is more, other research reviewed by Hennessey & Amabile (1988) demonstrates that creative problem solving is lessened under conditions that emphasize materialistic, extrinsic rewards. Such conclusions are bolstered by recent research showing that individuals who focus on materialistic goals sometimes process the information needed to complete tasks in less than optimal ways (Vansteenkiste, Simons, Lens, Soenens & Matos, 2005). Specifically, when an activity is executed with a materialistic mindset, people have more difficulties conceptually integrating the learning material (i.e., processing at a deeper level), although no performance decrements are notable if all that the task requires is a superficial level of processing and rote learning. Such results suggest that individuals with a materialistic mindset are more likely to approach activities in a "strategic" fashion or as a means towards attaining their materialistic goals. As a result, they become more likely to engage the activity in a more rigid, less flexible fashion. Such a strategy may work fine when superficial memorization or rote learning is all that is called for, but is antithetical to the conceptual integration and creative use of the material necessary for optimal performance.

Although the experiments supporting this conclusion were conducted in classroom and exercise settings, the results have clear implications for business environments. If managers place a more materialistic focus on particular job tasks (e.g., by emphasizing salaries for employees or the financial success of the company), their employees may do more poorly on the job task. Such effects are likley because rather than focusing on the intrinsic motivators that are known to facilitate performance on the job

(Baard, Deci, & Ryan, 2004; Deci, Connell, & Ryan, 1989; Deci, Ryan, Gagne, Leone, Usonov, & Kornazheva, 2001; Ilardi, Leone, Kasser, & Ryan, 1993; Kasser, Davey, & Ryan, 1992) employees will adopt a strategy towards the task which makes them more extrinsically motivated (Deci & Ryan, 2000). As a result, they are less likely to become fully absorbed in the task, and will instead engage in the more superficial types of information processing described above and be more focused on others' opinions relevant to obtaining the promised rewards (Vansteenkiste, Simons, et al., 2005). Thus, they may perform more poorly. This poor performance may be considered an ethical problem if it is brought on by the structure of the work environment or by the messages conveyed by superiors.

Manipulative Treatment of Others

In addition to problems with unhappiness and performance deficits, materialistic values are also associated with the sine qua non of problematic ethical behavior in business: the manipulation of others. Many anecdotal accounts from the history of business scandals clearly show that when individuals are in the grip of greed, other important considerations in life, such as honesty, equality, and concern for the well-being of other people and the quality of the environment, are ignored and downplayed. As shown below, empirical research supports the idea that a focus on materialistic values can lead to such problematic ethical behavior.

To begin, cross-cultural research on the structure of people's values clearly shows that concerns for financial success and wealth directly oppose and are in conflict with values relevant to ethics and to others' well-being. For example, Schwartz's (1994) work, validated in numerous nations around the globe, shows that the aims for money and power oppose concerns such as "social justice," "equality," "a world at peace," and "protecting the environment," as well as being "helpful," "loyal," "responsible," and "honest;" recent work by Burroughs and Rindfleisch (2002) has extended Schwartz's model by incorporating a more direct measure of materialism (Richins & Dawson, 1992), yielding the same results. Our own work examining aspirations in fifteen nations (Grouzet et al., 2005) has similarly found that financial success aspirations oppose "community feeling" concerns for helping others and improving the world, as well as "affiliation" concerns for having close, caring, intimate relationships. This cross-cultural research thus demonstrates that when people emphasize materialistic aims in their value or goal systems, they will care less about how their actions might detrimentally impact other people and the environment.

Other research more directly shows that materialistic values are associated with expressing less care about others' well-being and desires. Kasser

(2002) called this an "objectifying" stance, for materialistic values seem to lead people to treat others as instruments to be used for one's own desires, rather than as fully experiencing, subjective beings in their own right. Consistent with this reasoning, materialistic values are associated with being more disagreeable (Roberts & Robins, 2000) and engaging in more antisocial activities (Cohen & Cohen, 1996; Kasser & Ryan, 1993; McHoskey, 1999) that violate the rights of others and go against society's rules. Other research shows that materialistic pursuits are associated with less empathy (Sheldon & Kasser, 1995), with more competitive and less cooperative behavior (Sheldon, Sheldon, & Osbaldiston, 2000), and with a more Machiavellian, manipulative, and socially dominant attitude towards interpersonal interactions (Duriez, Vansteenkiste, Soenens, & De Witte, 2005; McHoskey, 1999). Materialistic individuals are also less nurturant and often express their care for other individuals in a contingent way, i.e., only when the other person acts in a way consistent with the materialistic person's own desires (Kasser, Ryan, Zax, & Sameroff, 1995; Khanna, 1999). Further, some recent research (Duriez et al., 2005) demonstrates that materialism is associated with less tolerance towards others, a more authoritarian attitude, and more racist attitudes. Essentially what all of this research demonstrates is that materialistic values are associated with treating others in more objectifying and manipulative and in less caring and empathic ways.

How these ethically-questionable interpersonal attitudes might transfer to a business context is made quite clear by Tang and Chiu (2003). These investigators assessed the "love of money" in a sample of 211 white collar employees and business students in Hong Kong by asking participants how much they agreed with statements such as "Money is good," "Money is a symbol of my success," and "I want to be rich." These business people also read 15 scenarios presenting ethical quandaries of different sorts that are frequently experienced in business situations (Robinson & Bennett, 1995), and rated the probability that they would perform each unethical action. The actions included deviant behaviors such as charging customers too much, using one's expense account inappropriately, selling company secrets to competitors, and stealing merchandise. Even after controlling for other variables such as income, pay satisfaction, and organizational commitment, Tang and Chiu (2003) found a direct effect of love of money on deviant behavior. Thus, as materialistic values increased, business people were more likely to report that they might engage in ethically unacceptable business practices.

Most of the ethical problems associated with materialism discussed thus far involve behavior in which the business, other people, or societies at large are the victims. It is important to note that some research suggests that materialistic behavior can lead to ethical problems affecting the environment as well. For example, just as materialistic values oppose certain positive social values, Schwartz (1996) has shown that the power and achievement values that are most similar to materialistic concerns oppose concerns for "protecting the environment" and attaining "unity with nature" (see also Burroughs & Rindfleisch, 2002). Similarly, Saunders & Munro (2000) reported lower "biophilia," or love of all life, on the part of individuals highly focused on materialism and consumerism. Other work more directly studied the kinds of problematic environmental behaviors associated with materialistic pursuits. For example, Richins and Dawson (1992) and Brown and Kasser (2005) found that materialistic individuals engage in fewer positive environmental behaviors and use more environmental resources to support their lifestyle.

Two studies investigating the ecological consequences of a materialistic value orientation in a business context have been conducted. Both Kasser and Sheldon (2000) and Sheldon and McGregor (2000) asked subjects to pretend that they owned logging companies that were bidding against other companies to harvest wood from state land. In both studies, materialistic individuals were more likely to report being motivated by greed, i.e., the desire to make more money than other companies. Consequently, they made larger bids to cut down more of the available land, to the detriment of the health and sustainability of the forest. Clearly this is an ethical problem in the sense that our great-grandchildren's well-being could be quite lower if business decisions made today on the basis of materialistic values create unsustainable practices that further degrade the environment on which our progeny will depend for life and happiness.

CAUSES OF A MATERIALISTIC VALUE ORIENTATION

As we hope is now evident, businesses interested in being more ethical have good reason to be wary of practices that might encourage a materialistic value orientation. Organizations who care about their employees' well-being and performance and who believe in social justice and environmental sustainability might thus want to consider how they may be encouraging, emphasizing, or taking undue advantage of their members' materialistic values. Substantial research and theorizing has been conducted that might shed light on how people become materialistic in organizational settings. Specifically, Kasser, Ryan, Couchman & Sheldon (2004) discussed two main processes that conduce towards the development of a materialistic value orientation. After briefly reviewing evidence supporting the importance of both of these processes in encouraging materialistic values, we apply this approach to different organizational practices in general, and to pay structures in particular.

Social Modeling and Materialism

A substantial body of psychological research demonstrates that individuals take on the important behaviors, values, and goals modeled by others around them (Bandura, 1977; Miller & Dollard, 1941). Not surprisingly, this is also the case for materialistic pursuits. That is, one of the processes through which people become materialistic is by imitating important individuals such as parents, peers, and people they frequently see in the media who behave in ways that imply materialism is an important striving to pursue in life.

Regarding parents, at least three studies document an association between parents' materialistic values and those of their children. For instance, Kasser et al. (1995) and Flouri (1999) both found that when mothers highly valued materialistic goals, their children did so as well. More recently, Vansteenkiste, Duriez, et al. (2005) assessed whether adolescents felt their parents were emphasizing the attainment of materialistic goals in their child rearing; both mothers and fathers also indicated how much they highlighted these goals vis-à-vis their children. Results showed that when parents promoted extrinsic, materialistic goals, their children tended to care more about such aspirations.

Some evidence is also beginning to accumulate suggesting people other than parents also influence the adoption of materialistic values. For instance, Ahuvia and Wong (2002) found that people were more materialistic when they believed that they grew up surrounded by more materialistic parents, peers, heroes, other adults, and local communities. Sheldon et al. (2000) found that individuals more focused on materialistic values tended to have friends who held similar aspirations. Finally, Flouri (1999) showed that individuals who communicated with their peers more about consumption issues also tended to be more materialistic.

A final important socializing model with regard to materialism is the television, which of course conveys numerous messages, both explicitly and implicitly, about the worth of materialistic pursuits. That is, not only do commercials explicitly state that happiness to some extent depends upon the purchase of advertised products, many shows also implicitly contend that happy people are like the wealthy, beautiful, high status individuals who are the stars or who win prizes through their knowledge or skills. Several studies using different age groups show that materialism is indeed associated with greater ingestion of television (Cheung & Chan, 1996; Kasser & Ryan; 2001; Rahtz, Sirgy, & Meadow, 1989; Sheldon & Kasser, 1995). In fact, a particularly impressive recent study by Schor (2004) used path modeling to show that children's use of television and other media predicted high levels of "consumer involvement," which includes concerns with obtaining money and possessions.

Insecurity and Materialism

In addition to these rather straightforward modeling and reinforcement processes, a more dynamic explanation of the causes of materialism has also garnered substantial empirical support. Specifically, when people experience situations that make them feel psychologically insecure, they tend to orient towards materialism, assumedly as a means of trying to cope with this unpleasant feeling (Kasser, 2002; Kasser et al. 2004). Several types of evidence support this conclusion.

Family environments are of course one of the main situations we encounter in life that can either help us to feel safe and secure, or not. And research shows that individuals are more materialistic when they grow up in family environments that do a poorer job of satisfying needs for safety and security. For example, Kasser et al. (1995) found that materialistic teenagers were more likely to have mothers who were less warm, more critical, and more controlling toward the teenager. Other studies show that materialism is associated with parents who are less communicative (Moore & Moschis, 1981), less autonomy-supportive (Williams, Cox, Hedberg, & Deci, 2000), and more punitive (Cohen & Cohen, 1996). Relatedly, individuals who experienced the divorce of their parents report stronger materialistic values (Rindfleisch, Burroughs, & Denton, 1997). All of these familial experiences are of the sort that would make children feel less secure about the predictability of their world and their worth as people; as such, they apparently attempt to cope with these feelings by pursuing materialistic goals and aspirations at a relatively high level.

Broader socio-economic circumstances that conduce towards feelings of insecurity are also associated with stronger materialistic tendencies. Both Cohen and Cohen (1996) and Kasser et al. (1995) reported that teens were more materialistic when they grew up in socio-economically disadvantaged situations. Broader, cultural experiences of economic insecurity are also associated with materialistic tendencies. For example, Abramson and Inglehart (1995) report that when people are raised during eras when their nations are experiencing economically difficult times, they tend to become more materialistic in terms of their concerns for the priorities they believe their society should be pursuing.

Some experimental evidence exists that more strongly suggests that insecurity is indeed a causative factor in making people place more importance on materialistic values, at least temporarily. For example, Kasser and Sheldon (2000) asked participants to write short essays about either death or music; afterwards, participants who had written about death (and assumedly had their insecurities raised) reported stronger materialistic desires for 15 years in the future (Study 1) and became more greedy and bid to chop down more of a state forest in a resource dilemma game (Study

2). More recent experiments by Sheldon & Kasser (2005) similarly find that death, economic concerns, and imagined interactions with people who are more controlling than supportive can all lead people to shift towards materialistic tendencies, presumably because they all invoke a sense of insecurity within individuals.

APPLICATIONS TO A BUSINESS CONTEXT

The research literature reviewed above suggests that people are likely to become more materialistic when they are exposed to environments that model materialistic values or to experiences that make them feel psychologically insecure. Although to our knowledge no studies have directly examined these processes in a business context, we nonetheless believe that both modeling and insecurity should have similar effects in organizational settings, with resulting increases in materialism and thus the ethical difficulties described earlier in this chapter. Next, we briefly sketch out some of the ways that we see these processes operating generally in businesses, and then focus in more depth on how organizational pay systems may influence materialistic tendencies.

The modeling of materialistic values in an organization could occur through a variety of channels. For example, other employees may act in ways that are materialistic and suggest to newer employees that such values are normative within the organization. Bosses may also strive largely for materialistic gain or use materialistically-oriented ways of interacting with and attempting to motivate their employees. Finally, boards of directors and shareholders might place "the bottom line" above other potential concerns of the organization (e.g., equality of pay, environmental impact, etc). Any of these types of organizational social norms could lead employees to believe that materialistic values should be primary among their own concerns.

Organizations might also induce feelings of insecurity on the part of employees that could enhance materialistic tendencies. At more distal levels, hostile takeovers, poor quarterly reports, pressures from boards of directors, downsizing, and the unbridled competition of contemporary capitalism may lead individuals at all levels of the organization to feel insecure, and thus perhaps more materialistic. At a more proximal level, bosses who are threatening and controlling, as opposed to warm and autonomy supportive (Deci et al., 1989) and competition within divisions of a corporation may increase materialism by enhancing feelings of psychological insecurity. Indeed, some practices are even *designed* to create feelings of insecurity. For example, the increasingly popular "rank and yank" performance rating systems, used by such companies as Enron and General Electric, require that a certain percentage of the workforce be designated for rehabilitation or termination each rating period (e.g., Meisler, 2003); clearly such systems are very likely to make most employees feel that their situation is unstable and unpredictable, as even those who survive one year probably know that next year they may not be so lucky. To the extent companies use practices such as these, materialistic tendencies are likely to become more prominent and the untoward ethical problems described above may become more in evidence.

Pay Systems and Materialism

As a way of demonstrating more specifically and concretely how materialism might increase due to modeling and insecurity, and how these processes might be minimized, we next focus on one of the basic features necessary to any business: pay systems. All businesses must develop some form of pay system in order to attract, retain, and motivate their employees (Milkovich & Newman, 2005), and some of these pay systems may increase materialism through the processes described above, whereas others may lessen the modeling of materialism and employees' experiences of insecurity. As such, different pay systems are likely to have different ramifications for materialistic values, and thus for ethical behavior as well. Below, we discuss pay systems that our analysis suggests would create high, moderate, and low levels of materialism, respectively.

The highly materialistic systems. If an organization attempted to design a pay system to create and exploit materialism, it might start out, as some experts recommend (e.g., Bates, 2003; Ghosn, 2002), by making pay a central element of the corporate culture. By doing so, it would become clear to members of the organization that materialism is a primary value, that management principles are likely to be based on such values, and that employees are likely to be rewarded to the extent they pursue such values (Lawler, 2000; Pfeffer, 1998). One key way to move pay to the center of a corporate culture is to create large differences in pay between organizational levels, e.g., between top executives and lower level managers. Such a strategy characterizes many businesses in the United States, where high pay dispersion has been on the increase: for example, the income of chief executive officers (CEOs) increased from 42 times that of average hourly workers in 1982, to 301 times in 2003, to 431 in 2004 (Anderson, Cavanagh, Klinger, & Stanton, 2005). High pay dispersion creates a very concrete and visible way in which employees can "keep score" of success within the organization and makes it increasingly likely that employees will come to believe that there is an instrumental link between money and the outcomes of power, status, and respect that they might also value. Thus, as employees come to believe that a materialistic value orientation is prerequisite to advancement in the organization, those who hope to rise to higher level managerial jobs will try to fit in to the corporate culture by taking on the trappings of a materialistic lifestyle, as those who resist the draw of such values are likely to be seen as deviants unworthy of higher level and more responsible positions in such organizations. Such a social dynamic may even lead the organization to prefer those whose extrinsic goals match the values of the organization rather than the individuals whose intrinsic goals help them reach the high level of performance we have shown is typically associated with such a task orientation.

Of course, the likely result of such a dynamic is that those employees who take on materialistic values will be more likely to rise to positions of power in such corporate cultures, and thus to make the decisions that will maintain a corporate culture that emphasizes pay and materialism. Further, as highly materialistic individuals gain more power and responsibility, their decisions will have larger effects on more of the organization's stakeholders, including employees, customers, competitors, the community, and the environment. Consequently, materialistic values will become even more deeply embedded and resistant to change in that organizational culture, raising even further the likelihood of the negative ethical behaviors associated with materialism that we reviewed earlier.

Another effect of high pay dispersion is to create a competitive "tournament" in which only some managers will win the prize of executive promotions and high pay, with most losing (Bloom, 1999). Such competition is likely to create feelings of insecurity through at least four processes. First, those highly competitive plans in which bonuses and/or adjustments to salary are based on some measure of employee performance (e.g., "pay-for-performance" plans) inherently create a situation in which individuals can never be completely sure what their level of pay will be. Such unpredictability is compounded when employees are in competition with one another over a fixed sum of money, whether it is a bonus pool or a pool related to raises in salary. Other, so-called "earnings at risk" plans even *reduce* base pay and offer employees the opportunity to recoup their base pay level and more by yearly bonuses tied to productivity improvements (Brown & Huber, 1992). As a result, if the organization has a good year, employees can fare well financially, but if the organization has a bad year, employees can see a significant decline in pay from prior year levels. What each of these plans has in common is the creation of uncertainty, risk, and insecurity in workers, all of which are likely to breed materialism.

A second reason why earning-at-risk plans often create feelings of insecurity is that many of the factors that affect performance and assessments of performance are not under the employee's control, thus leading some employees to question their ability to achieve the standards imposed by management (Deckop, Merriman, & Blau, 2004; Igalens & Rousel, 1999).

For example, if pay decisions depend on group or organizational performance criteria, numerous factors (such as the actions of competitors, fellow employees, and the political, social, and economic environment) can affect performance, and thus employee's pay. If the performance criteria are at the individual (employee) level, employee performance may be affected by the work of fellow employees and various features of the employee's work environment, including working conditions and equipment, not to mention the various competing demands related to work-family balance that can affect employee performance. Finally, the well-documented difficulties of accurately measuring employee performance, supervisory biases in performance appraisal, and employee misperceptions of their own performance (e.g., Meyer, 1975; Murphy & Cleveland, 1995) can also lead individuals to feel that whether they attain the required standards is not entirely within their control; this, in turn, might create uncertainties and insecurities that further exacerbate feelings of risk under such pay systems.

Third, only a limited number of individuals can be the winners in pay systems based heavily on competition. As such, there are many losers, and these individuals are likely to begin to doubt their skills and feel insecure about their competencies. Such feelings of doubt and questions about one's competence, in turn, are associated with more materialistic tendencies (Kasser, 2002). For example, in samples of business students and entrepreneurs, Srivastava et al. (2001) found that materialistic values were associated with wanting to earn money in order to overcome self-doubts and in order to compare favorably to other people; these motives for making money, in turn, predicted lower well-being. Such "insecure" motives are likely to be heightened under conditions of competition, in which self-doubt is probably endemic among losers and social comparison is probably present in most employees. In turn, such motives apparently are associated with higher levels of concern for materialistic ends.

Fourth, individuals who are in competition with their peers for a fixed sum of money that only some will win are probably wise to be suspicious of the behavior of their competitors; such suspicion will create a form of relational insecurity. Recall, for instance, the research findings that materialistic values are associated with placing less value on honesty, good friendships, and helping others and with acting in more competitive, antisocial, and Machiavellian ways. Now imagine that the pay system of your organization forces you to compete with materialistic individuals for the very pursuit that they value highly: money and prestige. Such a situation is pre-determined to create insecurity, as it may be unwise to totally trust others' motives and behaviors, or to act in a more pro-social, cooperative manner that materialistic individuals might view as weakness to be exploited. Indeed, Sheldon et al. (2000) found that when people high and low in materialistic values were placed together in social dilemmas, the former often took advantage of the cooperativeness of the latter. As such, less materialistic individuals must remain wary in competitive situations, which will increase their feelings of insecurity, and thus may lead them to take on the values and behaviors of their more materialistic competitors as a way of surviving within the organization.

In sum, the pay systems most likely to create insecurity would be those in which a significant portion of an employee's pay is continually at risk. Such systems can be expected to create more feelings of insecurity, and thus more materialism, and thus more ethical problems. Some indirect support for this conclusion comes from past research showing that high risk pay plans produce the types of outcomes previous research has associated with materialism, including pay dissatisfaction (Brown & Huber, 1992), emotional distress (Shirom, Westman, & Melamed, 1999), and, where employees are risk averse, lower productivity (e.g., Yukl, Latham, & Pursell, 1976), pay dissatisfaction, and lower organizational citizenship behavior (Deckop et al., 2004).

The moderately materialistic systems. Several features of the systems just described could be modified or eliminated to lessen the likelihood of creating or exploiting employee materialism. For example, pay dispersion could be lowered by, among other things, controlling top executive pay or setting maximum ratios of CEO to average worker pay. Such a strategy would result in fewer losers (Bloom, 1999), as well as less social modeling of a materialistic lifestyle as an indicator of success.

As we described above, the most materialistic systems encourage competition among employees by providing fixed sums to be awarded based on relative performance, or by threatening the loss of pay. Better systems would eliminate many aspects of competition by providing group or organizational level rewards in which employees have incentives to cooperate with one another rather than compete. Such group-oriented systems not only support the types of cooperative values that oppose and thus provide an antidote to materialistic values (Grouzet et al., 2005; Schwartz, 1994), but also represent a "win-win" situation for employees and their organization, thereby lessening feelings of insecurity.

One group-level pay plan that probably has more positive (or at least less negative) features from a materialism standpoint is "gainsharing," which provides bonuses to employees based on the degree to which employees as a group increase productivity and lower labor costs (Welborne, Balkin, & Gomez-Mejia, 1995). In most gainsharing plans, all employees, from managers to production and clerical workers, receive the same bonus, thus working against income dispersal. Another important feature of gainsharing plans is employee involvement, whereby workers and their managers collaborate to develop ways to solve problems and lower labor costs. These plans are intended to tap employees' "hidden" knowledge of the production process (Locke & Schweiger, 1979) and to improve employee motivation by helping them feel more control over their own work lives and more identification with the organization (Miller & Monge, 1986). Thus, employees under gainsharing plans focus less on the pursuit of materialistic goals, and more on intrinsic goals such as those for cooperation, connection to others, and personal growth (Kasser & Ryan, 1996). As we saw earlier, when people have an intrinsic focus on their activities, they experience greater task engagement, persistence, and better performance, as compared to those who are more focused on extrinsic, materialistic goals. It should therefore not be surprising that research shows many performance benefits of gainsharing plans, whereas the results are quite mixed on how productive people are under individual incentive systems (which encourage employee competition and the pursuit of materialistic goals; Milkovich & Newman, 2005).

The problems associated with materialism should also be reduced under gainsharing systems because the crucial performance measure, i.e., reduced labor costs, is more under the control of employees than are performance measures used in many other group level pay-for-performance systems. As such, there is less uncontrollable risk associated with gainsharing, and thus less insecurity about future income. In fact, any pay system should have fewer problems associated with materialism to the extent it reduces the amount of risk experienced by employees. Other ways of reducing materialism would involve eliminating or otherwise accounting for factors that affect employee performance but are not under employee control. Such performance measurement design issues are typically discussed as ways of improving productivity effects of pay for performance (e.g., Beer & Cannon, 2004; Milkovich & Newman, 2005); these issues become all the more urgent when considered from the standpoints of insecurity, materialism, and resultant unethical behavior.

The least materialistic systems. Organizations that want to design pay systems that are least likely to exploit or induce materialistic values might start by making sure that pay is not positioned as an important element of the organizational culture, and thus not use pay to represent how the organization is managed or what the organization values. How might this be done most effectively? Over the years the academic and popular management literatures have proposed numerous such models of organizational design, including "total quality management" (Deming, 1986), "learning organizations" (e.g., Kofman & Senge, 1993), and "good to great" organizations (Collins, 2001). All of these designs explicitly exclude paying for performance, and instead focus on factors such as quality improvement, continuous learning, good hiring practices, and management that is proactive and supportive rather than reactive and fearful. Rather than raising the most self-interested and materialistic individuals to places of leadership, systems such as learning organizations propound the notion of "servant leadership," in which leaders choose to serve both other employees and a higher purpose (Kofman & Senge, 1993). Similarly, good to great organizations encourage leaders who are self-effacing and humble (Collins, 2001). Such conceptions of good leadership are antithetical to the materialistic values of other systems that model high pay and wealth accumulation as indicators of accomplishment, and as sources of respect, power, and authority.

Best organizations from the standpoint of materialism would not use pay for performance systems, and would thereby lessen problems related to competition, the creation of losers, risk, and insecurity. Instead, organizations could focus on other, more intrinsic sources of employee motivation and satisfaction in the work environment, such as skill development, meaningfulness, and autonomy in work. Although eliminating pay for performance in favor of a focus on these intrinsic sources of work motivation is hardly a novel suggestion, most other organizational thinkers typically present such recommendations as a means of improving employee and organizational performance (e.g., Beer & Cannon, 2004; Kohn, 1993); we contend that such changes could also improve an organization's ethical standing, as materialism and thus the ethical problems described earlier should also decrease as a result of such changes.

Of course, such proposals are sometimes met with the rejoinder that employees, particularly managers, want their pay adjustments to be based on performance, and believe this to be a just and fair basis for reward (e.g., Milkovich & Newman, 2005). For these employees performance contingent rewards may provide some competence feedback, and thus not necessarily reduce intrinsic motivation and productivity (Deckop & Cirka, 2000). Consistent with this view, Malka and Chatman (2003) found that increases in income for extrinsically oriented individuals predicted greater job satisfaction. On the other hand, Malka & Chatman found that higher incomes predicted lower subjective well-being and job satisfaction for intrinsically oriented individuals, and Srivastava et al. (2001) found that after controlling for income, materialistic entrepreneurs still reported decrements in their well-being.

These issues are relevant to three final points we would like to make. First, we must note that many extrinsically oriented workers who might say that they want their pay adjustments to be based on performance have in fact developed this particular motivational style in part as a result of living in popular culture that models material wealth as a measure of success, in family and community environments that create insecurity, and in organizational situations where pay is the way the score is kept. Thus, rather than thinking that such desires are "natural" and to be rewarded, managers might consider that the expression of such desires is the result of a value system that has been actively socially inculcated into these individuals, and that may not be ideal for the variety of reasons specified above. Second, we should mention that most Americans work under pay systems designed to meet the motivational proclivities of extrinsically oriented rather than the intrinsically oriented workers. Because such systems may work to the detriment of the latter's well-being, it is imperative from an ethical perspective to better understand the types of systems that may support the well-being of those who care less about the extrinsic, materialistic values typically modeled in society and organizations. Finally, even if income might somewhat ameliorate the negative well-being consequences of a materialistic value orientation, it seems unlikely that the questionable social and environmental behaviors associated with materialism would disappear with higher incomes. As such, organizational structures that reinforce materialistic value systems should still be considered ethically questionable.

CONCLUSION

We hope to have shown that the celebration of materialistic values that characterizes the contemporary form of American capitalism (and thus culture) is also associated with several types of ethical difficulties that, unfortunately, also seem to characterize our culture. Specifically, when people are more focused on extrinsic, materialistic goals, the research indicates that they report lower personal well-being, perform at lower levels, and exhibit behavior that damages social equality and ecological sustainability. Thus, an ethical organization would do well to strive to minimize how much it models materialistic values and how much it induces feelings of insecurity in its employees, for these processes are known to influence how much individuals value materialistic aims. Happily, approaches currently exist, and more can certainly be developed and researched, that hold promise for decreasing materialistic tendencies in organizations and employees, and thus for benefiting employees' well-being and performance, as well as the quality of life of other organizational stakeholders, other species, and future generations of humans.

REFERENCES

Abramson, P. R., & Inglehart, R. (1995). *Value change in global perspective.* Ann Arbor, MI: The University of Michigan Press.

Ahuvia, A. C., & Wong, N. (2002). Personality and values based materialism: Their relationships and origins. *Journal of Consumer Psychology, 12,* 389–402.

Anderson, S., Cavanagh, J., Klinger, S., & Stanton, L. (2005). *Executive excess 2005: Defense contractors get more bucks for the bang.* Institute for Policy Studies and United for a Fair Economy, August 30.

Baard, P. P., Deci, E. L., & Ryan, R. M. (2004). Intrinsic need satisfaction: A motivational basis for performance and well-being in two work settings. *Journal of Applied Social Psychology, 34,* 2045–2068.

Bandura, A. (1977). *Social learning theory.* Englewood Cliffs, NJ: Prentice-Hall, Inc.

Bates, S. (2003). Top pay for best performance. *HR Magazine, 48*(1), 30–38.

Beer, M., & Cannon, M.D. (2004). Promise and peril in implementing pay for performance. *Human Resource Management, 43*(1), 1–20.

Belk, R. W. (1985). Materialism: Trait aspects of living in the material world. *Journal of Consumer Research, 12,* 265–280.

Bloom, M. (1999). The performance effects of pay dispersion on individuals and organizations. *Academy of Management Journal, 42*(1), 25–40.

Brown, K., & Huber, V. (1992). Lowering floors and raising ceilings: A longitudinal assessment of the effects of an earnings-at-risk plan on pay satisfaction. *Personnel Psychology, 45,* 279–303.

Brown, K. W., & Kasser, T. (2005). Are psychological and ecological well-being compatible? The role of values, mindfulness, and lifestyle. *Social Indicators Research, 74,* 349–368.

Burroughs, J. E., & Rindfleisch, A. (2002). Materialism and well-being: A conflicting values perspective. *Journal of Consumer Research, 29,* 348–370.

Chan, R., & Joseph, S. (2000). Dimensions of personality, domains of aspiration, and subjective well-being. *Personality and Individual Differences, 28,* 347–354.

Cheung, C., & Chan, C. (1996). Television viewing and mean world value in Hong Kong's adolescents. *Social Behavior and Personality, 24,* 351–364.

Cohen, P., & Cohen, J. (1996). *Life values and adolescent mental health.* Mahwah, NJ: Erlbaum.

Collins, J. (2001). *Good to great: Why some companies make the leap...and others don't.* New York: Harper Collins.

Deci, E. L., Connell, J. P., & Ryan, R. M. (1989). Self-determination in a work organization. *Journal of Applied Psychology, 74,* 580–590.

Deci, E. L., Koestner, R., & Ryan, R. M. (1999). A meta-analytic review of experiments examining the effects of extrinsic rewards on intrinsic motivation. *Psychological Bulletin, 125,* 627–668.

Deci, E.L., & Ryan, R.M. (1985). *Intrinsic motivation and self-determination in human behavior.* New York: Plenum.

Deci, E. L., & Ryan, R. M. (2000). The "what" and the "why" of goal pursuits: Human needs and the self-determination of behavior. *Psychological Inquiry, 11,* 227–268.

Deci, E. L., & Ryan, R. M. (Eds.) (2002). *Handbook of self-determination research.* Rochester, NY: University of Rochester Press.

Deci, E. L., Ryan, R. M., Gagné, M., Leone, D. R., Usunov, J., & Kornazheva, B. P. (2001). Need satisfaction, motivation, and well-being in the work organizations of a former Eastern Bloc country. *Personality and Social Psychology Bulletin, 27,* 930–942.

Deckop, J.R., & Cirka, C.C. (2000). The risk and reward of a double-edged sword: Effects of a merit pay program on intrinsic motivation. *Nonprofit and Voluntary Sector Quarterly, 29*(3), 400–418.

Deckop, J.R., Merriman, K.K., & Blau, G. (2004). Impact of variable risk preferences on the effectiveness of control by pay. *Journal of Occupational and Organizational Psychology, 77,* 63–80.

Deming, W.E. (1986) *Out of the crisis.* Cambridge, MA, Massachussetts Institute of Technology Center for Advanced Engineering Study.

Duriez, B., Vansteenkiste, M., Soenens, B., & De Witte, H. (2005). Evidence for the social costs of extrinsic relative to intrinsic goal pursuits: Their relation with right-wing authoritarianism, social dominance, and prejudice. Manuscript submitted for publication.

Flouri, E. (1999). An integrated model of consumer materialism: Can economic socialization and maternal values predict materialistic attitudes in adolescents? *Journal of Socio-Economics, 28,* 707–724.

Ghosn, C. (2002). Saving the business without losing the company. *Harvard Business Review, 80*(1), 37–45.

Grouzet, F. M. E., Kasser, T., Ahuvia, A., Fernandez-Dols, J. M., Kim, Y., Lau, S., Ryan, R. M., Saunders, S., Schmuck, P., & Sheldon, K. M. (in press). The structure of goal contents across 15 cultures. *Journal of Personality and Social Psychology.*.

Hennessey, B. A., & Amabile, T. M. (1988). The conditions of creativity. In R. J. Sternberg (Ed.), *The nature of creativity: Contemporary psychological perspectives* (pp. 11–38). New York: Cambridge University Press.

Igalens, J., & Roussel, P. (1999). A study of the relationships between compensation package, work motivation and job satisfaction. *Journal of Organizational Behavior, 20,* 1003–1025.

Ilardi, B. C., Leone, D., Kasser, T., & Ryan, R. M. (1993). Employee and supervisor ratings of motivation: Main effects and discrepancies associated with job satisfaction and adjustment in a factory setting. *Journal of Applied Social Psychology, 23,* 1789–1805.

Kasser, T. (2002). *The high price of materialism.* Cambridge, MA: MIT Press.

Kasser, T. (2005). Frugality, generosity, and materialism in children and adolescents. In K. A. Moore & L. H. Lippman (Eds.), *What children need to flourish?: Conceptualizing and measuring indicators of positive development* (pp. 357–373). New York: Springer Science.

Kasser, T., & Ahuvia, A. C. (2002). Materialistic values and well-being in business students. *European Journal of Social Psychology, 32,* 137–146.

Kasser, T., Davey, J., & Ryan, R. M. (1992). Motivation and employee–supervisor discrepancies in a psychiatric vocational rehabilitation setting. *Rehabilitation Psychology, 37,* 175–187.

Kasser, T., & Ryan, R. M. (1993). A dark side of the American dream: Correlates of financial success as a central life aspiration. *Journal of Personality and Social Psychology, 65,* 410–422.

Kasser, T., & Ryan, R. M. (1996). Further examining the American dream: Differential correlates of intrinsic and extrinsic goals. *Personality and Social Psychology Bulletin, 22,* 280–287.

Kasser, T., & Ryan, R. M. (2001). Be careful what you wish for: Optimal functioning and the relative attainment of intrinsic and extrinsic goals. In P. Schmuck & K. M. Sheldon (Eds.), *Life goals and well-being: Towards a positive psychology of human striving* (pp. 116–131). Goettingen, Germany: Hogrefe & Huber Publishers.

Kasser, T., Ryan, R.M., Couchman, C.E., & Sheldon, K.M. (2004). Materialistic values: Their causes and consequences. In T. Kasser & A.D. Kanner, (Eds.) *Psychology and consumer culture: The struggle for a good life in a materialistic world* (pp. 11–28). Washington, D.C.: American Psychological Association.

Kasser, T., Ryan, R. M., Zax, M., & Sameroff, A. J. (1995). The relations of maternal and social environments to late adolescents' materialistic and prosocial values. *Developmental Psychology, 31*, 907–914.

Kasser, T., & Sheldon, K. M. (2000). Of wealth and death: Materialism, mortality salience, and consumption behavior. *Psychological Science, 11*, 352–355.

Khanna, S. (1999). *Corrosive messages and capitalist ideology: Well-being, objectification, and alienation from a cross-cultural perspective.* Unpublished Honors Thesis, Knox College, Galesburg, IL.

Kim, Y., Kasser, T., & Lee, H. (2003). Self-concept, aspirations, and well-being in South Korea and the United States. *Journal of Social Psychology, 143*, 277–290.

Kofman, F., & Senge, P. M. (1993). Communities of commitment: The heart of learning organizations. *Organizational Dynamics, 22*(2), 4–23.

Kohn, A. (1993). *Punished by rewards: The trouble with gold stars, incentive plans, A's, praise, and other bribes.* Boston: Houghton Mifflin.

Lawler, E.E. (2000). *Rewarding excellence: Pay strategies for the New Economy.* San Francisco: Josey-Bass.

Locke, E.A., & Schweiger, D. M. (1979). Participation in decision-making: One more look. In B. Staw (Ed.), *New Directions in Organizational Behavior, Vol. 1.* (pp. 265–339). Greenwich, CT: JAI Press.

Malka, A., & Chatman, J.A. (2003). Intrinsic and extrinsic orientations as moderators of the effect of annual income on subjective well-being: A longitudinal study. *Personality & Social Psychology Bulletin, 29*(6), 737–746.

McHoskey, J.W. (1999). Machiavellianism, intrinsic versus extrinsic goals, and social interest: A self-determination theory analysis. *Motivation and Emotion, 23*, 267–283.

Meisler, A. (2003). Dead man's curve. *Workforce, 82*(7), 44–48.

Meyer, H.H. (1975). The pay-for-performance dilemma. *Organizational Dynamics,* Winter, 39–50.

Milkovich, G.T., & Newman, J.M. (2005). *Compensation.* Boston: McGraw-Hill.

Miller, N. E., & Dollard, J. (1941). *Social learning and imitation.* New Haven, CT: Yale University Press.

Miller, K. I., & Monge, P. R. (1986). Participation, satisfaction, and productivity: A meta-analytic review. *Academy of Management Journal, 29*(4), 727–753.

Moore, R. L., & Moschis, G. P. (1981). The effects of family communication and mass media use on adolescent consumer learning. *Journal of Communication, 31*, 42–51.

Murphy, K. R., & Cleveland, J. N. (1995). *Understanding performance appraisal.* Thousand Oaks, CA: Sage Publications.

Pfeffer, J. (1998). Six dangerous myths about pay. *Harvard Business Review, 76*(3), 109–119.

Rahtz, D. R., Sirgy, M. J., & Meadow, H. L. (1989). The elderly audience: Correlates of television orientation. *Journal of Advertising, 18*, 9–20.

Richins, M. L., & Dawson, S. (1992). A consumer values orientation for materialism and its measurement: Scale development and validation. *Journal of Consumer Research, 19*, 303–316.

Rindfleisch, A., Burroughs, J. E., & Denton, F. (1997). Family structure, materialism, and compulsive consumption. *Journal of Consumer Research, 23*, 312–325.

Roberts, B. W., & Robins, R. W. (2000). Broad dispositions, broad aspirations: The intersection of personality traits and major life goals. *Personality and Social Psychology Bulletin, 26*, 1284–1296.

Robinson, S. L., & Bennett, R. J. (1995). A typology of deviant workplace behaviors: A multi-dimensional scaling study. *Academy of Management Journal, 38*, 555–572.

Rokeach, M. (1973). *The nature of human values.* New York: Free press.

Ryan, R. M., Chirkov, V. I., Little, T. D., Sheldon, K. M., Timoshina, E., and Deci, E. L. (1999).The American dream in Russia: Extrinsic aspirations and well-being in two cultures. *Personality and Social Psychology Bulletin, 25*, 1509–1524.

Sagiv, L., & Schwartz, S. H. (2000). Value priorities and subjective well-being: Direct relations and congruity effects. *European Journal of Social Psychology, 30*, 177–198.

Saunders, S., & Munro, D. (2000). The construction and validation of a consumer orientation questionnaire (SCOI) designed to measure Fromm's (1955) 'marketing character' in Australia. *Social Behavior and Personality, 28*, 219–240.

Schmuck, P. (2001). Life goal preferences measured by inventories, subliminal, and supraliminal priming and their relations to well-being. In P. Schmuck & K. M. Sheldon (Eds.), *Life goals and well-being: Towards a positive psychology of human striving* (pp. 132–147). Goettingen, Germany: Hogrefe & Huber.

Schmuck, P., Kasser, T., & Ryan, R. M. (2000). Intrinsic and extrinsic goals: Their structure and relationship to well-being in German and U.S. college students. *Social Indicators Research, 50*, 225–241.

Schor, J. B. (2004). *Born to buy: The commercialized child and the new consumer culture.* New York: Scribner.

Schwartz, S. H. (1994). Are there universal aspects in the structure and contents of human values? *Journal of Social Issues, 50*, 19–45.

Schwartz, S. H. (1996). Values priorities and behavior: Applying a theory of integrated value systems. In C. Seligman, J. M. Olson, & M. P. Zanna (Eds.), *The psychology of values: The Ontario symposium, Vol. 8* (pp. 1–24). Hillsdale, NJ: Erlbaum.

Sheldon, K. M., & Kasser, T. (1995). Coherence and congruence: Two aspects of personality integration. *Journal of Personality and Social Psychology, 68*, 531–543.

Sheldon, K. M., & Kasser, T. (1998). Pursuing personal goals: Skills enable progress, but not all progress is beneficial. *Personality and Social Psychology Bulletin, 24*, 1319–1331.

Sheldon, K. M., & Kasser, T. (2001). "Getting older, getting better": Personal strivings and psychological maturity across the life span. *Developmental Psychology, 37*, 491–501.

Sheldon, K. M., & Kasser, T. (2005). *Psychological insecurity pushes people away from intrinsic goals and towards extrinsic goals.* Manuscript under review.

Sheldon, K. M., & McGregor, H. (2000). Extrinsic value orientation and the tragedy of the commons. *Journal of Personality, 68,* 383–411.

Sheldon, K. M., Sheldon, M. S., & Osbaldiston, R. (2000). Prosocial values and group assortation in an N-person prisoner's dilemma. *Human Nature, 11,* 387–404.

Shirom, A., Westman, M., & Melamed, S. (1999). The effects of pay systems on blue-collar employees' emotional distress: The mediating effects of objective and subjective work monotony. *Human Relations, 52,* 1077–1097.

Solberg, E. C., Diener, E., & Robinson, M. D. (2004). Why are materialists less satisfied? In T. Kasser & A. D. Kanner (Eds.), *Psychology and consumer culture: The struggle for a good life in a materialistic world* (pp. 29–48). Washington, DC: APA.

Srivastava, A., Locke, E.A., & Bartol, K.M. (2001). Money and subjective well-being: It's not the money, it's the motives. *Journal of Personality and Social Psychology, 80*(6), 959–971.

Tang, T. L., & Chiu, R. K. (2003). Income, money ethic, pay satisfaction, and unethical behavior: Is the love of money the root of evil for Hong Kong employees? *Journal of Business Ethics, 46,* 13–30.

Vansteenkiste, M., Duriez, B., Simons, J., & Soenens, B. (In press). Materialistic values and well-being among business students: Further evidence for their detrimental effect. *Journal of Applied Social Psychology.*

Vansteenkiste, M., Lens, W., & Deci, E. L. (2006). Intrinsic versus extrinsic goal contents in self-determination theory: Another look at the quality of academic motivation. *Educational Psychologist, 41,* 19–31.

Vansteenkiste, M., Neyrinck, B., Niemiec, C., Soenens, B., De Witte, H., & Van den Broeck, A. (in press). Examining the relation between intrinsic versus extrinsic work orientations, basic need satisfaction, and the "bright" and "dark" side of job functioning: A self- determination approach.

Vansteenkiste, M., Simons, J., Lens, W., Sheldon, K. M., & Deci, E. L. (2004). Motivating learning, performance, and persistence: The synergistic role of intrinsic goals and autonomy-support. *Journal of Personality and Social Psychology, 87,* 246–260.

Vansteenkiste, M., Simons, J., Lens, W., Soenens, B., & Matos, L. (2005). Examining the impact of extrinsic versus intrinsic goal framing and internally controlling versus autonomy-supportive communication style upon early adolescents' academic achievement. *Child Development, 76,* 483–501.

Vansteenkiste, M., Simons, J., Lens, W., Soenens, B, Matos, L., & Lacante, M. (2004). "Less is sometimes more": Goal-content Matters. *Journal of Educational Psychology, 96,* 755–764.

Vansteenkiste, M., Simons, J., Soenens, B., & Lens, W. (2004). How to become a persevering exerciser? The importance of providing a clear, future intrinsic goal in an autonomy-supportive manner. *Journal of Sport and Exercise Psychology, 26,* 232–249.

Welborne, T.M., Balkin, D.B., & Gomez-Mejia, L.R. (1995). Gainsharing and mutual monitoring: A combined agency-organizational justice interpretation. *Academy of Management Journal, 38*(3), 881–899.

Williams, G. C., Cox, E. M., Hedberg, V. A., & Deci, E. L. (2000). Extrinsic life goals and health risk behaviors in adolescents. *Journal of Applied Social Psychology, 30,* 1756–1771.

Yukl, G.A., Latham, G.P., & Pursell, E.D. (1976). The effectiveness of performance incentives under conditions of variable ratio schedules of reinforcement. *Personnel Psychology, 29,* 221–231.

CPSIA information can be obtained
at www.ICGtesting.com
Printed in the USA
JSHW012320160121
10989JS00004B/56